"COMBINING SERVICE AND LEARNING is an essential resource for all those interested in establishing their own community service programs. This comprehensive book successfully blends some of the most thoughtful perspectives on service to date, with practical advice from those in the field. A 'must' for those who wish to connect learning to life." — *Ernest Boyer, President, Carnegie Foundation for the Advancement of Teaching*

"This is a useful distillation of the lessons learned in the last two decades about programs that combine service, citizenship, and education. Practical examples and the principles that seem essential for success are highlighted. As the nation seeks opportunities to provide this kind of experience to more of our people, this is a valuable resource." — *David Broder, National Political Correspondent and Columnist, THE WASHINGTON POST*

"COMBINING SERVICE AND LEARNING is an excellent resource for both teachers and community persons interested in expanding students' awareness of social concerns. Of special interest to me are the sections on successful and unsuccessful programs, and what factors contributed to their success or failure. We as educators must encourage young people to become more involved in meaningful activities that will break down pre-conceived cultural prejudices."
— *Ninon H. Cheek, 1989 Wake County Teacher of the Year and 7th Grade Language Arts Teacher in Raleigh, North Carolina*

"COMBINING SERVICE AND LEARNING is an impressive, comprehensive book on service programs. The massive task of assembling this reference work will pay real dividends as Americans recognize the benefits which accompany programs for service and learning." — *Bill Clinton, Governor of Arkansas*

"This is a valuable and important book — one much needed at this time, when community service is becoming more and more a part of the lives of so many young people."
— *Robert Coles, Professor of Psychiatry and Medical Humanities, Harvard University, and Pulitzer Prize winning author, CHILDREN IN CRISIS and THE MORAL LIFE OF CHILDREN*

"At a time when many in our country doubt our ability to tackle our social ills, these volumes appear and give us example after example of how we can take charge and build a more productive and humane society. These volumes reflect the rich diversity of creative community leadership. Seldom does one see combined in one work such an array of best practices *and* scholarly analysis of the dynamics behind such successful cases."

— *David DeVries, Executive Vice President*
Center for Creative Leadership

"This extraordinary book looks at service-learning from all the angles that matter. It shows how our democracy might become better when students are properly prepared to take civic action. It shows how our colleges and universities might engage more fully in learning — and in life!"

— *Zelda Gamson, Professor of Sociology,*
University of Massachusetts at Boston;
Author, LIBERATING EDUCATION; and
Director, New England Resource Center
for Higher Education

"Instilling good citizenship is fundamental to a high-quality education. COMBINING SERVICE AND LEARNING offers a thorough and thoughtful roadmap for those who seek to enrich students' understanding of the communities and nation in which they live."

— *Senator Nancy Kassebaum (R-Kansas)*

"Community service deserves to become part of the education of every student in America, from kindergarten through college. In COMBINING SERVICE AND LEARNING, the field's leading experts explain why — and how to make it work effectively in every community. This essential handbook can help educators bring the concept of community service to life for millions of students across the country."

— *Senator Edward Kennedy (D-Massachusetts)*

"COMBINING SERVICE AND LEARNING breaks new ground by offering the most comprehensive rationale and in-depth presentation yet for service-learning. Rather than extending broadly and sometimes superficially, as have many recent publications, this three-volume set reaches deeply to the roots of service-learning, demonstrating its well-developed theory and wide-ranging practice. It gathers from among the liveliest and best informed writers, making the exercise of reading this ambitious collection an enjoyable task.

The entire set is a 'must' for those who are serious about the integration of this important method into the mainstream of education." — *James Kielsmeier, President*
National Youth Leadership Council

"An important, impressive, and inclusive compilation of information about programs at all levels of education that use experience in serving our communities and fellow citizens as a basis for learning. This comprehensive handbook is an essential reference and guide for all who seek to actively engage young and old to learn through service. I can't think of a better way for people in a democracy to learn." — *Ed Meade, Chief Program Officer (retired)*
Ford Foundation

"An excellent resource for the research and practice of education. This collection provides a wealth of information for creating effective service-learning programs at all levels. NSIEE has done a yeoman's task in compiling what will be an invaluable tool to everyone interested in teaching and learning."
— *Suzanne Morse, Director of Programs*
Kettering Foundation

"COMBINING SERVICE AND LEARNING is an important and unique contribution to the community service efforts taking place in schools and colleges across the entire country. I hope it will be used extensively in colleges and schools because these volumes represent the most comprehensive collection of information on the educational value of community service."
— *Frank Newman, President,*
Education Commission of the States, and
Co-Founder, Campus Compact

"The spirit of young people and the practical examples and ideas in this book will make community service a trademark of future generations." — *Brian O'Connell, President, Independent Sector*

"The student community service movement of the '90s truly stands on the shoulders of giants. You will find no other collection of essays like this one where service-learning leaders speak out critically, historically, and with deep conviction. COOL is proud to be a collaborating organization for this vital text."
— *Julia Scatliff, Executive Director*
Campus Outreach Opportunity League

COMBINING SERVICE AND LEARNING

A Resource Book for
Community and Public Service

FOR DISPLAY ONLY

Volume II   NS EE COPY

DO NOT REMOVE

by Jane C. Kendall and Associates

A publication of the
**National Society for Internships
and Experiential Education**

in partnership with the
**Mary Reynolds Babcock Foundation
and the Charles F. Kettering Foundation**

and in collaboration with
91 national and regional organizations

National Society for Internships
and Experiential Education

Jane C. Kendall and Associates, *Combining Service and Learning:*
A Resource Book for Community and Public Service,
Raleigh, North Carolina: National Society for Internships
and Experiential Education

International Standard Book Number (ISBN): 0-937883-09-3
Library of Congress Catalog Number: 90-060427

Cover design by Tracy Wang, Sabine Moore, and Carol Majors
Production by Publications Unlimited
Printed in the United States of America

Table of Contents for Volume II

PART I: PRACTICAL ISSUES AND IDEAS FOR PROGRAMS AND COURSES THAT COMBINE SERVICE AND LEARNING

Faculty Issues and Resources

Robert Coles
reference

Community Issues and Tips

Evaluation

PROFILES OF PROGRAMS AND COURSES THAT COMBINE SERVICE AND LEARNING

PART II: PROFILES OF PROGRAMS AND COURSES THAT COMBINE SERVICE AND LEARNING: COLLEGES AND UNIVERSITIES

PART III: PROFILES OF PROGRAMS AND COURSES THAT COMBINE SERVICE AND LEARNING: K-12 SCHOOLS

PART IV: PROFILES OF PROGRAMS THAT COMBINE SERVICE
AND LEARNING: COMMUNITY-BASED ORGANIZATIONS,
GOVERNMENT, AND YOUTH-SERVING AGENCIES

Important: See the Other Two Volumes!

This volume is only part of a three-volume resource book on combining service and learning. All three volumes are intended to go together as a coherent whole. Volume I contains essential principles, theories, rationales, research, institutional and public policy issues and guides, and the history and future of service-learning. Volume II contains practical issues and ideas for programs and courses that combine service and learning, as well as case studies of programs in diverse settings. Volume III is an annotated bibliography of the literature in the field.

Important: See the Other Two Volumes!

Preface

COMBINING SERVICE AND LEARNING is a treasure trove of practical guidance for addressing the national crisis of public disengagement. The 1980s' celebration of individual gratification robbed our young people of a vision of the rewards of active citizenship. As we enter the 1990s, all Americans concerned about our future are asking how we can prepare today's youth to meet the unprecedented challenges of the 21st century. COMBINING SERVICE AND LEARNING is a major contribution to answering this question. It offers both inspiration and concrete lessons for re-engaging young people.

COMBINING SERVICE AND LEARNING pulls no punches. It does not romanticize learning through community experience. It clearly poses the toughest questions. Leaders in the field ask what is necessary to turn a community service activity into a practice that builds the capacities and ongoing commitments of all involved.

In one place, COMBINING SERVICE AND LEARNING is the collected wisdom of decades of experience and reflection. It can well serve to spur a national dialogue on the meaning of democracy itself. As a people we simply can no longer afford to teach our youth that being a good citizen means not causing trouble and that democracy is merely a set of fixed institutions we have inherited. This impressive work can go far in helping to redefine democracy as the problem-solving practices of active citizens, and schools as places where citizens learn the rewarding arts of democracy.

— *Frances Moore Lappé*
Author, DIET FOR A SMALL PLANET
Director, Institute for Food and Development Policy
and Project Public Life

Cooperating Organizations

Combining Service and Learning: A Resource Book for Community and Public Service is a publication of the National Society for Internships and Experiential Education (NSIEE). This massive, three-year project was done in partnership with the Mary Reynolds Babcock Foundation in Winston-Salem, North Carolina, and the Charles F. Kettering Foundation in Dayton, Ohio. NSIEE and the users of this resource book are also grateful to the following organizations which graciously cooperated with NSIEE in this project:

ACCESS: Networking in the Public Interest
American Association for Higher Education
American Association of State Colleges and Universities
American Association of University Women
American Council on Education
American Institute for Public Service
American Political Science Association
American Sociological Association
American Youth Foundation
Association for Community-Based Education
Association for Experiential Education
Association for Volunteer Administration
Association of American Colleges
Association of Episcopal Colleges
Association of Voluntary Action Scholars
Campus Compact
Campus Outreach Opportunity League
Carnegie Foundation for the Advancement of Teaching
Center for Creative Community
Center for Creative Leadership
Center for Global Education, Augsburg College
Center for Youth Development and Research, University of Minnesota
Commission on Voluntary Service and Action
Community Service Volunteers, United Kingdom
Constitutional Rights Foundation
Cooperative Education Association
Council for Adult and Experiential Learning
Council for the Advancement of Citizenship
Council of Chief State School Officers
Council of Independent Colleges
Council on Social Work Education
Education Commission of the States
Educators for Social Responsibility
Executive High School Internship Association
Facing History and Ourselves National Foundation
Fund for the Improvement of Postsecondary Education, U.S. Department of
    Education
Great Lakes Colleges Association, The Philadelphia Center
Higher Education Consortium for Urban Affairs
Independent Sector

Institute for Food and Development Policy
Intercultural Development Research Association
International Christian Youth Exchange
The Johnson Foundation
Maryland Student Service Alliance, Maryland Department of Education
Michigan Campus Compact
Minnesota Association for Field Experience Learning
Minnesota Campus Service Initiative
Minnesota Youth Service Association
National Association for Equal Opportunity in Higher Education
National Association of Independent Schools
National Association of Partners in Education
National Association of Schools of Public Affairs and Administration
National Association of Secondary School Principals
National Association of Service and Conservation Corps
National Association of State Boards of Education
National Association of Student Employment Administrators
National Association of Student YMCAs
National Center for Effective Schools, University of Wisconsin
National Civic League
National Coalition of Alternative Community Schools
National Commission on Resources for Youth/Institute for Responsive Education
National Commission on the Public Service
National Community Education Association
National Conference on Governors' Schools
National Crime Prevention Council
National Governors' Association
National Institute for Work and Learning, Academy for Educational Development
National Service Secretariat
National Youth Leadership Council
New York State Cooperative and Experiential Education Association
North Carolina Youth Advocacy and Involvement Office
Operation Civic Serve
Overseas Development Network
Partnership for Service-Learning
PennServe
Project Service Leadership
SerVermont
Society for Intercultural Education, Training and Research
Society for Values in Higher Education
Southern Regional Education Board
Thomas Jefferson Forum
United Negro College Fund
VISTA/Community Service, ACTION
VOLUNTEER: The National Center
The Washington Center
YMCA of the USA
Youth and America's Future: The William T. Grant Foundation Commission on
  Work, Family, and Citizenship
Youth Policy Institute
Youth Service America

About the
The National Society for Internships and Experiential Education

THE NATIONAL SOCIETY FOR INTERNSHIPS AND EXPERIENTIAL EDUCATION is a national resource center and professional association that supports the use of *learning through experience* for civic and social responsibility, intellectual development, cross-cultural awareness, moral/ethical development, career exploration, and personal growth.

NSIEE's mission: As a community of individuals, institutions, and organizations, NSIEE is committed to fostering the effective use of experience as an integral part of education, in order to empower learners and promote the common good.

NSIEE's goals are:
- to advocate for the effective use of experiential learning throughout the educational system and the larger community;
- to disseminate information on principles of good practice and on innovations in the field;
- to enhance professional growth and leadership development in the field;
- to encourage the development and dissemination of related research and theory.

Experiential education includes community and public service when combined with learning, internships, field studies, intercultural programs, leadership development, cooperative education, experiential learning in the classroom, outdoor education, and all forms of active learning.

NSIEE's services include conferences, workshops, publications, newsletters, the National Resource Center on Service and Learning, professional network services, and in-depth consulting for program and institutional planning. See pages 641-651 for membership information and a publications list.

NSIEE was founded in 1971 as the National Center for Public Service Internship Programs and the Society for Field Experience Education. NSIEE's national office is in Raleigh, North Carolina.

Principles of Good Practice in Combining Service and Learning

IN 1987 THE NATIONAL SOCIETY for Internships and Experiential Education (NSIEE) began a process of articulating and refining principles of good practice for programs that seek to combine service and learning effectively. This was in response to the burgeoning growth of community service programs for youth, students, and adults and the increasing awareness among thoughtful practitioners that effective service and learning do not necessarily happen automatically.

As programs of the 1980s experienced the same challenges about program *quality* that programs of the 1960s and 1970s had also faced, NSIEE began a broad-based process of articulating the principles learned by experienced practitioners. We reviewed the advice of leaders in the community and public service movement of the late 1960s and early 1970s. We asked members of the NSIEE Service-Learning Special Interest Group to reach into their group's 15-year reservoir of experience. We asked more than 75 other national and regional organizations to do the same; the staffs and members of most of the organizations responded by adding their diverse perspectives, experiences, and advice. Nine drafts were circulated over an intense, 12-month period of refinement.

Then in the spring of 1989, the Johnson Foundation generously agreed to host a Wingspread conference to hammer out the final product. Several national organizations co-sponsored the May 10-12, 1989, working session: the American Association for Higher Education, Campus Compact, Constitutional Rights Foundation, Council of Chief State School Officers, National Association of Independent Schools, National Association of Secondary School Principals, National Society for Internships and Experiential Education, and Youth Service America.

The 75 national and regional groups that had participated in the review process also provided examples of the implementation of the ten principles that resulted from the Wingspread working session.

What follows here are the Introduction, the Preamble, the ten principles refined from this two-year collaborative process, and an explanation of each. Examples of each principle as used in actual programs are provided in Volume I of this resource book. Ellen Porter Honnet and Susan J. Poulsen of The Johnson Foundation graciously produced the final copy.

We invite you to use these principles in the context of your particular needs and purposes. You may decide to reject some of them, but we hope this work at least helps you ask some of the right questions about combining service and learning in an effective, sustained way.

— Jane Kendall, NSIEE

Introduction

The level of interest and sense of urgency in community and public service grows greater every day. In every community, programs are being designed for participants from kindergartners to the elderly. Is there a set of guiding principles by which service programs can be designed and by which their effectiveness can be judged? Is there a set of ideas which have the potential for deepening and sustaining the current movements?

The principles described in this section reflect the grassroots experience and the thinking of thousands of people, hundreds of programs, and numerous national organizations over the last two decades. They are offered with the hope that current initiatives to create service programs will benefit from this rich history.

The combination of service and learning is powerful. It creates potential benefits beyond what either service or learning can offer separately. The frequent results of the effective integration of service and learning are that participants:

- develop a habit of critical reflection on their experiences, enabling them to learn more throughout life,
- are more curious and motivated to learn,
- are able to perform better service,
- strengthen their ethic of social and civic responsibility,
- feel more committed to addressing the underlying problems behind social issues,
- understand problems in a more complex way and can imagine alternative solutions,

- demonstrate more sensitivity to how decisions are made and how institutional decisions affect people's lives,
- respect other cultures more and are better able to learn about cultural differences,
- learn how to work more collaboratively with other people on real problems, and
- realize that their lives can make a difference.

The emphasis on learning does not mean these Principles are limited in any way to programs connected to schools. They relate to programs and policies based in all settings — community organizations, K-12 schools, colleges and universities, corporations, government agencies, and research and policy organizations. They relate to people of all ages in all walks of life.

Preamble

We are a nation founded upon active citizenship and participation in community life. We have always believed that individuals can and should serve.

It is crucial that service toward the common good be combined with reflective learning to assure that service programs of high quality can be created and sustained over time, and to help individuals appreciate how service can be a significant and ongoing part of life. Service, combined with learning, adds value to each and transforms both.

Those who serve and those who are served are thus able to develop the informed judgment, imagination and skills that lead to greater capacity to contribute to the common good.

The Principles that follow are statements of what we believe are essential components of good practice. We invite you to use them in the context of your particular needs and purposes.

Principles of Good Practice in Combining Service and Learning

An effective and sustained program:

1. Engages people in responsible and challenging actions for the common good.

2. Provides structured opportunities for people to reflect critically on their service experience.

3. Articulates clear service and learning goals for everyone involved.

4. Allows for those with needs to define those needs.

5. Clarifies the responsibilities of each person and organization involved.

6. Matches service providers and service needs through a process that recognizes changing circumstances.

7. Expects genuine, active, and sustained organizational commitment.

8. Includes training, supervision, monitoring, support, recognition, and evaluation to meet service and learning goals.

9. Insures that the time commitment for service and learning is flexible, appropriate, and in the best interest of all involved.

10. Is committed to program participation by and with diverse populations.

See the following pages for an explanation of each principle.

Principles of Good Practice in Combining Service and Learning

1. An effective program engages people in responsible and challenging actions for the common good. Participants in programs combining service and learning should engage in tasks that they and society recognize as important. These actions require reaching beyond one's range of previous knowledge or experience. Active participation — not merely being a spectator or visitor — requires accountability for one's actions, involves the right to take risks, and gives participants the opportunity to experience the consequences of those actions for others and for themselves.

2. An effective program provides structured opportunities for people to reflect critically on their service experience. The service experience alone does not insure that either significant learning or effective service will occur. It is important that programs build in structured opportunities for participants to think about their experience and what they are learning. Through discussions with others and individual reflection on moral questions and relevant issues, participants can develop a better sense of social responsibility, advocacy, and active citizenship. This reflective component allows for intellectual growth and the development of skills in critical thinking. It is most useful when it is intentional and continuous throughout the experience, and when opportunity for feedback is provided. Ideally, feedback will come from those persons being served, as well as from peers and program leaders.

3. An effective program articulates clear service and learning goals for everyone involved. From the outset of the project, participants and service recipients alike must have a clear sense of: (1) what is to be accomplished and (2) what is to be learned. These service and learning goals must be agreed upon through negotiations with all parties, and in the context of the traditions and cultures of the local community. These goals should reflect the creative and imaginative input of both those providing the service and those receiving it. Attention to this important factor of mutuality in the service-learning exchange can help keep the "service" from becoming patronizing charity.

4. An effective program allows for those with needs to define those needs. The actual recipients of service, as well as the community groups and constituencies to which they belong, must have the primary role in defining their own service needs. Community service programs, government agencies, and private organizations can also be helpful in defining what service tasks are needed and when and how these tasks should be performed. This collaboration to define needs will help insure that service by participants will: (1) not take jobs from the local community, (2) involve tasks that will otherwise go undone, and (3) focus their efforts on the tasks and approaches that the *recipients* define as useful.

5. An effective program clarifies the responsibilities of each person and organization involved. Several parties are potentially involved in any service and learning program: participants (students and teachers, volunteers of all ages), community leaders, service supervisors, and sponsoring organizations, as well as those individuals and groups receiving the services. It is important to clarify roles and responsibilities of these parties through a careful negotiation process as the program is being developed. This negotiation should include identifying and assigning responsibility for the tasks to be done, while acknowledging the values and principles important to all the parties involved.

6. An effective program matches service providers and service needs through a process that recognizes changing circumstances. Because people are often changed by the service and learning experience, effective programs must build in opportunities for continuous feedback about the changing service needs and growing service skills of those involved. Ideally, participation in the service-learning partnership affects development in areas such as intellect, ethics, cross-cultural understanding, empathy, leadership and citizenship. In effective service and learning programs, the relationships among groups and individuals are dynamic and often create dilemmas. Such dilemmas may lead to unintended outcomes. They can require recognizing and dealing with differences.

7. An effective program expects genuine, active, and sustained organizational commitment. In order for a program to be effective, it must have a strong, ongoing commitment from both the sponsoring and the receiving organizations. Ideally, this commitment will take many forms, including reference to both service and learning in the organization's mission statement. Effective programs must receive administrative support, be an ongoing part of the organization's budget, be allocated appropriate physical space, equipment, and transportation, and allow for scheduled release time for participants and program leaders. In schools and colleges, the most effective service and learning programs are linked to the curriculum and require that the faculty become committed to combining service and learning as a valid part of teaching.

8. An effective program includes training, supervision, monitoring, support, recognition, and evaluation to meet service and learning goals. The most effective service and learning programs are sensitive to the importance of training, supervision, and monitoring of progress throughout the program. This is a reciprocal responsibility and requires open communication between those offering and those receiving the service. In partnership, sponsoring and receiving organizations may recognize the value of service through appropriate celebrations, awards, and public acknowledgement of individual and group service. Planned, formalized, and ongoing evaluation of service and learning projects should be part of every program and should involve all participants.

9. An effective program insures that the time commitment for service and learning is flexible, appropriate, and in the best interests of all involved. In order to be useful to all parties involved, some service activities require longer participation and/or a greater time commitment than others. The length of the experience and the amount of time required are determined by the service tasks involved and should be negotiated by all the parties. Sometimes a program can do more harm than good if a project is abandoned after too short a time or given too little attention. Where appropriate, a carefully planned succession or combination of participants can provide the continuity of service needed.

10. An effective program is committed to program participation by and with diverse populations. A good service and learning program promotes access and removes disincentives and barriers to participation. Those responsible for participation in a program should make every effort to include and make welcome persons from differing ethnic, racial, and religious backgrounds, as well as varied ages, genders, economic levels, and those with disabilities. Less obvious, but very important, is the need for sensitivity to other barriers, such as lack of transportation, family, work and school responsibilities, concern for personal safety, or uncertainty about one's ability to make a contribution.

PART I

Practical Issues and Ideas for Programs and Courses that Combine Service and Learning

Project Ideas for Combining Service and Learning for All Age Groups

This listing of community service projects done by college and high school students can provide ideas for new or established programs. It can also be helpful for middle and elementary schools as well as for programs for any age group based in community organizations, youth-serving agencies, service corps, and other non-school settings. Reprinted from Service-Learning: A Guide for College Students, *National Center for Service-Learning, ACTION, pp. 87-91.*

Project Ideas Related to Fields of College Study

This section lists specific projects that have been done by college students as part of their courses in the particular fields of study listed. It is intended to give examples and is certainly not exhaustive.

Accounting

- Work with community groups to investigate patterns of loan-credit discrimination against persons with low incomes.
- Instruct halfway house residents in the management of personal finances.
- Organize a fund-raising effort to support community mental health.
- Organize grassroots efforts to encourage the business community to provide jobs for unemployed youth.
- Develop a system to help low-income people prepare tax returns.
- Develop an accounting system for a food co-op.

- Organize an energy audit team to prepare cost estimates for improving the energy efficiency of homes in low-income areas.
- Help obtain financing for community improvement efforts.
- Establish a community credit union.

Agriculture

- Establish a community gardening project for retired people.
- Study nutritional needs/habits of a low-income community.
- Study cooperative food costs in stores serving low-income neighborhoods.
- Assist older persons with home canning and food preparation.
- Organize an emergency food program.
- Draft legislation to regulate quality of meals served in nursing homes.
- Assist Outreach Programs run by the county health division.
- Develop educational materials on sound dietary habits for pregnant women.

Anthropology

- Help people in halfway houses explore their "roots."
- Document the need for mental health care services for Native Americans.
- Become involved in efforts to preserve the heritage of Native Americans.

Architecture

- Help older persons with home improvement.
- Survey care facilities for older persons, comparing these to the standards set by local building codes.
- Design a community center.
- Organize retired carpenters to winterize homes of people with limited incomes.
- Plan the renovation of older homes for use as halfway houses.
- Design economically feasible energy saving plans for homes in poor neighborhoods.
- Assist energy environmental groups to prepare cost and feasibility studies for solar recovery units.
- Investigate the need for improved housing (e.g., using community meetings, door-to-door-canvassing, home visits).
- Find emergency and permanent housing for community members in need.

Biology

- Design a biological park as part of a community center.
- Conduct classes on "What's Happening to My Body" for retirees.
- Study medical and nutritional practices in homes for older persons.
- Organize groups to lobby for adequate medical attention for people with low incomes.
- Bring pressure on the community zoo to make it accessible to persons with special physical challenges.
- Design a system to help people who are blind to experience zoos, parks.
- Assist neighborhood groups with non-contaminating pest control programs.

Business

- Organize workshops and informal meetings where those already in business show others how to start a business.
- Assist grassroots groups that advocate for the rights of persons who have low incomes or other disadvantages — help them establish bookkeeping and other fiscal procedures that meet their needs; help the groups consider the advantages and disadvantages of incorporating.
- Assist nursing homes with an audit of their records.
- Assist in establishing sound business procedures for a food co-op.
- Document practices of local businesses that discriminate against poor people; set up a mechanism for handling complaints.
- Organize a neighborhood credit union.
- Help people with limited incomes to utilize sound financial planning practices.
- Sponsor workshops on fund-raising and organize activities to generate resources (e.g., a clothes sale, a yard sale, a hot dog roast).
- Use contacts in government, business and in other local organizations to obtain funding and donations for community members (e.g., free use of facilities, transportation).
- Refer community members to groups that can provide technical assistance in organizing community business (e.g., the Small Business Administration).

Chemistry

- Assist in counseling of "substance-abusers."
- Publish information about dangers of alcohol, nicotine and other drugs in a community newsletter.
- Study the effects of artificial foods on emotional and mental states.
- Work with community mental health cooperatives to plan to meet nutrition needs.
- Develop rooftop vegetable gardens, community gardens, inexpensive methods of fertilization.
- Monitor levels of pollutants in local air and water; bring pressure on polluting industries to abide by regulations.

Computer Information Sciences

- Develop computerized learning modules for use by youngsters and adults with mental illnesses.
- Create a data processing format and analysis service for non-profit, community-based service agencies.
- Develop a community workshop on how to deal with computers: straightening out mistaken billings, removing names from mailing lists, etc.
- Help youth from families with low incomes to explore careers in computer sciences.

Economics

- Encourage business and industries to open job positions to persons who have been chronically unemployed.
- Form a consumer protection service: publicize its availability to people who need it most; train others to investigate complaints about auto repair, insurance, medical care, deceptive credit practices and deceptive advertising techniques.
- Work to encourage consideration of needs of low-income people in local/regional economic development plans.
- Produce materials to help low-income families institute sound financial planning practices.
- Arrange training for people so they can qualify for better jobs (e.g., workshops on language skills, job-seeking techniques and job-related skills).
- Arrange workshops for potential employers to familiarize them with the skills of community members and encourage them to hire community members.

- Serve as a work referral agent for teenagers and others who want work in the community (e.g., refer community members who need babysitters or gardeners to those teenagers who want work).

Education

- Arrange for retired persons to serve as learning resources for younger people.
- Work with local school board to develop educational programs appropriate to all community residents.
- Organize a program to provide needed educational experience to prison inmates.
- Tutor children with learning difficulties.
- Provide plant therapy, art therapy, exercise therapy in nursing homes.
- Work with high school students to develop a plan to clean up the high school, to remove graffiti and to stop vandalism.
- Establish a life skills program for adults.
- Organize a tutoring center.
- Set up role playing sessions that will train and prepare community members for situations they will encounter in applying for services at a community agency.

Engineering

- Help increase the self-reliance of community cooperatives by building compost makers, solar energy panels or waste-recycling units.
- Develop devices for people with disabilities to help them achieve mobility.
- Design a typewriter for kids with cerebral palsy.
- Build a playground for people with special physical challenges.

English and Journalism

- Assist community groups with the preparation of a newsletter that publishes concerns and suggestions of community members.
- Utilize techniques of the folklorist to learn "folklore" of an area from longtime residents.
- Investigate forced retirement in your community and develop a series of news articles based on findings.

- Develop attractive, hard-hitting brochures for use with various kinds of outreach programs.
- Help the library increase its services to low-income neighborhoods.
- Establish an alternative community magazine.
- Develop a "Guide to Access to Buildings" for the persons with special physical challenges.
- Establish an adult literacy project.
- Refer community members to public officials who can help them with their problems — this will involve compiling a directory of officials according to their areas of influence.
- Organize letter writing campaigns (including committees to write group letters to their political representatives).
- Assist community agencies with proposal writing.

Environmental Studies

- Investigate feasibility of developing solar heating for schools, community centers.
- Conduct survey of interior design needs of nursing homes.
- Document incidence of lead-paint poisoning in low-income neighborhoods.
- Document violation of environmental quality regulations by local industries.
- Bring information about needs of low-income community to the attention of local mass transit authorities.

Fine and Applied Arts

- Use art therapy techniques in tutoring persons with mental illnesses.
- Plan to display work of community residents in community buildings.
- Design attractive pamphlets containing nutritional information as part of health division's educational efforts.

Foreign Languages

- Use translation skills to help new immigrants articulate needs.
- Work with local media to develop programs using foreign languages.
- Translate consumer information for speakers of foreign languages.
- Work as a bilingual aide in the public schools.

- Translate information concerning agency programs into languages or dialects common among community members.

Forestry and Horticulture

- Help community groups operate a vegetable garden on a previously vacant city lot.
- Organize "Outward Bound" experiences for city youth with special problems.
- Work through city parks bureau to involve residents of halfway houses in landscaping and maintaining parks and recreational areas.

Health and Recreation

- Plan illness prevention activities involving diet and exercise with community mental health center residents.
- Work with center staff to get funds from city parks and recreation department so activities can be provided for youngsters from families with limited incomes.
- Investigate adequacy of medical care available to those with mental illnesses.
- Document need for dental care in low-income neighborhoods.
- Plan health and nutrition activities that can be used in Head Start programs.
- Organize a community health fair.
- Gather data on needs of youngsters for vaccinations.
- Identify major health problems in the community and plan a campaign to educate community members about these concerns (e.g., diabetes, lack of needed immunizations, malnutrition, high blood pressure, venereal disease).
- Help reorganize existing health programs to meet the particular needs of community members (e.g., extend their hours in the evenings and on weekends, arrange for a mobile clinic to be at different locations on various days of the week).

History

- Document the history of a neighborhood or town using oral history techniques.
- Gather background on the history of treatment of low-income people in your city or state.

- Work with public organizations to establish displays that recognize the achievements and contributions of various ethnic groups to the culture of the area.
- Develop and publish a cultural journal that reports on unique aspects of the community.
- Develop ways to help children of various ethnic heritages understand their own background and ancestry.
- Set up workshops to inform community members about the history of an issue and possible strategies for resolving the issue, so that they will be better able to evaluate the opinions and actions of local government officials.

Law

- Conduct workshops to inform people of their rights and legal remedies for their grievances.
- Operate a legal assistance program for persons with limited incomes or mental illnesses.
- Counsel (advise) non-profit community organizations on matters of liability, property ownership, incorporation.
- Provide paralegal assistance to minors.
- Provide support for groups who seek to prevent outlawing community-based treatment facilities and halfway houses in residential areas.
- Conduct "Street Law Classes" to familiarize residents of correctional institutions with the legal system and with their rights.
- Organize victim assistance programs.
- Provide aids such as transportation, babysitting and emotional support to witnesses of crimes whose lives may be disrupted by the need to testify.
- Develop a program of tenant education through researching the housing code, and rights and responsibilities of tenants and landlords. Make the information available to tenants and tenants' groups.
- Study laws and regulations relating to nursing homes and other health care facilities for older persons; help willing administrators with matters of compliance.
- Assist grassroots groups with development of model utility regulations. Advocate to keep utilities from discontinuing services to poor and older citizens.
- Set up a petition drive to show community support of a legal action.

Music

- Document local or indigenous folk music of an area.
- Develop music therapy programs for children with disabilities.
- Stage concerts or other musical performances at nursing and retirement homes.
- Work with local musicians to find ways to provide music lessons to children who otherwise could not afford lessons.
- Raise funds to purchase instruments for children from families with limited incomes.

Physics

- Develop devices that help persons with arthritis or rheumatism to do such things as open food cans.
- Gather data that support excluding poor and retired citizens from planned utility rate increases.
- Develop solar heating systems for installation in retirement homes.
- Work with community groups to check and repair the wiring in homes of older people.

Political Science

- Help citizens with physical disabilities travel to and from their polling places.
- Work with groups to lobby for legislation to meet older people's needs.
- Help organize opposition to mandatory retirement policies in your college/university and in places of business in your community.
- Assist with the formation of neighborhood action groups: provide assistance to such groups as they make their needs known to appropriate governmental units.
- Organize an "awareness day" for community members during which activities are encouraged that promote a better understanding of community problems (e.g., ask community members to keep a record of what they learn during the day and publish the excerpts in a newsletter).

Psychology

- Provide assistance to grassroots groups conducting research on the extent to which mental health care needs are being met in the community.

- Establish a crisis hotline or work with an existing one on its community outreach.
- Assist with programs that provide family counseling as part of a delinquency prevention program.
- Assist with programs that provide counseling for battered wives, husbands and children.

Sociology

- Assist with counseling services for alcoholics.
- Work with grassroots groups to increase community acceptance of halfway houses.
- Work with a drug abuse clinic to counsel teenage drug users.
- Help recently released prisoners adjust to life through counseling, group meetings, problem solving.
- Establish a "clearinghouse" of volunteer services to direct clients to needed sources of assistance or help with research at existing clearinghouses.
- Serve as a catalyst to establish pooling of resources with other community groups (e.g., share office space, staff, buses; present a united front when requesting or protesting city services).

Project Ideas for Young People Aged 12-18

This section describes briefly a number of possible and actual service projects for students in high schools, middle schools, or elementary schools. The ideas are also valuable for programs based in community organizations, service corps, and other non-school settings. Reprinted from *High School Student Volunteers*, ACTION, pp. 47-51.

While no attempt has been made to be exhaustive — students and communities are coming up with original projects every day — the list should give you some idea of the range of opportunities available. It may help in generating ideas for your program. Some of the educational projects involve students working in their own elementary and junior high schools. Schools which have never sponsored student service in the community may want to begin their programs with these school-oriented projects, in which students will be working close at hand and under the direct supervision of professional educators.

Education

Sesame Street. Using Sesame Street as a nucleus, the students improvise plays, puppet shows and other devices to enhance the effectiveness of the televised presentation.

Teacher Aides. High school students volunteering as teacher aides in an elementary school serve as small group discussion leaders and researchers.

Language Lab. As the "laboratory" portion of a language course, students teach English to Italian and Mexican-American employees in local businesses. In turn, students benefit from the opportunity to converse in Italian and Spanish.

Health

Project Turn-Off. A student-organized drug education program informs parents how young people feel about drugs and teaches teenagers the dangers of drug abuse.

Drug Drag. Students design and present a drug education program for elementary school children, including a play, a puppet show, comic books, and mini-lectures.

Hospital Aides. Visiting patients, helping run the gift shop, and assisting in children's wards are among the duties performed by student hospital aides.

Hospital Interns. Working as interns in the various departments of a hospital — the kitchen, the laboratory, the physical therapy room — students assist hospital workers while learning health-related occupations.

High School Red Cross. Under the auspices of the local Red Cross chapter, students volunteer in hospitals, disaster relief efforts, and blood drive registrations.

4-H Volunteer Corps. Organized through the high school's 4-H Club, this project develops and presents a nutritional education program for children from families with limited incomes, using puppets and other creative techniques.

Aging

Benefits for Older Persons. As part of a study of the Social Security program, a social science class works in conjunction with the local Social Security office to bring information about benefits to older people and shut-ins through neighborhood canvassing.

Senior Summer Festival. An arts and crafts fair displaying the work of older persons is organized by students.

Adopt a Grandparent. Each student adopts an older person. Telephone calls, letters, visits, and social activities all give the "grandparents" a sense of being wanted and the students a sense of responsibility and value.

Children

Library Aides. Assisting in the local public libraries, students hold story hours and help children select books.

Neighborhood Paint-In. Students enrolled in art courses organize children to decorate interior and exterior walls of a community center building.

Day Care Corps. Students act as recreation leaders and teacher aides at a day care center, allowing it to operate at substantial savings.

Music Instruction. Music students and choir and orchestra members give free music lessons to children from families with limited incomes.

Nature Study Center. High school biology classes furnish guides, helpers, and animal handlers at a non-profit nature study center which provides free education programs and tours for inner-city children.

Inner-City Football League. Coaches and team members from city high schools organize an inner-city football league for boys from 9 to 12 years of age, with a championship game to be played on the same day as the high school championship game.

Housing

Project Reclaim. Students in the field section of an industrial arts course repair rundown dwellings in the community, using materials donated by local merchants and under the supervision of members of the local building trades unions.

New Housing Aides. The city housing authority uses home economics students as aides to instruct new residents of housing developments in the use and care of household facilities.

Environment

Environmental Action. In conjunction with local and national ecology groups, students campaign for neighborhood clean-up and trash collection; run pick-up centers for bottles, cans, and paper; and support environmental legislation.

National Parks and Forests. Students work on recreation projects, build camps and shelters, and create play areas in nearby parks.

Consumer Services

Project Price Watch. Students survey food and drug stores in and around the community to establish the relative prices and quality of essential items. They issue a monthly listing of this information, which helps prevent stores in low-income communities from raising their prices above those found in surrounding areas.

Neighborhood Co-op. Students in an accounting class assist in running and staffing a cooperative food store and credit union.

Quantity Buying Club. In conjunction with community residents, home economics classes organize a quantity buying club in a low-income area. Students take orders for food and clothing so as to enable residents to buy in large quantities at reduced prices.

Community Organization

Vest-Pocket Parks. Working with a citizens' group and the city parks department, students help raise funds to turn vacant lots into miniature playgrounds. The students also assist in clearing the land, constructing play equipment, and supervising recreational activities once the parks are completed.

Cross-Cultural Arts Fair. Organized by a language club, this project closes off a side street on Saturday for the exhibition and sale of arts and crafts, ethnic foods, and other homemade items. Dancing and costumes are also featured.

Social Action News. Students from English and journalism classes assist a community group in running its own newspaper.

Community Libraries. Students organize a book drive to set up community libraries in community centers in low-income neighborhoods. They also staff the libraries.

Volunteer Patrol. Students work in the office and patrol the streets with police in a project aimed at improving student understanding of the Police Department and increasing community support and participation in combating crime.

Community Services

Meals on Wheels. A student group delivers hospital-prepared meals to people confined to their homes.

Free Breakfasts. In a project sponsored by the school district, students use home economics facilities to prepare free breakfasts for elementary school children.

Car Pool Corps. Working afternoon and early evening shifts, students supply transportation for persons who need assistance in getting around.

Cool-Line Committee. A clearinghouse for short-term volunteer requests from agencies and individuals (such as clean-up campaigns, shopping for shut-ins), the Cool-Line Committee keeps a roster of students willing to serve on an "on call" basis.

Senior-Student Service Corps. Students team up with older persons to volunteer at a local orphanage. The project gives both the older persons and the students a feeling of being needed.

Sick Car Clinic. Students in the auto mechanics class at a vocational high school staff a sick car clinic where families with limited incomes can have their automobiles repaired in the school's automotive shop for the cost of materials only.

Office Staff. Advanced typing becomes a field course as students get on-the-job experience in agencies short on staff and long on need.

The Service-Learning Educator:
A Guide to Program Management

The National Center for Service-Learning (NCSL) was a vital part of the federal ACTION agency until the early 1980s. NCSL produced a number of excellent publications for college, K-12, and community-based programs that combine service and learning. When NCSL was dismantled, the National Society for Internships and Experiential Education (NSIEE) became the disseminator of NCSL's materials. In addition to the outstanding Synergist *magazine (contact NSIEE for an index to* Synergist*) and numerous guides, NCSL published* The Service-Learning Educator: A Guide to Program Management *in 1981. The table of contents is reprinted on the following pages along with a few selections from this useful guide. While the language here is geared toward college- and university-based programs, the principles discussed are also applicable to K-12 and community-based programs. For a copy of the full guide, contact NSIEE, 3509 Haworth Drive, Suite 207, Raleigh, NC 27609.*

Table of Contents

*The sections marked with an asterisk are reprinted in whole or in part in this section of the resource book. Each chapter listed in this Table of Contents also has an "Introduction" and "Additional Readings" provided.

Needs Analysis Tool*
Planning Site Visits*
Project Evaluation
Sample Form for Documenting Student Achievement of
 Learning Objectives
Sample Job Description
Sample Letter to Organizations*
Sample Project Description
Sample Site Visit Record
Sample Timeline
Some Ways of Demonstrating Project Impact*
Training Interviewers*

Special Forms and Charts

Areas for Evaluation
Common Uses of Evaluation*
Levels of Leadership Development*
Personal Development Plan
Sample Planning Sheet to Meet Reporting Needs
Sample Recordkeeping System
Service-Learning Agreement*
Transportation Schedule

Involving the Community in Assessing Needs for Service

Description and Rationale: Assessing community needs is where service-learning begins. Many programs flounder because they fail to find out what the service needs truly are. They may assume that certain needs exist, but they may overlook less obvious needs. Periodic assessment of community needs will keep you aware of changes that may be occurring, and may lead you to a need that no one else is serving. By meeting such a need, your program will gain in identity and purpose. By keeping track of changing needs, you will be able to widen the repertoire of opportunities and provide service experiences on target for students—*and* students who are on target for the community.

Your principal question in assessing community needs is, "If students were available to help solve problems, what kinds of tasks would they be doing?" You can train student interviewers to approach community people directly, or you can concentrate your efforts on checking with major community service agencies and advocacy groups. It is crucial to follow up your survey by informing respondents of the results and how you plan to address the needs identified. [See the "Principles of Good Practice" at the front of this book for important principles about enabling people to address their *own* needs.] If you are going to concentrate on only one need, it is important to explain why you made that decision.

How to Do It: The tasks associated with conducting a needs survey are similar whether you are surveying members of a single group or an entire community. A community survey can be a valuable student or class project. Education, sociology, psychology and math departments are full of potential helpers. Here are some steps to consider in planning a survey:

1. Decide what kind(s) of information you want. Some typical questions are: What are the most pressing problems in our community? How could you use students in this organization? How could you use students in new ways in your organization?

2. Determine who has the information you need. Begin by listing the information and the persons who are most likely to have it.

3. Determine whom you are going to survey. This can be done in conjunction with selecting a desired survey method, since some techniques allow you to reach more people in less time, while others allow you to get better information, but require more survey time.

   The key to effective surveys is choosing a representative *sample.* Usually you won't be able to question everyone in the community, so make sure your sample is representative of the entire community population. When you survey an agency or community organization, sampling may not be necessary because your population is usually small enough to survey in its entirety. But if you want to survey a neighborhood to determine the kinds of help students might provide, you'll have to study various types of *sampling* procedures. (See Tool #2.)

4. Decide who will conduct the survey and when, and provide appropriate training. (See Tool #2.)

5. Prepare materials

6. Conduct survey.

7. Analyze, publish and distribute the results.

Tool #1. Advantages and Disadvantages of Survey Techniques

Kind of Survey	Advantages	Disadvantages
Telephone Survey	Get direct responses to questions.	Lose advantage of face-to-face contact with respondent.
	Good way to get through to busy agency people.	Time consuming.
	Get information immediately.	Not everyone has a phone, especially in low-income communities.
		Requires skill to record responses accurately.
Mail-Out Questionnaire	Can survey great numbers of people this way.	Response rates almost always low; data may represent feelings of only a small group.
	Data easy to tabulate.	
	Takes little time to conduct.	Can be impersonal.
	Good way to survey agencies with established offices.	People may interpret questions differently, may be difficult to interpret responses
Personal Interviews	Yields most accurate information.	Most time-consuming method of surveying.
	Can establish good relations with community members.	Requires skill to record responses accurately.
Visits to Large Group Meetings	Can conduct on-the-spot survey of large number of people.	Other business of group may be distracting; you may distract group.
	Opportunity to answer questions.	May not be able to clarify issues for all participants.
	Not time-consuming.	May omit segments of the population.
Community Meetings	Can be used within neighborhoods.	Impractical for any but small communities.
	Can reach large numbers of people quickly with on-the-spot survey.	Requires skill.
		Requires logistics, unless meetings occur regularly.

Tool #2. Training Interviewers

If your needs assessment will be conducted by interviewers, it may be helpful to offer them training in interviewing skills. Training should give them practice in:

- Putting the respondent at ease
- Explaining the purpose of the survey
- Explaining how the information will be used
- Recording answers *in the respondent's own words*
- Minimizing the influence of bias created by the interviewer

The easiest way to develop these skills is to have interviewers pair off and role-play the interview. Have the interviewee give feedback to the interviewer, then reverse roles and repeat the process.

Tool #3. Sample Letter to Organizations

Dear _____:

For many years, students in Sun College have been providing services to our community. Examples are:
- An art major has created an after-school program for elementary school youth designed to help them see the art that is all around us, not only in museums.
- Teams of students, with training from IRS and the State Department of Taxation, assist low-income taxpayers to file their annual tax returns.
- Counseling and psychology students operate a 24-hour hotline that offers crisis intervention services.

Under Sun College's Service-Learning Program, students also consciously explore the learning that results from providing service. Many of our students earn credit for the learning that results from their work in the community.

We are hoping to involve large numbers of our students in the Service-Learning Program, and so we are asking you, along with other individuals and community organizations, to help us by letting us know whether you could benefit from student assistance. If so, please let us know what your priority needs are, and whether you would like to arrange a meeting to discuss further how our Service-Learning Program could assist you.

Please complete the enclosed form and return it to us as soon as you can. If you have any questions, we would be happy to have you call us at 123-4567. Thank you for your assistance.

Sincerely,

Reed Wright, Director
Sun College Service-Learning Program
Riverton, Arizona

Determining Which Needs to Address

Description and Rationale: A survey will usually uncover more needs than you can effectively meet. Once your program develops a good reputation, community organizations may besiege you with requests for assistance. These requests can be used to involve greater numbers of students; however, a good service-learning experience rarely comes from simply sending bodies in response to the request: "We need five students." You need to specify what needs you will help to meet — and what needs you will not presently deal with. Much can be gained by focusing your program's efforts in specific areas.

You might try to find needs that no other community organiza-tion is meeting. Doing so gives your program a clear focus, lessens the chances you will be perceived as competing with other agencies, and provides excellent opportunities for making a real difference in the community.

How to Do It: Construct an instrument to set priorities among needs (See Tool #1). Then, analyze the information you gather with your instrument, and determine which needs you will assist in meeting. This analysis becomes the basis for organizing projects and recruiting students.

Tool #1. A Needs Analysis Tool

This tool can be used to choose among or prioritize several needs. The first step is to determine the criteria you will use to select needs you will address. List these vertically. List needs horizontally. For each criterion develop a ranking scale (for example 1-5) making sure that the scales are consistent. Needs with the greatest combined scores are candidates for high priority attention.

Sample criteria for selecting among needs \ Sample Needs	Help elementary school children learn about recycling	Assist older people in their homes	Do market research for a food co-op
1. No other agency is meeting need (1=many agencies; 5=no agencies)	5	2	4
2. Our office doesn't have to acquire new resources (1=many new resources; 5=no new resources)	3	5	1
3. There is high potential benefit to the community (1=no benefit; 5=high benefit)	5	3	4
TOTAL	**13**	**10**	**9**

Developing Projects and Service Sites

Description and Rationale: After assessing community needs and prioritizing those you will help to meet, begin to plan the projects your program will undertake by developing clear project purpose statements, long-term and short-term objectives, and tasks.

How to Do It:
Setting Purposes: A good statement of purpose tells in general terms whom you serve and what you do for or with them. A purpose statement provides a boundary that allows you to determine if a suggested activity falls within the purpose. Purpose statements usually tell why you are doing what you are doing: they do not have a time limit. A sample statement of purpose is: *The Spring College Home Repair Project provides materials and training to enable low-income families in the metropolitan area to become skilled in home maintenance.*

If your project has been in existence for some time, be sure its purpose statement satisfies the criteria stated above and accurately describes the purpose of your project.

Setting Long- and Short-Term Objectives: Long- and short-term objectives grow directly out of the purpose statement. Both long- and short-term objectives need to be:

- *Feasible* — There must be a reasonable expectation they can be accomplished.
- *Dated* — A specified end date indicates when they will be achieved.
- *Measurable* — You need to be able to tell whether you've hit the target.
- *Indicative of an acceptable level of achievement* — They tell you how much must be achieved for the effort to be considered successful.

A sample long-term objective is: *By the end of the school year, six apartments in an uninhabited building will be ready for occupancy as a result of our neighborhood rehabilitation project.*

Short-term objectives refer to those activities you must carry out within the time frame established by the long-term objectives. Sample short-term objectives are: *(1) By the middle of September, 30 students will have been recruited; (2) By the middle of October, each student will have completed a certified training program in housing rehabilitation; and (3) By the end of January, two (of six) apartments will be available for occupancy.*

Written plans become an important reference to keep projects on course and running smoothly. Dates and statements of expected results will help you determine whether projects have succeeded. After planning is completed, you can use your project plans to build project and job descriptions and service-learning agreements.

Monitoring Project Activities

Description and Rationale: The purpose of monitoring project activities is to assure that they are meeting the needs identified. Monitoring involves checking regularly the attainment of short-term objectives and making any necessary adjustments. Be alert to unanticipated negative results so you can counteract them. When a project is adequately monitored, its impact on the community is more easily measured as part of evaluation activities. Normally, the project coordinator is responsible for project monitoring.

How to Do It:

1. Using short-term objectives, develop a timeline for your project.

2. As each objective is attained, use a simple form to record its attainment; if modifications have been made, use the same form to record these.

3. Keep in touch on a regular basis with students on projects and with the community people involved in the project. Site visits are good mechanisms for keeping in touch.

Site visits can provide direct information about what a student is accomplishing. They can be a useful community relations device to let others see the benefits of service-learning firsthand, as well as a technique for orienting other students. The following steps can assure a productive site visit:

1. Define your purpose for making a site visit (e.g., to gather information about student accomplishments, to monitor the quality of the learning and the service).

2. Contact the student's supervisor and the student to arrange a convenient time for a site visit. Explain the purposes of your visit and allow plenty of time between the initial contact and the proposed visit. It's best to pay a visit after the student has had ample time to become accustomed to the site.

3. Prepare a list of things to look for or questions to ask during the site visit, such as:

For Supervisor:
- Is the student meeting the objectives of his/her service-learning agreement? Should the agreement be modified?
- Has the student made any notable contributions?
- What problems have been encountered?
- What steps are you taking to solve these problems?
- Would you like outside assistance?

For Student:
- What objectives of your service-learning agreement have you met thus far?
- Should the agreement be modified?
- How have your learning activities helped you carry out your tasks?
- What objectives do you intend to concentrate on over the next two weeks? The next month?
- What difficulties have you encountered?
- Which of these difficulties were not anticipated?

Ending Projects ... and Beginning Again

Description and Rationale: Most colleges and schools operate on a nine-month schedule so students are often not available during the summer to work on projects. Consequently, work on projects usually terminates before final exams. Activities should be organized so this does not come as a shock to the community. Be sure it is clearly understood at the outset when a project will terminate. If the project is long-term take steps to allow it to continue over the summer with or without student help. If it is not possible to continue without students, try to bring activities to a point where they can "rest" until students are again available.

In addition to bringing closure to projects for the summer, there will also be cases in which projects are completed — and not only at the end of a school year. One of the biggest pitfalls is failing to end projects at the right time. Sometimes the same organization requests the same number of students year in and year out to do the same tasks. When this happens, it can be as much a detriment to the community as to the students involved. You can avoid the "tired project syndrome" by attending *early* to two important matters.

First, define projects clearly, so that you and community people will know when they have been completed. Resist the urge to respond to requests that fail to define clearly what students will be doing. Second, build into each project, especially if it is long-term, steps that lead to takeover of the project by community people as soon as possible. The old proverb has lost none of its truth: "If you catch a fish for someone, he will have dinner; if you teach him to fish, he will eat for the rest of his life."

How to Do It:

1. Review long-term objectives for each project, and determine whether each was met. Gather documentation of demonstrated impact on the community. Consider these ways of demonstrating project impact:

   - Photographs (especially before-and-after pictures)
   - Newspaper reports
   - Products of student efforts, such as research studies, that have been used to effect community change
   - Outcomes of hearings, court cases, deliberations of local governmental units in favor of citizens
   - Existence of new agencies and services with records of community members served
   - Statistics of record: health, crime, employment
   - New policies that come into being as a result of project efforts
   - Before and after surveys

2. Analyze the situation and prepare recommendations for future action.

3. Share your findings with the community people and students who have been involved so that there is mutual understanding and agreement.

4. Let those involved in the project know, either by letter or telephone, of your appreciation for their efforts and of plans for future activities.

Preparing Students for Learning

Description and Rationale: A service project in the community is a rich learning resource, and there are several steps you can take to ensure that learning is maximized. Helping the student to think about learning objectives, to negotiate a service-learning agreement, and to explore the project's relationships to classroom theory are all ways you can facilitate student learning.

Learning Objective: For many students, learning through service is a chance to learn about themselves and their own learning styles. For others, the learning involves refinements of conceptual knowledge. Still others gain exposure to new values and new ways of thinking about social problems and civic responsibilities. You can help students become oriented to the learning possibilities of service projects by asking them to think about their own learning objectives. Learning objectives are brief statements that define the results expected in a specified period of time and can be considered similar to project objectives discussed previously. Some persons define learning objectives like this:

- Objectives state exactly what is to be accomplished.
- They include a definite period of time for accomplishment.
- They define results to be accomplished, not activities leading to the results.
- They state the expected results in measurable terms.
- They are realistic, yet challenging.

A quick test of a learning objective is whether it contains:

An Action Verb + A Measurement + A Result + Time

For example: "I will **identify** at least **eight existing city resources** to use in **measuring/surveying** by **May 31**." The student who wrote this learning objective left open the methods to be used to accomplish it (the student might locate the resources through a textbook or by interviewing professional surveyors). Only the result was specified.

One useful introduction to learning objectives is Robert Mager's *Preparing Instructional Objectives* (Fearon Press, 1962). *(Contact the National Society for Internships and Experiential Education for more information on learning objectives.)*

Service-Learning Agreements: Because of service-learning's educational approach, designing appropriate methods of specifying and monitoring what is to be learned is important. In the typical classroom course, the professor sets the learning objectives for all

Sample Service-Learning Agreement

Student's Name	Telephone

Student's Address

Project/Community Organization	Telephone

Supervisor	Telephone

Project Address

General Purpose of Project

Beginning Date	Hours	Completion Date

Summary of Service Objectives

Please describe the service objective(s) you intend to pursue in this project, the methods you will use to achieve your objectives, and the evidence you will present to show you have achieved your objectives. Attach additional sheets.

Summary of Learning Plan

Please describe your learning objectives for this project, the methods you will use to achieve your learning objectives, and the evidence you will use to show you have achieved your objectives. Attach additional sheets.

Student: As a student committed to a service-learning component in my education, I agree to devote _____ hours per week for the time period from _____ to _____ in the fulfillment of the service objectives described here to meet the academic requirements of this service-learning experience.

_____   _____   _____
Signature   Name (print)   Date

Student's Supervisor in Community Organization: As supervisor to _____, I hereby agree to guide this student's work done under my direction (as outlined above), and to submit a final evaluation of his/her work.

_____   _____   _____
Signature   Name (print)   Date

Project Coordinator: I agree to monitor the progress of _____ and to assist the supervisor in any capacity pertaining to the student.

_____   _____   _____
Signature   Name (print)   Date

Faculty: I have examined _____'s learning plan and find it satisfactory. Upon satisfactory completion and my evaluation of _____ and other classroom requirements as listed below or on an attached sheet, I will award ____ credits for the class: _____.

_____   _____   _____
Signature   Name (print)   Date

students. Because the service-learning experience is often unique for each student, a way must be found to help students plan and monitor their own service and learning objectives. One practice is to design a service-learning agreement in which the student specifies what he or she hopes to accomplish, the activities to be carried out, and how the accomplishments will be demonstrated. These three components — objectives, activities, demonstration — are applied both to the service the student will give and to the learning the student wants to gain. Agreements are put in writing, and in most cases signed by all those involved in the student's service-learning plans: the student, the supervisor, the project coordinator, and the faculty member.

How to Use Service-Learning Agreements:

1. Develop a standard form for recording service-learning agreements. Change the sample service-learning agreement on the following page to fit your needs. For example, if the service project is not with an established community organization, the section requiring a signature from a community supervisor may be inappropriate. If the student is pursuing self-directed learning objectives and not expecting credit, the section requiring faculty sign-off may be inappropriate. If a faculty member is sponsoring the service-learning experience as part of a class, there may be no project coordinator involved.

2. Develop standards for acceptable service-learning agreements. For example, what kinds of evidence will you accept to demonstrate that learning has been achieved? You may also want to clarify the level of specificity you want for both service and learning objectives.

3. Also consider:
    *   When does the student file a service-learning agreement? Most programs require the agreement prior to beginning a project; some also find it helpful to ask students to review and revise it as needed when they have been with a project for two or three weeks, so they have a more realistic perspective from which to fashion their service and learning plans.
    *   Who should receive copies of the agreement?
    *   What provisions should exist for modifying the agreement if necessary?

Assessing Learning in Service-Learning

1. As part of your overall evaluation efforts, you and the student will want to: (1) assess the achievement of each service and learning objective; (2) examine the experience in relation to the student's personal and career development; (3) explore future steps the student can take to build upon the service-learning experience just completed; and (4) generate information that can improve your program or course.

2. To assess the learning from a service-learning experience, choose with the student's help one or more methods by which the student's learning will be demonstrated. Arrange the necessary meetings and schedules that will allow the student to demonstrate the learning. Assess the extent to which the demonstration represents mastery of what was to be learned. Then document the student's accomplishment. One of the most useful approaches to assessment has been developed by the Council for Adult and Experiential Learning (CAEL). The steps listed below have been adapted from CAEL's approach (Whitaker, 1976):

a. Document the student's participation in a service-learning project.

b. Identify the learning acquired through the service experience.

c. Relate this learning to the longer-term educational objectives of the student.

d. Measure the extent and character of the learning acquired.

e. Evaluate whether the learning meets an acceptable standard and determine its credit equivalence.

3. Examples of ways learning can be assessed include (Forrest, Knapp and Pendergrass, 1976):

a. Demonstration of skill. **Example:** Student demonstrates tutoring skill in a real situation. Faculty member or supervisor observes and certifies competence in skill area.

b. Journal, essay or report describing knowledge, understanding or insight gained by student. **Example:** Student uses locally available resources (e.g., old newspapers, city records, interviews with long-time residents) to write a report about the decline of a neighborhood.

c. Assessment using same means that would be used in a class-room course. **Example:** Student who has worked on a project involving victims of child abuse is given a test in deviant psychopathology.

d. Certification of student accomplishments by the service-learning supervisor. **Example:** The student's supervisor in a community organization agrees to review the student's learning objectives, and at the end of the student's involvement with the project, gives evidence of the student's progress toward each objective.

e. Observation of a student in a simulation. **Example:** Student demonstrates skill in staffing a crisis hot-line by responding to a simulated call.

f. Assessment of a product the student prepares in conjunction with, but not as a part of, a service project. **Example:** Student submits a research paper describing the history of the Chicano struggle for civil rights while working as a community organizer in a Chicano community.

g. Interview. **Example:** Faculty member interviews student, who describes what has been learned.

Relating Learning to the Classroom: If faculty are not working directly with students, a project coordinator can still help students explore their experience in relation to classroom theory. Reading lists for various projects can be compiled and shared with students. Perhaps professors on campus and experts in the community can be persuaded to present talks to students working on a particular project. You can also involve experienced service-learners in helping students who are new to service-learning to focus on their learning needs. *[See the sections of this resource book on faculty and learning issues.]*

References

Forrest, Aubrey, Joan E. Knapp and Judith Pendergrass, "Tools and Methods in Evaluation," in Morris Keeton, ed., *Experiential Learning: Rationale, Characteristics and Assessment,* Jossey-Bass, 1976, pp. 169-170.

Whitaker, Urban G., "Assessors and Their Qualifications," in Morris Keeton, ed., *Experiential Learning: Rationale, Characteristics and Assessment,* Jossey-Bass, 1976, pp. 194-198.

Whitaker, Urban G., *Assessing Learning,* Council for Adult and Experiential Learning, 1989.

Developing Student Leadership in Your Program ... or in General

A careful plan for developing student leadership can repay enormous dividends by providing a significant increase in the staff time available to manage your program. It can also provide new and important dimensions of learning for the student.

Conceived at the broadest level, building student leadership is a process that stretches across the entire four or five years the student spends in college. It implies a continuing, growing relationship between the student and the service-learning program, beginning perhaps with a part-time placement; followed by a full-time, intensive service-learning experience; and culminating in an opportunity to supervise, orient and train other service-learners, coordinate projects, or develop new projects.

Student turnover is often a major problem for service-learning programs. Graduation can affect your program as seriously as it affects the football team. If you can develop a smoothly functioning process for passing the skills of one generation of students to another, the problem will be considerably lessened.

The chart provided here describes five levels of increasing responsibilities that students might assume.

Levels of Leadership Development

Levels	Representative Project	Characteristics of Tasks	Typical Learning
Level I: Beginning	Supervised tutoring Researching a well-defined topic	Work under supervision with well-defined tasks Limited opportunity for exercising judgment	Meeting schedules and commitments Recognition of importance of service Understanding needs in community
Level II: Intermediate	Interviewing Documenting case histories Bookkeeping for a community organization	Less direct supervision Some opportunity for independent judgment	Application of knowledge to a situation Confidence in own skills Increasing ability to define problems and locate resources to solve them Understanding situations from community residents' viewpoint
Level III: Experienced	Counseling Organizing	Independent judgments necessary Some supervisory responsibilities	Problem-solving skills Importance of initiative Importance of enabling people to help themselves Role of leadership Interpersonal and analytical skills
Level IV: Project	Developing projects based on community needs	Administrative and supervisory responsibilities Independent judgments about the application of policy	Skill in translating goals into reality Understanding relationships between individuals and institutions
Level V:	Developing and administering service-learning program	High degree of leadership and management responsibility Mutual goal-setting with directors of community organizations, institutional staff	Confidence in functioning autonomously Ability to inspire value of service-learning in others

Common Uses of Program/Course Evaluation

What and how you evaluate depends in large measure on how you plan to use the results of your evaluation and with whom you will share them. Some common uses of evaluation follow:

Purpose of Evaluation	Audience	Typical Kinds of Evidence
1. To improve services to the community	Service-learning program staff	Documentation of changes brought about by projects; suggestions from community persons about needed changes, improvements, new services; evaluation of students by community organizations
2. To justify continuation of service-learning program	Administrators	Documentation of impact of projects in community; costs of providing services; evidence of interest from faculty; evidence of students' learning
3. To improve office support for project	Service-learning program staff	Student assessments of service-learning program staff; additional resources/support necessary
4. To gain support from the community	Community residents	Documentation of impact of projects in the community; evidence that community support will result in better services

Creating a Service-Learning Advisory Committee

Description and Rationale: Working with a service-learning advisory board can be one of the most effective ways of gaining broad support for a service-learning program. Depending on the strength and representation of the board, it can offer the advantages of: (1) community and university advocacy for the program; (2) wide consensus on program policy; (3) quick and efficient communications links with the community; and (4) the resources of board members. The ideal service-learning advisory board would consist of influential representatives of the university and community dedicated to solving community problems and to the concepts of service-learning involvement for students.

If it is your goal to create an advisory board, be prepared for some hard work, but also be aware that the payoffs may be handsome.

An advisory board often performs functions such as the following:

- Brings new ideas to your program
- Suggests new projects
- Suggests areas where research is needed
- Acts on behalf of the community to point out existing needs
- Advises faculty groups on matters of academic accreditation, curriculum design, and faculty involvement
- Helps recommend policy on emerging issues
- Involves the community more widely in the service-learning program
- Serves as an advocate for the program within the community and college or university.

How to Do It:

1. Have two or three people from the community and the university work with you in planning for an advisory group. With this "planning task force," identify what groups ought to be represented on a policy or advisory board.

2. Generate the names of at least one representative of each group.

3. Contact each person suggested. Introduce yourself and your program and explain who suggested the individual's name.

4. Explain that you are exploring the possibility of creating an advisory board and are looking for suggestions about what groups and individuals should participate.

5. Determine with your planning task force:
   a. How many members should be on the board,
   b. Which groups should be represented,
   c. How many representatives each group should have,
   d. Who should be asked to serve,
   e. How long they will be asked to serve,
   f. What their expected tasks will be (The first task will be to establish a purpose and a set of procedures.), and
   g. A target date for the first meeting.

6. Call or visit the persons selected. Explain carefully what you are asking them to do, why, and what kind of a commitment you are asking for. Follow up with a letter and get their commitment in writing, if possible.

7. Convene the first meeting and assist the group to select a chairperson or convener.

Legal Issues in Combining Service and Learning

Michael B. Goldstein

A basic guide to the legal issues involved in programs that combine educational goals with direct involvement in the community — essential reading for any program administrator. The term "school" is used throughout to indicate any educational institution — elementary, secondary, or postsecondary, public or private — which may sponsor a student service-learning program. The term "agency" denotes any public or private community-based organization which may provide work opportunities or training or supervision of students at work sites. Portions of this analysis of legal issues in internships and experiential learning first appeared in Legal Issues Resource Booklet, *by Michael B. Goldstein and John Laster, a publication of the National Center for Service-Learning, a former ACTION Program.*

Introduction

THE TRADITION OF service-learning is a venerable one, with roots in both the American concept of community service and the ancient apprenticeship system, which understood that one became accomplished in the arts or skilled in crafts only by engaging in them with guidance from masters. For over two decades now, organized programs of service-learning for high school and college students have proliferated, taking on a wide variety of forms and features. Some programs emphasize the value of community service, others stress the educational component, with many attempting to strike a balance between the two. Such programs may be sponsored by schools and colleges, public service agencies, nonprofit organizations and even for-profit companies.

Service-learning embodies many different forms; even the names of programs indicate this variety; internships, practica, work-learning, cooperative education, community education, volunteering. While these names may denote different types of activities, for the purposes of this chapter, I will consider all of them to be included under the term, "service-learning," the common denominator of which is the combining of a service component with learning. The work may be compensated or unpaid; it may be on behalf of a public body, a nonprofit or profit-making organization, a community, or a group of individuals; the learning may be formal or informal, for credit or not, and at any educational level from elementary school to postgraduate. Each of these characteristics creates certain legal issues, and each needs to be dealt with both separately and as part of an overall approach.

In this summary I will look at the implications of service-learning from the perspective of the student both as a learner and as a worker. Within each of these roles, I will review the particular characteristics, such as compensation or discrimination, that create legal responsibilities and liabilities. While it is often an anathema for those involved in service-learning to look upon the service component as "working," the law fails to draw neat distinctions in this area; a student volunteer's efforts may be legally construed as "work" even though the intent was only to "serve." For the purpose of this chapter, except as otherwise noted, I will assume that the service component of service-learning is *legally* parallel to working.

In looking at the legal issues of service-learning, it is important to consider all parties involved and the relationships among them. There are almost always three key parties in service-learning programs; the student participant, an organization which provides the work site, and an educational institution (high school, college, etc.) The relationships between and among these parties create and carry with them certain legal relationships and obligations, which vary considerably depending upon the particular circumstances of the service-learning program and the perspectives of each party.

This guide is intended to identify legal issues of concern to service-learning educators, administrators, and practitioners, to permit them to know when to seek expert advice and what general steps may be taken to gain the maximum feasible protection, consistent with the educational and social purposes of the program. Of course, at one extreme the ultimate safe course is to avoid all risk by not doing anything at all! In the case of service-learning, however, the social values so far outweigh the limited risks that the application of some basic "preventive law" is usually all that is needed to make the risks that do exist very manageable.

Because much of the law relating to service-learning is based on state *statutes and decisions, involvement of legal counsel in re-*

viewing individual programs or activities is strongly encouraged. The information provided in this monograph is not intended to substitute for qualified legal advice. It is particularly important to recognize that laws vary from state to state both in their substance and their interpretation. Counsel should always be consulted regarding questions concerning the legal rights and responsibilities of students, institutions and work sites and before entering into any form of contractual relationship. Particular care should be taken not to adopt documents and forms used by other institutions or programs without the advice of counsel as to whether the form is appropriate under the applicable law.

Responsibilities of the Educational Institution

Many service-learning programs are related to a school, college, or other educational institution. This relationship may be limited to the sponsorship of a program that is peripheral to the educational goals or program of the institution or it may be an integral part of the school's course of studies. But regardless of whether the service-learning activity is directly related to the academic program or whether academic credit is rewarded or participation is required, certain unique legal relationships have been found to exist.

Expectations and "The Contract of Enrollment"

When students enroll in educational institutions, they enter into what has come to be called a "contract of enrollment." At the collegiate level, the institution's catalogue usually embodies the elements of that contract, although application forms and other materials may supplement or modify it. The contract may also be modified by action of either the institution or the student, and become legally enforceable when relied upon by the other party.

The consequences of this concept are especially significant when applied to experiential learning. In a conventional course, the student and the institution have (or should have) relatively clear expectations of requirements and outcomes. In service-learning, however, this is not often the case. Here, students may assume learning outcomes that are very different from those envisioned by the institution. Likewise, the requirements for the award of credit may be understood quite differently by the two parties. The result of such misunderstandings may be confusion and a diminution of the value of the learning experience. At worst, they may result in law suits, with the student alleging a breach (violation) of the contract of instruction. It is important to note that these conflicts may occur at any educational level and type of institution. Indeed, the courts have been more than ready to enforce a responsibility to teach on primary and secondary schools than they have on colleges. While most courts still try to avoid entangling themselves in academic decision-making, there are cases that point to a new willingness to impose obligations upon schools that in the past were never seriously considered.

To avoid such conflicts, service-learning educators should seek a mutual understanding of expectations, preferably in writing. These may take the form of descriptions of the service-learning program, similar to a catalogue entry, or as "learning contracts" entered into between the student and the institution.

But is a "learning contract" a true contract? The answer is simple: if it establishes mutual rights and responsibilities between the parties entering into it, it *is* a contract. It is essential to recognize that while contracts are often written in highly legalistic form, they may also be in the form of brief letters or even verbal agreements: the critical issue is whether they establish *mutual* rights and responsibilities binding on all parties. (An agreement that establishes rights and responsibilities for only one party may be unenforceable for what is called "want of consideration," that is, the party binding itself gets nothing in return.)

Since learning contracts can, and indeed should be, binding agreements, they must clearly set forth the rights, responsibilities, and expectations of the student, the school, and the organization providing the work site. The better and more complete this agreement the less likely it is that problems will arise over misinterpretations or misunderstandings. Whether certain of the understandings between the parties in service-learning programs may be intended to be no more than *guidelines* which set forth *expectations* rather than *requirements*, that distinction must be clearly stated and understood. An outline of recommended elements of a "Learning Contract" is provided here.

Liability for Acts of the Student

If a service-learning program is considered part of an agreement between the student and the school, then the question arises whether the school would be held responsible for the acts of the student. This is an important question: If, for example, a student is involved in an automobile accident, injuring herself, some clients for the agency for which she is working, *and* other persons, under certain circumstances the school or college sponsoring the program could be held responsible.

Elements of a "Learning Contract"

1. the specific responsibility of the student and the institution in identifying and consummating the internship placement;
2. the nature of the relationship between the student and the institution arising out of the internship placement;
3. the nature of the student's status vis-a-vis the placement site, i.e., volunteer, employee or independent contractor;
4. the duration of the internship placement, as well as the starting and ending dates;
5. the anticipated learning outcomes arising out of the placement;
6. the academic benefit arising out of the student's participation in the internship program (i.e. the credits awarded and the conditions of their award);
7. the method and frequency of evaluations and the manner through which such evaluations will affect the credits earned or grade received;
8. a description of the relative rights and responsibilities of the student, the institution and the work site with regard to acceptance, duties, supervision and termination; and
9. a description of how disputes between the student and the work site coordinator, or between the student and the institution arising out of the placement, will be resolved.

Ordinarily, the organization controlling the work site is responsible for acts of student interns, and injured parties would not, in most cases, be able to successfully sue the school or college. But suppose that, in the above example, the student suffered from epilepsy and was prone to frequent lapses of consciousness, a fact known to school officials but not revealed by them to the agency. If such a loss of consciousness was the immediate cause of the accident, then it is indeed possible that the school could be held responsible. This liability might exist *regardless* of whether the student was receiving credit or compensation; the key issue is whether the school had (or *should* have had) information or knowledge which, if disclosed to the work site would have been likely to have prevented the injury.

There is an interesting and difficult problem when one speaks of a school or an agency "knowing" something. Of course, organizations cannot "know" anything; their knowledge is nothing more than the collective knowledge of their personnel. However, under the law, such an organization is deemed to have knowledge of a fact *if that fact was known to an employee or agent, and that person had a duty to the organization to do something with that information.* Thus, if a service-learning coordinator at a school knows of a disability that should disqualify a student from engaging in certain activities and yet fails to use that information to protect either the student or the public, then the *school* may be held responsible. The principle is simple: generally an organization will be deemed to know what its employees, in the conduct of their work, know. It is therefore essential that the school or other sponsoring agency inform the organization at which a student will be working of any information that might bear upon his or her capacity to perform the likely tasks, and particularly of any potential risks, either to the student or those with whom he or she will be working.

Remember, however, that it is important to respect the privacy of the student. Particularly when dealing with a student with a mental or physical handicap the school needs to strike a balance between protecting them and the public from potential harm and protecting their rights of privacy. The *Family and Student Educational Rights and Privacy Act,* commonly known as the *Buckley Amendment,* forbids an institution receiving *any* Federal funds from releasing all but the most rudimentary information about a student to most third parties without the student's consent. While a student with a physical ailment may require special consideration in being placed, as would be the case with a student with a history of seizures, and Federal law mandates a school to seek to accommodate those needs in affording access to its programs, the Privacy Act limits the ability of the school to divulge information about the student's infirmity without his or her consent. If the student will not consent to the release of information about his or her physical limitations, and if the school considers divulging that information to be essential to protect the student's health and welfare as well as that of others around him or her, then the only prudent course of action is to decline to make any placement of the student where there is any likelihood that the student will be required to perform hazardous work.

To the extent that third-party risks do exist, they can usually be protected against by insuring that the service-learning program is expressly included under the institution's liability insurance policy. However, whether or not a particular activity is covered by existing insurance is a complex issue which must be determined by professionals. If the existing insurance does *not* cover activities performed under the service-learning program, it is generally possible to obtain an extension of coverage either under the present policy or through a separate one. In either case, the cost of such additional coverage is usually minimal.

While the school must take reasonable care to insure that the assignment of students to service-learning activities does not pose unreasonable risks, at the same time, neither the student or the agency can, or should, attempt to guarantee the ability of students to carry out specific tasks; they are only required to act with care and prudence.

Liability for Injury to Students

What if the *student* is injured while performing a service-learning job? Traditionally, it has been assumed that a school has no liability for injuries which may occur when students are beyond the school's direct control. Recent cases, however, have challenged this interpretation; thus the prudent school will act with care in this area.

As discussed above, the key element is *prior knowledge*: if the school (or its employees) knew, or should have known, of a risk to the student, the school may be responsible if the student is injured. For example, assigning students to work sites known to be dangerous may open a school to liability for resulting injury. However, this is not to say that students cannot be assigned to relatively hazardous activities. For example, many types of service-learning programs involve physical activities and some, particularly outdoor wilderness experiences, may encompass significant risks. Other programs may send students into industrial sites, where work-related injuries are not uncommon. There is also the possibility of students suffering mental harm, as in cases of service-learning interns at a mental health center. While schools *should* ascertain that there are no *unusual* hazards, they cannot expect to protect students against *any* risk. The degree to which the school seeks to ascertain the safety of the work depends on both the type of program and the resources of the school. Administrators should be aware, however, that the more responsibility the school assumes for investigating the safety of activities, the *more* closely it may be held accountable. On the other hand, failure to aggressively determine if an activity is safe may itself make the school responsible. There are, however, several ways to minimize these risks, and one way that actually *increases* them.

A. The Wrong Approach: *Waiver of Liability.* The most frequent suggestion is to ask (or require) students and their parents to sign *waivers of liability.* Unfortunately, these are almost useless, because as a matter of law no one can waive the consequences of someone else's negligence. For example, if one person negligently runs down another on the street, the fact that the victim previously signed a waiver of liability would be meaningless. Indeed, the use of waivers has proved extremely dangerous, since it creates a false sense of security.

B. The Right Alternatives:

1. Assumptions of Risk. This is a quite different concept from that of waivers, with far more value in the service-learning area. It permits individuals to knowingly engage in conduct which may involve certain risks *without creating unlimited potential liability.* For example, a student playing on the school football team assumes the very real risk of injury that goes with playing football, and he and his parents usually sign a statement to that effect. But that assumption of risk is limited to the *ordinary* risks of playing ball. If the student is injured because the school issued him a defective helmet, the school will almost *surely* be held responsible, whether the student signed an assumption of risk statement or not, because he did not accept that risk.

To take advantage of the protection afforded by an assumption of risk, the student must be fully informed, in advance, of any risks inherent in the activity, must knowingly consent to undertake such risks, and must have the requisite level of knowledge and maturity to make an informed judgment accepting the risk.

In the case of minor students, parental consent will also be required, although the age varies from state to state. Examples of service-learning assignments in which informed consent is important are medical and psychiatric placements, criminal justice activities, and field expeditions.

2. Insurance. Most risks can be covered by appropriate commercial insurance. However, school or college policies will very often *exclude* from coverage liability arising from activities of students beyond the direct control of the institution. The school's risk management officer or attorney must be consulted to determine the extent to which present insurance provides sufficient protection, and the propriety of obtaining additional coverage for any unprotected risks.

3. Indemnification. This is nothing more than a form of insurance in which a private party agrees to protect the "indemnified" party from loss, just as an insurance company agrees to do for a policy holder. An agreement between a school or college and an organization which provides volunteer experience may provide for one party to indemnify (protect) the other from any loss, *regardless* of who was at fault. Unlike waivers of liability, indemnification agreements are generally enforceable. They also create complex legal issues, and should be entered into only with the advice of counsel. In considering an indemnification agreement, it is important to determine if:

- The indemnifying party has sufficient resources to protect against the potential loss (a poverty stricken agency with no assets is a poor choice to protect a school);
- Insurance policies that are expected to protect against loss cover liability arising out of an indemnification agreement (most do not); and,
- State law forbids or limits particular types of institutions or agencies from agreeing to indemnify other parties (this is particularly important for public agencies or institutions where such restrictions are common).

Equal Opportunity and Civil Rights

With very few exceptions, schools and colleges engaged in service-learning are subject to the non-discrimination requirements of federal laws, such as those relating to discriminations based on race and sex, discrimination against the handicapped, and laws protecting veterans and other "protected classes." The administration of service-learning programs must therefore take into account the requirements of these laws.

Very simply put, the basic premise of all of the civil rights statutes is: *No organization receiving federal support can deny access to, or the benefits of, its services to persons on the basis of race, sex, or handicap.* Two things are implied by this requirement: first, service-learning programs themselves cannot discriminate on the basis of any proscribed characteristic, and second, where service-learning programs are operated under the auspices of schools, colleges, or other organizations covered by civil rights legislation, prohibited discrimination on the part of a cooperating agency can be attributed back to the school or college. The following summary of issues provides guidance for the service-learning programs:

1. **Racial Discrimination** in any form except in the limited context of an institutional affirmative action program, is unquestionably a violation of the law. This is particularly important in placing students in service-learning positions with other organizations which may discriminate on the basis of race. Because participation in service-learning programs may be considered a benefit afforded students by schools and colleges, they can be held responsible if a student is denied access to a placement because the *receiving* agency discriminates.

2. **Sexual Discrimination**, or the use of sex as a criterion for placement, is a more complex issue. Unlike race, which is virtually never a *bona fide* qualification for a job, there are some situations in which sex may indeed be a valid criterion. Thus, a rape counselling project could legitimately request the referral of only female students. However, job specifications that are not related to the actual work but have the effect of eliminating access for women are illegal. For example, being able to lift a 50-pound sack is a proper qualification *only if the job actually requires such work.*

3. **Disabilities**, whether physical or mental, pose the most difficult problems. The law requires recipients of federal funds to offer access to their services in such a fashion as to not exclude those with disabilities. This "reasonable accommodation" text means the school or college must attempt in good faith to *reasonably accommodate* the special needs of persons with disabilities. When it comes to work, this accommodation must permit the person to carry out the task despite the disability, so long as the disability itself does not preclude the work. Thus, a wheelchair-bound student who seeks an internship in a social service agency may reasonably expect not to be excluded from consideration because the office is two steps above the street. On the other hand, a student who is blind could not expect to qualify for a volunteer job that would involve driving a vehicle. The problem becomes more difficult if the placement agency declines to make a reasonable accommodation, in which case the school or college may have to decline to place *any* students there or risk facing a potential legal challenge.

4. **Affirmative Action Programs**, especially if established as a result of a formal finding of prior discrimination, may legally include an institution's service-learning program as a way to provide special opportunities for minorities or women. However, the degree to which an institution can provide *favorable* treatment to protected classes remains to be defined, and caution must therefore be exercised in this area. The advice of experienced counsel is strongly recommended.

5. **Reverse Discrimination** on the part of a receiving agency poses an extremely difficult dilemma. Even if an organization requesting interns has an affirmative action plan under which it seeks only women or minorities, a school or college would be at risk in agreeing to refer *only* such persons. The reason for this is that while the receiving agency may be carrying out a permissible affirmative action program, the school or college would be *im*permissibly discriminating by denying access to persons *other than* minorities or women. There is, however, a difference between a preference and a *requirement*: an agency that *encourages* the referral of minorities is showing good citizenship. However, an agency that insists on *only* interviewing members of a certain protected class may put the institution in considerable legal jeopardy, and may have to be excluded from participation!

Responsibilities of the Work Site

An increasingly common concern of agencies and organizations that provide work sites for service-learning students revolves around the applicability of the federal minimum wage law. It is *not* automatically true that declaring a student's activities to be part of an "internship" or "volunteering" renders them exempt from minimum wage and other requirements of the Fair Labor Standards Act. Indeed, a student may receive no compensation whatsoever and yet conceivably come under the provisions of the law. The correct answer to this question depends in large measure upon the nature of the particular program, and particularly the relationship of the program to the *learning* component.

Minimum Wage Laws

As a general rule, the U.S. Department of Labor has agreed that uncompensated *community service* activities do not fall within the purview of the minimum wage laws. Likewise, interpretations of Labor Department rulings and court decisions support the position that service-learning activities, whether performed for non-profit *or* profit-making entities, do not require payment of the minimum wage *if* they are part of a *structured academic* program administered by an educational institution, the work site does *not* receive substantial benefit from the student's efforts, *and* there is no promise of a job after the completion of the program. The "substantial benefit" test is not as difficult to meet as it may at first seem since it has been interpreted to mean that the agency or organization providing the

work experience is providing "learning" services to the student that
tend to offset the value of the work performed.

An explicit statement to that effect in the school-agency agreement will usually be sufficient to avoid minimum wage problems
for uncompensated work.

The issue becomes more complicated when the student receives
some monetary reward, but still less than minimum wage. Many
organizations provide students with small stipends, intended to
defray the cost of meals or transportation. If such funds are paid on
an actual reimbursement basis, there is no problem. But if the
agency decides to pay the "reimbursement" on the basis of a certain
amount per hour of service performed, the Labor Department may
well decide that what is being paid is compensation rather than
actual reimbursement, and may require minimum wage levels.
Worse, a failure to pay minimum wage can result in the assessment
of *treble* damages: *three times* the amount that would have been due
under the minimum wage law. Thus, it is important to make sure
that the program is so configured as to fit within the exemption to
the Fair Labor Standards Act afforded experiential learning programs. Counsel should be consulted to ensure that all the agreements and program operations conform to these requirements.

It is also important to determine whether the work performed
falls within the limitations of state and federal child labor laws.
While this is not a concern for college-level programs, the increasing
number of service-learning activities at the secondary and even
primary grade levels makes this an issue that should be carefully
considered.

Employer-Employee Relationship

One of the most important elements of the relationship of the
service-learning student to the work site is the existence of an
employer-employee relationship. The existence of such a relationship depends only in part upon the payment of compensation. The
cases are divided as to whether a person may be "employed" without being paid for the work: the Fair Labor Standards Act implies
that one cannot, but the decisions remain unclear. Payment of
compensation generally *does* create an employment relationship,
although in certain circumstances the recipient may be deemed an
independent contractor and not an employee. While liability, tax,
and other consequences are different (and often preferable) for an
independent contractor situation it is not enough to simply declare
that a student *is* an independent contractor and therefore not an
employee. The level and manner of control over the work to be

performed, the power to hire and fire, the provision of the workplace and instruments of work, and the manner of payment and calculation of rate all figure into the determination of whether one is an employee or independent contractor. Generally, in order for a person to be deemed to be an independent contractor, he or she must have great latitude in the manner through which the work is performed, have a relatively high level of skill in the performance of the particular work, provide his or her own tools and equipment, and function on a project-specific basis. It is obviously difficult for a student engaged in a service-learning program to meet these tests, and except in rare cases it is not worth the effort to try. Note particularly that work-study students are almost always deemed employees.

Taxes. Unless a compensated student is an independent contractor, he or she *is* an employee, and appropriate taxes *must* be withheld from compensation and remitted to the appropriate government agencies. Declaring that payments are "stipends" or "scholarships" rather than compensation is in itself virtually meaningless: the form of payment and the nature of the involvement must meet certain very narrowly defined tests in order to be considered scholarship or fellowship aid and therefore exempt from taxation. The terms "scholarship" and "fellowship" are increasingly narrowly defined in the tax code, and unless payments meet these rigid definitions the tax exclusion will not apply. Likewise, the term "stipend" should not be construed to render payments free from tax. Unless counsel has advised that payments to a student are specifically not includable as taxable income, it is wise to advise students that payments are taxable. (*Note that payments made to students under the College Work-Study Program are virtually without exception considered to be compensation for work performed and are fully taxable, regardless of whether payments are made by the institution or by the agency to which the student is assigned.*)

Liability for the Acts of Student Workers. Unlike the case of schools or colleges, the agency that provides the service-learning experience will, in most cases, be responsible for the acts of students assigned to it. An agency may avoid liability for the acts of students only if it can show that the student was acting entirely outside the scope of his or her assignment or as an independent contractor rather than as an agent for the organization. However, insuring against liability is relatively easy and, in most cases, inexpensive. Counsel should be consulted, however, to assure that existing coverage is sufficient.

Liability for Injuries to Students. The agency providing the service-learning opportunity will generally be held liable for injuries arising from its negligence. Where students are deemed to be employees, Workmen's Compensation statutes provide protections regardless of who is at fault. In a few states, certain *volunteer* activities are also protected under Workmen's Compensation laws; these tend to be very narrowly defined and should be reviewed carefully with counsel.

As discussed above, liability may be shifted back to the school or college, both for injuries to students and for damages caused by students, if the institution can be shown to have acted carelessly in improperly assigning students. Where both the institution and the agency share the supervision of students, the determination of liability becomes considerably more complex.

A special case arises out of injuries incurred by students while travelling to or from service-learning activities. Generally, where students make their own travel arrangements neither the school nor the agency will be held responsible for injury. However, if the school or agency either *provides* the transportation or *requires* a particular type or manner of transportation, there could be liability, but only if the injury arose out of the negligence of the agency or school. Where the student travels to a service-learning activity during the school day, *as part of his or her educational activity,* then the responsibility of the school to assure the student's safety becomes more apparent. Since most of this risk will involve the use of motor vehicles, liability insurance should usually protect all parties. As noted earlier, however, the policies should be reviewed by counsel to make certain that service-learning students are covered.

School-Agency Agreements. Because of the potential complexity of the relationship between institutions and agencies providing service-learning experiences, it is always advisable for these parties to enter into written agreements describing their mutual rights and responsibilities. Elements to be included are: determination of the existence of an employment relationship, identification of the employer, liability and indemnification, control of activities, the role of the school's service-learning coordinator, student report and writing requirements, confidentiality of information, duration of assignments, the right to suspend or dismiss students, supervision, training, evaluation, transportation, and the nature and manner of compensation, if any. Institution-agency agreements can create important legal rights and responsibilities, and therefore they must be prepared with the advice of counsel. It is appropriate for each student to receive a copy of such agreements and to signify his or her understanding by signing a copy. Regardless of whether there is compensation, a written understanding between school and agency can avoid many problems and misunderstandings. A minimum amount of time and effort expended in establishing the rights and responsibilities of all parties before the service-learning program begins may save vast amounts of time, effort, and money later on.

Student Responsibilities

The fundamental purpose of any service-learning program is to promote the educational, social, and intellectual development of the participating student. Thus, it is essential that students fully understand their rights and responsibilities as participants in the service-learning program. The growing willingness to seek legal redress makes this understanding not just ethically correct but also economically imperative.

Students have responsibilities to both their school and to the agency which provides the service-learning experience. They are responsible to the school for completing all service-learning assignments in a manner consistent with all educational or other requirements. This may require reading assigned materials, keeping journals and other records, attending classes, and preparing papers or oral presentations. If academic credit is involved, students must be fully aware of credit requirements before entering the service-learning program; otherwise the school may have difficulty enforcing its requirements.

Students are also responsible to the agency which provides service-learning experiences for completing all assigned tasks in a proper manner. The more this relationship is that of employer to employee the more obvious it is that students must work under the direct control and supervision of agency personnel. Problems may arise if this relationship is ill-defined, for example, if there is a lack of clarity about who is responsible for training or supervising the students.

Written Agreements. As discussed earlier, the inclusion of students as parties to the written service-learning agreements can help resolve such ambiguities, especially if the agreements are clear and simple. To be effective, such agreements should specify: (1) the student's responsibilities and to whom they are owed; and (2) the student's rights and how these can be exercised. For example, an agreement should provide a mechanism for students to deal with problems of their conduct on the job.

While it is probably unnecessary to apply full due process procedures to the assertion of student rights, neither is it appropriate to assume that either the school or the agency can act without regard for them. The courts have become very serious about student rights and are more willing than ever to enforce them against institutions or other parties. Even if students are not being paid, they may have rights that must be protected, especially with regard to the learning component of their programs.

Students also have an obligation to inform their schools or agencies of any special or unusual characteristic, such as illness, allergy, or other limitation, which might restrict their participation in service-learning programs. If a student (or his or her parents) knows that a particular activity, although generally safe, might pose a special problem, but fails to inform the school or agency of this fact, the student may be unable to recover for injuries that might result. Furthermore, students or their parents could be held personally responsible for injuries to others if these result from undisclosed incapacities. However, as noted above, once the student or parents notify the school or agency of such limitations (or once these have been discovered through independent means), the school or agency *must* take them into account or bear the possible consequences.

Legal Implications for Sponsoring Organizations

Since the operation of service-learning programs may bring with it certain legal obligations and potential liabilities, the issue of how the sponsoring organization is organized becomes important. Service-learning programs that are administered by educational institutions (public or private, secondary or postsecondary) will usually be considered activities or programs of those institutions and thus will fall within their corporate or public body structure. Similarly, service-learning programs sponsored by government agencies (federal, state, or local) or by private corporations (profit or non-profit) would be considered activities of those corporate bodies. Liability would generally be limited to corporate assets and, in the case of public bodies, may be even further limited by law. However, conduct by trustees, directors, officers or employees that show a flagrant or negligent disregard for the protection of the public or the students may puncture this insulation and make such persons directly liable.

Every organization sponsoring a service-learning program, including corporate bodies, must determine whether it has the power to carry out the program and whether it is authorized to do so, either by law, its own by-laws, or its governing body. A teacher who establishes a service-learning program on his or her own initiative may be personally liable if that activity is found to be outside the scope of his or her employment. To protect against this risk, it should be made clear that the teacher's supervisor or superior is aware of, and has condoned the service-learning program. Since such programs are often outside the normal scope of an institution's program, such approval should not be taken for granted; preferably, there should be written authority to undertake such an effort.

Some service-learning programs are operated on an *ad hoc* basis, by groups or organizations that are not incorporated. In these cases, *each and every officer or member of the organization could be held personally responsible for damages.* Incorporation as a non-profit organization is usually easy to accomplish, and is a very prudent step to take.

Legal Issues Checklist for Schools and Colleges

The following questions should be asked — and answered — to insure that basic legal issues have been covered.

1. **Is there a clear understanding of the learning responsibilities of the student participant?** Does the student know what is expected, and what he or she must do to receive any specific academic reward? (See list of recommended contents of a "Learning Contract" earlier in this chapter.)

2. **Does the experience provider understand and share responsibility for that learning?** Is this also in writing? Has counsel reviewed it?

3. **If there is a learning agreement or contract, is everything stated in that agreement intended to be enforceable?** Has counsel reviewed the agreement?

4. **Does the teacher or faculty sponsor have express authority to supervise the program or activity?** If school facilities are used, is the use authorized?

5. **Does the school or college liability insurance cover the activities of the student participants?** Are teachers and staff protected, particularly when off campus?

6. **Does the school or college offer the opportunity to take part in the program on a nondiscriminatory basis?** Does it place students with organizations that discriminate? Does it insure that reasonable accommodation is made for students with disabilities? Does it insure that requests for male or female students are based solely on a *bona fide* requirement of the work, and that other requirements, such as physical size or strength, are actually related to the expected activity?

7. **Does the school, college, or any employee or agent with responsibility for the service-learning program, have any information about the student participant that should either keep him or her out of the program, restrict his or her activities, or require notification to the experience provider?**

Legal Issues Checklist for Community Agencies
and Other Providers of Work, Training or Supervision

1. Is there a clear understanding as to whether an employment relationship exists between the student participant and the experience provider? If so, are the legal requirements of employment being followed?
2. Is there a clear understanding as to whether any money is to be paid to the participant? Does the student understand the terms of such payment? If the payment is compensation, have taxes been withheld and the student apprised of his or her obligation to report the earnings to the IRS? If the payment is a scholarship or fellowship, is there clear IRS authority in the current tax laws to exclude it from taxable income?
3. Does the liability insurance of the experience provider cover the activities of the student participants?
4. Does the experience provider offer the degree of supervision and support necessary for the participant to adequately and safely carry out the activity? Is there a clear understanding as to who is responsible to provide such supervision and support?
5. Does the experience provider understand the conditions upon which a student is participating in the activity, particularly as to changing the nature of the assignment or terminating the student's assignment entirely?
6. If the experience provider has agreed to protect or indemnify the school or college, is it financially capable of doing so? If relying on insurance, will its insurance policy cover losses arising out of an indemnification agreement?
7. Is the experience provider organized in a manner to properly conduct the program? Does its corporate form protect the individual officers, trustees, and members (if any) from personal liability?
8. Has the experience provider asked the school *and* the student whether there are any special problems, medical conditions or other circumstances that may affect the student's capacity to participate in the intended activities? Knowing of any such limitations, has the experience provider acted to insure that they are respected?

Legal Issues Checklist for Students

The following list may be provided to students and their parents, or used as the basis for insuring that legal issues are being adequately explained to them:

1. Do you know *exactly* what is expected of you in performing the service-learning assignment? By your school and by the experience provider? Is it in writing?
2. Do you know who is responsible for supervising your activities?
3. Do you know what you can do if you have a problem with your assignment? Who has the right to change your activity?
4. If you are getting credit or any other kind of academic reward, do you know what you must do to qualify? How is your performance to be measured?
5. If you are getting any form of payment, do you know whether it is compensation, reimbursement for expenses or a scholarship or fellowship payment? Do you know if it is taxable income that must be reported to the IRS?
6. Do you know who is responsible if you are injured in the performance of the service-learning activity? Do you have your own insurance?
7. Have you informed your school or the experience provider of any special problem or medical condition that should limit or be taken into account in your participation in the service-learning activities? Are they respecting your needs?

Michael B. Goldstein is a partner with the Washington, DC law firm of Dow, Lohnes & Albertson, where he is in charge of the higher education practice. He was the first Executive Director of the New York City Urban Corps and in the early 1970s under a Ford Foundation grant worked with many cities and states in the establishment of urban internship programs. Prior to joining his firm he was an Associate Vice Chancellor for Urban and Governmental Affairs and Associate Professor of Urban Sciences at the University of Illinois-Chicago, and before that was Assistant City Ad-

ministrator and Director of University Relations in the Office of the Mayor of the City of New York. He has served as President of the National Center for Public Service Internship Programs, a predecessor of NSIEE, and has been NSIEE's general counsel since its creation.

References

The following materials were consulted in the preparation of this chapter.

Berte, Neal R., general editor, *Individualizing Education Through Contract Learning*, University of Alabama Press, 1975.

Experiential Education Advisory Panel, *Experiential Education Policy Guidelines*, National Center for Research in Vocational Education, 1979.

Far West Laboratory, *Legal Issues Study*, National Institute of Education, undated.

Gaffney, Michael et al, *A Guide to Operating an Off-Campus Work-Study Program*, National Association of Student Financial Aid Administrators and American Association of Community and Junior Colleges, 1975.

Goldstein, Michael B., "Academic Internships: Can Cash and Credit Coexist?," *Synergist*, National Center for Service-Learning, ACTION, Vol. 5, No. 1, Spring 1976, pp. 27-29.

_____, *Federal Policies Towards Experiential Education*, Institute for Educational Leadership, December 1977.

_____, "Liability for Volunteers' Injuries," *Synergist*, National Center for Service-Learning, ACTION, Vol. 7, No. 3, Winter 1979, pp.

_____, "Using Federal Work-Study Funds," *Synergist*, National Center for Service-Learning, ACTION, Vol. 10, No. 1, Spring 1981, pp.

_____, "Injured Volunteers: Who is Liable?," *CASE CURRENTS*, Winter 1981.

_____, "Legal Issues in Experiential Education," Panel Resource Paper No. 3, National Society for Internships and Experiential Education, December 1981.

_____, "Policy Issues in Experiential Education," National Society for Internships and Experiential Education, March 1982.

_____, "Achieving the Nondiscriminatory Recognition of Experiential Learning," *Learning by Experience*, New Directions in Experiential Learning, No. 1, Jossey-Bass, 1978.

_____ and Wolk, P., "Legal Rights and Obligations of Students, Employers and Institutions" in Kenneth Ryder, James Wilson, *et al, Cooperative Education in a New Era*, Jossey-Bass, 1987.

Hollander, P. A., *Legal Handbook for Educators*, Westview Press, Inc., 1978.

Jennings, E. K., "Breach of Contract Suits by Students Against Postsecondary Institutions: Can They Succeed?" 7 J. Coll. & U.L., 1980-81, pp. 191-121.

Larson, A., *The Law of Workmen's Compensation*, Matthew Bender, 1980.

Nordin, V. D., "The Contract to Educate: Toward a More Workable Theory of the Student-University Relationship," 8 J. Coll. & U.L., 1981-82, pp. 141-181.

Riesman, David, *On Higher Education*, Chapter 9, "Student Consumerism and Educational Change," Jossey-Bass, 1980.

Stark J. S., *The Many Faces of Educational Consumerism*, D. C. Health and Co., 1977.

U.S. Department of Labor, *Child Labor Requirements in Nonagricultural Occupations Under the Fair Labor Standards Acts*, WH Publication 1330, Revised 1978.

_____, *Employment Relationship Under the Fair Labor Standards Act*, WH Publication 1297, Revised February 1973.

_____, *Employment of Full-Time Students at Subminimum Wages Under the Fair Labor Standards Act*, Employment Standards Division, WH Publication 1250, Revised February 1980.

(Note: All Synergist articles listed here are available from the National Society for Internships and Experiential Education, 3509 Haworth Drive, Suite 207, Raleigh, NC 27609, (919) 787-3263.)

Youth Program Models

Dan Conrad and Diane Hedin

Reprinted with permission from Youth Service: A Guidebook for Developing and Operating Effective Programs *by Dan Conrad and Diane Hedin, published by Independent Sector, 1987, pp. 14-18. The term "youth service" as used here includes an emphasis on combining service and learning.*

Community Service in Youth Organizations

THIS SECTION ADDRESSES the ways in which community service can be made to fit into the organizational structure of a school or youth agency. We begin with youth-serving agencies, since they face fewer barriers.

First, community service is compatible with responsible citizenship, a central mission of many of them. These agencies want their members to see themselves as part of the human community and to develop the capacity to care for and care about others. For some organizations, citizenship education remains the main goal. For others, a focus on personal growth and development has almost eclipsed the service ethic. But for nearly all youth-serving programs, there is a tradition of and commitment to devoting some attention and resources to community service.

Second, a structure already exists in many youth organizations and clubs for allowing participants to do service. For example, in the Red Cross youth program, involving youth in community service is the organization's central activity, permeating all aspects of programming. Similarly, the Boy Scouts encourage boys at all levels of the organization to perform some daily act of service to others as part of their basic commitment as Scouts.

In other organizations, such as 4-H, Boys Clubs, Girl Scouts, and the Congressional Award program, students are required to complete a certain number of hours of service to earn awards, badges, ribbons, or other forms of recognition.

In some of these traditional youth-serving organizations, service activities are performed sporadically, as "events" at a district, council, or county level. Nevertheless, staff of youth agencies typically can identify both an organizational mandate and a programmatic structure for doing community service activities.

Third, since youth agencies usually are not constrained by the rigidities of a six- or seven-period school day, they often have more options as to where and when they provide service. This is especially valuable for projects requiring large blocks of time to complete, or which demand the use of evening or weekend hours, or which are cooperative ventures with adult volunteers.

School-Based Programs

Incorporating community service into the school is often more complex and challenging. Therefore, we are devoting more detail to the way in which schools around the country have achieved this goal. One way of distinguishing among types of school-based programs is to examine how closely they are integrated into the regular academic program of a school. The continuum below represents a movement from least integration into the school curriculum on the left to most on the right. Distinctions between programs are based on their structure, not their merit.

Club or Co-curricular Activity	Volunteer Clearing-house	Community Service Credit	"Lab" for Existing Courses	Community Service Class	School-wide Focus or Theme
1	2	3	4	5	6

1. *Club or Co-curricular Activity*. Schools are the most likely to offer this type of program in which students perform community service through joining an after-school club or co-curricular activity. About 15 percent of all high schools in the United States report having this option.

In one sense, this may be the purest form of service, since the activities are strictly voluntary with students receiving neither academic credit nor time off from school. But the lack of incentives beyond the intrinsic value of serving others means also that the population of those who participate is a rather narrow one: mostly those who already possess a service ethic.

There are certain clubs that nearly always incorporate community service into their programs. These include such organizations as the Future Homemakers of America, which frequently sponsors peer education around family issues such as pregnancy prevention; National Honor Society chapters, which often require their members to participate in some school-related service such as teaching, tutoring, or collecting books for school libraries; and Key Clubs, whose main service activity is helping the needy.

Typically, the school provides a faculty adviser — sometimes paid, sometimes volunteer — to guide the students. In one large city school system, a staff person attached to the central administrative office works full time to help students and school staff establish after-school clubs and programs in individual high schools so that a city-wide emphasis on serving the community can become a reality.

That approach is atypical though, and most school districts provide only minimal resources to this type of community service program. The plus side of this arrangement is that students often carry significant responsibility for making the programs happen, and in this way leadership skills among the youth members are developed.

2. *Volunteer Clearinghouse.* Some schools have created a "volunteer bureau" to serve as a central clearinghouse for a number of school-community interactions, including volunteer service. This is a more comprehensive approach than the first in that students can learn about a wide array of involvement opportunities within the wider community, which may include voluntary clubs in the school but certainly are not limited to these.

Just as in voluntary clubs, students receive no academic credit for their service. The work may be done during the student's unscheduled time or during a study hall, especially if it can be placed near lunch or at the end of the school day.

Students with time and interest come to the bureau to obtain information about service opportunities. If they find a suitable placement, they check it out personally and then sign a "contract" to carry out the volunteer service. Follow-up and review often are carried on by both the students and faculty members of the volunteer bureau.

In one school a Department of Community Involvement, staffed by students and faculty, developed a central resource list by employing students during the summer to investigate opportunities. During the school year, students staff the department, along with a regular faculty member who serves primarily as a supervisor to the student staff.

In other schools, the office is staffed by a non-school employee — someone from a Voluntary Action Center or from organizations which promote community service such as the Junior League, Red Cross, or Jaycees.

3. *Community Service Credit.* Here, community service not only is facilitated and encouraged by the school, but also is accredited. Often a community service credit is given for an established number of hours. (For example, 100 hours equals one semester credit.) In some schools, students are required to perform a specific number of hours of volunteer service in order to graduate. In others, they are awarded elective credit and in some cases these credits may be used in lieu of some other credit, such as social studies or humanities.

A common procedure is for a student to prepare a proposal outlining what he or she wants to do, for how long, for what purposes, and what product is to be produced. This proposal is reviewed by a faculty adviser or program coordinator. If approved, the student acts on the proposal in the time blocked out.

"There is a strong assumption in this model that whereas experience can be educational, it is neither necessarily nor automatically so."

For some, it may be one full school day a week; for others it may be after school; and in some cases, students may be given from a month to a semester away from school to complete their service projects. In structure, this model is very similar to the various independent study options available on most college and some high school campuses.

The key point as far as our continuum is concerned, however, is that the community service is not performed within the context of a regular school course. It is essentially an off-campus experience with minimal supervision by school personnel. There may be an occasional discussion with an adviser and/or other participants, but the learning is seen as being in the doing.

Formal training of students is the responsibility of the receiving agency. The role of the faculty adviser is to check occasionally on the student's progress and provide an opportunity to talk about what he or she is doing and learning.

4. *A Laboratory for an Existing Course.* This kind of program has enabled many schools to introduce community service into their academic program with little or no immediate change in curriculum, school structure, or staff deployment.

In this model, students in existing courses do community service as a way to "reality test" course content, gather data and examples, and make use of what is learned in the class. In a social problems course, for example, students might read about the growing gap between rich and poor in America, but gain personal insight into this phenomenon by volunteering in a program for the homeless, providing child care in a deprived neighborhood, or painting the home of a person too poor to do it himself.

A typical time requirement is two hours per week of community service during the quarter or semester, which can be performed during school hours or after school depending on the student's schedule and agency needs. This often is done in lieu of some other requirement, such as a research paper.

Generally, the classroom teacher is responsible for helping students find appropriate off-campus experiences and for the general supervision of students. In one school, a student involvement office staffed by students who do this as their community assignment, identifies service opportunities and helps match students to experiences. In another school, a community fair is held early in the year, where community agencies desiring student assistance set up tables or booths and students shop around for a placement that interests them and meets their time and transportation restrictions.

It is important to note that even though this procedure does not require curriculum changes, the practical consequence of including an involvement component may be a gradual altering of topics and approaches to coincide with the kinds of experiences students are having. A healthy pressure develops to provide more practically useful information and more techniques for integrating the rich but varied data gathered through the community experiences.

5. *Community Service Class.* This model, found in approximately seven percent of U.S. high schools, represents an attempt to combine the strongest features of the previous two into a course which exists as an integral part of the school's academic program.

Here the community experience forms the heart and is the central focus of the course, but it is combined with an ongoing classroom experience where the emphasis is on providing information, skills, and generalizing principles to assist students directly in interpreting their experiences to operate more successfully in their placements.

There is a strong assumption in this model that whereas experience *can* be educational, it is neither necessarily nor automatically so. This approach assumes that it is the role of the teacher to help make community service educational.

A typical example would be a one-semester social studies class meeting two hours per day. Students spend four days (eight hours) in the field and one day (two hours) in class.

The additional hours per day (for teacher and student) are gained by giving the student double social studies credit or an additional elective credit by making the course multidisciplinary. The most typical combinations involve English, home economics, humanities, and social studies. In parochial schools, community service often is done in the context of a religion class, where students are able to apply moral teaching to real hardship and suffering.

A two-hour time block for such a course is ideal, allowing students to have enough time at their field site to make a real contribution, and lessening or eliminating the need for extra staff, students missing other classes, and so forth.

6. *Community Service as a School-wide Focus or Theme.* A rare, but highly desirable, approach is for community service to permeate a school's curriculum. In one large city system, a special magnet school on the human services has been created in which all students are in field placements in human service agencies. Their volunteer work has two purposes: career exploration and preparation and the development of social responsibility.

In a parochial school, service to others is woven into many courses and serves as an organizing principle for the total academic program. For example, biology students work in a food co-op, where they teach nutrition to low-income elderly people; home economics students run a day-care center several mornings a week for neighborhood preschoolers; and advanced math students offer their computer skills to small businesses to manage inventories and do financial projections.

In all these examples, the students are practicing "the humane application of knowledge." In this model, community service is not just for the selected few motivated students who choose to become community service providers, but rather is viewed as a key organizational principle which affects all students.

Collaborative Models

While either schools or youth agencies can offer high-quality volunteer service programs for teenagers, neither can do the job as well alone as they can when these and other organizations concerned with volunteerism work together. Though there are only a limited number of examples of collaboration among schools, youth organizations, Voluntary Action Centers, and adult civic organizations such as Rotary or the Junior League, those that do exist are noteworthy.

In several communities, staff members of the Voluntary Action Center or some clearinghouse on volunteer opportunities work directly with the high school student volunteer program. The program works efficiently because the teachers or school counselors concentrate on what they do best — recruiting, motivating, teaching, and supporting students in their work in the community — while the person from the volunteer clearinghouse brings expertise in training community service providers, matching students to appropriate field sites, and knowing the community agencies and their needs. As one director of a Voluntary Action Center said: "We're just like Willy Sutton. He said he robbed banks 'cause that's where the money is. Well, we're in the schools, 'cause that's where the young volunteers are."

A national program in which Junior League volunteers work with teams of high school students to help them design community projects is another example of effective use of talents and resources. Four students from a school, along with a teacher or counselor and a Junior Leaguer, form the Project LEAD team. The Junior League volunteer, because of her knowledge of the community and experience in volunteerism, helps students launch new projects or become involved in existing League or other community programs. The youth members' expertise lies in knowing their peers and designing strategies to recruit them into community service efforts. The teacher knows how to connect the project to the ongoing structure of the school, helping the students receive credit for their work, integrating their volunteer experience with the academic program, and so on.

In other cases, a youth organization and a school have joined to develop and operate community service programs. In one city, the Red Cross needed people to teach a basic first-aid course for fourth graders and also felt pressure to increase the number of teen members in the organization. The youth director of that agency set up a program with a high school in which the members of a community service course became Red Cross volunteers who spent six hours each week teaching basic first aid. Both the teacher and the youth director benefited. The teacher was able to place students in high quality volunteer experiences with a minimum of effort, since the Red Cross staff member trained, monitored, and transported the students. The youth director solved her twin problems of low teen membership and not enough volunteers to fill requests for the first-aid course.

Dan Conrad directs community involvement programs at Hopkins High School in Minnesota. Diane Hedin is former Director of Community Relations at the Pillsbury Foundation and is now a professor at the Center for Youth Development and Research at the University of Minnesota. Over the past 17 years, Conrad and Hedin have co-directed several research and publications projects in experiential education, youth participation, and service-learning.

Journals:
Diaries for Growth

Keeping journals enables students to practice basic writing skills, analyze service situations, and evaluate their own actions and reactions. Reprinted from Synergist, National Center for Service-Learning, ACTION, Vol. 10, No. 2, pp. 46-50.

IN THE CONTINUING SEARCH for ways to enrich the service-learning experience, journals — sometimes called logs, diaries, or simply notebooks — have emerged as one of the most flexible, useful tools available to teachers. Many service-learning educators have developed special forms of the journal to increase its value as a practical device for monitoring progress and as a tool for long-term personal development. These journals often are very structured and seek to take maximum advantage of the opportunities for personal reflection and self-evaluation that service-learning experiences elicit.

The following cluster of brief articles give various approaches to using journals. Jane Zimmermann describes journals as a written dialogue between professor and student. Vicki Zawacki gives the framework of an informal diary that enables a coordinator to monitor and direct high school students. The third article describes a thematic approach to keeping journals. Jan Bird tells how journals provide a link between coursework and fieldwork, and Virgil Peterson introduces the highly structured, self-analytical technique developed by Ira Progoff.

Journal as Dialogue

Jane E. Zimmermann

The PULSE program at Boston College offers undergraduates the opportunity to combine community service with academic study, primarily in philosophy and theology. For many students, the PULSE experience represents the first serious challenge to the opinions, values, and priorities that they have established over the years. PULSE courses provide a structured context in which students can examine firsthand the failures of institutions and the lives of the people who have suffered. At the same time, the courses encourage students to formulate new ideas and insights while analyzing their own role and identity. By using journals, students find an outlet for their troubling questions about society, and for their feelings about their own prejudices, limitations, and inhibitions.

The effectiveness of the journal depends, to a great degree, on the PULSE professor, for the journal is a written dialogue between professor and student. The self-searching aspect of the student's entries places a heavy responsibility on the professor to respond in an appropriate manner. Comments must promote trust at the outset, aiming not at critical judgment but at recognizing achievements and challenges. ("Standing up to that supervisor required real courage.")

Once trust has been established, a professor may pose alternate ways of looking at problems. ("Have you considered the possibility that, despite the child's behavior, he might really be interested in your affection?") Or the professor may restate what the student has said in such a way as to encourage the student to question his or her assumption. ("So, are you saying that legal services should always operate *against* apartment owners?") Since most PULSE courses have a philosophical base, the professors may use the experiences recounted in the journal to link the students' experiences with the principles of the humanistic tradition expounded in their readings. ("The lawyer you are discussing sounds rather like Callicles in the *Gorgias*. Would you say he is an example of a new sophist?") Some PULSE professors use the journals as a vehicle to enhance small group discussions. After first consulting the students, the professor invites them to share with their peers a situation or problem from their journal. Verbalizing a conflict and having others contribute similar experiences is reassuring. It creates trusting relationships within the group.

Journals count as a percentage of students' grades in some PULSE courses. The program has not set guidelines or instructions for writing them, however, for fear that students will concentrate too heavily on the rules rather than on their own thoughts. Ideally, a journal will be, or will become, a student's personal, unstructured exploration — an opportunity to write freely.

To this end, the professors encourage students to develop their techniques of observation and writing. Students often tend to speak in generalities, possibly avoiding underlying feelings or issues, so the professor may direct the student to be more conscious of the specifics of events. A professor may urge students to avoid simple reporting, concentrating instead on their judgments, feelings, and observations.

Each journal differs as much as the individuals who write them, but one can see the general pattern in the following excerpts from the journal of a student who was coping with managing the children in an afterschool day care program on a trip to a bowling alley. The professor's words are in italics.

Up to about the first three rounds, they were behaving as well as could be expected. Then Kathy organized a game of follow the leader which involved jumping over bowling balls into other lanes. Other bowlers were going crazy. 'Will you get these kids out of here?!' I could tell that the others would have been willing to cooperate, but when they saw Kathy was not listening or caring, they didn't either.

In a situation like this one, perhaps it would have been good to just cancel the game, take them back, and say that that's what will happen when they act that way.

Coming outside after paying, I thought we were ready to leave. Then I saw that Kathy was again running up the street yelling that she was going home. By now it was almost 5:00 and my patience was wearing quickly. Luckily the others were willing to cooperate, and waited at the corner until I returned. When I reached Kathy I was infuriated. Grabbing her by the arm, I dragged her down the street to the van. Feeling both annoyed and upset, I spoke to the driver, who is also a supervisor, and explained the day's events. She told me not to worry about it, that Kathy's mother was going to receive a phone call about her behavior of late. I'm anxious to see the results of that if any.

Later on, reflecting upon the day, I wondered if I correctly handled Kathy. I don't know what else I could have done at the point. I felt I had no other alternative.

Understanding in a "playroom" is one thing; at a bowling alley, it's another. You probably have to draw some pretty definite limits for Kathy, and I think that's what you started to do.

Realizing she's got problems, by then I was not in a very understanding mood. I'm afraid that this may have a devastating effect on the beginnings of a relationship that I had built with Kathy. It will probably take a while to break the ice. To be honest, I'm not looking forward to seeing her on Wednesday. It's not so easy for me to forgive and forget.

Relationships cannot be built out of chaos (as we'll see in Transformation of Man), which is what you've got on your hands. Perhaps with Lisa's help, you can work out limits — like sending her home, etc. — to keep chaos from running wild. Slowly then, you can work on building something. She evidently wants your attention, complicity, etc. enough that, when you withhold it, she either gives in or makes things worse. So just "ignoring" her won't always be successful. But perhaps sending her home would. Patience and forgiveness are very important in this situation. (You can't let her make you think you're not doing a good job — letting her get to you.)

A Structure for Reflection

Vicki Zawacki

The student practicum is one of the alternative programs at New Canaan (Connecticut) High School. The coordinator of the practicum placements, most of which are in service agencies, needs to communicate regularly with the students in the program for two reasons: to make sure that the experience is going well, and to see that the student is directed enough to be getting the most out of it. Individual weekly meetings with the coordinator help to meet that need for communication, but the student journal has proven to be the most effective tool to ensure success and avoid potential problems.

We allow the students a fair degree of latitude in how they keep their journals, which are primarily informal diaries in which students make daily or weekly entries. A longer interval between the experience and the journal entry seriously affects a student's recollections. When the reactions in the journal are fresh and immediate, the students can use them as reminders of what they want to discuss in the weekly sharing meetings. Our most important general direction on how the journals are kept is to encourage the students to be themselves and to express their feelings freely. They are assured that no one but the coordinator will read the journal without their permission. We are sometimes astonished at how honest the students can be in their journals.

To record one's feelings and experiences can be enormously difficult without a framework within which to work. The framework we suggest has the added benefit of encouraging the self-exploration and improvement of skills that the service activities make possible. The steps outlined below are accompanied by actual journal excerpts:

1. *Describe what you did in your volunteer service today.*
"Today I worked with a small group of the slow learners in reading readiness (vocabulary)."
Observation: "John sat in his seat studying vocabulary for twenty minutes."
Interpretation: "John has a long attention span."

2. *Describe your reactions to what you did today.*
"I thought that I was successful in getting the children to go over our lessons."

3. *Describe the feedback you received from people you work with.*
"Ms. Smith, the teacher, told me today I was using good communication in talking with the children. I listened to them, showed them that I understand what they say and felt, and told each one of them how nice they were."
"Joyce said that some of the children we both worked with really enjoy the Elephant Word Game. This is a game that I invented. That makes me feel really good."

4. *Describe your feelings and attitudes.*
"I think it's wrong for the teacher to yell at the kids for the whole class time."

5. *Describe what you learned.*
"I found that I have to use the progress sheet in my daily lessons or the kids don't say as much."

6. *Describe what you would have changed about today's activity.*
"I ignored Billy today when he spoke to me. It was the first time he had said anything to anyone in three days. Next time I will be more careful."

7. *Include any comments from your sharing meeting.*
"Mr. Caputo suggested in one of our sharing meetings that I keep a record of 'the things that work' and the 'things that don't work.' I did and I found that I can see what I'm doing wrong

because I'm doing the same thing over and over. I realize that I have to change."

8. Describe the things that are bothering you or important things that you are thinking about.
"Mr. Plank doesn't talk to me. He never offers advice or ideas. I wish he would say something."

A coordinator can read the journal at the weekly meeting or the student may submit it for monthly review. The student and teacher then may use the journal as a springboard for assessing progress and for discussion. The journal also allows the student an opportunity for the kind of self-analysis that leads to a better understanding of involvement in the program. Students frequently comment that when they read their own journals a week or so after writing them, they are surprised at how they felt and reacted in certain situations. The writing not only has helped with recall, but also has aided in clarifying new feelings and attitudes.

Journal as Discipline

Charles Norman, director of the Learning Skills Center at Macalester College, St. Paul, has devised a model for keeping journals that is widely used in Macalester's Community Involvement Program. Norman recommends organizing a journal thematically, with themes selected to reflect the journal keeper's interests. A looseleaf notebook makes a particularly good vehicle, since pages and sections can be rearranged at will. Some themes or sections of the journal may reflect aspects of the purely personal life, such as dreams, fears, and relationships. Other sections may reflect aspects of relationships with institutions, job, or education.

For areas of particular importance the individual may want to organize a specialized journal with detailed subcategories that relate to aspects of either academic work or service work. Categories may include goals, tasks, strategies, and self-evaluation of development. This journal can interface with service activities, since the user may want to include memos or evaluations from professors or supervisors as they relate to the journal objectives. Norman suggests that learning contracts may be a logical organizing point for one part of the journal.

A system of organization does not a journal make. "Now that I've got it, what do I put in it?" a student just embarking on the journal process may ask. "Be ritualistic," says Norman. "Set aside a time every day for reflection and writing. Be analytical. Allot 20 percent of writing time for stating a problem and 80 percent for solving it. Be optimistic. Just because an internship falls apart does not mean you cannot learn something valuable from it."

Different modes of writing and different allowances of time should be considered within the process. A student may find that a half hour is not too generous an allowance for working through and reflecting on the experiences of each day. A technique worth considering in conjunction with some of the others is to allow a short period each day — perhaps 10 minutes — for free writing. With no heed to logic, form or organization, scribble down the most impulsive thoughts that arise. According to Norman, "The sheer spontaneity of free writing may surprise you with what you come up with — strange ideas and rich oddities that you might otherwise pass by if you are thinking too clearly or cannily about what you should be writing."

Concentration, regardless of what combination of techniques or structures is used, will remain the single most important key to constructive journal keeping. The journal user must *want* it to work, and must be willing to work at it, truly seeking to understand, through self-analysis, some aspect of self.

To illustrate the kind of basic progress that takes place in the journal process, Norman cites an example of a student trying to cope with a difficult relationship with a supervisor. The student's first journal entry was: "S. doesn't seem to like me, or maybe he is too indifferent toward his work to pay attention to me and let me get involved. *I want to work!* I didn't come here to get lost at a desk with nothing to do."

Norman sent the student back to the placement with the admonition to make sense of the situation, even if he couldn't make the placement a success. The student came back a week later with the following entry: "I think S. would like to use me — God knows he could shift some of his work load to someone else. But he is so disorganized that when he has a tough deadline to meet, he doesn't have time to tell me what to do and have me do it too. So he ends up doing it himself, badly ... The trouble is, he's beginning to resent me because he knows that he's inefficient and he knows that I know. How do I do this? If I tell his supervisor I'll be going over his head and if I tell *him* he'll get mad. Maybe if I tell Norman, he can do something. I'll tell Norman."

Norman, by his own account, was unable to do much about the situation, and the student's internship went poorly much of the time. But, as the journal showed, the student learned a great deal about coping with a difficult situation.

The Bridge to Curriculum

Jan E. Bird

The purpose of Project Action at Wylie Groves High School, Birmingham, Michigan, is for students to apply classroom knowledge and skills to community service. To accomplish this, the community service must be infused into courses throughout the curriculum.

In many cases, teachers are enthusiastic about having their students involved in community service but need suggestions on how to forge the vital link between service and classroom learning. We have found that journals are one of the most useful, flexible tools for accomplishing that link when the fieldwork does not *directly* use what is learned in the classroom but enhances the overall knowledge of the students.

The situation in a recent English course is an example of how the journal was used in a Project Action program. After attending one of our workshops, the English teacher was excited about the possibility of adding another dimension to the learning experiences of her students. The students spent one class period a week working in a nursing home, an elementary school, or a district court probation department. To meet Project Action criteria for using classroom skills, the teacher chose the journal option. After each period in the field, the students wrote what they did, what they felt they learned from the experience, and their own reactions to the experience. This allowed them to exercise their writing skills and to make their own evaluation of their volunteer experience.

Further use of their journals came at the end of the semester when the teacher conducted group discussions so that the students would have an opportunity to reflect collectively on their experiences and assess what they had done. Journals facilitate this kind of discussion at the end of a project, or at any time in between, by reminding the students of what was important.

In another instance, we recommended journals as the vehicle for a course in human development. In this case, the journals were used primarily as factual records of observations by students doing research projects.

When students in a social psychology course worked in a court, a nursing home, and an elementary school, they used the journal to record personal reactions, attitudes, and values. These observations contributed greatly to their study of cultural, class, and social differences.

These examples show how successful the journal has been as a tool for integrating service experiences into the curriculum, allowing teachers in many courses to use Project Action as an option without sacrificing the academic goals they need to accomplish.

A Psychological Workbook

Virgil Peterson

When I was in my early teens, my sister gave me a five-year diary complete with lock and key. During the ensuing years, I crammed my daily activities, along with a few rites of passage, into the inch and a half of space that the diary allowed for each day.

In college, inspired by the journals of writers I read as an English major, I began a journal — this time, a record of events accompanied by my reflections. Those entires sometimes ran to many pages. That journal lasted for three decades and is still a precious possession. Meanwhile I became a teacher and experimented with journals as adjuncts to the courses I taught. For students engaged in field experiences, I asked for a developmental journal in which they listed goals for the course that they checked at mid term and end of term. They also wrote regularly of their service experiences and the feelings that accompanied the service performed.

Then about four years ago, I learned of the Intensive Journal, developed by Ira Progoff, a psychotherapist whose credentials include work with C. G. Jung, the directorship of Drew University's Institute for Research in Depth Psychology, and the founding of Dialogue House, which publishes his books and organizes journal workshops.

Introduction to Progoff's method was, for me, like a leap to another sphere. It accomplished everything I had previously known in my journal experience, and so much more. Progoff's journal is a psychological workbook — a basic instrument for personal development. Its several parts enable the user to be in touch with the most fundamental aspects of his or her life. Its processes evoke creative possibilities for future growth and development. Using the journal independently with occasional participation in group workshops permits careful monitoring of personal growth. Its processes allow creative possibilities for development that the user might never have found in any other way.

Progoff's journal has four major parts and each part has subdivisions. Each part represents a different kind of life process. Life History is the place for evoking one's past. In Inner Resources, the journal user works with dreams and other spontaneous experiences. Dialogue Dimension contains a set of exercises for deepening the relationship with other persons, one's own body, work, events, and society. The Process Meditation section provides a place for taking meaningful events from the past and using them as starting points for new, and often unpredictable, inner experiences.

What distinguishes the intensive journal from all other forms of journal writing that I know is its sensitivity to complex processes and the practicality of its methods for exploring and enhancing our lives. Each of the exercises involves, in one way or another, a mediation between our conscious, thinking selves, and our nonconscious, intuiting selves. The world of our conscious thoughts speaks in the language of words. The world of our nonconscious selves speaks to us in a variety of languages — feelings, dreams, hunches, and even the muscular tightness that occurs wherever we physically register stress. Progoff's methods enable us to bring all those languages together in a comprehensible whole by evoking the links between our conscious and nonconscious minds.

The method is too intricate for complete explanation here, but perhaps the experience of one person with one exercise will convey the sense of how it works. This person wanted to write about experiences in a service-oriented job in which he had been working for about six months. Dialogue with Work was the exercise we chose to use. That exercise consists of five steps: writing down what he thought and felt about the job at that moment; writing a life history of the work, i.e., putting down a series of brief statements recording the origin and course of development of that work; imaging, i.e., in a relaxed state, inviting whatever may come spontaneously to the mind; comparing what was written deliberately and thoughtfully with what occurred spontaneously; and writing a dialogue between him and his work.

The effects of the method are best illustrated by what occurred during the imaging stage. After diligently going through the first three stages, he looked up with a mix of puzzlement and disappointment. "All that came was the image of a fireplace."

I asked what his associations with fireplaces were. He answered that fireplaces are warm and nurturing, that they give a sense of coziness and security. He found it interesting, as he thought about it, that a fireplace nurtures, but it also must be nurtured, fed, and attended to. The relationship is, in a sense, mutual. Suddenly his jaw dropped as he realized that the fireplace symbolized how he thought of his job. It was warm and gratifying;

it nurtured and needed to be nurtured. The dialog came easily. He could "write to his job," and listen to what his job had to say to him. And when I saw him a few weeks later, he said that the image of the fireplace came frequently to his mind as he went about his work.

The Intensive Journal method deepens our relationships, whether with our work, with other persons, or with the other dimension of our lives. It is a process that is particularly appropriate to those of us in service-learning. Few avocations demand as much self-knowledge and fortitude, or profit as greatly by the nourishment of those attributes.

At the time these articles were published, Jane Zimmermann was an administrative intern with the PULSE Program at Boston College, Vicki Zawacki directed the student practicum at Canaan (Connecticut) High School, Charles Norman directed the Learning Skills Center at Macalester College, Jan Bird coordinated Project Action at Wylie E. Groves High School in Michigan, and Virgil Peterson was a professor of literature at West Virginia University.

Tools for Journals and Debriefing

Three short pieces for use by participants (or staff and faculty) in service-learning programs.

Examples of Analysis and Debriefing Questions

These questions could be used by any human service program. The language used is from a social science perspective and could be adapted for other fields or approaches. Reprinted with permission from "Learning through Questioning in Field Programs" by Barbara A. Hursh in Field Study: A Sourcebook for Experiential Learning, *Lenore Borzak, ed., Sage Publications, 1981, pp. 262-263.*

A. **Professionals' Perspectives on Themselves and Their Agency**
    1. What do the professionals say are their personal goals in working with clients? Are these goals ever in conflict with the purported definition of the agency?
    2. What motivates someone to go into community service work? Why is s/he doing that instead of something else?
    3. What qualifications does the professional think are necessary for community service work?
    4. When a question of agency, policy, procedure, or new direction arises, is a professional's position on the question ever influenced by factors other than commitment to the welfare of the client? If so, what are some of these other sources of influence?

B. **Professionals' Views of Clients**
    1. How do the professionals define who their clients are or should be?

2. What do the professionals think their clients need? Can the professionals meet all the needs of their clients? Where and how do they draw the line?
3. What words or labels do the professionals use to refer to clients when talking to you? to other professionals? to clients? What functions (intended or unintended) are served by these labels?
4. What do the professionals view as a "success" with a client? What criteria do they use to evaluate successful interactions with their clients? unsuccessful interactions?
5. What factors do the professionals feel might prevent or interfere with successful interactions with clients? Can these difficulties be resolved? How?

C. *Clients' Perspective*
1. What reasons do the clients give for being at the agency? Do they like being there?
2. Do the clients ever make suggestions (to the professionals, to other clients, or to you) for improvement of staff and/or facilities and/or agency policies? Why or why not?
3. Are the clients dependent on the agency services? Do they have any alternatives?
4. For the clients, what constitutes a successful interaction with a professional? unsuccessful? (Compare with B4)
5. What words or labels do clients use to refer to the professionals and/or to other clients among themselves? in the presence of professionals? in your presence?
6. What is the client's view of the professional(s) with whom s/he is most often in contact?
7. Is there much (any) informal interaction between clients and professionals? What form does it take? What impact does this have on the formal organization? What factors either inhibit or facilitate informal interaction?
8. What are clients' needs, and do they perceive that these needs are being met? What is their level of satisfaction?

D. *Your Perspectives*
1. What do you think are the goals and means of your agency in theory? Is there any difference between the theory and the practice?
2. What do you think the clients need? How did you develop your opinions? How well does the agency meet clients' needs, as you see it?

3. What impact does client contact have on you? on your
    assumptions about what they need? on your assumptions
    about how the agency should serve the clients?
4. What do you think is the major problem the professionals
    face in attempting to satisfy clients' needs? How would
    you resolve it?
5. How would you define a successful professional-client
    interaction? (Compare with B4 and C4)
6. In what ways are the professionals attempting to socialize
    you into their culture?

Additional Resources for Service-Learners

College-Sponsored Experiential Learning: A CAEL Student Guide by
Hadley Nesbitt, Council for Adult and Experiential Learning, 226
South 16th Street, Philadelphia, PA, 19102.

*The Experienced Hand: A Student Guide for Making the Most of an
Internship* by Timothy Stanton and Kamil Ali, National Society
for Internships and Experiential Education, 3509 Haworth Drive,
Suite 207, Raleigh, NC, 27609.

Service-Learning: A Guide for College Students, National Center for
Service-Learning, ACTION (available from NSIEE, address
above).

Some Answers to that Nagging Question: "What Should I Write in My Journal?"

Written for K-12 students, this list can be useful for learners of any age. Reprinted with permission from Reaching Out: School-Based Community Service Programs, *National Crime Prevention Council, 1988, p. 101.*

What?! You say you don't know what to write for your daily journal entry? Cheer up! Journal writing can be easy and fun once you get the hang of it. Here are a few questions that might help get you started:

- What was the best thing that happened today at your site? How did it make you feel?
- What thing(s) did you like the least about today at your site?
- What compliments did you receive today, and how did they make you feel?
- What criticisms, if any, have you received? How did you react to them?
- How have you changed or grown since you began work at this site? What have you learned about yourself and the people that you work with?
- How does volunteering make you feel? Happy? Proud? Bored? Why do you feel this way?
- Has this experience made you think about possible careers in this field? What jobs might relate to this experience?
- What kind of new skills have you learned since beginning to work at this site? How might they help you in future job searches?
- What do people do who work at this occupation? Describe a typical day at your site.
- What are some of the advantages and disadvantages of working at this occupation?
- If you were in charge of the agency, what changes would you make? How would you improve it?
- How has your work changed since you first started? Have you been given more responsibility? Has your daily routine changed at all?

- What do you feel is your main contribution to your service site?
- How do the people you work with treat you? How does it make you feel?
- What have you done this week that makes you proud? Why?
- Has your experience been a rewarding one for you? Why or why not?

Reflecting on What You're Learning

A short, basic summary for service-learners. Reprinted from Service-Learning: A Guide for College Students, *ACTION, 1979, p. 43.*

The highly individualized learning that you're doing in the community requires time for reflection so you can take a look at what you're learning, relate it to yourself and generalize from it to other experiences. Reflection is an essential part of "experiential learning" — learning from direct experience.

There are several ways of reflecting on your experience that can be useful to you in service-learning; hopefully you can provide for all of these and possibly others as well:

1. Keeping a journal of the experience
2. Regular meetings with supervisor and faculty advisor
3. Interaction with other service-learners

Keeping a Journal

One useful way of keeping track of what you're learning and the kind of service you are providing is to keep a personal journal or log of your activities. Keeping a journal may, in fact, be required for field experiences directly related to course work.

Whether a personal journal is required or not, it's a good idea to keep one. It causes you to think about your experiences and can help give you insight into what you are experiencing and how you are feeling about it. It can also give you a useful record of your service and learning.

To be most effective for you, the journal should not be merely a log of events. It should be a means for you to analyze the activities you are performing and the new things you're learning, to recognize important events and to relate your stated service-learning objectives to what you perceive you're learning and doing.

Making Journal Entries

Make daily entries in your journal, if possible.

1. *First, write an objective account of the daily events that occur.* Try to remember everything that happens. Don't make any inferences, just write the facts.
2. *Next describe your feelings and perceptions about what happened during the day* — *about your behavior and the behavior of others.* This is your subjective account of the day.
3. Look back at your service-learning agreement and *reflect on how the day's events relate to your service and learning objectives.* Are stated objectives still appropriate? Do you see the need for changes? Maybe a concept in a class came alive for you out in the field, or maybe you'd like to test a theory the next time you go to your service-learning site. These are generalizations you can draw from the experience. If you do begin to alter your objectives, be sure to inform your supervisor and professor of the revisions. Your objectives can change as your perception of the situation changes, but it is essential that you make note of what is changing so that it can be taken into account when you review the entire experience.
4. Finally, while you have the day's events fresh in your mind, *outline actions for your next contact* based on what you feel you learned during the day or any problems or needs that have surfaced. Use your log as an "agenda-setting" tool.

You might format these four kinds of information as follows:

Daily Events	Perceptions	Generalizations	Action

By using columns, you can add to the journal in the appropriate place as more information and experience come into play. For example, in the "Daily Events" column you may note some interesting perceptual behavior by a small child. Two weeks later in a Child Growth and Development class you may be introduced to some developmental theories that explain the child's behavior. Then you can easily go back to your journal to note the linkage between the "Daily Events" observation and "Generalizations" that can be made. Generalizations might also be initiated by a lecture, something you've read, a television program, conversation over a meal or lying awake in bed staring at the ceiling.

Exercises for Cross-Cultural Learning

Center for Global Education

A travel seminar can be a good way to prepare learners for a service experience in another culture. Although the term "travel seminar" is used here, this chapter presents useful reflection questions and exercises that can also be adapted for service-learning programs in a neighborhood across town, in a rural or urban setting in the U.S., or in another country — anywhere that learners need skills in reading a culture different from their own. These questions can help people separate their experiences and observations from their interpretations about the new culture. Allowing time for reflection and discussion is essential for developing skills in critical thinking within a cross-cultural context. Reprinted with permission from Crossing Borders, Changing Boundaries, *pp. 5.1-5.6, 11.3-11.4, 11.7-11.8; available from the Center for Global Education, Augsburg College, 731 21st Avenue South, Minneapolis, MN 55454.*

Travel Seminar Reflection Questions

THE FOLLOWING ARE SAMPLES of questions appropriate to be asked of all seminar groups. They are grouped according to style or when they might be best used during the travel seminar. Combine with references to "widening the lens" and begin to work on the question of "How do you separate the experience from your interpretations (so that when people interact with you they can draw their own conclusions)?"

Early in the Travel Seminar

Several elements of critical thinking and cross-cultural experience may be helpful to introduce early in the travel seminar; participants may return to these questions during the course of the trip as

they deepen their own learning and awareness. Some samples of
these:

- Talk about how our own experience and values influence the
  way we experience and interpret the world, creating for each of
  us a filter. How does your general background and experience
  influence your filter? What is your background? How does this
  influence how you see the world?

- Whom do you believe and why? What is truth? What criteria do
  you use to decide who is telling the truth? Of the speakers we
  have heard today, who do you think is telling the truth? What
  signals did they send that made you believe them? Was it body
  language, words, data, sincerity? What criteria can you identify
  that you use to judge a situation, and how does this change
  during the course of the trip?

- In small groups or individually: Come up with a definition of
  democracy (or justice or freedom, or some other appropriate
  concept or category). How is your definition challenged or
  changing as the trip progresses? How would the different
  sectors with whom we are talking define this? How does that
  affect their responses to the current situation?

- What we expect to see or experience can often filter what we
  actually experience, so it is important that we are aware of our
  expectations — both conscious and unconscious. At or near the
  beginning of the experience: What are your expectations for this
  trip? As the trip progresses: How is what we are experiencing
  different from what you expected? How did your background
  influence your expectations? Have you modified some of your
  expectations during the course of the trip? Why or why not?

- This exercise should be done in two phases. First night: Write
  what you think are the most important things you need to learn
  from this experience. At the end of the trip: Is what you thought
  to be most important the same as what you heard from the
  people of the host country as being the most important? What
  were the similarities and differences? Why do you think this is
  so? What are some of the different insights you have gained
  from the people of the host country or community?

Role Playing and Viewing from Another Perspective

A way to assist people in understanding an issue or viewpoint is
to help them to see it through another perspective. Role plays can be
especially helpful in areas where they give participants permission

to ask questions or make observations that they might not ask in their own voice.

- Take a concept that we all know, like capitalism or democracy, and have people represent some of the perspectives they have heard on the trip, such as: landowner, landless peasant, urban worker, professional or bureaucrat. Have each perspective describe *their* experience of capitalism/democracy/etc. and tell what they see as positive and negative about it. As a group analyze the different perspectives. How are their experiences and perspectives similar or different, and why? Are there conflicts inherent in their differences, and are they resolvable? What would it take to resolve them? Who stands to lose? Gain?

- An exercise to be used in Nicaragua: Divide the group into small groups representing different sectors of Nicaraguan society such as Sandinistas, Campesinos, Private Business, Church Hierarchy. Have each group reflect on questions such as: What has the Revolution done for you? What do you stand to gain from the Revolution? To lose? Where do you find groups that support you? Oppose you? Have small groups report to the larger group and write their responses on the chalkboard. Help the group to reflect on and analyze the results. Work at developing tools of analysis and identifying key questions.

- What problems do you see in the host country? How do you usually respond to these problems? What do the people with whom you have met say are the responses to the problems?

Making the Connections

One of our goals as educators is to help participants make connections between what they experience in another context such as Latin America and their own experience and issues in their home environment. These reflection questions can aid this process:

- What do you want for your children? What did the person we talked with today want for her/his children? What are the resources that you have available to accomplish your goals and hopes? What are the resources that the people here have to accomplish their goals and hopes? How does this help shape your and their responses and actions?

- Many of the sectors we visit are those who traditionally have been powerless in society. Who in your own culture has similar levels of powerlessness? What are the similarities and differences between the two groups and their contexts? How can we confront these issues in our own context?

- Review the people and groups with whom you have talked and identify the sectors they represent. Who do you know (know *personally, not* know *of*) at home that would represent the same perspective or same group? If there are sectors at home with whom you have no contact, why is this? How could you meet and learn from people in these sectors? What similarities and differences do you see in the relationships and dynamics between the different sectors you have met on the trip and those "back home"?

U.S. Policy and Regional Analysis

Many travel seminars have a distinctive focus, style or group make-up (such as church, academic, or policy), and reflections appropriate for one group may not be for another. In designing discussions that help participants better understand the dynamics of U.S. policy and form a regional analysis, keep in mind the following:

- Ask questions that help people see the contradictions.
- Examine the definitions and assumptions of commonly used terms and concepts such as democracy, human rights, and communism. Are these terms used to help clarify the issue or to mask the reality?
- Ask questions that help expose the structural relationships in society, such as: Who has access to power? To land? To media?
- With which sectors/governments is the U.S. aligned? Against whom? Why? Who are the primary beneficiaries of U.S. policy? Who is harmed by U.S. policy?
- What are the economic interactions and interests in the society? In the region? Which sectors wield economic power, and how is this power maintained?
- What are the roots and forces leading to militarization in the region, and what impact does this have on the larger society?
- Who are the major role players in the region? What are their goals? How do they interact with each other between countries and within each country?

Closing Reflection and Discussion

The final or closing reflection serves many functions, providing closure as well as beginning the transition back to home life. It is important that this reflection is carefully planned. Among the elements to consider incorporating:

- Ask questions that highlight key themes.
- Ask questions that help participants summarize and articulate their experience.
- Provide an opportunity to note new truths discovered and myths debunked.
- Acknowledge the unanswered or new questions.
- Where appropriate, acknowledge feelings: What has touched you the most?
- Acknowledge and begin the transition back home: What are your expectations upon returning home? Greatest fear? What are you most excited about?
- Open the door to action: How do we respond in our own context?

Each closing reflection will be unique according to the group and their shared experience. Here are some examples:

- What three or four things stand out most clearly from your experiences here? (Take five minutes, then go around the room and hear each person. Get a sense of what four or five key things have merged for the group.)
- What three or four things remain most unclear? (same format as above).
- What do you tell the neighbors? In a single sentence write down what message you plan to take back home from your experiences here (five minutes, then hear each person. See what kind of consensus emerges, if any; discuss from there.)

On the board list all experiences and talks during the stay in that country. Out of these experiences:

- What has affected you most deeply?
- What has disturbed you most deeply — most challenging to the convictions, assumptions, or values you hold?

- Tabulate these ... to get a sense of which experiences have been most important to the group.

- What about these have affected you or been disturbing to you? List these on board.

- In small groups: How do you feel challenged by what you have seen and experienced? (Have each group sum this up in one sentence; write on board.)

- What new themes or understandings are emerging for you?

Reflection on preparing to go home: Role play what you think it will be like to go home. What kind of questions will people ask, and how will your respond? Different people can play different roles, but everyone should play the returnee at some time. After the role playing, reflect upon what you need from others, in the group or at home.

Samples of Reflections

Sometimes it is helpful just to see what other groups have used for reflection on previous occasions. Here are samples to give you ideas for reflection:

Early on in travel seminar, after exposure to poverty or suffering:
- What did you observe?
- What feelings did you have as you entered the settlement, in the home, as you left?
- What barriers do you see to the people's future, hopes? (This is a question you may or may not want to use, understanding that any answers at this point are tentative.)

After visits to squatters' settlement, campesino family, base ecclesial community family: Taking into account our three visits with [Mexicans] who are poor so far, answer the following questions.
- What similarities/differences do you see in the way they perceive reality?
- What is their source of hope and what vision of the future do they have? (Suggestion: have groups break up into groups of 3 or 4, then gather back together in a large group to see what conclusions people have reached.)

Mid-point in the seminar:
- What questions are emerging for you?
- How has your perspective or the base from which you ask questions changed, developed, or remained the same?

Samples of Reflections, *continued*

- How has your perspective or the base from which you ask questions changed, developed, or remained the same?
- What connections and differences do you see emerging between your lives and those of the people with whom we have spoken?
- From your experiences so far, what images are emerging?

After visits with agencies and organizations, such as Social Security, an orphanage, and church relief groups, divide into groups of four or five and ask:

- How do you think each agency or organization defines the problem with which they are dealing?
- Using a consensus style, decide which agency has the most potential for bringing about long-term, fundamental changes to benefit those who are poor.
- Bring the group together and ask each small group to state its decision and reasons. If there are different conclusions, encourage the groups to discuss these differences.

Discussion session on the meaning of justice:

- In a large group, brainstorm, then come up with a definition of the word "justice."
- Break into small groups and talk about what it means to be on the side of justice.
- How do you determine what is the "side of justice," especially when others of differing viewpoints may also claim to be on the "side of justice"?
- Are there examples of "doing justice" or not "doing justice" within your trip group? (For example, are there instances of racism, sexism, ageism, or classism within your group?) If so, how are they being dealt with?

After visits in homes, neighborhoods or refugee camps:

- Suggest that the group close their eyes and silently reflect on people they have met. Ask them to put themselves into the people's situation. You may want to create an image through names and places.
- Then set the scene of a group of North Americans who come to their homes to ask questions and take photos. How do you feel about them? What kind of questions do you respond to favorably? Negatively? Why are you speaking to these gringos? What could be improved during these visits?
- Bring the group back to the here and now. Ask for their reflections. Do they have any insights or suggestions for the visits or for the group?

At the end of the travel seminar:

- Have people draw a picture of a struggle they are going through as a result of the experiences on the seminar.
- After about 15 minutes, form groups of four or five and have them show their pictures and talk about them.

Cross-Cultural Exercises

The Blindfold Game

Goal: The Blindfold Game is a simple exercise that can help participants identify the feelings and dynamics that result from interacting in a foreign environment where familiar forms of communication don't work. It can also be a good ice-breaker in a group where many people don't know each other.

Materials: Blindfolds for each participant and scraps of paper.

Time: 20-30 minutes, including debriefing.

Directions: Use an open space with no obstacles so the group can move around. Ahead of time, write two-digit numbers on pairs of scrap paper; i.e., one pair of scrap paper might have 36, another 72, and so on. There are only two rules to the exercise: participants can't see (because you blindfold them) and they can't talk or make sounds (because you ask them not to). Give each person one of the papers with the number on it, and make sure that one other person in the group has the same number. Tell each person they are to find the one other person who has the same number, without speaking or seeing. It there is an uneven number, ask one person to be the observer and comment on what is seen after all partners are found. As people find their partners, they can remove their blindfolds, move to the side of the room and watch the remaining members of the group.

Debriefing: Ask the group what they learned, how they felt, and how this might apply to an experience in another culture. In particular have them note:

- What feelings or emotions did you experience?
- How did you try to communicate? How did others communicate with you?
- What differences in style among others did you notice in your interactions? How did you react?
- What does this say about your interacting and communicating in a culture where you don't know the language or some of the cultural norms?

Ask people to jot down some of their insights in their journals and to keep track of their reactions and insights during the trip.

* * *

Bafá Bafá

Bafá Bafá is a cross-cultural learning game that gives insights into the dynamics that can develop between two different cultures with different values systems. It creates different interactions between members of the two cultures that reveal the role that values, assumptions, and stereotypes play in cross-cultural communication. It is especially helpful at showing the dynamics of power and the role power plays in racism and sexism. Contact the Center for Global Education for further information on Bafá Bafá.

Time: 1.5 -2 hours.

Materials: The Bafá Bafá game, cassette tape player, 2 facilitators, newsprint and markers, or chalkboard and chalk for debriefing.

* * *

There is No Such Thing as Immaculate Perception: Developing Tools for Observation and Interpretation

This exercise was developed by Meredith Sommers Dregni in 1986 and reprinted here with her permission.

Goals: To help participants develop better observation skills and differentiate between observation, emotion, and interpretation.

Materials: Short film and projector, slides and projector, photographs, or poster; chalkboard or newsprint.

Method: Use a short film, slides, photographs or a poster that depict people living in poverty. Give the group time to study the visual image, and then ask the group, "What did/do you *see?*" Write this down on the chalkboard or newsprint. Divide their comments into two columns, but do not label the columns. Put actual *observations* in one column, such as "thin children" or broken window." In the other column, write down their statements that you think are *interpretations* of what they saw, such as "hunger" or "despairing mothers." When comments are completed, draw their attention to the columns and label them.

Now ask the group how they *felt* when the viewed the pictures. Differentiate between *emotions* and *thoughts*. A statement such as "I felt sad and guilty" expresses that person's emotions. A statement such as "I feel the church should be more responsive to their needs" uses the language of feelings to express a thought.

Debriefing: Explain that there is no right or wrong in this exercise. The purpose is to understand the different components to our experience: observation, interpretation, and the accompanying feelings or emotions. All three will be present; knowing how to distinguish between them and paying attention to how they affect you will help deepen your learning about another culture.

Warn of the danger of generalizations, interpretations, and analysis with insufficient data or understanding of the rules and norms of another culture. For example, in some cultures women laugh when they are deeply embarrassed. Upon seeing this occur we might conclude — using our own cultural norms — that these women are happy, when in fact the opposite may be true.

In addition to culture, what we observe and how we interpret are influenced by our own understanding of ourselves, our history, gender, race, class, and sexual orientation. No one observes from a neutral stance, so it is important to be aware of the unconscious influences on us and what criteria we use to make judgments and interpretations.

Upon entering another culture it is important to take time to begin to understand the culture before trying to analyze or interpret it. Much of North American culture trains us to look for solutions to problems. In another culture this can cause us to jump to solutions without really experiencing or understanding the problem. Encourage participants to focus on observations and living with the questions, especially toward the beginning of the trip, before moving into analysis.

* * *

The Shape of the World:
An Exercise on Observation and Perception

This exercise was adapted from "The Shape of the World," MDI Group, 1975, in Training for Transformation *by Anne Hope and Sally Timmel, Mambo Press, Zimbabwe, 1987.*

Background: This is a stimulating exercise that helps a group share their perceptions of the most important things happening in the world (or some other reality, such as Central America). It develops interest in the forces which are shaping and changing the world, for better or for worse. For groups whose members come from very different backgrounds, it may be helpful to do a listening exercise before starting to ensure that people try to understand each other's points of view. If done in this spirit, it can lay a basis of trust in a very diverse group and provide a common experience for many types of analysis.

Time: 2.5 - 3 hours

Materials: Newsprint, markers or crayons, individual papers, tables at which groups can work.

Method: Ask the participants to form mixed groups of five and sit around tables where newsprint, markers, crayons and individual papers are provided. Explain that there are five steps in the exercise, and that you will explain each, one at a time, and illustrate on newsprint on the wall.

1. Main Illustration
   - Ask each person to draw a circle on a plain piece of paper. Explain that this circle represents the world in which the participants live.
   - Ask: "If you could draw a picture or symbol of the world, what would be its main illustration?" Give time for each person to reflect on this and make his or her own drawing on a separate sheet of paper.
   - Now ask each person to share the drawing and what he or she was trying to express with the other group members.
   - Then ask each group to make a common picture on newsprint that includes everyone's ideas. They can either plan a new picture which includes all the ideas, or draw different ideas in different parts of the circle. (Warm them not to draw the circle too large, or to draw outside the circle, since they will have to use the space outside the circle later.)

2. Future Impacts
   - Ask each small group to discuss: "What do you believe is having an impact on the world now, and over the next few years will continue to affect it strongly?"
   - Have the groups show this by drawing arrows into the circle and labeling them. Arrows directly into the center show the most direct impact while arrows into the periphery describe a less direct impact. Groups may want to use one color for negative forces and another for positive forces.

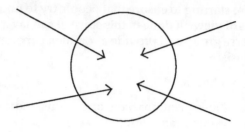

3. Influences Dying Out
   • Ask each small group: "What things are dying out in the world [or other reality] or will die out in the next few years?"

   • Have them show this by using arrows going out of the circle and labeling them.
   Arrows leaving from the center represent important influences dying out; arrows leaving from the periphery describe weaker influences fading away.

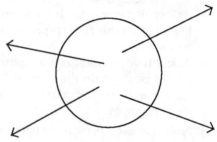

4. Long-Range Impact
   • When the group finishes the above task, ask each group: "What things do you believe will one day have an impact on the world but which are now five or ten years, or more, away?"

   • Show these by arrows adjacent to the circle and label them.

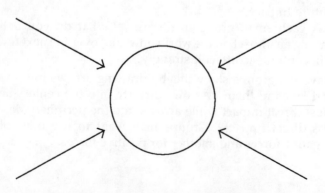

5. Implications
- When all the above tasks are completed, put the names of the group members in the corner of the drawing and hang the drawings around the room. Take about ten minutes for each person to look at what the different groups have drawn.
- Now ask each person to take about five minutes to reflect quietly and write: "What is the major insight this process has given me?" or "What are the implications of this for me and our group?"
- Now ask the small groups to discuss their points, and then write on newsprint a summary of the insights and implications they have discussed. Have each group try to summarize these in one sentence that can be attached to their drawing.
- *(Optional)* Pair up with one other person and take 10-15 minutes to talk about the implications for you.
- Debrief the exercise in a large group. Allow people to ask questions of each group about their drawing. What do people perceive overall is the shape of the world? What are some of the important implications of this? How was this exercise? Was it helpful? What helped, what blocked the experience? What does it say about how we communicate as a group?

The Center for Global Education at Augsburg College in Minneapolis is committed to education which helps people expand their world view and deepen their understand of international issues. The Center offers a variety of international and domestic experiential education programs for undergraduate, graduate, and continuing education credit. For more information about these programs or the consulting services offered by the Center, contact: Center for Global Education, Augsburg College, 731 21st Avenue South, Minneapolis, MN 55454, 612/330-1159.

Practical Issues for Youth Programs:
Recruitment, Liability, Transportation

Dan Conrad and Diane Hedin

Reprinted with permission from Youth Service: A Guidebook for Developing and Operating Effective Programs *by Dan Conrad and Diane Hedin, Independent Sector, 1987, pp. 32-38. The term "youth service" as used here includes an emphasis on combining service and learning.*

Recruitment

RECRUITMENT OF VOLUNTEERS is a task faced by the leader of every youth service program — whether it is a club activity or a program in a school where service is required for graduation. While there will be differences in the degree of voluntariness, the level of commitment demanded, and the type of incentives that can be offered, there are certain principles and approaches that are relevant to any effort to recruit young volunteers.

Designing the Appeal

1. A good rule of thumb is to *be as concrete and specific as possible*. A few people may respond to the invitation to "Be a Volunteer," and a few more may jump at the chance to "Help Make Someone's Day." But many more are likely to respond to a request to do a specific job.

One young man who had shown no interest in joining a volunteer group responded immediately to a request for someone to replace a broken lamp socket for an elderly woman. His only comment on why he never got involved before was: "I didn't know you wanted lamps fixed."

Of course you cannot always be as specific as that, but your recruiting message can at least provide examples of the kinds of things volunteers will do in the program.

Potential volunteers also should be told as soon and as plainly as possible how many hours they will be asked to put in, over what period of time, and what other requirements there may be (such as keeping a journal). The more informed the volunteer's choice, the less likely it is that there will be complaints, problems, and drop-outs later.

2. Try to *convey that community service is enjoyable*, that helping others needn't be — and most often is not — a dull and dreary affair performed with long faces and heavy hearts. That story needs to be told, and it usually can be told most effectively by previous volunteers or shown through snapshots, slides, or videotapes.

"Few young people will be scared off by a significant challenge."

Some activities are fun, and filled with promise of adventure (going horseback riding with retarded children for example). Most often the source of enjoyment is people: meeting new kinds, forming new friendships, being part of a close-knit and spirited group.

3. *Stress the challenge* of tackling a tough job *and the satisfaction* of completing it creditably. This is not a contradiction of the previous point. An activity can be good fun and hard work, and indeed in many ways the fact that it is hard makes it more rewarding.

Few young people will be scared off by a significant challenge, particularly if it is also made clear that they will have ample help and support in facing it.

A point to keep in mind when forming your own recruitment campaign is that your task is similar to that of a Madison Avenue executive designing an advertising campaign for teenagers. The secret of success is to know the customers' interests and motives, and what it is about a product or organization that will appeal to them.

It is no accident that the recruiting messages of the armed services and fast-food chains both feature young people having a really great time taking on new challenges with the exuberant support of some wonderful new friends.

Making the Appeal

Successful recruitment is not a one-shot, short-term event in the life of a program. More often it is the product of ongoing efforts to make the program visible to those who ought to know about it. Anything that draws positive attention to the program will help attract new volunteers, and some ways to attain recognition that have special implications for recruiting volunteers are listed below.

1. *Use the school newspaper or agency newsletter.* Run a regular column on new volunteer opportunities, and suggest occasional articles about newsworthy projects or profiles of student volunteers.

2. *Produce a video presentation* on the program. Students in one program made an MTV-type music video that was very effective in recruiting new volunteers. Others have done documentaries of specific projects. If your school or agency does not have adequate equipment, contact the cable TV company serving your area. Usually it is part of the company's franchise agreement that it make equipment and expertise available to community groups.

3. *Set up a bulletin board* in a high traffic area of the school or community with pictures, notices of current needs, and anything else that will draw attention. In some schools the same kind of information is transmitted through a *video monitor*. It also would be possible to put relevant information into an *interactive computer program* that would give passers-by updated information on available placements.

4. *Keep people who make referrals* (such as counselors, social workers, administrators, and teachers) *informed* and up-to-date on the program so they feel some ownership.

5. Take a hint from other school groups. *The school P.A. system* could as easily give periodic information on the volunteer program as it does on the soccer team, and volunteers might wear *pins and badges* as appropriately as do members of the school pep club.

6. *Use previous and current volunteers* as much as possible in any activities, particularly in making presentations to classes or youth groups. They always will be the most credible witnesses for the program.

7. *Produce a printed brochure* or other attractive handout that is easily (and cheaply) distributed to interested people.

8. *Think about new ways to reach large numbers of people.* Mass assemblies are seldom effective, but large numbers might be reached by other means. One school with a large volunteer program hosts a *Community Volunteer Fair* each fall at which agencies desiring

student help set up booths in the festively decorated library, where they talk to students and make clear by their very presence that young people are needed and wanted in this community.

9. If possible, *have a conveniently located central office* where students can find out what volunteer opportunities are currently available and get other information about the program. Staffed by a coordinator and/or students, it will be welcomed by community people as well.

10. In some programs *parents also must be "recruited,"* or at least persuaded that their son or daughter should be allowed to participate. Some youth organizations telephone parents to explain what their child will be doing, or even stop in to meet the parents personally.

Some groups encourage teenage volunteers to bring a younger brother or sister and let them get involved in community service too. That approach may persuade parents that their son or daughter can help with child-care responsibilities while still being involved in community service.

It is a good idea to *require parents to sign a permission form* that includes basic information on the program. Beyond asking for parents' permission, many groups actively solicit the help and involvement of parents, from assisting with transportation of volunteers to joining the students in projects requiring the adults' special expertise. One good way to get parents involved could be to *hold an informational "potluck" dinner* hosted by the young people.

Directing the Appeal

The aim of any recruitment effort ought to be to attract as varied as possible a group of volunteers: male and female, good students and poor, older and younger, model citizens and renegades. This is a goal not only for the program leader but one which needs to be made clear to counselors, youth workers, teachers, and others who are in a position to channel people into the program.

It can be the death of a program to have it be seen as just for troublemakers, or just for honor students, or just for girls, etc. Part of the power of the experience is in young people working alongside kids they might never associate with otherwise. More importantly still, the community needs the contributions of all kinds of people, and everyone has something to contribute somewhere. Most importantly, since service is an experience that can benefit all young people, all young people ought to have equal access to it.

Liability

The threat of lawsuits is the current Achilles' heel for organizations serving children and youth, and community service programs are no exception. Yet fears about liability do not seem justified in light of the very few cases of injuries or negligence ever reported in these programs. While it is reassuring to know that the chances of legal problems occurring are extremely small, your agency or school does need to understand its legal responsibilities and liability.

A good starting place is to *discuss your individualized insurance needs* with your administrator or organization's legal adviser. Some of the key factors to consider in designing the right insurance package are:

• *Transportation arrangements.* Whether students drive their own cars to their volunteer placements or the coordinator drives students in a personal car or agency vehicle will determine what kind of automobile insurance is needed. In some cases, the student's or teacher's personal automobile insurance is deemed sufficient; in some circumstances, schools or agencies should purchase supplemental coverage.

• *School or agency's current insurance coverage.* You may be able to amend your organization's ongoing insurance policy to include coverage for community service activities.

The best way to think about this issue is to identify similar kinds of activities already under way and simply incorporate what you are doing under the coverage. For example, many schools have a work experience or cooperative learning program in which students leave the school building and work for pay a part of the school day. A community service program is not very different in its general approach, in that it involves students leaving the school building, working at a variety of community sites, driving to their work sites, and not being under the direct, personal supervision of the teacher.

Since almost every school in the country already has addressed liability concerns surrounding work-study programs, you may be able to use the same procedures and policies.

• *Volunteer sites' insurance coverage.* Some of the sites to which your students go, such as hospitals, day-care centers, etc., have insurance to cover volunteers.

The second key consideration in the liability issue is to *establish procedures and policies that reduce risks and dangers* to the participants, thereby reducing potential liability for negligence. The section on "Evaluation" outlines some key elements of a record-keeping system, which helps to do just that. For example, parent permission slips are helpful in documenting that parents have consented to have their child in the program.

A master chart showing where volunteers are working indicates that you have taken steps to supervise those students in your charge. These charts, ID cards, parent permission forms, etc., all are indicators that you have established procedures to exercise care and concern for the students' welfare. It is the concept of exercising due care that is at the heart of the negligence issue.

The National Association of Secondary School Principals has outlined a series of principles pertaining to liability for negligence by school administrators generally, and for cases in which injuries have occurred to students while away from the school building. Many of the principles are applicable to youth-serving agencies when they undertake community service. They are useful in developing the appropriate policies and procedures for reducing negligence:

1. The exercise of due care requires an administrator to attempt to foresee dangers to students in his charge and to take whatever precautions seem reasonable to avoid them.

2. Specifically, an administrator is expected to establish rules for the guidance of his or her staff, and to assign adequate supervision for any student activity, but the school and its staff are not expected to be an insurer of the health and safety of students.

3. The greater the possibility of injury, the greater the efforts that should be made to assure student safety.

4. The closer the relationship of a student activity to the purposes and educational program of the school, the more likely a principal or other administrator is to be held accountable to the students for their well-being.

5. In circumstances where supervision and control of student welfare is infeasible, extra care should be taken to assure that the circumstances into which the student is placed are not fraught with inherent dangers. Any necessary risks should be brought to the attention of both students and parents in advance.

6. The degree of care required, and the consequent amount of supervision expected, increase as the age and maturity of students involved decrease.

7. The location in which a student is injured is only one factor in the consideration of whether there was negligence and consequent legal liability on the part of the principal or other educator.

Transportation

Transportation can affect significantly the overall success of a community service program. While it seems like a small issue, it can drain the energy from the most enthusiastic coordinator if it is not successfully resolved. Three factors should be considered in devising a strategy: resources of the sponsoring organization and participants, student safety, and scheduling.

Resources

1. Student Resources.

Some programs have relied on the resourcefulness of youth to solve the transportation problem. Some students have cars and can drive other students, as well. Others have the pocket money to travel by public transportation. Try to remain alert, though, to the problems that may be created. For some students, having to be responsible financially for their own transportation may be an obstacle to participation. If this approach denies opportunities to students, then some of the alternatives below ought to be tried.

2. School District or Youth Agency Resources.

Some schools and youth-serving agencies will be able to supply the funds necessary to cover student travel. Some of the ways this can be done include:

• *Using a school district bus with a regular bus driver*, or with a parent or teacher as driver. (The driver must have a chauffeur's license.) Buses often are free during school hours, thus making it possible to obtain their use. However, getting them on a regular basis does require persistence.

• Having the coordinator or teacher *use a personal car*. On the plus side, it's one of the most convenient arrangements, giving the most direct control over moving students around the community. A drawback is that it limits the number of sites to which students can go. Driving students hither and yon also can be tedious. Yet, the opportunity to help students solve a problem or hear about a triumph enroute can break the tedium of any trip!

• *Purchasing mini-buses or vans* specifically for community service programs, sometimes through a grant or gift from a service group (Rotary, Kiwanis, etc.). Since other school or agency programs may find a mini-bus useful, it may be possible to fund its purchase and maintenance through several sources.

• *Supplying bus tokens or fares* to students. Usually, schools and youth agencies can get special rates on public transportation or provide participants with identification cards that enable them to get reduced fares.

• *Having parents or volunteers drive.* Parents sometimes are willing to drive, and it may be possible to organize their time so that different parents drive on alternating days. The PTA may be willing to take on such a project. Such arrangements can be complicated to organize. The more people who are involved, the greater the chance for miscommunication and missed rides.

> *"Part of the power of the experience is in young people working alongside kids they might never associate with otherwise."*

• *Gathering together a fleet of used bicycles* so that the more energetic students can ride to their community service placements.

• *Borrowing vehicles.* School-owned driver education cars might be available. Some agencies are able to persuade local automobile dealers to contribute vehicles to the programs. Some businesses, particularly large corporations, have vans for transporting their employees to and from work; some schools have arranged to use those vans during the school day when they are not ordinarily in use.

Safety

It seems obvious that students should not travel in areas or at time that may threaten their physical safety, but the point is so crucial to a program's longevity that it's worth repeating. When students must travel in high-crime areas, it is best to have them travel in groups of two or more.

When students are being driven to a site, the driver (whether an adult or young person) should be reminded of his/her responsibility for the safety of the passengers. Just one accident caused by the careless driving of a program participant could cause great damage to a program's reputation.

Scheduling

Transportation is a major problem for programs that allow students to volunteer during the regular school day because of the very limited amount of time available for participants to go to and from their placements and back to their next class.

Arranging a two-hour block of time by offering double credit in one subject area or one credit in each of two subjects (English and social studies, for example) is one solution. Another is to schedule the field experience either at the beginning or the end of the school day. This way, students can travel directly from home to the community agency or directly from the site to home.

Dan Conrad directs community involvement programs at Hopkins High School in Minnesota. Diane Hedin is former Director of Community Relations at the Pillsbury Foundation and is now a professor at the Center for Youth Development and Research at the University of Minnesota. Over the past 17 years, Conrad and Hedin have co-directed several research and publications projects in experiential education, youth participation, and service-learning.

Reference

"Responsibilities for Student Injury Occurring Off School Property, A Legal Memorandum," National Association of Secondary School Principals, Reston, Virginia, March-April, 1975, p. 6.

Establishing Agency Relationships

William R. Ramsay

Bill Ramsay discusses practical steps in initiating lasting relationships with representatives of community service organizations. Reprinted from Synergist, National Center for Service-Learning, ACTION, Vol. 4, No. 3, Winter 1976, pp. 14-18.

PART OF THE MANAGEMENT JOB of a director or coordinator of a student community service program is establishing and maintaining productive agency relations. A variety of agencies, situations, and personalities may call for different approaches, but all require attention if effective assignments are to result. This article raises questions, makes observations, and provides examples which may be helpful in managing agency relationships.

The comments are directed primarily to directors, coordinators or counselors for student community service programs. The agencies discussed are assumed to fit the general definition of community service, be they governmental or nongovernmental, large or small. It is also assumed that the program has both service and learning goals. Students are expected to perform services that are real and important, rather than simply observing or pursuing an academic exercise. At the same time, conscious learning is also expected of the students in their community placements.

In working with agencies it is essential to understand the realities of the world in which they operate. One of these realities is imperfection. The agency, its personnel, its programs, and its clients will sometimes be incompetent, wrong, and unfair, but simply to discover this is not enough for either the program director or the student.

A willingness to work with imperfection is basic to effective agency relationships. Nothing closes an agency door faster than unconstructive criticism, given in a condescending way by a self-satisfied program director. Problems that agencies face are complex. They are not served by simple answers or settled within a short time. Community service agencies usually have limited resources — one good reason why they use student volunteers.

Preparing for Agency Contact

Before contacting an agency, prepare yourself. A first step is to know your objectives. Be able to articulate concisely your program's goals, service objectives, and learning expectations.

Knowing your students is also critical. It is helpful if you are prepared to give information about the types, range, interests, limitations, and talents of your students, along with examples of what they can do. Are your students of urban or rural experience, graduates or undergraduates, local or out-of-state, experienced or new to community service? This information will be of interest to the agency you call.

Your program may have other resources important to a potential assignment. Access to a library, campus research bureau, or technical resource is important. Transportation, duplication, or publicity services may be of interest to small agencies without them. The director of a day care center came in recently and said, "I've taken 13 of your students, but I need a way of duplicating notices and training materials for them. Can you help?" Such simple things loom large in day-to-day agency operations. It is useful to describe in package format, in a simple brochure or single sheet, all your program resources, including your students, their pre-assignment training, and your campus resources.

Prepare for an agency contact by doing preliminary research on the agency and its programs. It helps if you know the agency's structure, mission, and activities — at least well enough to ask intelligent questions. Familiarity with legislative or administrative provisions governing a public agency (or the board and corporate structure of a private one) can make planning easier for all concerned. In dealing with governmental agencies, knowledge of this sort can keep you from getting an automatic "no" because you asked the wrong question of the wrong person in the wrong way. Bureaucracies do have "no sayers," but they are also populated with positive public servants. Researching an agency in advance can result in your reaching quickly those administrators who can help you.

In addition to preliminary research, it is important to be prepared administratively before contacting an agency. Prepare in advance your answers to questions about administrative relationships between the student, the agency, and your program. Who will make the final selection? Who will notify the student? What reports will be needed? What records must be kept? Prepare forms, instructions, and information on procedures in advance.

If possible, the student himself should be involved in approaching an agency. In some programs the student has the chief responsibility for finding her own placement, with support from the campus office in the form of literature and counseling. In many cases, agency identification and contact occur before a specific student has been identified, but as a general rule a student should become involved in his or her prospective assignment as early as possible.

The sum of these observations on preparation for approaching an agency is that an agency representative will appreciate and respond better to your approach if it is obvious that you have done your homework. Time has been saved. The agency's first impression of the program is one of competence. You have established a solid basis for building effective relationships.

Initial Contacts

Being well prepared does not mean going to an agency with a complete plan of what you think it should do. Knowing in advance your program and resources and something about the agency, you are now ready to listen effectively as well as to inform. On first contact, allow enough time for more than superficial communication. In discussing the agency's structure, programs, and problems, a good listener can pick up important clues to potential assignments for students. One is not likely to find an agency that feels overstaffed or a professional person who doesn't have a list of unmet needs. A gold mine of possible projects can often be discovered among these unmet needs.

Avoiding Misunderstandings

Unless you take care to listen well and creatively, time will be lost or misunderstandings will arise. Unless you make deliberate efforts, it sometimes takes three contacts to begin to communicate. At first contact people tend to jump to conclusions and respond to the image they have quickly formed about what the other is saying. At a second meeting, the differences between these initial impressions and what was really meant come to light, and it takes a third session to start hearing what is really being said. If you listen carefully, question creatively, and make sure that your responses are genuinely responsive, you will be on your way to a good agency relationship.

Many agencies have a need for students to fill "positions." Staffing a station in a bloodmobile, answering a phone for a consumer agency, or playing with children in a day care center are examples of positions where a specific operation is carried out by a student. Often a problem-solving approach, where the student is given a task defined by objective or need, may be coupled with a specific service-learning position. Identifying agency needs (for both filling positions and solving problems) and then relating these needs to your student resources is a basic task of fostering agency relationships.

As new needs which might be served by students are identified, organize them into general descriptions. The description at this point needs to be enough to give a possible assignment form and direction, but should not be very detailed. Knowledge of the students, program resources, and time limits is important.

It helps to have a simple form on which to record potential assignments. Describe the position by a general title and include basic information on location, names and addresses, and telephone numbers. Three simple questions can serve to develop a preliminary outline for an agency assignment:

1. How does the general need or goal of the assignment relate to the purposes of the agency?
2. What are the specific objectives (outcomes) of the assignment?
3. What are the first steps in its accomplishment?

With this kind of preliminary statement, a student, agency representative, and program coordinator can move toward getting an agency relationship and a particular student assignment off to a good start.

As you discuss goals and purposes of your program, the agency, and specific assignments, you will be making assumptions about values. It is helpful, exciting, and most often appreciated when these values are discussed rather than just assumed. Most agency personnel who participate in programs like yours share with the students and you a commitment to service, a sense of duty, and ideals of integrity and human worth.

Too often these sentiments are expressed only in the rhetoric of speeches and publicity. They tend to be pushed aside in day-to-day routines by the matters of efficiency, economy, skill, and accountability. Agency personnel are as eager as students and program directors to find kindred spirits who share values and commitments which underlie their motivations. Keeping shared values alive adds meaning to assignments and enriches agency relationships.

During initial contacts with an agency, review the roles and objectives of the various parties in a general way. The fact that program, agency, and student objectives are somewhat different, or at least vary in emphasis, is important to discuss. Varying objectives should be expected, acknowledged, and respected. They are usually not incompatible, and in fact lend vitality and realism to a program. Likewise the roles of student, agency supervisor, and program director are different and need to be understood, at least generally, from the time of first contact.

Establishing Procedures

Assuming that a general understanding has been reached that an agency is interested in cooperating with your program and potential assignments are feasible, the final step of the initial contact is to arrange the next meeting. Both agency and program considerations are involved in establishing procedures. Who will serve as the primary contact person? What written confirmation of relationships and records is needed? Is further approval needed from personnel within the agency?

Getting and giving accurate and complete information on names, titles, addresses, telephone numbers, and schedules will save time later on. In general the initiative for next steps should be assumed by the representative of the student community service program. A budding relationship can die very quickly if the agency finds that it has been asked to take responsibility for another set of initiatives.

In summary, the goal of the initial contact with an agency is to establish a relationship of mutual understanding of missions and resources, possible assignments, value assumptions, roles and objectives, and follow-up procedures. This requires advance preparation. Set aside time to give your undivided attention to these matters because they will be the basis of future relationships.

Establishing Relationships

The most critical point in establishing and maintaining effective agency relationships is the need for clarity of expectations. Knowing what is expected is essential in knowing how to respond and in evaluating responses. This is true of agency personnel, students, and program directors.

As suggested above, the objectives and motivations of the various parties will likely be different, and tensions can develop if these differences are not understood. The agency is apt to be primarily concerned with accomplishing a task or perhaps looking over a future employee. Students want to learn and to express themselves in service. They are apt to ask questions which may seem to agency personnel impertinent or annoying if learning objectives are not appreciated.

While understanding the objectives and roles of others is important, it is also important for each party to execute his or her assigned role. Sometimes agency supervisors, in deference to learning objectives, are lax in performance requirements, with the excuse that the volunteer is "just a student." Likewise, a program counselor whose primary role is to help a student interpret a service experience may overplay the supervisory role by giving directions rather than making observations.

Clarity about scheduling and administration is also essential. An effective agency relationship rests on the confidence that each party knows what commitments it has made and the degree to which it can be counted on to meet them. After a schedule and administrative responsibilities have been established, any changes must be cleared with all parties. Effective internal communications within an agency should not be assumed. If more than one agency person is involved, as is often the case, coordinate schedules, arrangements, and changes with all. It is particularly important to keep the agency head or primary contact person up-to-date on progress and changes, even though your day-to-day work may be with another person.

Placement, another important function of establishing a relationship, involves more than placing a student in an assignment. Ideally, placement means placing the "right" person with the "right" situation. A professional personnel approach can be used to analyze both the student's qualifications and the position. The tools of job analysis can identify duties, levels of supervision, working conditions, skills and experience needed, and other technical aspects of a placement. Professional personnel techniques, such as interview, reference, and review of application, can help program director and agency representative select a qualified student. Personnel techniques can also help to work out a procedure for supervision.

This process of review of person and of position can also be of value to the student as she participates in an assessment of her abilities, interests, and potentials in relation to specific tasks to be done. Agencies appreciate a professional personnel approach to placement and take student volunteers more seriously if their program director assumes the initiative.

In establishing agency relationships, questions about legal responsibility, financial demands, and administrative relationships are often the most difficult. These will range from who is liable for an injury to a student to who must approve news releases regarding a student's activity. Here again the more prepared the program director is, the greater the respect agency personnel will have for the program. These questions and answers will depend on many individual factors, and each agency relationship can be examined individually in light of these matters. If transportation is involved, who carries the insurance? Can a student commit his host agency by acting as its agent? Should an agency that uses a number of students report this fact to their liability insurer?

Identifying Administrative Questions

Lawyers, insurance agents, personnel officers, and other professionals in cooperating agencies can often be helpful in identifying the questions. Students can help research these questions. As experience builds, the basic questions and answers become known, and only exceptions and variations caused by unusual circumstances will need research and decision.

Some of the questions raised are answered by paper instruments such as contracts, agreements, forms, published policies and procedures, reports, and records. While many student community service arrangements are informal, most continuing agency relationships involve an exchange and maintenance of written records. A simple exchange of letters may be sufficient to record the basic conditions of cooperation agreed upon between a program and an agency. Larger programs may involve formal contracts. Legal phrasing need not be used for most agreements, but clarity about basic responsibilities and procedures is important. In general it is good to have a letter of agreement signed by both parties, with copies retained by each, so that if questions should arise later the document can serve as a reference point. If attachments of printed policies and procedures of either party (the agency or the program) are included as part of an agreement, refer to them in the agreement itself. See Michael Goldstein's chapter in this volume for more information about legal issues.

A reporting system is a useful tool in agency-program relationships. Deciding what information is significant, how it will be collected and reported, and when reporting should be shared between agency staff and service-learning program directors is a preliminary task. A reporting system tailored to each agency is preferable to a standardized system, but in any case set up a reporting timetable that is mutually acceptable to all parties concerned.

In the establishment of good relationships with an agency, the student himself or herself can play a significant role. The student's involvement in the definition of roles, placement, legal, financial and administrative questions, contracts, and reports can help him and help the relationships necessary to the program. If a number of students are involved, a group meeting with agency personnel is useful. The more each student knows of the relationships between the program and the agency, the better she will represent one to the other. The student is surely the person with the greatest stake in those relationships.

Orientation

Another important task in establishing good agency relationships is the development of an orientation that will serve the program, the agency and the student equally well. A joint effort at planning orientation is called for, although too seldom done. If the student can be involved in the development of his assignment and the administrative issues between program and agency, his orientation will be well along. The earlier and greater the involvement of the student, the better.

If a student cannot be involved in advance, it is a good idea to divide orientation to the agency and assignment into two steps. Students new to an assignment need basic information such as where and when to report, office procedures, and other immediate concerns. Orientation to general goals, purposes, and agency history is apt to be more effective if it comes after the immediate questions have been answered and the student is somewhat settled. General orientation, most often seen as the first thing on the agenda, may be more effective if parts of it are deliberately delayed.

Cultivating Relationships

Once established, an agency relationship needs to be cultivated. Basic to sustaining a good relationship is student performance. No matter what techniques are used to establish and maintain cooperation with an agency, the relationship will lose meaning unless the students produce positive results with reasonable consistency. Accordingly, primary attention is needed to those policies and services which bear most directly on performance. The student needs to be aware of the importance of his performance in relation not only to his assignment but to the continuity of the entire program. Success in new assignments with an agency is especially vital.

Many agency assignments are worthy of publicity. Agencies, as well as your program, can benefit from public knowledge and understanding of the joint activities and can thereby spread the impact to a larger population. In addition, recognition of service-learning projects by elected officials, agency directors, and other leaders can strengthen the student effort and the agency commitment. Work out a procedure for publicity and information flow with an agency to assure coordination, accuracy, and effectiveness of reporting. Some programs use a regular news format for releases sent to a student's home town newspaper and another format for releases sent to newspapers in the area of assignment. Including agency information and names can be very helpful in strengthening cooperation.

Established relationships tend to be taken for granted. This can be true in marriages, in friendships, in organizations, and in program-agency relations. If the relationship is remembered only when a need arises or a problem occurs, it will not be as vital or productive or able to survive difficulties as one which has been maintained more positively.

Taking time to visit by phone or in person without an agenda can lead to much stronger relationships and can uncover concerns before they become problems. Visiting also increases the enjoyment of both agency and program personnel and is worth doing for itself. Publicity and visiting are management techniques that serve to strengthen the interpersonal relationships upon which service-learning programs fail, survive, or flourish.

William Ramsay is Dean of Labor and Student Life at Berea College in Kentucky. He is also past President of the National Association of Student Employment Administrators and a participant in the early roots of the service-learning movement in the 1960s in the South.

Cultivating Agency Allies

William R. Ramsay

Ramsay presents techniques for educators to strengthen and sustain relationships with representatives of community and public organizations. Reprinted from Synergist, *National Center for Service-Learning, ACTION, Vol. 5, No. 1, Spring 1976, pp. 18-53.*

A WILLINGNESS TO DEAL with the imperfections of community service agencies is an important characteristic of effective directors of service-learning programs. Regardless of the excellence of your agency relationships and of your students' performance, problems can arise. Knowing this, the best way to prepare is to establish clear procedures for handling them. For example, an understanding of the procedures needed to terminate a student's relationship with a community service agency is necessary, whether initiated by the student or by agency staff. The situations are often highly emotional; therefore it is important to handle them quickly and professionally, without having to improvise. It is well to deal with the situation and the perceptions as they are, looking for solutions rather than someone to blame.

Dealing openly and constructively with a problem can provide an opportunity to strengthen your agency relationships. Some problems may not be so serious as they appear. If you carefully question those involved to clarify the elements of a problem, you can sometimes help to resolve it before it becomes a crisis on campus. Many reports of problems from student volunteers to program directors may not have been called to the attention of the agency supervisor. The first step in a trouble-shooting procedure is to report the problem directly to the agency supervisor. Until the student has done this, your intervention is generally unwise. A next step is to arrange a meeting with all parties concerned in as nonthreatening a setting as possible. Keep all parties informed and record key information. Make sure that this record is cleared with everyone present before it passes into your files, and give everyone present a copy of it.

Feelings of Exploitation

Concern about exploitation may be one of the issues about which your students are especially sensitive. A student's feeling that the agency is exploiting him or the population it serves may threaten your agency relationships.

Of course, it is important to avoid or to remedy situations where serious exploitation of any of the parties concerned is apparent. However, an interpretation of the relationships can often put what may be perceived as "exploitation" in better perspective. In the relationship between a student and an agency, each hopes to gain from and contribute to the other. This honest trade-off is important to understand and is not a form of exploitation.

More often a student's concern is about exploitation of an agency's constituent group. This feeling may come from an over-simplified view of the problems and a strong wish to do something significant in a short time. The realization that problems are not solved so simply and require more time than the student has may result in a search for someone to blame. The agency is a convenient scapegoat because it is accessible and often somewhat vulnerable. Why was support withdrawn from a program that was proving successful? Why was staff reduced when more were needed? How can agency officials spend money on travel to a conference at a resort when they claim they do not have enough funds to meet program needs?

Artistic Statesmanship

Such questions may be valid. But unless they get beyond rhetoric, they will likely serve no purpose other than to sever the relationship between student and agency. These situations call for artistic statesmanship on the part of program directors as they try to foster and encourage high hopes, standards, and ideals at the same time that they grapple with priorities and standards of conduct and performance. Agency personnel can help by avoiding a defensive posture and exhibiting patience in discussing such concerns.

It is often at the border of frustration that the most learning can occur. An enthusiastic group of students building a playground for children in a slum area may find it hard to sustain momentum if they are faced with delays caused by questions of zoning, security, safety, liability, supervision, and neighborhood feelings. The recreation agency with which the students work may have many other projects of higher priority that make immediate attention to the concerns of the students impossible. Students can help in these situations (with leadership from program directors) by researching and pursuing answers to some of the important questions involved.

Once you have established a good relationship with an agency, endeavor to raise to the highest possible levels the service and learning dimensions of your students' assignments. One good way to do this is to raise expectations. Beyond your students' expectations of doing a good job in a service assignment can be the expectation of contributing to the well-being of the service-learning program as a whole and the effectiveness of its operating procedures. Beyond your student's expectations of learning a specific task in a specific agency is the expectation of broader learning about the agency itself and about the people working in it — volunteers, staff and clients — with backgrounds and values different from his or her own. From this exposure your students will learn more about themselves and develop a thinking approach to service.

Interpreting Volunteer Experiences

You can enhance the learning dimension if you provide for interpretation of experience. Encourage the agency to set aside time, beyond necessary orientation, for the student to talk about his or her observations, to hear interpretations of experienced personnel, and to understand varying perspectives. This need not be done only in formal sessions but can become part of the student's day-to-day activities. It takes an understanding of the learning goals and a willingness to give time and thought to the student on the part of supervisors and other agency personnel.

Interpreting negative experiences can be especially meaningful and keeps a poor experience from being viewed as a total loss. A student can perform very useful services and learn very little. Conversely she can be unsuccessful in performance but learn a great deal. If a student serving in a hospital emergency room finds that he faints at the sight of blood, he at least has learned something about himself which should be useful in future choices. Helping a student interpret a negative experience is usually best done by a counselor outside the agency or at least apart from the immediate staff. At a more general level, however, it is important to work with agency personnel in understanding the potential value of negative experience.

A service-learner who has undertaken to tutor an adult in basic reading, for example, may find that, after initial progress, there is a loss of interest on the part of his tutee, who may have other concerns, such as getting a job, that interfere with his motivation to learn to read. The student may be frustrated in attempts to help in these areas by lack of resources, especially if he or she finds no interest on the part of the agency. The tutee may want to continue with the student because it provides some attention and sympathy, even though the original goal of literacy is not being served. Attempts by the student to persuade the tutee that finding a job can depend on literacy may be met with agreement but no additional effort.

At some point a decision may be made to drop the tutee from the program. To see this simply as a failure on the part of the adult reading program or just to write off the tutee as "no good" would be simplistic. The potential for understanding more about the cycle of poverty, motivations, and limitations of programs is considerable, and such a seemingly negative experience can contribute to improvements even though it may not be personally satisfying to the student.

Techniques to Improve Learning Experiences

A variety of techniques can be used to improve the learning experience. Establishing learning expectations has been mentioned as important. At Berea College, we use a learning description of an assignment that parallels the job description. Where a job description outlines duties and responsibilities, qualifications, and work environment, a learning description outlines areas of understanding to be gained, types of situations to be encountered, skills to be learned and applied, and outcomes, in terms of abilities, arising from the experience.

Keeping journals and making reports are more widely recognized tools for learning from experience. Seminars, supplementary readings, and individual consultations are also frequently used. The critical point is to provide some system that reinforces the learning side of the experience. Otherwise it tends to be haphazard and lost.

Educational Debriefing

The Christian College of Georgia in Athens, Georgia, and Berea College in Kentucky use a technique called "educational debriefing." Students who have participated in a specific service project are organized into groups of six or eight. A facilitator and a recorder conduct a series of debriefing sessions, usually two or three sessions of a couple hours each. The facilitator's job is to question and foster discussion so that students bring their learning to a conscious level. The basic assumption is that "You know more than you think you know." As students express what they have learned, what they can do now that they couldn't do previously, and what new questions they have, the recorder prepares a summary of learning for each which is later given to the student as a record of learning. Students continuing in an experiential situation or preparing to undertake a new one are much more alert to its learning possibilities.

Performance and Conduct Standards

It is generally assumed that a student will meet performance and conduct standards of the agency assignment. However, program directors and students also have their own standards of performance and conduct. Stay alert to potential differences in standards between agencies and the program and between agencies and students. Standards of health and cleanliness are especially important in some situations. Personal appearance and dress may be important in others. Behavior off the job is also important in a culturally different area with more rigid social customs. Your students should identify and understand standards that they are expected to meet *before assignments begin.*

If a conflict arises between a student and an agency over whose standards should apply, the program director is usually caught in the middle. Conflicts can occur in matters of personal appearance, techniques used, and, occasionally, in basic philosophy and integrity. The key to effective handling of these situations is the separation of matters of preference from matters of principle. Usually conflicts arise over preferences that are labeled principles by one or more of the parties. If a principle is truly at issue and cannot be compromised, a change in assignment is indicated, but this is rare, and most often the conflicts can be resolved. For example, a volunteer was working with a planning commission on a survey and found that the questionnaire to be used was not, in his opinion, sound. The student took the position that he could not be associated with the survey using that questionnaire. The commission took the position that it had spent a great deal of time and effort in developing the form and, in its opinion and the opinion of its trained staff, it was adequate. How should a program coordinator respond? The student could, of course, quit, but is that necessary? Is the conflict more a matter of opinion than principle? In this case it would seem that the program director should encourage the student to work with the agency on its own terms. Some assistance in interpreting the situation can also be helpful for the student.

Just as standards vary, so do goals. Most situations involve quite a list of goals, each valid and all seen with different priorities by the various participants. Resist the tendency to insist on one overriding goal applicable to all parties. List the various goals of student, agency, and your program and try to understand how they interrelate. Review these various goals from time to time because they change in priority. Which is most important? To do a job? To gain experience? To learn something? To give a young person an opportunity? To travel or live in a certain area? To serve your fellow man? To try out a career? To be a member of a group? Obviously there is no single answer unless it is, "It depends..."

Take the young hospital aide who volunteered because her friend had done so yet found great fulfillment in her service. The hospital's goals are to see that services are provided to patients. The program director's reason for encouraging this volunteer was to get her involved in a wholesome activity for personal development. During the course of the volunteer experience, the girl developed an interest in a career in medicine and sought to learn more about the medical field. The hospital in turn had an opportunity to identify a potential future employee.

All of these goals and motivations are legitimate, and the interplay among them can lend vitality and reality to the service experience. Allowing the "provision of service" goals of the hospital to predominate would be simple exploitation of students, and the program would not last long. Meeting social and personal needs of students as the exclusive goal could result in deficiencies in services performed and also would kill a program. It is up to you, as the program director, with the help of cooperating agency personnel and the students, to integrate various goals and motivations, to identify their limits, and to manage the choices of priorities.

Lasting Relationships

Relationships are among people rather than institutions, and the opportunities for finding enjoyable and meaningful relationships through work with agency personnel are almost unlimited. This is true of the students as well as program staff. A working relationship with an agency has potential beyond the time and program limitations of the specific reason for initiating it. This broader view is rewarding personally and adds a human dimension to your program.

Relationships between programs and institutions do continue, however, beyond the tenure of any one person. Therefore, they must be seen beyond the short-term, person-to-person ones to include the creation of attitudes, environment, procedures, and a record that will foster and sustain institutional relationships. Lasting institutional relationships are built on successful personal relationships supported by procedures, communications, and a shared record of accomplishment that comes from deliberate effort and a sense of responsibility for those who follow. This sense of responsibility should be felt and expressed in action by students as well as by program staff.

Bill Ramsay is Dean of Labor and Student Life at Berea College in Kentucky and past President of the National Association of Student Employment Administrators.

The Issue Of Pay

Organized in the spring of 1969, the Atlanta Service-Learning Conference explored the implications of the service-learning concept, defined the elements necessary for a successful program, and designed a program in the Atlanta area to serve as a model for similar programs in other urban centers. This summary of the discussion on one topic — reimbursement for service-learning participants — shows how similar the issues in the service-learning movement of the 1960s and 1970s are to the issues being discussed in the service-learning movement of the 1980s and 1990s. Reprinted from the Atlanta Service-Learning Conference Report, *Southern Regional Education Board, 1970, pp. 37-38.*

THE QUESTION OF REIMBURSEMENT for service-learning participants was one of the most difficult issues to resolve. Common ground was established early when all conferees agreed that lack of money should not be a barrier to a service-learning experience. For example, those students who have to work during the summer and academic year may simply not have enough free time to volunteer their services. They should receive sufficient reimbursement for their services so they do not have to hire themselves out for a job unrelated to their studies.

Even for students who have time to volunteer, there is some feeling that they too should receive stipends for accomplishing needed public service tasks. Several reasons were given for this position. First, the person would have a substantial basis for feeling responsible to the agency or for the task. Second, the agency would take a greater interest in the student if it had an investment in him or her. Third, paid personnel have more influence over agency policies and practices than volunteers. Finally, it seems inappropriate for this society to pay student labor for sales, clerical and other such jobs, but to insist that social service be done without monetary recognition.

On behalf of voluntarism, the most convincing argument was that some public service tasks would be left undone, and some students would be deprived of service-learning experiences, if volunteers were excluded. On the other hand, the argument that volunteers are more dedicated than paid personnel was not accepted by the conferees.

The conclusion was that service-learning programs should be underwritten financially, thereby permitting a variety of financial arrangements but assuring every interested student enough support to enable him to have a service-learning experience.

As to sources of money for service-learning programs, the Conference recommended that a broad base of support should be sought so that no single contributor would obtain control over the program. Ultimately the sources of financial support for the service-learning program should reflect the benefits received. Thus a program might draw its funds in approximately equal shares from the agency being served, the student or educational institution, and the government or public interest foundation. In some cases, the input of the academic institution would be academic credit or counselors instead of money.

Service-Learning and the Liberal Arts: Designing an Interdisciplinary Program

Barbara K. Hofer

Barbara Hofer provides a realistic step-by-step process for de-signing an interdisciplinary service-learning course that is part of the regular liberal arts curriculum. Reprinted from Syner-gist, *National Center for Service-Learning, ACTION, Vol. 6, No. 2, Fall 1977, pp. 38-41.*

THE ATTENTION OF MANY PROFESSIONALS in the field of service-learning has been directed toward gaining institutional ac-ceptance for the concept of service-learning, establishing the basic operation of programs, and seeking financial support. But many programs have passed through these initial phases and are entering more sophisticated stages of development. Staff members of more established service-learning programs face such questions as: How can service-learning strengthen the liberal arts? How can it become a more accepted and respected part of the liberal arts curriculum? How can you encourage more faculty to participate in service-learning programs? How can you obtain sustainable funding? What new alternatives can you design to meet student needs?

Interdisciplinary Focus

One way to address these questions is through the development of new, interdisciplinary programs which incorporate service-learn-ing as an integral component. Programs designed around a special focus are geared to a special student population, when coordinated by the service-learning office on your campus, can demonstrate the merits of service-learning as an instructional strategy. The design of a new service-learning program is an excellent opportunity for soliciting the advice and involvement of students, faculty, administrators, and community residents not previously involved with your office. More important, a special program with an interdisciplinary focus can increase faculty awareness of the potential of service-learning for revitalizing the liberal arts. New program models can then be shared with other institutions.

The Office for Experiential Education at the University of Kentucky designed such a program, called "Ethics and Decision-Making in Public Service." The Office for Experiential Education is a university-wide office which coordinated out-of-classroom learning. Established in 1973, the office was set up to facilitate, advocate, and develop experiential education as an important part of the educational activities of the university. Our staff counsels students about field placement possibilities and coordinates ongoing service-learning programs.

In 1975, as a result of a continuing discussion about the role of experiential education in the liberal arts curriculum, we decided to design an experimental, interdisciplinary program which would demonstrate the effectiveness of service-learning as a means for teaching liberal arts concepts and which would involve new participants in its design.

We were interested in a design that was both timely in its appeal to students and traditional in its academic basis, and we were motivated by interest in citizenship education and a desire to develop new methods for teaching ethics. Therefore, we decided to focus on ethics and public service. Our hope was that if the university taught ethics and public service through a combination of experience, reflection, and theory-building — which service-learning provides — perhaps students would be more likely to internalize the issues in a way that would be personally and professionally meaningful to them.

"Ethics and Decision-Making in Public Service," combines full-time internships in the public sector, a team-taught interdisciplinary seminar, and a field trip to Washington. It is open to both undergraduate and graduate students from all academic disciplines; we encourage diversity within the student group. Participants earn a full semester of academic credit, arranged on an individual basis. Most students work 30 hours per week in their field assignments. They earn three credits for the seminar and 12 credits for additional readings arranged contractually with faculty members in their departments. Currently about 15 students participate in the program each semester.

The objective of the program is to assist students to examine the ethical basis and value assumptions of decision making in preparation for their future roles as professionals and as citizens. The internships provide specific off-campus situations in which students can study decision making and examine ethical issues. They have been in local and state government and with organizations such as the state commission on women, a legal services group, the state legislature, the city-county planning commission, the local government public information unit, a farmers' cooperative, the county health department, the human rights commission, the police department, and a high school.

Weekly seminars, held on campus, provide the theoretical framework for discussing the "oughts" of decision making and offer social, historical, and philosophical context. The week in Washington enables the students to examine group and individual concerns in the context of national governmental processes.

The students who have participated thus far represented a variety of academic disciplines. In the first semester's program, for example, students were majoring in agriculture, economics, education, pre-law, accounting, philosophy, math, social work, journalism, hospital administration, urban planning, sociology, political science, and English. The seminar provided them with an unusual opportunity to share ideas with students from other disciplines.

Designing a New Program

The first step in designing an interdisciplinary program is to generate ideas for its focus. Most faculty and staff involved in service-learning have probably already fantasized about its myriad possibilities for addressing a special student population or to teach a special topic. For example, several new programs are currently geared toward older women who return to college and their particular needs for internship experiences; others focus on cross-cultural awareness or environmental issues. The range of topics which a university can offer is limitless.

Faculty Input. Once you have chosen a focus, involve as many people as possible in the process of developing your program. At the University of Kentucky, after our staff selected ethics as a focus, we made appointments with a dozen faculty members and department chairpersons whose professional interests were related to ethics — in the departments of philosophy, political science, classics, psychology, and education. We also consulted administrators, such as the Vice President for Academic Affairs and the Dean of Arts and Sciences.

In open-ended sessions, these individuals shared their general views of experiential education, its potential in their particular field, and how they conceived of an ethics program with an internship. These discussions covered academic content of the program, format, placement suggestions, and inevitably led to the names of several more faculty who would enjoy contributing to the process of program design. In this manner several dozen faculty members were tapped. For many of them it was their first personal contact with our office. These visits served, then, not only to help design the program, but also to increase awareness of our office and to reinforce its purposes.

Student Input. Students should play an important role, too. Contact former interns, ask their advice, and discuss your proposed plans with student leaders, who generally have a good sense of what would appeal to other students. Student leaders can also be helpful in reviewing your plans at various stages.

Community Input. Community residents can offer an invaluable perspective. In designing a program which focused on ethical issues in public service, we contacted selected community leaders, including a retired state legislator and a city council member known for her concern for political reform. This is also a good time to begin scouting around for potential placement.

From among those faculty interviewed in the initial planning stages, we selected three (who had varying but compatible views) to design the first seminar. Representing the departments of political science, philosophy, and social and philosophical studies in education, the three met weekly for two months to forge a synthesis of purpose and objectives for the seminar and to design a syllabus.

Seeking Financial Support

After the framework of your program begins to coalesce, your next step *may* be to seek funding. See "If You Think a Grant Is the Answer" in Volume I of this resource book. Check out local as well as national sources of funding. We secured funds for our project from the Lilly Endowment, a national foundation, but many state and local foundations support educational projects with strong community ties.

Any of the available handbooks offering suggestions for locating sources of funds and preparing proposals may be helpful to novices. Most educational institutions also have development or research offices on campus which can provide assistance. The *Catalog of Federal Domestic Assistance* (available from the Government Printing Office) lists all sources of grants from the federal government and is helpful if your proposed project falls within the range of any of these sources.

Identify several foundations whose general aims are compatible with your proposed idea and write for their annual reports. These reports describe the foundation's major areas of interest and list projects supported that year along with dollar figures. This helps you to determine which foundations would be interested in your project and how much money you can realistically plan to request.

Planning the Budget

In planning the budget, you must answer a number of questions. Will a current staff member be released to direct the program or should a new staff member be hired? Should you request stipends for students? What about overhead, publicity, telephones, printing? At the University of Kentucky we decided that two current staff members in our office could be released part-time to develop the project, and that we would request funds to hire faculty to teach the seminar.

We also budgeted a small amount of money to offset expenses for students, such as transportation and research, and to defray the costs of the field trip to Washington. Because the topic was complex and had not been taught before in this format, it required thorough pre-planning; therefore we requested funds for training and staff development — books and workshops. We budgeted consulting money in order to bring in several experts to assist us in planning the program.

Service-Learning and the Liberal Arts

Our program, as it evolved at the University of Kentucky, has been an exploratory attempt at demonstrating that service-learning can be a fresh and meaningful part of liberal arts instruction. With funds for three pilot semesters, the Office for Experiential Education has offered the program to two groups of students and is currently planning for a third group.

The first group covered topics such as the nature of citizenship, interpretations of the concept of justice, the idea of community, participation in a democracy, and alienation in the modern world. The second group focused on current social and ethical issues, social policy, and the meaning of "morality." Professors who teach the seminar grade each student on the basis of an individual paper and a detailed journal.

In addition to a strong academic content, we structured the course so as to promote cohesiveness and community among its members. Orientation to the program consists of introductions, role-playing, and drawing up learning objectives. A dinner session often precedes the class, which meets in the evenings because the students intern during the day.

Additionally, the Washington field trip at mid-term has played an important role in group cohesiveness. Here the students attend group seminars and individual meetings with national leaders involved in areas specifically related to the students' internships. Students have met with Congresspersons, officials of the Civic Rights Division of the Justice Department, and with leaders of consumer protection organizations.

Managing the New Program

Developing and managing a new program takes considerable time and involves numerous decisions about the role of your office within the academic processes of the institution. For example, in order to establish a seminar for credit at our university, we had to propose a new course — an unusual step for an administrative office. But this in an important way to increase faculty awareness of the benefits of experiential education.

In addition to the usual recruiting techniques, such as stories in the campus newspaper, we send a memo to every faculty member on campus requesting assistance in identifying appropriate students. We ask interested students to complete an application describing their academic background, interest in the program, and the type of internship desired, and to submit two letters of recommendation from faculty members along with a transcript. Our office interviews each applicant. Selection criteria are interest, recommendations, and the contribution the student can make to the group in terms of academic diversity, thus ensuring the multidisciplinary nature of the seminar.

In addition, our office is able to identify appropriate service-learning placements for the students because this is our area of expertise. After students begin work in their placements, field supervision, which is often shared by staff and faculty members, depends on the degree to which faculty will commit themselves to this process, the needs of the students, and the demands of the sponsoring agencies. Our goal is to generate as much faculty involvement as possible, and we encourage faculty to visit students at their field sites and meet their supervisors. Our office plays a strong supportive role.

Faculty teach the seminar with as much assistance from our office as they request. This assistance ranges from simply reserving the room for the class and planning films to teaching sections of the course. The course is team-taught, and therefore the coordinating function is crucial. Two of the major roles that our staff have played so far are organizing the orientation at the beginning of each semester and planning the Washington trip. In offices where staff have less time, these program components could be dropped. Another option would be to give students the responsibility of planning the orientation or the field trip, with your office providing support.

Evaluation

The final stage of developing an interdisciplinary service-learning program is evaluation. Did the program meet its objectives? What happened to the participants as a result of the program? The way in which these questions are answered can range from simple questionnaires completed at the conclusion of the program to a full-scale research design. How do you plan to use the results of your evaluation? The answer to this question and the costs involved are two factors to consider.

At the University of Kentucky, because the program was experimental, evaluation became an important concern and emerged as a project in its own right, with separate funding from another organization. Under the direction of a faculty member, we created an evaluation design which drew upon the work of Lawrence Kohlberg on moral development, Jane Loevinger on ego development, William Perry on intellectual and ethical development, and Charles Hampden-Turner on psychosocial development.

We interviewed participants before and after the semester on a range of questions correlated to dimensions of psycho-political development. Now we are considering the use of evaluation designs such as the Watson-Glaser Critical Thinking Measure. In addition, for overall critique, the students assembled after the program to offer informal feedback.

Institutionalization

As your program begins to operate smoothly — and your initial funding begins to dwindle — it is time to consider if the program merits institutionalization. At this point you might present a description of the program to the university and suggest that it be included in the regular curriculum. Since many of the initial costs are related to mounting the program, extra financial support may not be necessary to continue it.

The impact of a new program can be far-reaching. It offers faculty members from a wide variety of liberal arts disciplines an opportunity to become involved in service-learning and to gain a greater awareness of its potential to revitalize the liberal arts curriculum. For students, it offers a chance to explore timely issues in theory and in practice, to test their personal beliefs, and to exchange ideas with students majoring in other disciplines.

Barbara K. Hofer served as Assistant Director of the office of Experiential Education at the University of Kentucky. She was a pioneer in service-learning and education for social/civic responsibility in the southeast and nationally during the 1970s.

References

Hofer, Barbara K., Robert F. Sexton, and Ernest Yanarella, "Exploring the Psycho-Political Development of Liberal Arts Interns," in *Initiating Experiential Learning Programs: Four Case Studies,* Council for Adult and Experiential Learning and Educational Testing Service, 1976.

Stephenson, John B., and Robert F. Sexton, "Experiential Education and the Revitalization of the Liberal Arts," in Sidney Hook, ed, *The Philosophy of the Curriculum: The Need for General Education,* Prometheus Books, 1975, pp. 175-196.

PART I

Practical Issues and Ideas
for Programs and Courses
that Combine
Service and Learning:

Faculty Issues
and Resources

Increasing Faculty Involvement

Jane Kendall, John Duley, Thomas Little, Jane Permaul, and Sharon Rubin

This chapter discusses why faculty involvement in experiential education is critical for community service-learning, what the barriers and incentives for faculty participation are, and ways to increase faculty support and expertise. While the chapter is written about the college or university environment, the principles discussed can also be adapted to K-12 settings. You may want to substitute the term "service-learning" for "experiential learning" as you read. Excerpted and adapted from "Increasing Faculty Involvement" in Strengthening Experiential Education Within Your Institution *by Kendall, et al.,* National Society for Internships and Experiential Education (NSIEE), *1986, pp. 49-68. This chapter was written as part of the National Program to Strengthen Experiential Learning in U.S. Colleges and Universities, an ongoing program of NSIEE which has worked with over 450 institutions since 1983. The advice presented here comes from the experiences of hundreds of faculty and administrators at these institutions.*

"THE PRINCIPLE OF CONTINUITY OF EXPERIENCE means that every experience both takes up something from those which have gone before and modifies in some way the quality of those which come after.... As an individual passes from one situation to another, his world, his environment, expands or contracts. He does not find himself living in another world but in a different part or aspect of one and the same world. What he has learned in the way of knowledge and skill in one situation becomes an instrument of understanding and dealing effectively with the situations that follow. The process goes on as long as life and learning continue." — John Dewey (1984)

Experiential education is the pedagogy that underlies service-learning. It is a style of teaching and learning that engages students directly in the issues and needs of the larger community. Faculty who want to integrate service experiences into their courses use experiential education techniques to link the field to the classroom in dynamic ways.

Ever since John Dewey challenged traditional notions of the relationship between experience, work, and education, faculty members have been reassessing their roles as supervisors of how and where learning takes place. The assumption of most traditional educators is that "information comes from experts and authoritative sources through the media of books, lectures, audio-visual presentations.... Learning takes place in settings designated for the purpose, e.g., classrooms and libraries.... Problems are defined and posed to the learner by experts and authorities.... The emphasis is on solutions to known problems.... Favorable evaluation by experts and authorities of the quality of the individual's intellectual productions, primarily written work" are used as criteria of successful learning (Harrison and Hopkins, 1967).

In contrast, experiential educators assume that "information sources must be developed by the learner from the social environment. Information-gathering methods include observation and questioning of associates, other learners, and chance acquaintances." Learning settings are everywhere, and "every human encounter provides relevant information. In order to solve problems, the learner has to define the problems, generate hypotheses, collect information," and develop problem-solving approaches on the spot (Harrison and Hopkins, 1967). Criteria for evaluation of learning are frequently individualized and may be based on anything from work products to the perceptions of peers in the learning environment. In brief, traditional faculty see themselves as responsible for their students' ability to learn, while experiential educators see learning as student-centered.

The dichotomy between traditional and experiential learning is more apparent than real. Every good teacher knows that while the content presented is important, if the way in which it is presented does not make sense to students — if they cannot identify its relevance and application — no real learning will take place. They also know that students must be self-motivated in order to master any subject matter. Students, on the other hand, like the comfort of certainty that comes from expert presentation of content, but they know they must integrate it with what they already know and believe and figure out how to apply it if they are to understand it.

Therefore, it is not surprising that faculty struggle to understand what the balance between traditional and experiential learning should be.

Why Active Faculty Involvement is Critical

There are five reasons that active faculty awareness of, support of, and involvement in experiential education is absolutely critical for a vital and ongoing institutional commitment to this style of teaching and learning. These reasons are as follows:

1. The faculty is the primary group responsible for teaching. Experiential education is a method of teaching and learning. It is an essential method for effectively combining student community service and learning. Without faculty support and active involvement, experiential education will simply not be part of the primary teaching mission of the institution. Faculty are not the *only* group whose involvement is valuable and appropriate, but faculty participation is critical.

2. Faculty are needed in order to integrate experiential education [and service-learning] into the curriculum. Faculty in most institutions are the people who decide what the curriculum will be.

"The faculty has been extremely negative. Not all faculty, of course, but the general reaction has been, 'This isn't any of our business. Students aren't here to get into these frivolous things like learning citizenship and becoming able to function in American society. Students are here to learn mathematics or sociology. That's why they come to my class. The real issue is whether they learn the methods of sociology I am teaching them.' When you ask about the question of other values, they say, 'None of that ideological indoctrination in my class.' And people really have said to me over and over again, 'This isn't a function for higher education' — forgetting that the original function of education in this country was the development of civic leadership. We have a major task on our hands to convince the faculties of this country that they've got to change their ways on this issue. I think it's absolutely at the core of our problems."

— Frank Newman (1985)

3. **Faculty are needed for quality control.** Faculty are the only group that can take full responsibility for evaluating what students learn in service experiences.

4. **Students listen to faculty.** If faculty communicate the value of experiential learning to their students, the students are much more likely to participate. Faculty can help students see field experiences as part of the way learning ordinarily occurs.

5. **Faculty members are significant role models for students.** If faculty adopt the stance of active, self-directed learners [and committed citizens] themselves, they are more likely to motivate their students to take the initiative to learn experientially. The students will then be better able to incorporate active learning and reflection into their usual styles of approaching problems.

What Faculty Gain from Experiential Education

Experiential education is part of good teaching. Various types of learning are best fostered by direct, active engagement in the phenomena being studied. These educational goals are certainly a big part of why faculty support experiential learning. Faculty who are dedicated to effective teaching and who understand the importance of active engagement in the learning process will support experiential learning. If you are trying to motivate faculty to become involved or if you want to be supportive of faculty colleagues who are already involved, it is also important to understand what faculty gain from experiential education on a more personal level.

When we have asked faculty what they gain, we have gotten a variety of answers. For some, it has been the pleasure of taking on new roles — as facilitator of learning rather than expert, of listener as well as speaker, as consultant rather than authority. For others, it has been a sense of new clarity in their expectations of students. For still others, it has been the development of a new set of skills. For all, it has been the excitement of seeing students become less passive, more motivated, and empowered as learners and as members of society. Perhaps some of their own best learning was experiential — the semester in Spain, a stint in the Peace Corps, the volunteer position as chairperson of a community organization. Perhaps they were introduced to personality theory or cognitive development theory, which made a difference in their ability to reach their students. Perhaps they know that they learn best through doing first and conceptualizing later, or they have children who learn best that way.

When the Far West Laboratory for Educational Research and Development asked faculty what they gain from teaching experiential courses, it was clear that faculty develop a number of new skills from their involvement (Murphy, 1981). Of the 42 "new skills" they described, the following 10 were mentioned by more than one faculty member in a sample of 48 people:

- Putting control in students' hands
- Developing community contacts
- Dealing with small groups
- Supervising
- Dealing with site supervisors and agencies
- Learning patience to let students proceed at own pace
- Gaining knowledge about agencies
- Facilitating discussions
- Solving problems with students
- Appreciating curricular problems.

In the same study, 54 faculty members responded to the question, "Does the amount of personal satisfaction you get from teaching this course differ from other courses?" Of the 36 who responded "yes," 32 said their satisfaction was greater for the field experience courses because of the following:

- More personal contact with students
- One of few ways academic world related to the community
- Opportunity to see students grow and mature
- Contact with a superior group of students
- Seeing students become aware of career opportunities.

As you work to increase faculty involvement in experiential education and service-learning on your campus or in your department, keep these benefits in mind.

Faculty Concerns and Barriers to Involvement

At one liberal arts college, a consultant found that "the faculty need to become more aware of experiential learning as a pedagogy. Right now, faculty attitudes about experiential learning vary from annoyance to guilt that they do not participate more, to an uneasy perception that internships are being used for vocational rather than intellectual purposes by students, to lack of clarity about the appropriate role for faculty in the career development process."

At a discussion on experiential learning among faculty at the University of Virginia, they were both excited and anxious about their roles. Opinions ranged from the nervous, "This is great, but someone else ought to be in charge of students wanting experiential learning," to the quizzical, "If experience is the textbook, how do you make up the assignments?" Faculty wanted to know how to bridge the gap between classes and the real world, how to articulate liberal arts values to field sponsors as well as to students, whether the emphasis of experiential learning should be skills or subject matter, whether experiential learning should be used primarily to teach what faculty members cannot teach in the classroom, how to deal with the crises of confidence students may have in unfamiliar learning environments, and "Who controls what?" Most often, they went back to the issue of utmost concern: how to think about experiential learning as an integral part of the curriculum in a course or a department. Such concerns would be voiced at most colleges by most faculty.

In order to encourage faculty involvement in service-learning and other uses of experiential education, you must consider carefully the following concerns and barriers that faculty may experience:

1. *Concern about faculty control of academic quality.* Faculty have an important function that cannot be given over even to the most talented non-faculty coordinator: control of academic quality. It is this control that is most problematic to many faculty. For some, it is, "I don't have the expertise to assess experiential learning. I know about term papers and examinations, but I don't know about evaluating something I cannot see." For others, it is, "I think I know what I am doing with regard to experiential learning, and I think my colleagues do as well, but I'm concerned about all those other departments that are too loose in their standards. They may be giving away credit." The solutions to both of these concerns are trust in faculty colleagues and their continued education.

At some point, it is necessary for faculty to trust their peers in other departments, even though some will always be more trustworthy than others when it comes to academic quality. The variety will be extensive. We are used to great diversity in our students. Most faculty have had the experience of reading student examinations and asking themselves, "Were these students all in the same room? What each has gotten out of my lectures has been entirely different." Faculty will be similarly diverse, based on their own backgrounds and skills. Some faculty will take their responsibilities seriously, and some will sign off without using good judgment. Some will have a structured approach, and others will "go with the flow." There is no perfect model that will assure quality where human beings are concerned. However, it is important to understand that if departments have standards for the academic performance of faculty in the classroom, it is possible for them to set standards for nontraditional faculty performance as well. See the chapter of this book on assessment of learning.

2. *Lack of awareness of experiential education as pedagogy and lack of theoretical knowledge in pedagogy.* Faculty received their training in their disciplines. When they served as Teaching Assistants during graduate school and when they applied for teaching positions, the focus was on their knowledge of the discipline. Teaching as a skill received relatively little attention. Erik Midelfort at the University of Virginia makes the point well: "Even faculty who want to learn more about good teaching know they don't have a good theoretical base in pedagogy, and that's probably one area where they feel the most lack [and] ... a sense of frustration. I feel that there are a lot of faculty members who are ready to study theory, but they just have not had the opportunity, nor the proper surroundings in which to do it."[1]

However, an institution can increase the chances that faculty will be able to become good experiential educators by giving them as many opportunities as possible to learn from more experienced faculty, and to discuss issues of teaching and learning frequently and seriously.

3. *Lack of familiarity with techniques for assessing experiential learning.* Closely related to the issue of unfamiliarity with pedagogy is the lack of faculty awareness of appropriate methods for assessing experiential learning. Most faculty feel particularly vulnerable when asked to evaluate students' understanding of something that the faculty have not organized and presented. A number of helpful works have been written on the topic, including *Efficient Evaluation of Individual Performance in Field Placement* by Stephen Yelon and John Duley and *Assessing Learning* by Urban Whitaker. The Yelon and Duley book contains an excellent chart that lists assessment mode performance tests, illustrations and examples, advantages, indications of appropriate cases for use, problems, and special considerations. Such a chart can be the beginning of a faculty development process that makes faculty confident about their abilities to use assessment methods consistent with the goals of experiential learning *and* with the maintenance of good academic standards. See also the chapters of this book on issues of evaluation and assessment.

4. *Lack of understanding of how experiential learning helps students test the concepts of the discipline.* One humanities professor observes, "I have heard real words of skepticism in the departments that have little contact with the community, like the government department. They send students to Washington for summer internships, but they have never given credit for it. They say people

should not get credit for learning how to live away from home or learning how to get around on the subway. They think classroom learning is the only type worthy of academic credit. I think the only way to surmount this attitude is by showing how internships help students apply the concepts of the discipline."

5. *A belief that application is only useful when it follows theory.* Like #2-4 above, this concern of many faculty reflects a lack of familiarity with theories of how people learn and a lack of awareness of multiple learning styles. An Academic Dean laments, "Faculty tell me, 'Look, a student is taking my course. That's the most important thing he could be doing because for the rest of his life he's going to be applying things. But he only has these four years to listen to me. He's not going to get the theoretical/conceptual base anywhere else. In the world it doesn't exist.' I think that's foolish because many students don't learn until after concrete experience."

6. *Concern about faculty compensation for sponsoring students in experiential education.* At many schools, faculty members may sponsor one or two students a semester in intensive experiential learning activities, so the work load is not particularly heavy. Just as faculty supervise doctoral students, sit on committees, and advise undergraduates in the course of their normal duties, they give students individual attention through independent research opportunities or experiential learning.

However, when a faculty member sponsors several students every term or is in charge of experiential learning for a department, both the administrative work and the academic mentorship can add the equivalent of one or more courses to the ordinary course load. There are several ways around this dilemma. For instance, Mars Hill College has developed a faculty compensation system that attempts to take into consideration the many different kinds of duties faculty have (Hoffman, 1976). At other institutions, such as the University of Maryland, faculty who sponsor a number of students may organize a seminar for all students instead of seeing each one individually each week. Not only can the seminar then become part of the faculty member's regular course load for the semester, but students can benefit from each others' experiences. However, it is clear that faculty who enjoy the gains their students make from active learning will continue to be involved, and those who are most concerned about the dissemination of content will prefer the lecture format. Developing educational models which come closest to compensating faculty adequately for the particular skills they must use as experiential educators should be a matter of concern for all faculty. For more information, see the chapter of this book entitled "Supporting Service-Learning in the Economic System of the Institution."

7. *Concern about whether involvement in experiential education helps with tenure, promotion, and merit increases.* Creative faculty in institutions that value teaching find ways to include their involvement in experiential education when they present themselves to department chairs and review committees that make decisions about tenure, promotion, and merit increases. Faculty often do not have models for how to present this involvement, however. Therefore they often miss opportunities to use their work in experiential education to show good performance in teaching, in public and community service, and in public relations for the institution. They may also miss opportunities to point out how experiential education helped them identify problems that led to research projects and publications.

This concern about tenure and promotion can be especially difficult for young faculty members who feel the pressure to publish and do research. They may feel that just finding time to teach can be a difficult challenge. They need special help to see how experiential education can create research and publishing opportunities as well as substantiate their teaching performance. Jeff Chinn, former Assistant Provost at Illinois State University, offers another suggestion: "We offer senior faculty the opportunity to be departmental leaders in the program. They often don't have the same time constraints as untenured faculty, and the experience has become an opportunity for professional renewal for them. It can be almost like a new career."

8. *Fear of the world outside the campus.* Many faculty have never worked in settings other than classrooms, libraries, and faculty offices. Like anyone facing a completely foreign culture, they may feel unsure how to talk with field supervisors, how to assess the learning potential in a service site, how to communicate their expectations and concerns, and even what to wear. As one philosophy professor (who now sponsors 15 students each semester) says, "I can lecture confidently to a room of 200 students, but I came down with an excruciating case of nerves when I called a judge to ask about setting up an internship on ethics in the judicial decision-making process. Fortunately, it was easier the second time."

9. *Lack of priority on student development.* In a national study of faculty goals and priorities, Richman and Farmer found that "student intellectual development" and "student personal development" came eleventh and fifteenth, respectively (1974).

Because experiential education is a method of teaching and learning, it also falls low on the list of priorities for many faculty. A faculty member who does not value students' intellectual and personal development is not likely to become involved in experiential education.

10. *Limitations of the 50-minute class.* Most class schedules are set up in 50-minute blocks three times a week, or in longer blocks two times a week. Even a professor who wants to integrate experiential learning may be stymied by the lack of time to put it into effect. It is a highly unusual college that attempts to arrange the school day or the school week to encourage experiential learning. Emory and Henry College in Virginia set aside Wednesdays as a day for field trips and other experiential learning opportunities, extended laboratory research, and other campus activities. Colleges such as the State University of New York at Stony Brook coordinate scheduling of a number of classes so that students participating in Federated Learning Communities can take advantage of blocks of time for special learning activities. By and large, however, the scheduling systems most colleges use make it a great challenge for faculty to extend learning beyond short time blocks.

The question of how to proceed once such concerns as these have been voiced is, of course, crucial. Even faculty quite intrigued by the idea of increasing their use of experiential learning processes are tempted to retreat into the comfort of what they already do well. The benefits of experiential education are substantial, however, and the process of becoming better at understanding and encouraging experiential learning can be exhiliarating for faculty.

Building Faculty Support and Involvement in Experiential Education

Consider before you decide on your approaches whether your goals are to increase: (1) overall awareness of the value of experiential learning and service-learning, (2) awareness of what is already happening in your institution or department, (3) attitudinal support, (4) active involvement in using experiential education, (5) commitment to experiential education as an important part of the entire curriculum, (6) the number of faculty who act as advocates and clear leaders for experiential education on campus, or (7) faculty knowledge and skills in utilizing experiential learning. Most likely, your goals include some combination of these.

The following ideas can be successful whether the initiative comes from an individual faculty member, a faculty committee, a director of a departmental or campus-wide program, an academic administrator, or another advocate. We have focused on the institutional level in the wording of these ideas, but most of the principles apply equally to a departmental or divisional effort. Be sure to see also the chapters of this book on strategies for institutional change.

1. Feed information about experiential learning to the faculty continuously. Use the campus newspaper and the faculty newsletter as avenues for periodic articles on experiential education and service-learning. You might take as an informal job for the next year the education of faculty about experiential learning. For instance, for liberal arts professors, some information from Paul Breen about the transferability of liberal arts skills might be just right. For others, syllabi from other institutions would be useful. It is important that they see examples and read literature that is geared toward their own disciplines. If you have a skeptical historian, send him or her something written by another historian. A speaker like David Kolb or Donald Schon would be impressive enough for any faculty member. If you cannot swing the expense, collaborate with another unit on campus that might be interested in co-sponsorship. Introduce faculty to each other, so that people sponsoring students in different departments get a chance to meet informally. Informal lunch discussions can also be effective.

> "It is very important that the faculty here see examples from other prestigious institutions. If a faculty member here reads that Podunk State University is doing a particular program, then that is reason enough *not* to do it at UVA — no matter how good the program is. The examples need to be from other comparable institutions."
>
> — H.C. Erik Midelfort,
> Professor of History and Associate Dean,
> College of Arts and Sciences, University of Virginia

2. Act as a catalyst to link faculty from different departments.

3. Organize informal discussions. A faculty member at a large university suggests: "Have an informal meeting of all the people you know are supportive. It could even be a brown bag lunch. Find out who else these faculty know (colleagues, neighbors, etc.) who are also supportive. Build on this."

4. Find out what people's concerns are. Douglas Boyce, Dean at King College, says, "I started by researching all the faculty who had sponsored internships over the last eight years. Then I talked with those people and listened to their concerns. Know who your allies are, and build on that."

5. *Work through supportive opinion leaders on the faculty.* One administrator suggests, "The faculty have to hear it from people they perceive to be their academic peers." Erik Midelfort, History Professor and Associate Dean of Arts and Sciences at the University of Virginia, says, "I think our first task is to see what kind of support we really have. Then we need to get the most respected faculty members among that group to be vocal about their support of good internships for discipline-based learning. These are the only people that other faculty will listen to."

6. *Establish a faculty committee on experiential education or service-learning.* Because of the absolute importance of a faculty committee at some point on almost every campus, an entire section of this chapter is devoted to ideas and examples for a strong, effective faculty committee.

7. *Let students speak for the value of experiential learning.* Margaret Schramm observed while she chaired the faculty's Internship Advisory Committee at Hartwick College that "One [of our most successful approaches] was to plan a meeting at which interns could discuss their experiences with faculty, with other students who have completed internships, and with students interested in doing internships. It was well attended and generated a great deal of interest in internships among faculty and students."

Erik Midelfort describes the University of Virginia's experience: "The strongest feature of the program is the seminar that pools students together and focuses on what they are actually learning during their internships. Watching those students would soothe any faculty member's objections [about experiential education] very effectively. Those students are really learning how to relate experiences back to theory. They are learning to articulate things that they observed that were just fuzzy ideas before."

8. *Conduct workshops or sponsor speakers on campus.* Listen to these tips from NSIEE consulting reports by Sharon Rubin:

> Workshops run by faculty for other faculty are very effective in the kind of informal 'technology transfer' that needs to occur much more at the University. (Report to the University of New Hampshire)

> Probably the easiest way for people to share their goals as experiential educators is through the medium of a workshop on curricular improvement. Many campuses offer a

To Do

21 Things to Do to Increase Faculty Involvement

1. Feed information about experiential learning to faculty continuously.
2. Act as a catalyst to link faculty from different departments.
3. Organize informal discussions.
4. Find out what people's concerns are.
5. Work through supportive opinion leaders on campus.
6. Establish a faculty committee on experiential education or service-learning.
7. Let students speak for the value of experiential learning.
8. Conduct workshops or sponsor speakers on campus.
9. Give away money and authority.
10. Reinforce excellence in faculty support of experiential education.
11. Help academic advisors to understand and promote experiential learning as an integral part of the curriculum.
12. Arrange faculty internships.
13. Have a summer study group of faculty focusing on experiential learning.
14. Create a rotating faculty position in the central office for experiential education.
15. Take faculty on site visits.
16. Ask faculty to design and implement research projects related to experiential learning.
17. Help key faculty members arrange sabbaticals that involve experiential learning.
18. Establish "Service-Learning Coordinatorships" like Teaching Assistantships for graduate students or advanced undergraduates.
19. Offer senior faculty opportunities to take on leadership roles in experiential education as a renewal experience.
20. Establish a library of resources for faculty about using experiential learning methods in courses.
21. Take faculty to professional meetings for experiential educators.

forum for faculty to hear experts from inside or outside the institution discuss good teaching, and it should be easy to arrange a topical workshop on experiential learning. Those faculty who are attracted by the topic may become the nucleus of an informal consortium.

Many of the NSIEE's member institutions have organized faculty workshops. Those schools offer these words of advice:

- Get someone who can communicate well with faculty. The speaker or workshop leader should be an intellectual peer of the participants.
- Publicize it well, not just by putting notices in mailboxes. Get opinion leaders to encourage their colleagues to come. Ask department chairs to bring key faculty members.
- Be sure the faculty want it. Do not expect someone with a briefcase to perform miracles. Workshops or even lectures can help for specific needs — presenting a conceptual overview of experiential education, facilitating an open discussion of related faculty interests and concerns, or working on particular problems that faculty have identified. As with any human beings, if faculty perceive that someone is bringing in an outsider to tell them what to do, the attempt will set you back a year or two.
- Use existing campus series for speakers, faculty lectures, or bag lunch discussions. These can all provide a good forum for periodic coverage of topics in experiential education.

9. *Give away money and authority.* In a time of scarcity, it may be difficult to find the money or the authority to hand out, but there is always some available. For instance, if you can fund a faculty member with a small summer stipend to prepare a handbook on experiential learning for a department, if you can fund a faculty member to prepare a paper on teaching processes for a disciplinary conference, or if you can ask faculty members to make policy decisions on experiential learning either informally or through a committee, faculty ownership of experiential learning will increase much more than the amounts given would suggest.

10. *Reinforce excellence in faculty support of experiential education.* Write thank you letters to put in the personnel files of faculty who are effective experiential educators. Offer to write letters when those faculty are considered for tenure, promotion, and merit increases. Issue certificates of appreciation for them to put in their offices. Take them along on the most interesting site visits.

Help them establish agency contacts that can support their research and publishing goals. Look for opportunities to give their work visibility among faculty, students, administrators, community leaders, and alumni.

11. *Help academic advisors to understand and promote experiential learning as an integral part of the curriculum.* Academic advising is a crucial — but often overlooked — link in helping students see experiential learning not only as volunteer service or as practice for a career, but as an alternative method of learning.

12. *Arrange faculty internships.* Faculty internships are a superb way to help faculty see the value of experiential education, especially if all the elements of a good service-learning experience are included. They can help faculty see the pitfalls and problems they need to address when they sponsor their students on field experiences. A number of schools, including Furman University, have used this method of teaching teachers.

13. *Provide other opportunities for faculty development.* See the special section of this chapter on faculty enrichment.

A Faculty Committee: Important Vehicle for Ownership and Involvement

A subcommittee on experiential learning in a department or an advisory committee to a campus-wide program offers faculty an opportunity to learn and to contribute their own ideas. A committee can also recommend changes in institutional policy to systematize course numbering and crediting throughout the institution. A committee can make sure that the educational role of experiential learning is documented in the catalog, schedule of classes, on transcripts, and in other materials representing the entire institution. Finally, an advisory committee can call representatives of different constituencies together from across the campus to develop consensus on broad policy issues that will then be acceptable to the entire institution. Rose Marie Springer of Westmont College's Urban Program suggests, "It is important that those who are affected by change have a part in developing those changes. Change takes a long time! I would advise other schools to begin working with NSIEE early, to seek administrative support as well as faculty support, and to form an ongoing advisory committee for the purpose of providing a forum where important issues can be discussed."

With a faculty committee, faculty members realize, "We own this program. We can make decisions about the policies and standards. We can make decisions about how this relates to our disciplines." In order to ground experiential education in the academic base of the institution, also use the existing reporting structures for both visibility and communication. For example, Adrian College's Internship Committee reports to the Academic Environment Committee (the major academic policy body) and uses this connection as a vehicle for advocacy and support of internships.

Who is appointed to a faculty committee determines its success or failure. At one college, a skeptical dean appointed mostly opponents of internships to a faculty study committee. The effectiveness of their recommendations was exactly what one would predict. A committee appointed at another institution was not given a clear sense of its responsibilities; it was also a predictable failure. The Dean of Arts and Sciences at the University of Colorado appointed mostly supportive faculty who were already somewhat involved in internships. Dean Samuel Schuman of Guilford College took the same approach. Doug Boyce of King College shares another idea: "I included half supporters and half skeptics. I chose opinion leaders in both groups. Their involvement on our ad hoc committee ensured that the committee's recommendations would be accepted when presented to the full faculty."

Finally, we must mention the choice of appointees for Hartwick College's Advisory Committee because of the proven performance record of this group of faculty and administrators. As Barbara Lilly, Director of Off-Campus and Experiential Programs, says:

> Our Advisory Committee on Internships was appointed by the Dean of the College ... [and] included faculty from the three divisions: two from the Humanities, two from the Physical and Life Sciences, and four from the Social Sciences. The larger representation from the Social Sciences reflected the greater number of internships undertaken through that division. The registrar and two students were also appointed. The charge to the committee was to advise the Dean and the Coordinator of Internships on all matters relating to the program, including establishing the goals of the program, defining 'internships,' and developing and modifying policies and procedures for implementing the program. Its function was to provide additional perspective and support to those responsible for the administration of the program.

Faculty Enrichment

As important as faculty support of experiential education and their active use of it for teaching is the faculty's ability to use it effectively. Teaching experientially takes a very different set of skills from traditional classroom teaching. Many faculty are not familiar with the pedagogy of experiential learning. In a classroom setting, faculty are accustomed to having complete control over the subject content, instructional methods (readings, lectures, papers, etc.), the criteria and methods of evaluation, and the exclusive decision about what valid learning was actually accomplished. The student is a participant observer, and the faculty member alone is in charge.

Experiential education, on the other hand, requires a completely different set of skills and roles. Objectives and goals are balanced among the student, the professor, and the site supervisor; the content is structured by the nature of the experience; the method of learning is defined by the community's needs and the student's own learning style; the faculty member acts as a facilitator and mentor; the student becomes a self-directed learner; and a community person shares the role of supervisor and performance appraiser. The faculty member's relationship to the student is more one-to-one than in the classroom arrangement, and more interpersonal skills are thus required. These are not easy adjustments for faculty who are used to the traditional role. See again the list of skills faculty gain from involvement in experiential education (provided earlier in this chapter). These are the very areas in which faculty often need help.

Some of our suggestions for offering opportunities for faculty enrichment in experiential learning are:

• *Have a summer study group* that examines what is known about experiential learning as pedagogy and recommends policy changes based on that knowledge. The group might begin with the works of David Kolb, William Perry, and Donald Schon and continue with discipline-related resources recommended by NSIEE and by faculty at other colleges and universities.

• *Establish a rotating faculty position* in the central office for experiential education or service-learning. Involve faculty from different divisions and departments every year or two. If a faculty member can spend even ten hours a week learning how to administer a program, from finding good sites to helping students prepare learning proposals to speaking to faculty groups about field experiences, that faculty member will go back to his or her teaching

ASSESSING FACULTY INVOLVEMENT ON YOUR CAMPUS

1. Are faculty aware of experiential learning as a learning process and as an option for students? Are they aware of the range of experiential learning varieties, from a set of discreet, short-term, out-of-class activities (like a science laboratory) to an intensive semester of full-time effort?

2. Are there several key departments on campus that offer experiential learning opportunities, whether for credit or not? How many? Are they among the larger, more powerful departments on campus?

3. In each department, do faculty discuss how to integrate experiential learning into the curriculum in order for it to make sense educationally?

4. Do faculty from different departments share their knowledge of experiential learning and exchange information about their practices?

5. Do faculty, in their roles as academic advisors, advocate experiential learning to students?

6. Do faculty discuss possible prerequisites for experiential education and the rationale for these requirements?

7. Are faculty involved in pre-field preparation of students or in debriefing after the experiences? Do they plan and carry out workshops, exercises, or other types of preparation? Do they expect, and come to, student presentations on their field learning?

8. Do faculty take seriously their responsibilities to students in the field and to site supervisors? Do faculty make site visits, or at least communicate with the student and supervisor by phone? Do faculty pre-screen placements, examine project descriptions, or in other ways involve themselves in the actual placement process?

9. Have faculty discussed and made departmental decisions about appropriate methods for evaluating experiential learning — about such assignments as journals, research papers, additional reading, the assessment of work products, or other evaluation materials?

10. Have faculty determined how grading options can be established and justified?

11. Within departments, are specific faculty expected to take major responsibility for working with students involved in experiential learning? Does one person work with all students, or does a coordinator assign each student to an appropriate faculty member? Do faculty receive pay or release time for work with students in field experiences? Is their involvement integrated with other departmental and committee responsibilities?

12. Does the department have an oversight committee? Is there a college-wide faculty advisory committee for experiential education? What are its functions? To whom does it report? Does it have an official relationship with the main curriculum policy committee?

13. Are there opportunities for faculty to participate in professional development activities related to experiential education on campus and at professional conferences, both as learners and as teachers?

14. Do faculty advocate experiential learning to colleagues across campus and at other colleges, and to administrators?

refreshed and changed as an educator. This also provides a discipline-based perspective to the central staff and builds a network of knowledgeable faculty advocates in the departments.

• *Take faculty on site visits* to current or potential field sites. Giving faculty the informal opportunity to learn more about the community, while making use of their scholarly expertise, is beneficial to students, agencies, and program administrators as well as the faculty themselves.

• *Ask faculty to design and implement research projects related to experiential learning.* If one of the primary values of the academic world is that research is important, then research is one of the most compelling reasons for faculty involvement in experiential education — and one of the best avenues for faculty enrichment. We make many assumptions about what students learn, how they feel about their experiences, the impact of experiential learning on their later academic and work accomplishment, the role of experiential learning in enhancing cognitive and moral development, the relationship of personality type and learning style to learning success, and many other important issues for which rigorous research is needed. At large universities in particular, there are always graduate students searching for dissertation topics and professors in the social sciences and education exploring new research areas. If the administrator of an experiential learning program is seen as a resource on campus, and not a barrier to interest in the field, successful collaborations can result in the kinds of publications faculty want to produce and the kinds that are sorely needed in the field of experiential learning.

• *Help key faculty members arrange sabbaticals that involve experiential learning,* perhaps a faculty internship and then a study of field experience as it relates to the discipline.

• *Set up a series of informal discussions* in which faculty can exchange ideas, syllabi, learning proposals, evaluation procedures, and journals. But be sure the faculty define their own needs. As Doug Boyce, Dean at King College, says, "I do not try to mandate to faculty what the issues are. They must come on their own to the need for more discussion."

If your faculty needs a catalyst for discussion, they may enjoy debating these principles hammered out by faculty and citizens at a school in Tvind, Denmark (Dalin, 1983):

1. You must go out and explore in order to make new concepts for yourself, and on further exploration to improve on those concepts.

The excitement of seeing students become less passive, more motivated, and empowered as learners and as members of society ...

2. You must get on intimate terms with things you want to learn about; the closer you get, the more you will learn.

3. You and your fellow students must be the driving force in your efforts to learn; life is too important to rely on the teacher's tricks to get you going.

4. You must learn that the more you start, the more you will finish; the deeper you look into problems, the more you will learn; it means hard work — but at least you will not be superficial or apathetic.

5. You can't learn everything at school, but only the top of the iceberg; the rest comes later.

6. Only Adam was alone in the world. The rest of us are here together.

7. What you learn is meant to be used, and preferably now, so that others can learn from you, but possibly also later, if the opportunity arises; you learn twice as well by passing things on to someone else.

8. You must be able to move about, so that you experience as much as possible; otherwise, everything will be at a standstill. Even if you have periscope eyes, the view from one spot is restricted.

9. Everything said here also applies to teachers.

- *Establish a library of resources for faculty* about using experiential learning in courses. Start with the resource materials published by NSIEE. Include examples of good materials from your own faculty. Each faculty member does not have to start from scratch.
- *Take faculty to professional meetings in experiential education.* Showcase their work while exposing them to issues, solutions, and practices at other institutions.
- *Establish "Field Study Coordinatorships" or "Service-Learning Assistantships,"* as is done at UCLA. By creating this new category for graduate student assistantships, you can involve regular faculty in teaching graduate students how to work with undergraduates by linking field experiences to the discipline. They can monitor and support undergraduate students' learning during internships, recommend readings, review journals and "reflection and analysis tapes," and evaluate what students learn on field experiences. The role of supervising graduate students who are supervising community service can create opportunities for regular faculty to dig into the literature on experiential education, recommend readings, and work with graduate students and faculty colleagues on research studies and publications concerning experiential education in the discipline.
- *Offer senior faculty opportunities to take on leadership roles in experiential education as a renewal experience.* The role of departmental or divisional coordinator can create a new career interest for tenured faculty. Illinois State University gives release time to a faculty member in each area to help locate appropriate experiential opportunities, publicize them to students and faculty in the department, help faculty design seminars, and help students prepare learning proposals.

Special Considerations for Those Who Are Not Faculty Members

Many people who run community service-learning programs are not faculty members. They may be student affairs professionals, graduate students, or administrative staff who one day find themselves trying to implement programs with significant educational goals from a position outside the departmental structure of the institution. To such staff members, the frustrations may be enormous and the challenges may seem insurmountable. Some people in this role withdraw from trying to reach faculty. They may begin to talk about "us" and "them," those who understand how to administer a program and everyone else. Sometimes there is only a "me" rather than an "us" on campus, and isolation and despair can result.

There are a number of particular approaches that non-faculty program administrators can take to reach out to faculty, to find opportunities for collaboration, and to extend the possibilities for experiential education and service-learning on their campuses. Besides the tips already presented in this chapter, consider the following special advice.

First, non-faculty administrators must redefine their roles. Often they see themselves as advocates for their students rather than advocates for the principles of experiential learning through community service. *Program administrators who see themselves as having the broadest possible mandate to extend the practice of experiential learning on their campuses will think of themselves as expert consultants and facilitators for the faculty, and they will seek out opportunities to be helpful to individual faculty members and to departments which have any interest in experiential learning.* One way of doing this effectively on a college campus is to become the catalyst for the exchange of information. If you find out what one faculty member is doing as an experiential educator, you can introduce it to another faculty member who might find it useful. Breaking down the barriers between departments and between faculty who do not know each other is one of the best ways of fostering an atmosphere where the discussion of experiential learning can take place. One approach is to assume the posture of a learner, that is to go to the faculty and learn how they manage community and public service, and then share those ideas with other faculty.

Second, working as a consultant to departments gives an important responsibility to non-faculty administrators. If you are going to have the background in pedagogy and the mental file of appropriate examples you will need, continued professional development is a must. Many administrators become stale running their programs because they do not seek out new ways to think about experiential learning as a vehicle for education for social and civic responsibility. Often, to persuade faculty that there is more to experiential learning conceptually than volunteerism or practical work experience takes both deep and broad knowledge of learning theory, cognitive development theory, and group process theory.

The single most common problem that we observe as we visit campuses and talk with experiential educators who are in central administrative positions is that they do not give away enough power and authority to faculty across the campus. Rather than stimulate and support departmental initiatives to build experiential learning into the regular curriculum, they may become protective of "their program" and unintentionally isolate themselves from the academic mainstream. Program administrators must acknowledge the central role of faculty in experiential education while they simultaneously explore their own roles as consultant, catalyst, and resource person to faculty. You will either choose to be part of the ongoing academic structure of the institution, or your program will remain on the periphery. As a non-faculty administrator, however, you must adapt to the faculty's culture and way of instituting change. You must also respect the faculty's rightful authority about curricular matters. This puts you in a unique role and one that offers tremendous opportunities and creative challenges if you understand the culture and the potential roles of faculty.

Jane Kendall is Executive Director of the National Society for Internships and Experiential Education. John Duley is Professor Emeritus from Michigan State University. Tom Little, founder of the Virginia Program, now works with socially responsible technology. Jane Permaul is Director of the Office of Field Studies Development at UCLA. Sharon Rubin is Dean of the School of Liberal Arts at Salisbury State University and President of the National Society for Internships and Experiential Education.

Footnote

[1] The quotes interspersed throughout the chapter come from discussions at the 20 pilot institutions that participated in the NSIEE National Program to Strengthen Experiential Education in U.S. Colleges and Universities during its pilot stage in 1983 to 1985.

References

Chickering, Arthur W., "Developmental Change as a Major Outcome," in *Experiential Learning*, ed. by Morris Keeton, Jossey-Bass, 1976. One of the best discussions of educational outcomes, student learning styles and teaching styles in relation to developmental theory. A good way for faculty to begin to think about their own roles.

Coleman, James S., "Differences Between Experiential and Classroom Learning," in *Experiential Learning*, ed. by Morris Keeton, Jossey-Bass, 1976. A very clear distinction between traditional and experiential learning; very basic information for faculty.

Dalin, Per, "An International Perspective," in *Learning from Work and Community Experience: Six International Models*, ed. Heather Chisnall, IMTEC, NFER-NELSON Publishing Company Ltd., 1983, p. 188.

Dewey, John, *Experience and Education*, 1938, quoted by David Kolb in *Experiential Learning*, Prentice-Hall, Inc., 1984, p. 27.

Duley, John S., and Stephen L. Yelon, *Efficient Evaluation of Individual Performance in Field Placement*, Michigan State University, 1978.

Harrison, R., and R. Hopkins, "An Alternative to the University Model," *Journal of Applied Behavioral Science*, Vol. 3, No. 4, 1967, pp. 437-438.

Hoffman, Richard L., "Encouraging Faculty to Invest Time in Service Learning," *Synergist*, Vol. 5, No. 1, Spring 1976, pp. 33-37 (available from NSIEE).

Kaston, Carren O., with James Heffernan, *Preparing Humanists for Work: A National Study of Undergraduate Internships in the Humanities*, The Washington Center, 1984 (available from NSIEE). An extensive exploration of the way in which some liberal arts disciplines use internships. The case studies are particularly meaningful for faculty.

Kendall, Jane C., John S. Duley, Thomas C. Little, Jane S. Permaul, and Sharon Rubin, *Strengthening Experiential Education Within Your Institution*, National Society for Internships and experiential Education, 1986.

Little, Thomas C., ed., *Making Sponsored Experiential Learning Standard Practice*, New Directions for Experiential Learning, No. 20, Jossey-Bass, 1983.

Murphy, Carol, *Integrating the Community and the Classroom: Instructors Describe the Results*, Far West Laboratory for Educational Research and Development, 1981, pp. 7-9.

National Society for Internships and Experiential Education, *PANEL Resource Papers Series*, 1980 to present. This series of monographs presents concise guidelines for faculty who want to establish or improve a course or program for experiential learning.

Newman, Frank, Catherine Milton, and Susan Stroud, "Community Service and Higher Education: Obligations and Opportunities," *AAHE Bulletin*, Vol. 37, No. 10, June 1985, p. 13.

Richman, B. M., and R. N. Farmer, *Leadership, Goals, and Power in Higher Education*, Jossey-Bass, 1974, pp. 119-120.

Thorburn, Neil, "Enriching the Liberal Arts," in *Enriching the Liberal Arts through Experiential Learning*, ed. by Stevens E. Brooks and James Althof, New Directions for Experiential Learning, No. 6, Jossey-Bass, 1979, pp. 13-22 (reprinted in this resource book). A chief academic officer's view of the liberal arts faculty's role in experiential learning.

Why the Resistance by Faculty?

Howard Seeman

A faculty member suggests reasons that faculty may be slow to incorporate experiential education — the teaching method behind combining community service with learning — into their courses. He also suggests ways to support faculty to adopt new approaches. Reprinted with permission from Experiential Education, *National Society for Internships and Experiential Education, Vol. 13, No. 4, September-October 1988, p. 22.*

Why is there still resistance to experiential education among many teaching faculty? We who promote this kind of education are often stymied by a lack of administrative and faculty support for field-based programs. We hear experiential learning derogated as "merely vocational [or merely voluntarism] and not scholarly," and we are told that budgetary constraints prevent the expansion of our work. This resistance, I think, stems from two basic facts: (1) Experiential education necessitates a redefinition of what academics usually honor as "knowledge"; and (2) experiential education requires some non-traditional teaching methods with which most faculty are not familiar.

Redefining Knowledge. We are still a society influenced by an epistemology dating back to Plato's "eternal forms" as the seat of Truth. Being informed by these fixed ideas was to have *real* knowledge of reality. Following Descartes, Hume and other philosophers, our society became infatuated with pure abstract concepts, cognition and quantification.

That stance has been challenged by Heidegger, among others, who rejected the myth that any knowledge can be purely cognitive: to have meaning, ideas must be involved with a network of affect. Dewey infused into our epistemology the notion that "knowledge" includes action, that "scientific knowing" is only one kind—and not the only kind—of human action that defines truth.

Though these more recent ideas open the door to experiential learning, we are still in a cultural lag. Purely cognitive learning is often deemed "real scholarship" and precludes subjectivity in education.

Experiential education demands that the instructor not, at least immediately, separate affect from cognition, that "knowledge" be defined as not just conceptual, but also potentially as non-verbal, emotional, even non-logical. The student's subjective comment may not be a digression, but may instead contain some phenomenological truth about the issue at hand.

For some faculty, this shift away from the traditional epistemology is very difficult. Of course, experiential content still requires analysis, synthesis and transfer of learning (concepts). However, we must overcome the resistance to the experiential as a legitimate component of education.

New Teaching Methods. Experiential education requires that faculty use non-traditional teaching methods which for many are new:

1. Student notes are not, by themselves, learning. Experience must be brought to sufficient awareness, felt and understood in all its affective complexity. Lecturing is not enough.

2. Teachers must facilitate the expression of affect in class. They must be values-clarifiers, facilitators of trust, even counselors. They must show their personhood so students can express theirs.

3. Experiential educators have to teach students how to give their experiences accurate language, to discover relationships within the data of their experiences, to see experience from perspectives other than the personal. They need to teach the application of these awarenesses.

4. Teachers need to learn to start their lessons with the student, not with their planned notes. They need to be able to teach inductively. As Freire says in *Pedagogy of the Oppressed*, knowledge is a process of empowering the knower through active reflection on his/her own knowledge.

5. Therefore, the instructor, not just the student, needs to take notes, to follow the class as well as lead it, and to formulate learnings almost on the spot.

6. Experiential education often involves role-play exercises and simulations. These methods help internalize and concretize learning, but they cannot be tried without training and practice.

7. These skills may require a non-traditional classroom setting such as teaching in a horse-shoe or circle, rather than in rows facing a podium. Many instructors feel uncomfortable with this change since it reflects a shift in power.

Dealing with Resistance. How can we deal with these forms of resistance? First, we must realize that our frustrations do not stem entirely from financial or administrative problems. Simply increasing our enrollments might handle those issues.

Second, as with any resistance, we must not fight it, but instead understand it, and calm the fears that block faculty support. We need to support their investments in cognitive learning while we point to the *enhancing* value of experiential learning. We need to encourage faculty to try new tools, and offer retraining workshops.

Faculty are used to beginning with their own notes. We need to help them go beyond the old epistemological heritage and pedagogy, to be comfortable with the non-traditional style of going from student experiences to analysis and on to new generalizations.

Howard Seeman, Ph.D., is Associate Professor of Education and Coordinator of Internships at Lehman College of the City University of New York.

Learning by Doing through Public Service: For Students and Faculty Alike

Robert Coles interviewed by Arthur Levine

Harvard psychiatrist Robert Coles, author of Children in Crisis, *talks about the role and meaning service can have in the education and lives of the nation's students — and faculty. Arthur Levine,* Change *Executive Editor and now at the Harvard Graduate School of Education, conducted the following interview with Coles in the summer of 1989 when President Bush was proclaiming national service as part of his mission and nine bills on the service issue were pending in Congress. From* Change, *Vol. 21, No. 5, September/October 1989, pp. 18-26. Reprinted with permission of the Helen Dwight Reid Educational Foundation, 4000 Albemarle Street, N.W., Washington, DC 20016. Copyright © 1989.*

LEVINE: I have been told that you are the most eloquent speaker in the country on the topic of community service for students. Not to put any pressure on you, but why is service important?

COLES: Service is important for many reasons. Educationally, because I think it is a tremendous way for students to learn sociology and anthropology, psychology and social ethics, and, in a sense, to learn about others and about themselves in the most effective way I know. One does learn by doing as well as by reading. Education is not only a function of books, but a function of experience and connecting what one reads with ongoing observations and experiences.

Service is also important, I think, morally and ethically, which, after all, is part of what I think universities are about. Harvard in the nineteenth century, for instance, used to say its mission was to develop the character of its students. One of its primary missions. I am just old fashioned and conservative enough to believe that's important, and that part of the mission of a university can be to help develop the character of its students. *And*, by the way, the character of its professors, because community service is important, not only for the students. It would be tremendous to have us professors doing this kind of work alongside our students, learning with them and being part of that world of learning by seeing and doing and hearing. We, too, could benefit from the kind of soul searching that goes on when one is in a particular set of circumstances with others — finding out about their lives, maybe trying to make a difference in those lives, and also, maybe, perhaps having one's own life thereby changed.

LEVINE: It shocks me how hot the topic is getting. As of July, nine different bills were pending in Congress on national service. Do you have any sense of why this topic is so hot right now?

COLES: We have had such a cold spell, now the pendulum is swinging from cold to hot, to pursue your image. There has been a kind of ebb tide of involvement, a moral ebb tide of sorts, that we have been remonstrated with recently, namely, that we should pursue our own interest and our own paths and be relatively uncon-cerned with others. This culture of narcissism and this emphasis on the "I" and the "me" has begun to wear thin in people, as, I think, instinctively it does. I think people are not only egoistic by nature; there is also a side of them that reaches out to others and thinks of others. Perhaps we go back and forth in our personal lives with those two sides of ourselves, and maybe politically, as well.

LEVINE: So do ideas like "a thousand points of light" seem appealing to you at the moment?

COLES: "A thousand points of light?" That expression and what it is about has always been a part of America. I think the phrase expresses a particular president's quiet, tactful notice to the country that this kind of value — that is, the value of thinking of others as well as ourselves — was going to make a difference to him and was going to be a part of his mission as a president. I think Bush is pursuing it and will pursue it. I do not think it is totally a political sham or a brazenly frivolous bit of rhetoric. I think he means it, and I think he will probably put some political capital into it, just as I think those representatives and senators mean it. At least, I hope so.

LEVINE: I sense that it is real. It is the beginning of the nation's moving into a more progressive agenda.

COLES: Right. After all, for 20 years this country has struggled with disappointment and loss and a feeling of betrayal. We lost our president in the early '60s. Another president was driven right out of office. We watched the deaths of Robert Kennedy and Dr. King and Malcolm X. We lost another president who had to resign. We lost a one-term president due to a complex series of foreign policy tragedies and perhaps his own ineptitude. So, we have had a lot of trouble in this country politically.

And then we got a president who for two full terms sent the message, "Hey, let's just stop all these notions of reform and let's see what we all can get for ourselves." Reagan endured politically and his ideology, I think, dominated an entire decade. I think now that is over and maybe the country is going to go back to some of the spirit — and I hope not the mistakes — of the '60s.

LEVINE: If you could design a service program for the nation, what would it look like?

COLES: I would like to see students of all backgrounds with their teachers involved in the projects where we are all needed — with the elderly, with children who desperately lack educational opportunities, on projects that would help the country ecologically and environmentally, in prisons — wherever there is a need for the kind of energy and intelligence that I hope both students and their teachers have.

I would like to see college students teaching in some of the schools. I teach, for instance, at a college and a medical school, but I also teach in a fourth-grade class in Cambridge. Those elementary school classrooms desperately need the kind of skills that college students have. Moreover, it would not hurt to have an occasional professor come in and help out. That professor might even learn something from these children, who are pretty sharp about what they see, including what they see about university life, because some of them walk right through the Harvard Yard on their way to school.

I would also like to see the range of activities be matched by the range of participation. I would like to see rich students as well as poor and middle class students doing community service. But this is a major problem. I would hate to see community service limited to minority students, for instance, who work out of their own sensitivity to their own personal experience. I would hate to see legislation written in such a way that only the poor students are being prompted into doing the service because it offers financial benefit. Some of the students who need community service the most, I think, come from well-to-do backgrounds, students who are so geared to competitiveness and greedy self-assertion that we really are in serious moral jeopardy. Community service is a means for us, perhaps, to get some kind of moral assistance. That is just as much our need as, say, psychological assistance.

LEVINE: I like that imagery. I do not think I have heard it before. What age is appropriate for service?

COLES: In some of my work in this country I have seen high schoolers help elementary school kids, but I think the best is college students. And graduate students, by the way; let's not neglect what medical students and law and business school students can do. I have worked with medical students who are working with the poor and the needy in Boston, with alcoholics, with the street people, with the homeless, with prisoners, with troubled children, and they are doing wonderful work. Law students can help people who have legal problems.

So, I would encourage voluntarism from maybe high school age on. I worked with high schoolers who have done tutoring, and it has been very helpful both to the children being tutored and to the high schoolers who have done the tutoring. Maybe I might wait until the junior year in high school, but I would not write off the high school years. I would encourage community service activities in our high schools as well as in our colleges and our graduate schools.

LEVINE: What about young people who are not in college? I am thinking that one finds in college a population more white than of color, richer rather than poorer. What about all of those young people who do not make the transition into college? Is there a service role for them?

COLES: That is a very good and important point, lest public service become connected only to the, relatively speaking, elite. When I worked in Appalachia in the '60s and early '70s, a marvelous group of volunteers there, the Appalachian Volunteers, were very sensitive to this. They had a wonderfully idealistic notion of their participation in this voluntary effort to work at some of the problems of the region — the educational problems, the environmental problems, serious environmental problems — the destruction of the landscape, really, by the coal companies. They tried to make connections with coal miners and with factory workers and with farm people — the younger farm people, the younger coal miners, the younger factory workers. And I thought that was a very important idea. They did forge some alliances with some working-class, blue-collar young people who helped participate in the environmental aspects of community service. This is something that could be done.

Maybe blue-collar youths are less interested in some of the cerebral sides of community service — the tutoring programs — but they have very serious concerns, I think, about the environment, about pollution and the nature of the water, the nature of the land, acid rain. I think they could be enlisted, and this would be important for the country.

When I worked in New Mexico, many of the young people I got to know had no interest at all in going to college. They were interested in blue-collar jobs, or whatever. But they had a sense of injustice, a sense of injustice connected to land use, to water use, to the quality of the air. Those are aspects, I think, of what community service might be in this country and ought to be. We ought to make an effort to get such young people involved. It would really pull the country together in a way that perhaps it needs to be pulled together, so that we do not have class against class and group against group, an elite against a group that feels neglected or ignored.

Oftentimes, when intellectuals talk about young people, they do not think of young people who are working in factories or on farms or in blue-collar jobs. Instead, they think of young people as college students and as future professional people. This is a rather narrow view of young people. I would hope that any community service program would include not only those young people in the colleges and graduates schools, but those who are not, as well.

By the way, it's at the high school level that we could really anticipate these class divisions. We could make efforts in high schools that are not primarily geared toward college admissions committees.

LEVINE: Very interesting. Now, let me ask you a few questions about mechanics. In your national plan, would there be incentives? What types of incentives? At some point, if you add incentives, it is not service anymore; it is paid work.

COLES: I have mixed feelings about this. On the one hand, I think there are some young people who really want and need those incentives, for all sorts of reasons. They need incentives about living successful lives, because some of them are demoralized and confused and without aspirations; yet they have to learn how to struggle out of their particular set of social and economic circumstances. Maybe they do not think there is any chance that they can successfully do so. But, having said that, I think there ought to be incentives for the well-to-do, too.

Maybe we ought to think of different kinds of incentives for different kinds of people. After all, we compel students to take languages; we compel them to take writing courses — there is a tradition of compulsion in our universities. Maybe we ought to think about the needs of some students just as we think about the tradition of scholarships and GI Bills. Perhaps some students do need some financial incentives or rewards, but those incentives or rewards do not necessarily have to destroy the sense of achievement and accomplishment that goes with voluntary service. Not necessarily.

Other students perhaps need different kinds of incentives. Perhaps they need the incentive of the college's saying, "Hey, this is what we stand for, and this is what we want you to be part of. We want you to be literate in many ways — educationally, morally — and we are going to put our money behind that. We will give scholarships to those who need them, and we are going to tell others that you need it, too. You have to learn how to speak Latin or Greek or Spanish or whatever. And, by golly, you are to go out there and do some work because it is educationally and morally part of our mission."

So let's flexibly reach out to all these constituencies with various "incentives."

LEVINE: Does a federal program make any sense in light of the kind of flexibility you are talking about?

COLES: The federal government has been a great prodder of the private sector and of the universities. The government pours money into the coffers of the universities, encouraging them in all sorts of ways, and I do not see why it cannot encourage them in public service, too. The more control the private sector has, including the university private sector, the better. The government has always been an important facilitator, and its cash has been welcome in many other areas. I mean, federal money is so earnestly sought for the humanities, for the sciences, for the social sciences. The universities have shown themselves able to survive this infusion of capital wealth from Washington without its destroying their integrity; they seem to welcome it. If they suddenly said, "We do not want it" now, I would want to know why.

*We cannot succeed in building
community spirit in our young people by
merely giving speeches, coining slogans
or exhorting them to stand tall. A
lasting concern for the community comes
from the chance to work for others, see
their needs and contribute to something
larger than oneself.*

— *Derek Bok*

LEVINE: There is talk in Washington of tying public service to, let's say, housing stipends, so you could use whatever money you make in service to buy a house; tying it to student financial aid, so students do not get any financial aid whatever unless they have done service. There are a lot of schemes. Do any of them stand out for you? Any to which you would say, "Yeah, let's go do that?"

COLES: I have mixed feelings about all of them. On the one hand, I hate to have financial aid so tied to service that students feel embittered. Do you know what I mean? That students feel, "Gee, I have to do this to get that money, but I do not want to do it, and I am really furious." Here is where, I think, the colleges and the universities have a mission. If the government is going to say, "This is what we want," the colleges and the universities have got to make clear to the students that it is not just the government behaving in a rather predatory and arbitrary manner. The universities have got to say, "Hey, we want this, too, and we *really* want it. And we want it out of our heart. And even if the government told you that they are going to give you these stipends without this kind of rider, we are telling you that this is an important part of your education, and it is an important part of our educational mission." There ought to be some way of getting that message to students.

LEVINE: In a lot of ways the universities and colleges are much more important actors than the federal government would be in the scenarios we have been talking about.

COLES: I wish our universities were more connected to this. The initiatives ought to be coming from them. They ought to be running down this road saying, "We not only want to be parties because we smell money around the corner, but we really believe that this is an urgent need of ours, an urgent intellectual need, an urgent moral need, an urgent educational responsibility that we, perhaps, have not taken as seriously as we might have over the decades and generations."

It is terribly important for more of us teachers to participate ... and to bring our intellectual skills and whatever nurturance and moral, intellectual, and emotional support we can offer to other people.

LEVINE: If a college were to come to you next week and say, "Yes, you are right. We think there is a moral requirement. Our students have got to do some of that. An intellectual requirement." What would you tell them to do? Do you have a favorite program that you would set up; some way you would organize this?

COLES: I would immediately go to some of the nearby schools and find out what kind of help they need from reasonably educated people. I would go to nursing homes. I would go to hospitals. I would go to places where the homeless are fed or find out whether there are homeless who are not being taken care of. I would then pull together my colleagues on the faculty and the students who are interested and see whether we could not respond to those needs.

It is terribly important — and I want to emphasize this as strongly as I know how — it is terribly important for more of us teachers to participate, to do the tutoring, to work in the soup kitchens, to visit the nursing homes or the jails; to bring our intellectual skills and whatever nurturance and moral, intellectual, and emotional support we can offer to other people. In so doing, we have a lot to learn that will help us to become better teachers. So, I would begin to talk to the faculty as well as the students and, pretty soon, I think we would have a cadre of people, both teachers and students, out there helping others — being helped as we help others because service is a mutual thing. It is not only helping others; it is being helped. Because we learn, we affirm ourselves in certain important ways, I think, psychologically and morally. We have everything to gain by doing this as human beings and as citizens and as people who are trying to learn about the world.

After all, what is an intellectual? An intellectual is someone who presumably acquires a body of knowledge in his or her head about the world, and this is one way of doing so.

LEVINE: Here is the question I've wanted to ask you all along. The students out there doing service — are they reading anything in addition, and, if so, what does the reading list look like?

COLES: Students who are doing these activities also need time to reflect upon what they have experienced, and there are wonderful books that can help them do that. By the way, not only do the books help them reflect on the experience, but the books help enrich the experience. The books give them pause for thought; after they have discussed some of these novels or poems or short stories, they go back to their work feeling a bit more savvy, maybe a bit more whole and healed, a bit wiser, even, and therefore better able to teach or work in the soup kitchen or whatever.

I have a reading list. Some of Tillie Olson's short stories or Raymond Carver's short stories. Tolstoy, struggling as he did with what it means to be old and sick and dying and to hold onto life and know that it is ebbing away. William Carlos Williams' poetry and stories talking about working-class people and their struggles and hopes and worries and doubts. Ralph Ellison's *Invisible Man*, trying to render what it means to feel invisible to others by virtue of one's race, and what it means to be blind — because for every invisible man, there is a blind person who does not see him. When you have read those books, I think you feel a bit more; I think you are somewhat better equipped to deal with some of the inevitable moments of doubt and inadequacy and hesitation and fear that are going to afflict people doing certain kinds of community service.

The book reading, I think, helps as one is going through the experience; conversely, the experience brings to the book reading a new intensity of intellectual response. So, it is a mutual thing. You can read Tolstoy or Dickens or Hardy in one way in a college library, emphasizing the symbolism and their use of language and imagery. But you can also get from those books a moral message, and that moral message is always intensified when one is having experiences very similar to those described in the novels.

Dickens' evocations of poverty, Hardy's evocations of what it is for someone to be an outsider and yet want to go to college and feel that he will never be able to go there. Tolstoy's struggles, not only to understand the poor, but to understand the arrogance and the selfishness and smugness in himself that kept him from understanding the poor and seeing them. On and on it goes.

There ought to be room in voluntary service and community service for the people involved to sit down and reflect. I do not mean overly self-conscious psychological analysis. God save us from that. But just plain old moral and personal reflection using novels, using short stories, using poems, and also using the experience itself.

LEVINE: What is the best way to organize a student service? Is immersion best? Do we say, "Go do this for a term full-time?" Do we tell them, "Do five hours a week for your four years of college?"

COLES: I would organize the service eclectically, with different possibilities. Some students may want to take a year or two off and do this full-time. Others may want to stay at school. I would respect diversity here, diversity of opportunities and diversity of participation. Different kinds of people doing different things.

LEVINE: Are you already doing this?

COLES: Yes. I work with students who are doing voluntary community service in the greater Boston area. They tutor, they work with the elderly, they work in soup kitchens, and then we have a seminar in which we sit and read Raymond Carver stories, William Carlos Williams poems. We read some social science like Anthony Lukas' book, *Common Group,* and we read James Agee's *Let Us Now Praise Famous Men.* We read some of Orwell's documentary writing, *Down and Out in London and Paris* and *The Road to Wigan Pier.*

Then we take up the matters that these writers take up. Namely, how does an outsider get involved in the community? At what personal cost or pain? How do you feel when you are working with others and having trouble doing so? What do you do with the sense of shame or guilt that may come upon you? How do you reach others who are different from you and establish relationships with them?

These novelists, these essayists, help us to have these discussions because they render some of the dilemmas and experiences that the young people are having in these stories.

After those discussions, the students have an opportunity to go through the experience again, remember what we talked about, and perhaps feel a bit stronger and more savvy about what they are going to do.

LEVINE: How many students do you have in your class at a time?

COLES: I have a seminar of 20, and then I give an undergraduate lecture course called "The Literature of Central Observation," which has about 6700 students in it. The lecture group then breaks down into sections of 20 students, so we have about 30 sections. I try to visit every one of those sections, but that is back-breaking work. The sections are led by a whole cadre of graduate students, medical students, law students, School of Education students (a lot of them, as a matter of fact). They discuss — as I do with my own undergraduate seminar — the reading, and they also discuss the community service.

LEVINE: Are the students required to do community service?

COLES: It's voluntary. About half of those sections are so-called "community service" sections, made up of students who are going to bring their community service work to the course as a topic of discussion.

LEVINE: How long have you been doing this?

COLES: About 10 years.

LEVINE: Was there a period in which the numbers were smaller, when fewer people were interested in the topic?

COLES: Suddenly, over the last four or five years, the community service participation has been growing. And last year I introduced my own special community service course in the seminar.

This fall, in the Harvard Extension school, I am also going to teach a community service course for people working in Cambridge. Some may be school teachers or community activists, maybe lawyers or doctors who have been involved in community service work and want to discuss it. A whole range of professional people exist to draw upon, but one can also draw upon ordinary working people who want to take a course in the Extension School.

For five years I have also worked with the medical students of the Urban Health Project, in which medical students work in the summer between their first and second or second and third years. For that summer they work in soup kitchens, or as tutors, or with the homeless, or with alcoholics, or whatever — doing voluntary work — but we also have weekly discussions about their experiences. I assign reading to them — short stories or novels or documentary literature from Agee and Orwell.

LEVINE: And there are no second-party payments for this?

COLES: No second-party payments. These are all heart payments.

I've another interesting thing to tell you. I know a group of Harvard Businsess School students who this summer are working at community service. They organized themselves to work with schools and with agencies that work with vulnerable people whether they are the homeless or troubled children. I find it remarkable. Who knows? Maybe the experience will wean some of them away from Morgan Stanley and they'll spend their time working in the development office at Covenant House, a wonderful place in New York City where street children are rescued.

LEVINE: How much of this have you been responsible for? I understand that you have taken these initiatives with the students. Perhaps that is what we need, a Robert Coles on every campus.

COLES: There are a number of people like me all over the country who would like to get involved. This is what I meant earlier: we need professors to get involved. Wouldn't it be great if we had deans and presidents and professors working alongside the students? What a tremendous educational moment in American life!

Robert Coles is a professor of psychiatry and medical humanities at Harvard and has been actively involved in community service as a teacher and a volunteer since the 1960s. He is the author of the five-volume Children in Crisis *series as well as* The Moral Life of Children *and* The Political Life of Children.

Arthur Levine is Executive Editor of Change: The Magazine of Higher Learning. *Now at the Harvard Graduate School of Education, he is the former president of Bradford College. He is the author of* When Dreams and Heroes Died *and other books.*

A Bit of History ...

... In 1966, the beginnings of a service curriculum were introduced through the initiative of Radcliffe's President Mary I. Bunting. The Harvard-Radcliffe service curriculum, Education for Action (EA), has all the necessary ingredients for providing educationally meaningful service opportunities for students. [In addition to] moral support from the administration, EA receives help from faculty in conducting seminars and teaching in orientation programs. EA also has a new full-time director.

Significantly, EA carries academic credit for one of its seminars. Begun as a seminar on "Teaching in Urban Areas" last year, the course, which requires field experience of the EA variety, was translated into "educationese" and now appears in the official Harvard register as "Social Sciences 121. Studies in Education: The Changing Function of American Education in the City." There were 75 qualified applicants for the 15 openings in the course last autumn.

The brief existence of EA has already led to the institutionalization of two aspects of the service curriculum. Providing information on summer service opportunities for students brought such a deluge of requests to EA that Radcliffe, with its own funds, has added a half-time staff member to cope with the demand. Deciding on financial awards to needy students proved both awkward and time-consuming for the student selection committee, so at its request, these decisions have been assumed by Radcliffe's Financial Aid Office.

In her first annual report on EA, President Bunting identified the major results:

> Summer service offered opportunities for students to develop capabilities not ordinarily called into play in the academic year or in summer jobs.
>
> Students expressed tremendous satisfaction in the fact that through EA the College seemed interested in giving them assistance to do things that seemed worthwhile to *them*.
>
> The college was made aware that summer service experience was available only to students from relatively well-to-do families, apart from those who benefited from EA financial support.
>
> Many students in EA summer service discovered problems and interests that helped to resolve their career decisions. This resolution generally led to academic improvement.
>
> Students who worked overseas and in new situations in this country emphasized the advantages of involvement in service projects for the person eager to [gain awareness of] unfamiliar cultures.
>
> Faculty members noted distinct contributions to student theses and classroom discussions as an outcome of EA summer service.

— from "Service Experience and Educational Growth" by Donald J. Eberly, in *Educational Record*, American Council on Education, Spring 1968, p. 4.

Service-Centered Learning: A Faculty View

Robert L. Sigmon

The public health practice program at the University of South Carolina illustrates two general principles of service-learning. Reprinted with permission from Redefining Service, Research, and Teaching, *Warren B. Martin, ed., Jossey-Bass, New Directions for Higher Education, No. 18, Summer 1977, pp. 65-74.*

MY FASCINATION WITH THE IDEA of service activities as an educational setting began in trying to relate three years of life in a village as a teacher and school administrator in Pakistan between 1958 and 1961 to the graduate work I was involved with from 1961 to 1964. Somehow, the human and institutional challenges I had faced in the Punjab were far richer for my learning and development than the knowledge and methodologies famous scholars challenged me to consider. What was the distinction between being saturated with situations that demanded action and immediate attention, such as malaria cases, rivalry between school leaders, death in the families of the students, floods, providing meals and shelter with limited resources, and institutional indifference, and the situation asking me to consider abstractions and precepts unrelated to what I had experienced?

My hunch was that being in the midst of difficult human dilemmas raised important questions for my learning and growth. The needs for shelter, food, opportunity, and hope created conditions for asking these questions. Why the cultural differences? Why the economic gaps? Why the injustices? What can be done by individuals? By institutions? By legislation and policy? How was I to live my life? What skills and knowledge did I need to do the work I was choosing to do? All these questions interwoven with the relentless day-to-day requirements of the work at hand created a richly textured learning environment. Although I did little formal reflecting on the learning consequences of those Pakistan experiences, my fascination with the idea of service settings as learning environments grew.

My odyssey with service-centered learning continued in the period between 1964 and 1966 as co-director with my wife of a two-year, domestic, Quaker, Peace Corps-type program in the Southeastern United States sponsored by the American Friends Service Committee. In this program, called Voluntary International Service Assignments, young college graduates lived and served for two years in isolated communities in rural Kentucky, South Carolina, Tennessee, urban Georgia, and North Carolina. The focus was on enabling communities to maintain their own well-being. Volunteers were invited to serve as aides to the communities in assisting with a day-care center controlled by the community, building a community center, and the like. The focus of the program for the volunteers was on the value question of what is worth doing. The total learning potential, just as in my Pakistan experience, was underrecognized.

At the conclusion of that two-year assignment, I was convinced that our educational institutions were missing a good bet by overlooking the learning potential in service-related activities. A job then became available in a new program at Oak Ridge Associated Universities in Tennessee that planned to engage college students in action programs in the new manpower areas of community development and economic development, known as the Resource Development Project. We developed a simple model that became known as the "service-learning internship" model. In 1967 this effort was transferred to the Southern Regional Education Board, which supported the development of service-learning internships throughout the Southeast. This model, which required support and administrative leadership from both colleges and public agencies, postulated that high school, undergraduate, and graduate students can all gain new skills and knowledge by serving specific public needs.

Eleven years, three states, and hundreds of associations with communities, agencies, universities, faculties, and students later, I have reached several conclusions about service as a significant context for learning, whether at the high school, college, graduate school, or lifelong learning levels.

Basic Premises

Programmatically, service settings used as learning environments require attention to two fundamental premises.

First, *the service is owned by those to be served.* That is, the ownership of identifying the service tasks — the actions intended to enable someone else to become stronger — as well as the processes used and the results obtained, must remain with the individuals or groups to be served. For educators who arrange service-learning activities for students, this means that the service to be provided has to be clearly differentiated from the learning outcomes expected, because if there is no service or work to be accomplished *as judged by the agency involved,* then the agency has no reason to be involved. My experience suggests that agencies and community groups are more interested in getting their objectives accomplished than in shepherding assorted students through activities associated with growing up and developing skills. As a result, the service-learning design that differentiates the service from the learning and places the service fully in their control is most consistent with their interests.

Second, *the learning is owned by those who plan to learn.* Thus the ownership of identifying learning objectives must rest with the learner, not a faculty member nor an academic department nor an accrediting body nor the agency. For educators who arrange service-learning activities for students, this means that students must have the initiative in identifying their learning needs and planning their learning experiences, since if there is no learning to be accomplished *as judged by the students themselves,* then they and the educational institution have no educational purpose in being involved.

A Program Model in Public Health Practice

Consider the application of these ideas in a specific case. In my role as director of public health practice with the School of Public Health of the University of South Carolina, I oversee an individualized service-centered learning program that comprises eight credit hours of a 38-hour program culminating in a Master in Public Health degree. Students, mostly practitioners in the sick cure and health care fields, are responsible for developing short-term service tasks with a community or organization and for identifying their own learning expectations.

The students can begin the development of their service-learning activity from either the basis of a task to be done or from competencies to be mastered; but the initiative in doing so rests with them. They then negotiate their learning objectives with a faculty member who serves as a counselor and adviser in helping them develop an adequate "fit" between the learning objectives they propose for themselves and the service tasks they plan to undertake. At the same time, they negotiate their service tasks with a "mentor" who represents the sponsoring agency and who provides sanction and supervision for the work activity. The mentor's chief role is overseeing the work or service dimension of the project and ensuring its usefulness for the agency. The mentor is not primarily responsible for the teaching and learning aspects of the project, but agrees to recognize and support the student's learning agenda.

Prior to developing their plans, students participate in planning workshops on assessing their learning styles, setting learning objectives, monitoring their performance and their learning, and reviewing ethical issues in service-centered learning. In addition to preparing their learning agreements and their service or work agreements, they prepare essays on "who will be served" by their activities and on "how I will monitor and keep track of how well I'm doing and learning." The paper on "who will be served" often has a sobering effect on the student as well as the faculty member and the agency mentor; it often leads to redoing both the learning and service agreements and opens up thoughtful dialogue among the three of them on fundamental questions.

During the service-learning activity, the mentor, faculty member, and student meet at least once to review the overall plan and clarify their expectations. The work or service aspects are regularly supervised and reviewed by the mentor. As a final exercise, students present their data or activity for review by the persons in the organization with whom they have done their project. The standards for assessing the quality of the service are generally negotiated at the time of initiating a project, but usually the mentor does not contribute to assigning the grade. The learning aspects are regularly reviewed by the faculty member through individual conferences or seminar sessions. A grade of either "satisfactory" or "not yet completed" is assigned by the faculty member based on the documentation provided by the student with respect to the original learning objectives and the criteria for this assessment spelled out in the original learning agreement negotiated between the student and the faculty member.

Examples from Public Health

The work of three students illustrates elements of this process.

Getting Started. A thirty-one-year-old black student, who just completed a B.S. degree after an interlude of nine years away from schooling, and who supports his family working nights as a computer programmer, is committed to helping poor black communities through health education. When he was ready for his individualized service-centered learning project, a planned parenthood agency had indicated an interest in having a male student work on their problem of not knowing how to involve males in their family planning activities. The student contacted the agency and found a good fit between his needs and those of the agency. With a staff member, he negotiated a set of manageable tasks designed to produce alternative plans for the agency to use to better serve males. He then evolved a set of learning objectives based on what he needed to know to be able to develop the alternatives.

He became heavily involved in conducting classes in cooperation with a white female staff member, steeped himself in the literature, became skilled and comfortable in discussing issues of sexuality with people, and developed skills in training and communication. His project was completed with his report to the agency and his critical reflections on how well he did his task for the organization and how he assessed and achieved his learning objectives, with special attention to the different areas of knowledge he brought to bear on the task.

Midterm Project Review. An experienced registered nurse who works with two others nurses as "Program Nurse Specialists" in a public health agency was concerned about the division of responsibilities among the three in terms of their personal interests and expertise and undertook a service-learning project to analyze their activities and relate these responsibilities to their interests and abilities. As she explained the problem in her mid-term project report:

> The present division of work load among the three Program Nurse Specialists is on specific program lines — Family Planning, Home Health Services, and Maternal and Child Care. This means that all activities related to that program fall under that Program Nurse Specialist's jurisdiction. She is the administrator, coordinator of activities, clinical worker, statistician, health educator, and supervisor of personnel assigned to that program.

But in its present form, the role of Program Nurse Specialist requires that the person holding that role must do all of these jobs, whether she is particularly competent in that area or not and whether or not her interests lie in that area. Equally important, other important roles do not fall into a specific program jurisdiction and thus jobs to be done sometimes "fall between the cracks."

I had heard that other organizations assign tasks according to the capability and interest of the individual, and I approached my fellow Program Nurse Specialists and the Assistant Director of Nursing to see if they thought this idea was feasible for us. They were all very interested, and we began to think how we could undertake an experiment in this area.

This student and her colleagues decided that she might begin by analyzing already existing data on their activities that is collected weekly and computerized, but eventually they decided that these data did not adequately cover all the information needed. Her report on the progress of her project illustrates the possible effects of a project on an organization:

I am currently at the point of role monitoring the activities of the other Program Nurse Specialists and conferring with them to explain my findings. In monitoring them, I have been able to see areas where roles could be combined and thus strengthened. I am finding that even though the job descriptions are nearly the same, the work involved with each job is quite different. I am better able to understand the "toils and tribulations" of my fellow workers and am able to empathize with them and be more helpful in offering concrete suggestions to them. In addition, it has been enlightening to observe firsthand their techniques of management and supervision. Because this experience has been most helpful to me, I would like to recommend that they in turn observe me and each other.

As a result of this project, the agency has created a new management system satisfactory both to the medical director and nursing director. The student has become the administrative agent, and her colleagues now specialize in clinical matters.

Final Learning Evaluation. Another nurse, in her mid-thirties, married and with two children, is responsible in a state health agency for evaluating home health service programs. One of her service-learning projects as a graduate student involved gathering epidemiological data from patients in a number of hospitals, analyzing the information, and reporting the implications to responsible officials. Here are some of her reflections about what she learned, from her report at the end of her project:

> The decision on an area for study was for me an easy one: I was seeking a project outside of my usual work responsibilities that would demand the application of epidemiological concepts and principles. The project I chose fulfilled this expectation for me. Actually living out the process of pinpointing a study topic, developing a study design, negotiating entry into a setting outside my usual work area, mobilizing resources, and implementing the study has left me with some areas of comfort with my skills and some of discomfort.
>
> I am now confident that I can do a better job of deciding on manageable projects and negotiating agreement with those persons who have an interest and investment in the outcome. I am much less confident of my skill in study design and analysis. I was left unsatisfied with the analysis portion of my project, partly because of a reluctance to accept the limitations of the project, but more because of my uncertainty as to how much analysis is enough and where it is reasonable to end.... Among my unexpected or incidental learning was the pleasant surprise at the reception of patients to being involved in the study. The cynic in me thought that, having lost so much control over their environment by being institutionalized, they would feel they had no choice but to participate. They convinced me to put aside that thought and appreciate their willingness to be helpful. One patient even requested a copy of the study. I feel an additional compulsion to make it useful and interesting reading as a result.

In this project, learning outcomes were reviewed in three ways: the student had a final conference with her faculty sponsor, met with the director of public health practice for an overview assessment, and received reactions to her report on her learning from the seminar group with whom she met regularly. In serving-learning, new questions for inquiry are framed continuously; this student is following up ideas stemming from her service-learning project and is now actively involving her own students in projects.

Implications

Service-centered learning, as illustrated by these cases, offers a format in which people can serve and be served by their performance in society. The major criterion of its success is that those who are involved in it grow stronger, healthier, wiser, more autonomous, and more disposed to serve. Service-learning participants are required not only to do a job well and learn through doing it, but also to contribute affirmatively to raising their capacity and performance as servants of individuals, groups, and institutions. I am indebted to Robert Greenleaf for his thoughts on the role of servant in society, which are contained in three brilliant booklets (see "References.")

Service-centered learning makes demands both on educational institutions and service agencies. For educational institutions, it means creating space and support alongside teaching and research for service-centered learning — not just service in terms of applying knowledge to social needs, but service as an appropriate educational activity. This requires a fresh look at setting up competency or certification requirements within academe independent of the situations to be served in communities. Faculty members need new skills in brokering learning opportunities and time to assist learners to reflect on service-centered learning. Students need sanctions and practice in realizing their capacity to define their own learning agenda, to see their experiences as basically sound for educational purposes, and to understand that service activities are legitimate for learning. These demands are stressful for most educational institutions.

For community groups and public agencies, service-centered learning often creates confusion about how to utilize students assistance effectively and provide learning environments. Because of wide disparities in the expectations of college educators, agencies often do not know whether they should offer simply raw work experience, let students observe, allow them to institute change or undertake research on the professor's terms, or even be responsible for teaching and grading of students. Differentiating service from learning and placing service fully in the agency's control can overcome this confusion and encourage their participation. In fact, for employers concerned about job enrichment for their employees, separating the service responsibility and control from the learning objectives suggests an opportunity to support their employees' own lifelong learning. Individualized, experience-centered, public need-based activities are a natural format for building an adult lifelong learning system; and by encouraging employees to design their own learning experiences in the context of improving their capacity to serve the interests of the constituencies served by the organization, the organization can undertake its own worker-based service-learning model.

Key questions remain about service learning. For example, does the quality of service improve with a service-learning program focus? What do learners in fact learn in this format? What is best learned by this format? What are workplace constraints on this type of learning? Can service be better conceptualized as an essential forum for learning and teaching? And what is gained by differentiating and then integrating the service and learning dimensions?

But already service learning is a widely used educational option for academic institutions as they seek alternative approaches to teaching, research, and service. It succeeds best when the service is owned by those to be served and the learning is owned by those who plan to learn.

Robert L. Sigmon was Director of Public Health Practice in the School of Public Health at the University of South Carolina and is recognized nationally as a pioneer in the development of service-centered learning. He directed the North Carolina Internship Office from 1970 until 1975, after helping to found the National Society for Internships and Experiential Education in 1971, and helping the Southern Regional Education Board launch its regional service-learning project in 1967. He now serves as Acting Director of the Wake Area Health Education Center in Raleigh, North Carolina.

References

Greenleaf, Robert, *Institution as Servant*, Center for Applied Studies, Cambridge, Massachusetts, 1972.

Greenleaf, Robert, *Servant as Leader*, Center for Applied Learning, Cambridge, Massachusetts, 1973.

Greenleaf, Robert, *Trustee as Servant*, Center for Applied Studies, Cambridge, Massachusetts, 1974.

Southern Regional Educational Board, *Service-Learning in the South: Higher Education and Public Service*, 1967-1972, 1973.

Carrots for the Faculty

Getting the support of fellow educators may mean rewarding them with money, time, professional status, or personal satisfaction. Reprinted from Synergist, *National Center for Service-Learning, Vol. 9, No. 3, 1981, pp. 2-5.*

SOMEDAY SOMEONE WILL DO A STUDY of service-learning programs that died. It will be a sad but enlightening collection of program post mortems showing fine ideas and good intentions overcome by a range of illnesses — failed finances, moribund morale, clotted community relations, and asphyxiated administration. Surely one of the most prevalent maladies (curable if treated properly) would turn out to be feeble faculty relations. Any program needs at least the good wishes of the faculty, and faculty sweat may be its life's blood.

Whether speaking on behalf of a program to the administration, recruiting students to participate, granting release time for fieldwork, or monitoring field placements, teachers make programs work. Their enthusiasm and dedication are the sine qua non of healthy programs, and it behooves service-learning educators to cultivate the art of developing faculty support.

What follows is a compendium of ideas from high school and college service-learning educators who have faced the task of building programs by meeting the needs of other educators and turning them into enthusiastic supporters of service-learning. Their advice runs the gamut from general techniques for creating a receptive atmosphere in the institution to devising specific rewards and incentives for faculty who participate.

The Beginning

In many cases, the most difficult phase of developing support is at the beginning, before a service-learning program has had the opportunity to demonstrate its ample benefits to all those who participate in it. Teachers and administrators have a great deal to worry about in the daily discharge of their duties. They are jaded with new educational schemes that promise to cure all their ills.

Generating support initially means fighting an uphill battle to credibility.

"You have to have institutional clout," says Robert Clifton, director of the Community Service Development Program at Metropolitan State College, Denver. For service-learning educators who are not major administrators in their institutions, that may mean enlisting the support of people who *do* have clout. A sympathetic administrator is one possibility. Another is to invite the chairman of an academic department to play a major role in the program, thus shifting some of the responsibility to shoulders that are institutionally broader.

At the high school level, principals are likely targets. They can make or break projects. In Dade County, Florida, Gina Craig manages a system-wide program involving thousands of students in a massive tutoring program. She says, "I have to face the fact that, when confronting the principal of a new school, I have less credibility than another principal. So I get a principal who's sold on it to convince the new principal of the value of the program."

For answering teacher anxieties about the value of her program to the students, Craig feels fortunate to have two major studies that show the measurable benefits that accrue to students in her program. "But before we had those we would use simple attitude surveys, anecdotal material — anything — to convince teachers that the program worked."

Ruth Bounous, director of the University Year for Action (UYA) project at St. Edward's University, Austin, Texas, says, "If you make teachers part of the planning process for a program, they have a chance to incorporate aspects into the program that they will enthusiastically support later on." Also, by being in on the early dialogue, they have a chance to have their misgivings explained away.

Where convincing teachers of the academic validity and high desirability of service-learning activities is not possible, educators should not leave a fledgling program a casualty on the philosophical battlefield. Elizabeth Anne Gilbert, who runs the Haverford Township (Pennsylvania) Career and Community Service Program, suggests making whatever concessions are necessary and possible to avoid generating initial opposition to a service-learning program's activities. "Because teachers need to feel that their coursework is not jeopardized, we schedule fieldwork during free periods and during the afternoon when regular classes are over."

Supplying Incentives

Now that the faculty is waving service-learning banners, singing the program's praises to the administration, and urging students to become service-learners, how does one get the fans out of the bleachers and onto the playing field? Experienced service-learning educators feel that, regardless of how enthusiastic teachers are about a program in principle, getting them to commit themselves to serious involvement is often a matter of allowing them to see some practical benefit to themselves.

Time or Money. Tom Little, director of The Virginia Program at Virginia State College, Petersburg, describes a number of institutions, including Mary Washington College in Fredericksburg, Virginia, that have financial reward systems. Under some systems, teachers get a sum of money — perhaps $100 — for each intern they manage. The money may be routed from a student's tuition directly to the teacher. Be forewarned that some institutions' comptrollers will not sanction this system because they feel that the college's ability to meet overhead is seriously jeopardized when it loses the collective buying power of the mass of tuition monies.

Money, then, may not be available, but time for writing, research, travel, further study, or tending the roses (or the children) is often as good as gold. Where an outright financial incentive is out of the question, Little recommends a voucher system whereby teachers can get a voucher that allows them to get a reduction in their teaching load for the time they spend supervising community service.

Technical Assistance. Talented, potentially dedicated faculty may quail at the idea of taking on participation in a service-learning program because they are not sure that they will be able to handle a new set of tasks and a new way of teaching.

In Miami, Craig stresses the importance of responding to the need for faculty training with workshops tailored to meet the needs of the high school teachers.

Ed Kult, director of the Social Service Program at Creighton Prep, Omaha, says, "We try to take as much of the time load off as possible. That means development as well as management. We provide as much information and assistance as possible to teachers who are getting involved. We set up placements for them. That can really make a difference."

Barbara Gardner, director of the Joint Educational Project at the University of Southern California, Los Angeles, repeats the same refrain in a slightly different key. "Remember that teachers are overworked. If they don't publish, they languish professionally. So, take away the nitty gritty stuff that wastes their time. They don't have time to be administrators. That's what we're here for."

Gardner's view raises a salient point. Barbara Keller, director of the Community Action Program at Niagara University, Niagara Falls, New York, says, "Looking at the areas that contribute to professional faculty growth, research is often emphasized. The service-learning office can assist faculty members in finding a research population for study in a variety of disciplines: health care or social service for all ages from infants to elderly. The service-learning office might even assist a professor in making a grant application for a specific project."

Patty Brandt, a graduate student working with the UYA program at Southern Illinois University, Carbondale, emphasizes that a service-learning program can be a great opportunity for a faculty member. "We keep track of people's pet research topics. That way, we can approach them when there are field placements relevant to their interests. Or, we can try to find field activities that will match what a faculty member is working on." In that way, teachers supervising students in field placements can use the opportunity of the student's work for their own research. Gardner of USC adds cautionary words. "We don't allow students just to go out as observers to report back to a faculty member doing research. There has to be a social benefit."

High School Variations. Because the professional life of high school teachers is different from that of college teachers, incentives are of a somewhat different nature. Research and publishing are not major considerations for the majority of high school teachers, although they may be somewhat more important to teachers in groundbreaking, innovative service-learning programs.

High school teachers are at least as overworked as those in college, and so are at least as likely to be impressed by the notion of being relieved of their paperwork. Gilbert spoke for the Haverford Township program and many others when she said, "One of the biggest things that a centrally run program can do is minimize the paperwork."

Rejuvenation

Some of the most effective incentives may be the least tangible ones. Whereas a good many college teachers, intent on research and publishing, would jump at the chance to be relieved of administrative tasks, the opportunity to dive into administration may be exactly what a high school teacher wants. To escape the routine of the classroom and make contact with the community can be a bracing tonic for high school faculty, not to mention an opportunity to write a new section in a resume and possibly move on to become an administrator. Gilbert says, "The work of the students connects the community to the school. Teachers can't help but be favorably affected by that as well."

Cheryl Willett, who directed a service-learning program that involves every department in two Livonia, Michigan, high schools, says, "Teachers are looking for rejuvenation. For people who have been teaching for 10 years or more, there is very often a need to bring the process back to life, to make it fresh and stimulating again. Teachers who might have been unsure about getting involved can see that service-learning has that effect — it reawakens them to the purpose of teaching."

That seems to be the crux of the issue in getting faculty involved in service-learning. The innate qualities of service-learning, once made clear to the receptive, committed teacher, stand a better chance of swaying that teacher than all the perquisites in the world. Service-learning educators overwhelmingly concur that service-learning sells itself because of its distinctive appeal to those teachers who see it as a way to vitalize education and serve society.

In discussing the Virginia Program, Little says, "The faculty who get involved have a value system that is aligned with service-learning; they are student oriented; they feel that knowledge should be useful and that it should have an ethical construct to it." Most conscientious teachers have a strong moral sense, want to be forces for good, and usually get their satisfaction on a deferred basis. They subsist on the belief that, by being morally constructive influences, they are turning out students who *may someday* contribute to the betterment of society.

But service-learning provides instant gratification for that need to do socially useful work. Payment comes in the form of seeing an immediate good for society. As Little says, "Let's face it, money is tight, so for the most part, extra involvement just comes out of a teacher's hide."

At USC, Gardner concurs. "Those who are seriously committed don't do it for money. And we don't pay people to participate, because then if you lose the money, you lose their participation."

Because of the current of altruism that runs through teacher participation, seeing the demonstrable benefit becomes an incentive for a teacher to push on. In fact, it's worth encouraging field site supervisors to express their appreciation openly from time to time.

Any time that appreciation becomes formalized into a testimonial that enhances the teacher's status with the school, so much the better.

The aura of good feeling that surrounds a learning program with a service component affects the students who get involved also. Teachers should be made aware of the enthusiasm that service programs generate in students. Service-learning can generate a great commitment in students — sometimes when nothing else will. Willett describes a service-learning social studies class in Livonia that has a high percentage of truant, delinquent, and otherwise troublesome students. "They may skip every other class they've got, but when it comes to *that* one, they're there every day."

Maintaining Enthusiasm

Initial enthusiasm or incentives may carry faculty into a program in its early stages. But for participation to continue, teachers need to receive nourishment along the way. Some of that support is part and parcel of service-learning and the dynamic that it creates — it comes with the territory. Other kinds of encouragement can be supplied by a program coordinator in order to keep enthusiasm high, and make a good program better.

Recognition — from the institution, the media, or the community — is something that gives teachers a special boost. "Tangible recognition means a lot to faculty members, for their ego, their sense of importance, and possibly their career," says Barbara Gardner. That might mean helping a teacher beat the bushes to find a publisher for an article or monograph about service-learning (an effort that can only benefit the program as a whole while it helps the teacher). It might mean trying to place stories with the local press about what teachers are doing, as Willett did in Livonia. Or it might mean publishing a newsletter, as Craig does in Miami. The purpose is not only to publicize the program but also to give credit where credit is due for the outstanding work of participants.

Most program coordinators who reflect on the issue of faculty support or faculty incentives run through the list of things that can be done and end in dwelling on the dimension that, more than anything else, seems to keep teachers going in service-learning.

Cheryl Willett's experience is indicative of how service-learning can have a self-renewing effect on faculty. When Stephenson High School first embarked on a campaign to introduce service-learning into every part of the curriculum, it faced the problem of dealing with a faculty that suffered from bad morale. With enrollments shrinking and faculty being laid off, most teachers initially were uninterested in a new, centrally managed program that was going to bring new people into the curriculum process.

As Willett and the coordinators — running a sustained awareness campaign and teacher-controlled inservice workshops — convinced more and more teachers of what service-learning could do for their students and the community, the teachers also began to see what service-learning could do for them. Willett recalls, "Some teachers never used to get out of their own department offices. With this program, they met faculty from other academic areas in discussions about curriculum. It was very energizing for them to have a dialogue about academics with people that they may never have talked with before. The program gives them stimulating experiences, just like it does the students. Community service attracts some pretty dynamic individuals; our teachers now get to meet and talk with those people. We have had some of those dynamic community leaders in to the school to speak. It gives all of us a shot of enthusiasm. Sometimes the presence of those people even attracts the press, which reflects well on the teacher that initiated the visit.

"When teachers first get involved, sometimes they start with a very modest kind of activity, like a little tutoring program or something. But as they move along, they get more confident. They try something more ambitious. They start making community contacts and building their own networks of associations. In the midst of that, they suddenly become aware of their own development. Service-learning creates an atmosphere that makes them think that way. And when teachers feel that they themselves are progressing and growing, they keep their enthusiasm. They want to keep going."

Continuum of Pedagogical Styles
in Experiential Learning

Faculty Role	Student Role
Disseminator of information and evaluator	Assimilate information
Mentor and evaluator	Apply knowledge and skill under supervision
Supervisor and evaluator	Receive instruction, observe demonstration, and practice under close supervision in worksite
Colleague [with] mutual involvement and evaluator	Participate jointly with faculty in research, study, or action projects
Designer or identifier of learning environment and evaluator	Apply knowledge and skill in simulations, role play or field placement and analyze experience
Consultant, adviser, and evaluator	Design and carry out learning plan for research, independent study or action projects
Facilitator, trainer, evaluator	Develop self-understanding, awareness, interpersonal skills or knowledge of transferable skills
Resource person and evaluator	Conscious effort to apply experiential learning theory
Evaluator	Action, reflection, documentation

The learner's role shifts from a dependent and passive one to one of greater independence and activeness.

Reprinted from "Nurturing Service-Learners" by John S. Duley in Synergist, *National Center for Service-Learning, ACTION, Vol. 9, No. 3, p. 15.*

Infusing Service-Learning into the Curriculum

Barry Fenstermacher

Edited for the National Center for Service-Learning, ACTION,
by Barry Fenstermacher from Dobbs Ferry, New York, as part of
"Curriculum-Related Volunteer Service," a concise guide that
is one of 14 in a series from NCSL now available from the
National Society for Internships and Experiential Education,
3509 Haworth Drive, Suite 207, Raleigh, NC 27609.

MANY COMMUNITY SERVICE PROGRAMS in high schools and colleges begin as extra-curricular activities designed primarily to provide community service and good will for the schools or colleges involved. As these program grow, coordinators often discover ways to meet community needs on a more consistent basis. They also become increasingly aware of the *educational* benefits inherent in community service. When teachers, program coordinators, and agency personnel cooperate to combine learning and community service in the same activity, many new opportunities emerge for students, institutions, and the community.

In these days of increasing concern about educational quality, educators want to be sure that traditional course offerings continue to cover all required material. Some are rightly critical of innovations that might lower quality or standards by reducing class time devoted to basic skills and other essential learning. Yet, classroom teachers and administrators have long been aware of, and committed to, certain types of experiential education that solidify and reinforce work presented in the classroom.

A Development Process

The success of "infusing" service-learning into a high school or college curriculum depends primarily on the ability of teachers, service-learning coordinators, and agency staff to work cooperatively on the process described below. Any member of this team can initiate the process; however, the beginning stages rely primarily on the special abilities of teachers or other educators, while the latter stages depend mostly on the skills of the community-based agency staff. Keep in mind that *the goal is to blend service and learning goals and activities in such a way that the two reinforce each other and produce a greater impact that either could produce alone.*

1. Examine the educational goals and objectives of the class or academic department involved. Identify specifically what students are required to learn: the knowledge, skills, understandings, or attitudes listed as course or curriculum goals.
2. Identify one or more specific concepts, objectives, or skills, the achievement of which could be enhanced, reinforced, or otherwise developed through participation in the community service activities.
3. Write one or more learning objectives that describes the desired outcome or impact on the students of a combined service-and-learning experience.
4. Describe in detail the activities that service-learning students might undertake, both in the classroom and in the community, to achieve the objectives listed in Step 3.
5. Design an evaluation procedure to measure student achievement of these objectives. Possibilities include written or oral exams, papers, interviews, questionnaires, observations, skill assessments, or other indicators of learning. (See the chapters of this resource book on assessing students' learning.)
6. Select the most appropriate activities from Step 4 above; if there are several, arrange them into a logical teaching order to fit the course outline.
7. Find or develop community service placements that will provide students with the activities or experiences listed in Step 6. Keep in mind the need to enable students to achieve the service and learning goals established above.
8. Develop a detailed teaching strategy for the course that includes both classroom and community service activities. These will probably include orientation to community service, specific job training, and on-site supervision.
9. Decide who will be responsible for each aspect of the overall service-and-learning experience. Assign appropriate tasks to the teacher, service-learning coordinator, agency personnel, on-site supervisor, and other participants.
10. Design student contracts, reference sheets, attendance records, supervision forms, and other materials required to define,

monitor, and evaluate the project in both its learning and service aspects. Distribute these to the appropriate parties along
with instructions for their use.

Program Examples

The two examples presented here, although very different, illustrate how teachers, service-learning coordinators, and agency officials can work together to create efficient and effective programs
that combine curriculum-related learning and community or public
service.

Case 1: The Department of Gerontology in a large, research-
oriented university requires an "Introduction to Gerontology"
course for all first-year graduate students. Although successful in
traditional ways, the course has recently been "infused" with a
community service requirement in order to meet one of the major
course objectives more successfully. The *learning goal* for the Gerontology students is to acquire a deeper understanding of the problems encountered by home-bound elderly citizens. The *service-
learning activity* through which students are to achieve this goal is a
series of weekly visits with home-bound seniors, to provide friend-
ship and personal contact, to identify medical or other needs, and to
locate services in the community that can meet the needs of these
citizens. This course has been designed in cooperation with the
university's Office of Service-Learning, which also assigns and
trains visitor teams, monitors their activities, and provides ongoing
evaluation for use by course instructors.

Case 2: The high school art department in a medium-sized city
recently sponsored student tours of the local art museum. In the
course of these visits, Latino students expressed interest in leading
tours of young Latino students, with an emphasis on viewing the
excellent collection of paintings by Latino artists. They agreed to
enroll in the high school's Art History course and to do special
preparation on the lives and works of the school's Art History
course and to do special preparation on the lives and works of the
Latino painters whose works were displayed in the museum. In
preparing to lead tours of younger children a year hence, however,
the high school students felt that it would enhance their project if
the identification signs near each painting were written in Spanish
as well as in English. They agreed to translate the existing signs and
to add a small amount of information to them if the museum would

pay for the signs. This was agreed to, and the signs now benefit both young and adult Spanish-speaking visitors to the museum. The *learning goal* for the high school students was to become familiar with the leading Spanish painters, their lives and works. The *service-learning activities* which reinforced and extended this learning was the research, writing, and production of the signs, and the leading of tours of Latino children.

Other examples of curriculum-related community service include:

• A high-school Ecology class learning to take and analyze water samples from the local river, offering the results to the town's Water Department, furnishing written reports of their findings to industries located on the river, preparing an article for the local newspaper and radio station, and surveying community attitudes on related ecological issues.

• College bi-lingual students teaching English to newly-arrived refugees.

• High school secretarial students teaching elderly citizens to operate duplicating machines and to lay out a newsletter so they can publish a periodical devoted to issues related to aging.

• University students helping mentally retarded citizens in a group home to dress themselves and to use public transportation.

The Learning Cycle

Glen L. Gish

The author suggests ways educators may apply Kolb's experiential learning model to service-learning. Reprinted from Synergist, *National Center for Service-Learning, ACTION, Vol. 8, No. 3, Spring 1979, pp. 2-6.*

ROGER, A HIGH SCHOOL JUNIOR WHO PRACTICES the piano two or three hours a day and hopes to become a composer, volunteers to take part in a new after-school project to teach developmentally disabled children to play musical instruments. Roger is eager to share his love of music with a child, but he takes no interest in setting up the program and seeing that it functions properly.

Janet, a college senior majoring in library sciences, likes nothing better than to take long walks in the woods alone. When she must carry out an assignment on using the public library as a community resource, she elects to work with a bookmobile that travels to nursing homes and senior citizen centers. She believes the service is valuable and enjoys talking to the older people about books, but when the city threatens to discontinue the service because of budget cuts, she is reluctant to advocate that the service be continued.

Anita, a college sophomore studying physics, enjoys working on complex problems. She takes part in a project to measure industrial pollution in a low-income residential area. She helps analyze the results and conceive a comprehensive solution. When it comes time to discuss the steps to be taken with those involved and test the proposed solution, Anita withdraws from the project.

Bob, a college senior, belongs to several clubs and likes to chair committees for such tasks as building parade floats and managing fundraisers. As a junior he became the chief organizer of a food co-op for students and low-income residents. He has been highly successful in getting people to participate. The bookkeeping, however, is becoming confused. Co-op members are beginning to complain about Bob's unwillingness to hold meetings or even to sit and talk about how they could have more control over the co-op and how it could be improved.

It appears that all of these students are well placed. They are doing valuable work, and they are using their preferred way of learning to put their abilities to use.

It also appears, though, that they are having trouble performing some aspects of their assignments. They are each uneasy with some part of the service-learning experience and each avoids certain activities by focusing on more comfortable ones.

Clearly each student (in fact, each person) prefers ways of learning that make it easier to perform certain tasks and obtain certain understandings. Each also avoids ways of learning that lessen effectiveness in doing and learning other things. Most people develop their preferred learning styles in school and use them throughout their lives. Thus students' life-long learning may be limited by an imbalance in learning styles.

Service-learning programs can — and should — offer great opportunities for students not only to use preferred learning styles but also to develop neglected styles, thereby enhancing both the service and learning functions of their experience. David Kolb, a developmental psychologist in the School of Management at Case Western Reserve University, has developed a way of looking at learning as a total experiential process. This model clearly portrays the different ways a person can learn in school, in the community, in a career, and in other facets of life. The experiential learning model provides some ideas for identifying how learning preferences impact service-learning. The model provides a view of how service-learning can become a vehicle for carrying students through significant development and can have a major effect on their careers and lives.

Experiential Learning

Traditionally, learning has been viewed as the accumulation of information and the development of concepts organizing that information into some coherent arrangement. This kind of learning is still to be valued. Learning, however, can also be seen as a process that includes all human experience. Active participation in others' lives is important to learning. Reflection on and orderly observation of human activity and the ideas that can define it are equally a part of learning. Creating concepts that organize the world so it can be understood and effectively dealt with is another important element. Finally, acting and experimenting allow us to test our experiences, reflections, and concepts — and thereby gain additional learning.

To state it another way, learning can be seen as a process in which a person experiences something directly (not vicariously), reflects on the experience as something new or as related to other experiences, develops some concept by which to name the experience and connect it with other experiences, and uses the concept in subsequent actions as a guide for behavior. Out of these four steps the person derives a new set of experiences that lead to a repeat of the learning cycle (see accompanying chart).

Kolb calls the four steps in the experiential learning process concrete experience, reflective observation, abstract conceptualization, and active experimentation.

Concrete experience involves direct, immediate (not past) experience, the stimulation of feelings and the senses as well as an awareness of the totality of one's environment. Someone who readily senses the mood of a group of people or responds kinesthetically to music appreciates and uses this mode of learning.

Reflective observation involves giving attention to certain experiences and thoughtfully comparing them or creating alternative meanings. Someone who sits back and absorbs experiences and begins to make sense of them — observing them intently and reflecting on their meaning — appreciates and uses this mode of learning.

Abstract conceptualization involves creating ideas and concepts that organize experience, action, and observations. Someone who builds concepts and models to explain things and likes to learn about others' theories gets a lot out of this mode of learning.

Active experimentation involves acting out one's ideas and theories, or at least using them as guides for experimenting in the real world. Someone who gets involved with people or tries out new — even risky — ideas takes advantage of this mode of learning.

The experiential learning model suggests that the four learning modes are followed in the sequence of concrete experience, reflective observation, abstract conceptualization, and active experimentation — which leads back into concrete experience. What seems to happen, however, is that individuals develop preferences for one or two learning modes.

Roger, Janet, Anita, and Bob are all good examples of such preferences. Roger, the pianist, tended to prefer concrete experience and, to a lesser extent, reflective observation. Janet definitely showed a preference for reflective observation in her desire for solitary walks and quiet talks. Anita seemed to favor abstract conceptualization in working out the solution to pollution. Bob indicated a preference for active experimentation by his choice of organizing a food co-op.

Responding and acting on the basis of preferences resulted in difficulties for each of these students when they needed to use other learning approaches for which they had not developed skills.

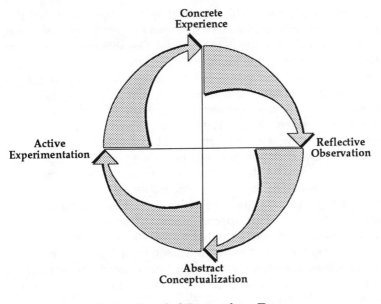

Experiential Learning Process

Service-learning can enhance students' academic learning by giving students like the four above opportunities to exercise both their preferred and neglected learning modes. The teacher or project coordinator must play a role in this, and the first step in the process is to diagnose each student's preferred learning mode(s).

One way to do this is by talking with the student about specific experiences that demonstrate a particular learning approach. Often two approaches will be combined. Another way is to use the self-profile instrument called the "Learning Style Inventory" developed by Kolb (see end of chapter for ordering information).

The following is an example of what happens when a faculty member works with a student in terms of completing the learning cycle. Bob went to Mrs. Witki, the co-op project coordinator, complaining that the harder he worked for the co-op, the worse things got. People were leaving the project and showing no appreciation for all he had done for them. She listened carefully and then asked Bob to describe fully his experiences on the project.

After a long recital of events and his feelings about them, Bob said, "You know, I bet those people are getting tired just watching me run around." The coordinator prodded Bob to consider how he might change his approach. After some thought he decided to relax and let some of the other co-op members take more responsibility.

The coordinator agreed with this strategy and suggested that Bob could learn and accomplish more if he spent more time just enjoying the people and the activity. He also might be able to come up with new ways of lowering the members' food cost.

Bob recognized that he needed to change his strategy or risk the co-op's failure. He came to that realization by fully identifying the elements of his *concrete experience* and *reflectively observing* the impact of that experience. Mrs. Witki helped him develop a new way to conceptualize the situation and develop a scheme by which he could *experiment* with new actions. Bob's scheme focused on being more reflective and on sharing the action rather than sticking to his preferred approach of active experimentation.

Not every situation can turn out so well. One cannot often try out all four of the learning approaches in a given situation. What is important is that service-learning be a vehicle for broadening each student's experience and skills in learning approaches other than the one each prefers and tends to use most in academic studies. If only one other learning approach can be tried out in a project, a student can gain much.

Really effective learning occurs most frequently when all four learning approaches come into play, with the mix depending on the requirements of the situation. In fact, if a person were to utilize thoroughly the four learning modes in the sequence suggested by the experiential learning cycle, the learning would be greatly enhanced. Such ideal conditions rarely occur, but those working with service-learning should be aware of the potential.

To make full use of the total learning cycle a person needs to practice each learning approach by itself and in tandem with the others. Finally all four learning approaches can be linked in a conscious application of the experiential learning cycle. Most people seldom achieve such complete learning on a regular basis, if at all.

Since academic learning usually focuses on only one or two approaches — which one(s) depending on the field of study — the service-learning setting offers a golden opportunity for students to try out the other approaches. One outcome could be a general broadening of the learning capacity of the student. Another could be the students' incorporation of additional learning approaches into their academic studies. This could result in students' more fully internalizing — and therefore retaining — the skills and knowledge learned.

Each time the experiential learning cycle is completed and begun again, the second cycle will represent learning at a higher level.

That higher level will involve more complexity in the content being considered and in the process by which the content is dealt with at each stage of the cycle. *The use of the learning styles in the cycle is seldom neatly sequential as the model suggests. People move through different styles in different ways, in different sequences, and at different speeds.*

Anita, the physics major, provides an example. In high school she was curious about many things, including why some objects sometimes would float on the surface of water and sometimes would sink. She thought of many possible explanations. When her physics teacher introduced the concept of surface tension, Anita tried out this concept in a laboratory experiment during which she discovered how strong surface tension could be. Her fascination with this phenomenon led her to begin considering what some of the factors mights be that contribute to this characteristic of fluids.

Anita has completed one cycle of experiential learning and begun a second, more complex cycle. She began with a concrete experience — watching objects floating on the surface suddenly sink when the water was stirred. She wanted an explanation. She needed a concept to organize this experience. She needed, in short, a way to move from experience to concept. Reflective observation, in the form of guessing possible explanations, prepared her for the moment when her teacher presented the concept.

Anita might have come to this on her own had she gone through several learning cycles, but she could jump several cycles based on the experience of others. Nevertheless, she had found a way — reflective observation — to bridge the gap between her experience and a concept. Anita needed to experience this new concept at a more complex level. An experiment in the laboratory provided the bridge between concept and experience.

Since then she has proceeded through literally millions of learning cycles involving not only physics but also all other elements of her life. Unfortunately, because of the "help" several very good physics and math teachers have given her, she has been able to dispense with the stages of active experimentation and concrete experience as she proceeded to higher levels of complexity in these subjects. To become a fully functioning scientist, she will need to reinstate those learning modes to create a complete learning process.

To have complete learning Anita needs to bridge the gap between experience and concepts that explain that experience. Experiences devoid of concepts become repetitious and empty. Concepts with no real basis in experience become sterile and meaningless.

In the project involving industrial pollution in a residential area, Anita's preference for conceptualization is obvious, as is her lack of preference for interpersonal contact and experience. For her to extract significant learning from the project, she — or the project coordinator — will need to find a way for her to use the complete learning cycle. Doing so will increase the chances for a successful project and greatly enhance the learning from it and, quite possibly, from the classroom work in which she applies this newly acquired, integrated approach to learning.

Service-learning represents a unique opportunity for students to practice and develop learning approaches not being fully developed in the classroom. As seen with Anita, the benefits may include not only a different set of experiences but also tangible flowback to academic and even life work.

Roger and Janet need to have different kinds of experiences from those Anita and Bob had in order to complete their learning cycles. The pianist and the future librarian represent two versions of a similar condition. Roger prefers to be quiet and uninvolved with others as he enjoys his music. Janet likes to be involved with the senior citizens on a one-to-one basis but dislikes the complexities of advocacy. Both favor concrete experience and reflective observation, with Roger leaning toward the former and Janet tending toward the latter. They need to practice their skills in active experimentation if their projects are going to succeed and if they are going to extract higher learnings from their work. If they do not, their service-learning experiences will be merely repeats of other experiences and their learning will be limited to a confirmation of what they already know.

Our four students represent four of the more common patterns of preference for particular learning approaches. All could enhance their learning by tapping the other approaches and eventually linking them into a comprehensive learning style.

The first step in achieving this goal of a complete experiential learning cycle is to find out what is the student's preferred learning approach. This preference should be valued and not lost.

The next step is to identify the complementary or alternative learning approach, which may be done by looking across the learning cycle depicted in this chapter. For Anita, who favors abstract conceptualization, the primary complementary learning approach is concrete experience. For Bob, the active experimenter, it is reflective observation. For Janet, who prefers reflective observation, it is active experimentation. For Roger, who is highly involved in expressions of concrete experience, it is abstract conceptualization.

When the complementary learning approach is known, the students can be encouraged to practice and develop that approach through specific actions. Coordinators may make work assignments or design projects on the basis of the learning approaches that need to be accented. Both the student and the teacher or coordinator must make some creative effort, and the first tentative steps need to be carefully monitored.

When two complementary approaches are beginning to be used well, the student and coordinator can turn their attention to the other set of complementary learning approaches. A student who has worked on being more active while retaining the valuable skills of reflective observation can, at some point, focus more attention on either concrete experience or abstract conceptualization. Eventually the student completes the experiential learning cycle and has skills from all four approaches to use in repeating the cycle on a more complex level.

The educator's role can be instrumental in this process. Students are under pressure to learn so many things that they cannot always gain the perspective that enables them to take full advantage of their opportunities. The educator can use the experiential learning model as a diagnostic tool, then as a guide to improve the education process. It is not easy to plan service-learning experiences so that students will use complementary as well as preferred learning approaches, but educators who take the time and trouble to do so will see better service and richer learning.

NSIEE publishes this article in memory of Glen Gish. He was a management consultant specializing in action research and large organizational change in urban transit systems. He wrote this article with the support and guidance of his adviser, David A. Kolb, originator of the theory of the experiential learning cycle. Copies of The Learning Style Inventory *may be ordered from McBer Company, Training Resources Group, 1137 Newbury St., Boston, MA 02116.*

Assessing Learning

Urban Whitaker

This checklist provides a summary of standards for use by service-learning educators who take the assessment of learning seriously. For a complete discussion, see Assessing Learning: Standards, Principles, and Procedures *by Urban Whitaker, 1989, available from Council for Adult and Experiential Learning, 226 South 16th Street, Philadelphia, PA 19102. Reprinted with permission, pp. 9-10.*

Standards for Assessing Learning

The first five **standards** are directly relevant to the assessment process itself:

I. Credit should be awarded only for *learning*, and not for *experience*.

II. College credit should be awarded only for college-level learning.

III. Credit should be awarded only for learning that has a balance, appropriate to the subject, between theory and practical application.

IV. The determination of competence levels and of credit awards must be made by appropriate subject matter and academic experts.

V. Credit should be appropriate to the academic context in which it is accepted.

The other five **standards** are related to the administrative context in which the assessment and the award of credit occur:

VI. Credit awards and their transcript entries should be monitored to avoid giving credit twice for the same learning.

VII. Policies and procedures applied to assessment, including provision for appeal, should be fully disclosed and prominently available.

VIII. Fees charged for assessment should be based on the services performed in the process and not determined by the amount of credit awarded.

IX. All personnel involved in the assessment of learning should receive adequate training for the functions they perform, and there should be provision for their continued professional development.

X. Assessment programs should be regularly monitored, reviewed, evaluated, and revised as needed to reflect changes in the needs being served and in the state of the assessment arts.

Urban Whitaker retired in 1979 as Dean of Undergraduate Studies at San Francisco State University, where he is Professor of International Relations. He has served on several accreditation teams for the Western Association of Schools and Colleges and on the Board of Directors of the National Society for Internships and Experiential Education.

Finding Time for Classroom-Based Community Service

Kate McPherson

Practical ideas for K-12 teachers. Reprinted with permission from Enriching Learning through Service *by Kate McPherson, Project Service Leadership, Seattle, WA, 1989, pp. 44-45.*

SCHOOLS HAVE APPROACHED the issue of time in a variety of ways. Many teachers simply use a series of regular class periods for planning a project, choosing projects that can be accomplished during the regular class period. This is particularly easy for projects that will later be donated to the community. For example, a class could build toys for younger children in latchkey programs during the class day, and those could be donated at another time. Or they could sew art smocks for younger children. This is easily accomplished during and does not interrupt the regular school day.

Infrequent Blocks of Time. Planning can happen during the school period, while actual community experience takes place only occasionally. A teacher can use classroom time for students to plan a project such as a visit to a home for the elderly, using important communication and planning skills. Once a month or every other month, an extended project time is used for the actual visit to the community site.

Chunks of Time. Sometimes teachers, especially those who are encouraging "in the community" experiences, find it helpful to explore these options:

• *Team Projects.* Interdepartment or department teams can plan and implement a project utilizing combined class periods.
• *Half-Day Community Experiences.* A number of schools have a half day once a week when students are involved in commu-

nity service projects. Central Park West in New York uses this time-chunk approach. While students are involved in community service, teachers have time for planning.

• *Two Periods for a Community Service Project Class.* A number of teachers who teach courses that regularly involve students in the community have established a two-period block of time for their program. Students receive one year's credit for a semester's work. Dan Conrad, a social studies teacher in Minnesota, offers his community learning class as an option to senior social studies. That class takes two periods a day, and students receive a full year's credit for the two periods put in each semester. Contacts: Dan Conrad, Teacher, Hopkins High School, Hopkins, MN; and Craig Sheets, Teacher, John Marshall High School, 1123 First Street SW, Rochester, MN 55902.

• *One-Half Day Two Times a Week.* In a variation on the above, one-half day of the week is spent with students in the community, volunteering in a variety of community projects linked to curriculum. Another day of the week, students are in the regular classroom reflecting on and examining the effects of those experiences. Contacts: Patti Hanni, Teacher, Forest Ridge, 100-140th SE, Bellevue, WA 98006.

Large Chunks of Time. Some schools organize themselves so there is a block of community service time available for either a class or a whole school. Sometimes, that block is available during a winter study period or during spring. One school even provides that chunk of time during seniors' last semester. While there is no best way of organizing time, it is hard to have a high-quality service-learning project with regular involvement in the community *without* a time structure that enables students to get to a site, become involved in a meaningful contribution, and return without becoming fragmented in the process. It also is helpful for teachers to have the time needed to make contacts and to facilitate student reflection.

On Students' Time. Frequently, teachers will encourage direct community service by students on their own after school, before school, on weekends, or during vacations. Sometimes it's required; sometimes it's optional. But it is left entirely to the students to plan when and how they will complete their task.

Kate McPherson is Director of Project Service Leadership in Seattle, Washington.

A Survey of Campus Compact Institutions: Major Findings and Recommendations

The Faculty's Role in Integrating the Issues and Practice of Civic Participation with the Mission and Values of Postsecondary Education

In 1988 Presidents Donald Kennedy of Stanford University and David Warren of Ohio Wesleyan University undertook a survey of Campus Compact institutions to examine the faculty's role in the public service initiatives on these campuses. Compact institutions were asked to convene representative faculty groups to consider a series of questions related to current and potential faculty involvement — both in supporting student interest and participation in service work and in integrating this participation with academic study. Each campus was asked to submit a report of its group's responses to the survey questions.

A summary of institutional responses to this survey, critical issues identified and descriptions of exemplary policies, programs and practices are included in the survey report, "Integrating the Issues and Practice of Civic Participation with the Mission and Values of Postsecondary Education: The Faculty's Role," published by Campus Compact in the fall of 1989.

In the following pages Presidents Kennedy and Warren offer their sense of the major findings of the survey and recommend action steps for Campus Compact and its member institutions.

Major Survey Findings

1. *Faculty must be active supporters and promoters of student participation in public and community service — as advisors, participants, and role models.* Most responding institutions expressed a conviction that faculty must support and promote student participation in public and community service. Several institutions described structures which enable faculty to participate with students in bringing public service issues to the attention of campus communities, to advise and support students in their service efforts, and in some cases to work alongside students in service projects. Perhaps most encouraging was a conviction expressed by several institutions that faculty must be effective role models of active citizenship, and that institutions must develop means for encouraging, documenting and publicizing faculty service off-campus. In so doing, as noted by one institution in its report, colleges and universities "communicate to students that one's life is radically incomplete without active concern for the welfare of individuals, institutions and communities here and throughout the world."

2. *However, the most important role of faculty in this initiative is an instructional one: assisting students to learn from their service experience and connect this learning with academic study.* Public service activities, when combined with reflection and in-depth analysis, promote cognitive development, knowledge acquisition, and intelligent behavior. With effective faculty guidance, facilitation, and assessment, public service-based learning can enhance students' mastery of both disciplinary subject matter and liberal learning skills.

Linking students' public service with academic study was the most often identified role for faculty in supporting an institution's public service initiative. Responding institutions viewed this role as central both to institutional responsibilities to help students strengthen the impact of their service in the community, and to assist students in integrating service experience with academic reflection and critical analysis.

Nearly every reporting institution identified one or more courses through which faculty encourage or require volunteer service and include analysis of this experience in the curriculum. The content, structure and labels (e.g., internship, service learning, practicum, action research) of these courses vary widely. They are found across the curriculum representing liberal arts, applied and empirical science, engineering, and professional school subject matter.

3. The academic curriculum is a principal means for developing in students an understanding of the importance, traditions and critical issues related to social responsibility. Nearly every responding institution reported some attention to placing the issues of social responsibility and civic obligation within the curriculum. It appears that increasing interest in public and community service has stimulated curriculum development and instruction in at least three areas: leadership development; issues of social obligation, democratic citizenship, and the concept of community; action research and community problem solving. These initiatives include establishment of new degree requirements, curriculum development, and implementation of new academic programs.

At several institutions faculty and administrators are seeking ways to strengthen the citizenship role of their institutions by sharing the research interests and resources of faculty and students with community organizations. The rationale here is both philosophical and educational. These institutions seek means to contribute their research-oriented resources toward the solution of community problems. They wish also to teach students how to use research knowledge and skills for the public good, and to instill in them a commitment to do so as professionals and scholars following graduation.

There is an important intellectual issue here which must not be overlooked. The drive to integrate public service into the academic life of an institution must not focus solely on adding service internships to existing courses or on developing new, interdisciplinary courses on citizenship or social obligation. We must match our interest in these efforts with a commitment to articulate a rationale accepted by faculty for including such questions as the relationship of scholarly achievement to the common good, or whether knowledge can be extracted through social exchange and participation, in the organization of the curriculum. We must engage faculty in an intellectual debate on how public service relates to the core, academic mission of postsecondary education.

4. Resources and structures are necessary to provide administrative support, recognition, rewards and incentives for faculty who participate in and support students' public service, and who help students integrate service work and its related issues with academic study. Through this project we have learned of numerous and varied efforts by faculty within Campus Compact institutions to support students' service efforts, and make the academic curriculum a place in which students can reflect on their service experience and on the complexities of social responsibility. A few institutions have policies or programs in place to support faculty in this work, and a few others have embarked on creative initiatives to implement new policies. Several institutions have established central offices or public service centers which assist faculty in developing and instructing courses which connect public service learning and academic study. They have provided resources for faculty to engage in new curriculum design or to develop skills in facilitating critical reflection on service experience.

However, much more must be done. Survey responses are nearly unanimous in stating that strengthening of faculty participation in public service will depend significantly on the extent to which institutions can find ways to recognize, reward, and provide stronger incentives for their involvement — particularly in the areas of review, promotion, and tenure.

5. *Leadership and advocacy from presidents and chief academic officers are critical elements in successfully strengthening the faculty's role in public and community service.* The convening of faculty to consider the questions articulated for this project served to stimulate interest on several campuses. In a few instances these meetings produced greater faculty participation and implementation of new programs and policies. Presidents have stimulated their faculty to consider establishing public and community service learning as a graduation requirement. Presidents have helped identify resources for supporting faculty as they develop public service-oriented academic programs.

Conclusion

There is an increasing sense that faculty must play an expanded, stronger role in the public service initiative — to help students serve effectively and integrate their service experiences into their intellectual and personal development. Through this survey we have discovered that a number of faculty within our member institutions are engaged in this important work. However, we have also learned that in order to build and sustain faculty participation, presidents may have to move beyond advocacy and exhortation to focus institutional attention on the curricular and structural issues identified here and in the full report of the survey results.

Recommendations for Action

Obviously, there are many steps to be taken. Below we list recommendations for immediate action by Campus Compact and its member institutions. [*These recommendations are useful for any college or university committed to public service.*] For member institutions:

1. *Those institutions which have yet to contribute a response to the questions presented in this project should do so.* We need to hear the views of colleagues at campuses not represented in this report. What are your concerns related to the faculty role in the public service initiative? What programs and practices can you share with other institutions? The process of convening faculty groups to consider the important issues articulated through this project has been very positive and fruitful for those institutions that did respond, and will surely benefit other campuses.

2. *Every Compact institution should review and respond to the issues raised here and in the full report.* There is need for much more dialogue and debate on the critical issues that have surfaced through this project, especially the need for a clear definition of public service and a sound academic rationale for faculty participation. Attention must be directed at establishing a closer alignment between the goal of increased faculty involvement and traditional recognition, incentive and professional development systems.

3. *Every Compact institution should be encouraged to provide public recognition and rewards to faculty who actively participate in the institution's public service initiative — whether as involved citizens, advisors to student service projects, or as instructors who help students connect their service with academic study.* We need to recognize and support our faculty who are already involved now. They should be provided opportunities to share what they are doing and what they have learned with colleagues on campus. They need time and resources in order to get better acquainted with the communities in which students serve and to design and instruct new curricula. They need assistance in shedding the sense of marginal or "second class" status that sometimes accompanies scholarship which is applied to social problem-solving, instruction which encourages active learning in the community, and general good citizenship on campus and in the community.

For Campus Compact:

1. Make available innovative course and program descriptions, and relevant incentive policies and practices identified through this project, or through other national organizations, such as the Association of American Colleges and the National Society for Internships and Experiential Education.

2. Make available to member institutions faculty opportunities to learn about and develop curricula which relate to social obligation and which effectively link public service experience with classroom instruction. If courses which address civic involvement and social responsibility are to increase in number, faculty need opportunities to share what they are doing with colleagues within institutions and across institutional lines. In addition, if faculty are going to more readily include volunteer service in the curriculum, they need opportunities to learn how to stimulate and structure student reflection on these experiences and to link these reflections with classroom instruction. Supervising, assessing, and linking experience-based learning to subject matter content are skills not normally learned or practiced by faculty. Campus centers for teaching assistance do not normally employ staff skilled in this area. In order for faculty to develop these skills, it will be necessary to reach beyond campus and discipline-based faculty development resources, and offer workshops for faculty led by skillful and experienced service-learning educators.

3. Conduct a national curriculum development project to support the development and instruction of courses which connect public service with academic study.

4. Stimulate and support discussion across the country on the importance of linking public and community service with liberal arts education.

Thanks to Timothy Stanton of the Haas Public Service Center at Stanford University and Susan Stroud of Campus Compact.

PART I

Practical Issues and Ideas for Programs and Courses that Combine Service and Learning:

Community Issues and Tips

Using Students Effectively in Your Organization

Jane C. Kendall

A short guide for staffs of nonprofit, government, and business organizations. The terms "student" and "internship" are used in this chapter, but the suggestions here also relate to young people, adults, and older persons who are not in school — anyone who provides service through your organization and who wants to learn in the process. The examples are drawn from environmental organizations, but they are applicable to any nonprofit, public, or for-profit organization. Adapted from A Guide to Environmental Internships: How Environmental Organizations Can Utilize Internships Effectively, *Jane C. Kendall, National Society for Internships and Experiential Education, 1984, pp. 12-24, 31, 33, 35-39, 43-45.*

Clarifying Your Needs

BEGIN WITH THE GOALS of your organization. Outline your current needs. What are your work priorities for the next six months? The next year? What are your research needs? What "organizational" activities need attention — membership development, bookkeeping, newsletter, media work, fundraising, citizen education, films, market research, computers? What about research on area schools that can provide you with more students? Students are handling responsibilities related to these functions for organizations of all sizes. The critical factor is that the students' work should be important for the goals and current priorities of your organization. Otherwise, why invest your time or the student's?

Many organizations have found it useful to have students focus on specific projects that can be clearly defined and completed within the designated period of service. Listen to what some other staff members say:

We choose projects that are of limited duration and which provide a definite product at the end.
— Ken Bossong, Citizens' Energy Project

Internships are most effective when the interns are assigned to a specific project and have specific tasks.
— Fred Annand, North Carolina Nature Conservancy

By giving the intern responsibility for an entire project, from planning to implementation and evaluation, the sense of purpose to deliver a product of high quality becomes very strong.
— Marshall Murphy, Atlantic Center for the Environment

Defining the Tasks

Rod Coggin of the Chesapeake Bay Foundation says, "The organization must clearly define its needs and then pass that clear definition on to the intern, so the intern is not doing makeshift, spur-of-the-moment tasks." Before your recruit interns, write down:

1. the purpose of the project(s);
2. the tasks to be accomplished and the important parameters that define the tasks *as clearly as you possibly can*;
3. how well the project will need to be done in order for it to be useful to you;
4. the completion date needed;
5. the knowledge it will take to handle the responsibilities successfully;
6. the types of work skills and qualities it will take, such as the ability to write so the general public can understand it, to get along with volunteers, to listen carefully to citizens' concerns, to communicate well by phone, to grasp the political implications of a project; and
7. what a person will learn by doing this project.

As you talk with prospective interns, also be sensitive to the students' learning goals. You can often negotiate for special projects when a student has particular interests and skills to offer. It is *still* important for you to be sure the project fits *your* goals and current needs. Lurrie Pope of Rock Creek Park says, "I have learned that the intern who is most interested will perform the best."

What About Routine Work?

In many organizations, all staff help out with clerical and administrative tasks. It is appropriate for interns and volunteers to carry their weight and do their part like other staff, but:

> Provide interesting work, not just drudgery. It is very easy just to assign jobs that no one else wants to do. If that is done on a regular basis, the program will die.
> — Joan Fordham, International Crane Foundation

> If interns are seen as just low-paid staff, the two-way learning exchange is no longer taking place. When this happens, it is nearly always to the intern's disadvantage.
> — Marshall Murphy, Atlantic Center for the Environment

> Give them challenging work as well as routine work. If their work is integrated into the main research projects at EAF, the intern feels a sense of importance more strongly than if doing only clerical work.
> — Sandy Green, Environmental Action Foundation

Recruiting

Some organizations report they get their best interns through informal, word-of-mouth referrals and unsolicited applications. *To get good referrals, you must stimulate the natural grapevines available to you.* The avenues for attracting students who can really help your organization are all around you. Your time in tapping these channels is worth every minute invested because good contacts bring good interns. And good internships mean that other strong candidates will want to work for your organization. Some suggestions from staffs at other organizations:

1. Contact relevant departments at schools in your area. Don't forget the departments for journalism, public relations, English, graphics, communications, media, library science, education, business, marketing, accounting, political science, sociology, planning, and others related to particular functions in your organization. Look in catalogs, call the schools, visit the departments, talk to your friends and members who work at the schools. Check with the two-year colleges, secondary schools, middle schools, youth-serving

agencies such as 4H and the YM-YWCA, programs for retired persons, and others who have access to people anxious to learn and serve. As one director says:

> We were surprised that the university faculty were so anxious to help us identify qualified students. I had hesitated because I thought they would not take our needs seriously. Now we have these same faculty helping us with other projects, and they are looking for good students to work here next semester.

2. Ask your Board of Directors and your members to help you make contacts. Fred Annand of the North Carolina Nature Conservancy says, "We get referrals from faculty on our own Board and from our members. They can *really* help identify appropriate students because they know our needs and goals, they are committed to our work, *and* they know the students." Don't overlook such resources right at hand.

3. Send position descriptions to schools and other organizations (see above) in your area. Some organizations type up a one-page flyer describing their opportunities for students and volunteers.

Many colleges, universities, and high schools have programs that can publicize your opportunities across the campus. Send your position or project descriptions to these offices. A phone call or personal visit to the staff there can go a long way toward getting you the interns you need year after year.

The names of these centralized programs or offices vary: community service, internships, public service, experiential education, service-learning, cooperative education, career planning and placement, career services, field studies, professional practice, practicum, applied learning, and others. Some departments or divisions also have coordinators for field-based learning, internships, community service, volunteers, etc.

Remember: It's hard to recruit a qualified student until *you* define what "qualified" mean for the project or task at hand.

Be as clear as possible when recruiting. Make prospective interns completely aware of their duties and responsibilities before they are chosen! Also, make sure the intern and the school have all the information needed.... No surprises. Start on the right foot.

— Bill Beatty, Brooks Nature Center

How Many Interns or Volunteers?

Start slowly with a maximum of one or two interns or volunteers in a small organization at the beginning. Have a good experience, sharpen your supervisory skills, and then assess whether your organization can handle more. Several factors — the interns' skills, the nature and duration of the projects, space, other projects — will determine how many people you can successfully integrate into your organization at one time.

It is important to get a good idea, in advance, how many interns you can handle. Because interns [or volunteers] can require a great deal of supervision and because it is important for both you and the intern to get the most out of the experience, make sure your present staff has ample time to work with them. [Don't] add on more and more interns, thinking, "What great free help!" Rather, be selective and accept fewer people to be more effective.

— Robert Percival, Environmental Defense Fund

The Arrangements: Who Does What, When and Why?

The student or other service-learner, the supervisor, and the educational institution or other sponsoring organization all get involved in internships or other service-learning programs for the same reason — because these arrangements help them meet their goals. The beauty of a good internship or service-learning arrangement is that it's a "win-win-win" situation because all three parties benefit.

The particular goals of each party are different, though. It is *essential* for you and the other parties to clarify your expectations for the internship, and communicate those goals and assumptions to each other. The agreements you reach about the respective roles and responsibilities of each party should be written down. *The internship will be only as good as the clarity of these understandings between the three parties.*

The basis of a successful internship [or other service-learning arrangement] is a clear understanding of what is expected by each party in work assigned, duration, periodic planning and evaluation, and amount of supervision.

— Ann Kenworthy, Partners for Livable Places

Make sure the students understand what is expected, who they are responsible to, and that they have the support of your staff and of their school's staff.
— Dennis Reeder, Partners for Livable Places

When working with interns, supervisors can also develop their own learning objectives which they want to fit into the internship experience.
— Harold Wood, Friends of the Earth

If students are receiving academic credit or are participating in a school-sponsored program, talk with the faculty member or program staff to be sure you understand the school's goals and requirements. The student will need to establish learning objectives for the experience. Be aware of your role in helping to support and evaluate his or her progress toward these objectives.

Review your initial agreements periodically, and revise the roles and responsibilities if needed. The project may take longer than you expect, or you may discover additional talents the service-learner can offer on other projects. Be clear with the student and the school about any adjustments agreed upon during the internship.

Orientation and Supervision

See the other chapters in this section of the resource book for ideas on orientation and supervision. These topics are vitally important, so separate sections are devoted to them.

Three themes run through most staff members' comments about supervision of interns: (1) take time for supervision on a regular basis so you can anticipate problems early; (2) the more clearly you communicate your needs and expectations throughout the internship, the more you are going to get the work you need from the intern; and (3) identify one person who will be each intern's primary supervisor. After the initial period of intense supervision, you can decide how much supervision is necessary and appropriate by the intern's performance and the nature of the project.

Evaluation

Also see the other sections of this resource book on evaluation. Some tips from staffs of other organizations give you a summary of the most important things to keep in mind related to evaluation:

Don't wait until the last day to inform the intern of shortcomings or to give praise where deserved. Take time at regular, stated intervals to meet with the intern to see how things are going.
  — Harold Wood, Friends of the Earth

In addition to informal evaluations throughout the internship, we provide a written evaluation at the end. Success is based on the expectations laid out in writing at the beginning of the internship. For internships with tasks like trail maintenance, we judge performance on behaviors such as attendance, cooperation, and demonstrated competency in the task.
  — Susan Spitzer, The Nature Conservancy

Apply professional standards even if they're high for a student. It becomes a learning experience.
  — Gordon Binder, The Conservation Foundation

Both positive and negative feedback enable interns to measure their performance against the standards you set. The most obvious factor to evaluate is the quality of the work. Equally important are less tangible factors such as the degree to which the intern assumes and handles responsibility, evidence of increased maturity, and demonstrated confidence in dealing with clients.
  — Massachusetts Internship Office,
    "A Guide for Intern Sponsors"

You may be asked later to provide references about the intern's work. Keep a permanent file on each person. Document performance, weeks worked, and responsibilities. You can be an important supporter of the intern's later career contributions to the field.

If the internship does not seem to be working out after several full efforts on your part and the student's, either party has the right to terminate it sooner than the scheduled completion date *if* the problems and decision are communicated directly with the other party. Be sure to communicate problems to the faculty advisor or other program representative, too.

Establishing Ongoing Relationships with the Schools

This section will use "schools" to refer to colleges, universities, and K-12 schools. (While the language used relates to schools and students, the *principles* outlined here for maintaining good relationships with sources of service-learners also relate to programs for retired persons, young people and adults who are not in school, employees who are doing community service, and others who are not students.)

Why is it important to establish and nurture these ongoing relationships?

1. The schools are anxious to maintain relationships with organizations that are doing meaningful work which can offer their students (or other clients) good opportunities to learn.
2. It is one of the best ways to ensure that your intern or volunteer program will continue and be successful.
3. The schools can help in deciding which of your projects are most suitable for student interns.
4. Recruiting and selecting interns will become easier as you have trusting relationships with faculty and program directors knowledgeable about your organization.
5. Schools can help students clarify their learning goals. Working toward intentional learning goals and having opportunities for critical reflection on the service experience can increase a student's motivation and improve his or her service. Academic credit can also mean that the student can be more flexible about financial arrangements.

Maintaining good relationships. After you establish relationships with selected schools, programs, and individuals, they can help you select projects and interns year after year if you nurture the relationships to keep them alive and healthy. Staff members at other organizations say:

Correspond regularly and thank the schools for providing the interns.
— Ken Bossong, Citizens' Energy Project

Keep them informed about projects and changes in your program. Provide feedback about interns from that school.
— Joan Fordham, International Crane Foundation

A good experience on the part of an intern is the best way of establishing sustained relationships.
— Gordon Binder, The Conservation Foundation

Look for opportunities other than internships to work together on shared concerns. The faculty members also help with our research and legislation. The internships helped us establish ties with the schools. Now we get multiple benefits from their participation. Volunteer to be a guest lecturer. Keep the schools on your mailing list. Invite the faculty to official and social functions.

— David Zahller, National Park Service

Remember that the schools need what you have to offer — important goals and meaningful projects that provide excellent opportunities for their students to learn from firsthand experience. So take the time to talk with them and follow up. It's one of the best investments you can make.

What's Next?

After each internship, reflect on the endeavor. What did you learn from the experience? Did it help your organization? What was good about the approach you used in defining the intern's responsibilities, recruiting, orienting, supervising, and evaluating? What will you change about your approach next time?

Look at your internship program as an evolving resource that you can adjust to fit the changing needs of your organization. What new initiatives could interns or other service-learners help you with in the coming year?

Jane Kendall is Executive Director of the National Society for Internships and Experiential Education.

Orienting, Training and Supervising Students: From the Agency's Perspective

edited by Marilyn Mecham

Three short guides to orienting, training and supervising students or other service-learners who work in your organization. The service-learners are referred to as "students" in this chapter, but the tips provided here also relate to others who serve and learn in your agency — youth who are not in school, adults, etc. Adapted from "Orienting Student Volunteers," "Training Student Volunteers," and "Supervising Student Volunteers," edited by Marilyn Mecham, National Center for Service-Learning (NCSL), ACTION. These three guides are from a series of 14 concise guides published by NCSL and now available from the National Society for Internships and Experiential Education, 3509 Haworth Drive, Suite 207, Raleigh, NC 27609.

Orienting Students

Orientation vs. Training

ORIENTATION INTRODUCES STUDENTS to community or public service in general and to the specific project in which they will be participating. This process should prepare them for the first day on the job or the first experience as an agency staff member. The overall goal of orientation is to insure that participants have some idea of what to expect and how to function, and thus to avoid any major mistakes during the first few hours or days on the job. But orientation is *not* a substitute for the more detailed and specialized process of training, in which specific job skills are imparted in a step-by-step process.

An Orientation Agenda

The following items need to be covered in most orientation sessions:
- the purpose, goals, and structure of the organization or agency receiving the students;
- a profile of the people acquiring the agency's services;
- the role of service-learners in the organization or agency;
- a description of key agency roles;
- what the students can expect to happen on the first day;
- to whom the students report;
- whom to notify if there are any problems;
- the identity of staff members and co-workers.

Types of Orientation

The preparation of students for community service may take place with individuals or with groups. Such sessions may be part of a lengthy interview or a walk-through of the student's job and role at the work site. They may also take the form of traditional group meetings or new volunteers with their supervisor or volunteer coordinator; such meetings are well-suited to students because they may be more comfortable in the company of other students. But some students will probably not be able to fit the orientation schedule and thus a back-up system — interview, handouts, a movie or slides — will be necessary to accommodate these students individually.

The Planning Process

Whether the orientation consists of group or individual sessions, the steps described below will help insure an effective preparation for service.

1. Assess the students' orientation needs. Find out what the students already know about the agency and what they think is important for them to learn. If it is not possible to personally question each new participant, study reports from past orientations to get ideas.

It may also be useful to ask the students to list everything they want to know before they begin their jobs. The answers will provide ideas for the orientation agenda. The same question may be asked of the agency and school staff members who will be involved with the students. Sometimes this needs assessment can be included in the orientation itself. Having the student group articulate their needs can help insure that the orientation agenda is on target.

2. Translate the information from the needs assessment into orientation goals. The following are examples:

- "By the end of the session, all students will have a clear understanding of what might happen on their first day on the job."
- "All participants will know where and to whom they are to report."
- "All students will be able to act in accordance with the posted rules for health and safety."

It may be helpful to rewrite these goals as precise objectives in order to indicate more exactly what the orientation sessions must include. For example, the first goal listed above might include the following specific objectives:

- "The participants will have talked with an experienced service-learner to learn about the first day on the job, and will have voiced their own expectations of the first day and received feedback from others. Their questions about the first day will have been asked and answered."

Making general goals into more precise objectives thus enables the planners of the orientation to understand exactly what kinds of activities and resources may be needed and to estimate more closely the amount of time required and the logistics, if any, that may be involved.

3. Determine methods for reaching the goals and objectives. Select a variety of methods of presentation and fit these to the points to be made. For example, the goal of "knowing what to expect the first day" could be presented via a lecture, a role-play or a group discussion. However, it is good general advice to avoid overusing the lecture format and to provide time for participants to absorb and question material rather than merely to receive it passively.

4. Determine the orientation schedule. If the agenda is too long, consider using different presentation methods, including written handouts and self-examinations that can be studied or completed later. Students usually have constraints on their time due to paid employment, class schedules, study time, and examinations. Schedule their orientations carefully after checking with student leaders and school officials. And be sure to consider the needs of older students as well (family, childcare, employment, etc.).

5. Assemble orientation resources. Select staff members to assist in the orientation. Involve as many people as possible so that key roles and viewpoints will be represented. Arrange for pleasant physical facilities, check lighting and seating arrangements. Duplicate handouts and other printed materials. Make sure that all the people involved in the presentation are clear about their roles and the goals to be accomplished.

6. *Invite the volunteers.* Check and double-check publicity for the training sessions. Clearly indicate its purpose. Tell everyone when and where it will be and how long it will last. Indicate any preparation required before the session or follow-up work to be done afterward. Ask the students to notify you if they are unable to attend.

7. *Conduct the orientation.* Begin and end on time. Keep in mind, and impress upon the students, that orientation is the process of familiarizing them with the organization so they can function on the first day on the job. It involves presenting in detail the nature of the organization, the students' place in it, and the basic roles, regulations, and expectations. But orientation is *not* imparting specific job skills — that important task will be done at another time.

8. *Evaluate the orientation.* Like other aspects of service-learning programs, orientation can be made more effective through evaluation by participants. A short evaluation at the close of the session, followed by a similar one six months later, can be a valuable tool for revising or upgrading orientation procedures.

9. *In planning subsequent sessions,* be sure to tailor orientation to the specific needs of the students, including their level of experience, type of work to be done, amount of responsibility required on the job, and expected methods of supervision available. Factor into these plans any changes in student attitudes, skills, or interests that you may have discovered since the last orientation was planned. Whatever the specific situation, individualize the orientation to help students feel wanted, welcome, and valued.

Student Contracts

Part of the orientation process is the completion of a student-supervisor contract. This form specifies the expectations of both the service-learner and the supervisor. It is completed after the student has been assigned to a placement but prior to his or her beginning work. Such contracts reiterate the job description and may be seen as the final version of the description of the student's role.

The exact format of the contract will depend on the mutual needs of the two parties, but it is likely to include the following items:

- the student's name, address, and telephone number;
- the supervisor's name, title, address, and telephone number;
- the work schedule agreed upon by the student and supervisor;
- the exact duties to be performed by the student and the specific objectives to be met in the performance of those duties (See other chapters of this resource book that discuss the importance of periodic renegotiation of duties.);
- the nature of the supervision to be provided: weekly meetings, daily debriefings, monthly reports, etc.;
- the nature and schedule of formal evaluations;
- detailed instructions and procedures regarding missed assignments or other changes from expectations, and reasons for justified absences;
- an indication of the student's commitment — the length of time he or she is expected to remain on the job.

Student-supervisor contracts are important in clarifying the mutual expectations of the agency, school, and student. They often help all three parties to formulate and agree on realistic expectations. Such contracts also make clear to the students the nature of formal evaluation and the steps leading up to it.

An Orientation Checklist for Educators, Agency Personnel and Students

1. Does your orientation give participants an understanding of what the agency is and how it operates?
2. Do the students know the people with whom they will work? the key agency staff members? the neighborhood in which they will be working? the larger community and its needs?
3. Do participants understand how their projects relate to the agency's overall goals and objectives?

Training Students

Training is imparting specific job skills to students and other service-learners. This key activity may take place before they begin their placements or while they are on the job. Either way, the goal is to provide them with the skills and leadership that will enable them to make a positive contribution and gain the maximum reward from their community service experiences.

Coordinators of student community service programs may or may not be personally involved in training activities, depending on

Developing School-Agency Relationships

What goes into developing good working relationships between schools and agencies? According to one explanation, such relationships are based on the sharing of emotionally charged experiences. For students, the service experience is often the most exciting, stimulating educational experience they have ever undergone. Thus, it's easy to see that these can be the basis for good relationships between the schools and agencies involved. It's equally easy to understand that poorly designed programs, uncaring students, unclear expectations, or uninvolved faculty can all create negative relationships that will destroy a program over time. From the practical point of view, then, the key to developing good school-agency relationships is having clear criteria for the performance and evaluation of all parties involved in the program. When we look at successful service-learning programs, we see well-structured, clearly defined programs with explicit expectations for all parties. Most of the steps that need to be taken to develop such relationships are during the planning stages of such programs, prior to the time that students actually begin their placements. Time spent on these issues during the early stages of a program will eliminate the need for time-consuming corrective steps later on. *Excerpted from "Developing School-Agency Relationships," edited by Ralph G. Navarre, ACSW, Whitewater, Wisconsin, for the National Center for Service-Learning, ACTION, pp. 1, 3. This is from No. 15 in a series of practical NCSL monographs on service-learning. This series is now available from the National Society for Internships and Experiential Education.*

the size of the program, the nature and location of the placements, the availability of staff resources, and the program's relationship to the cooperating agencies. But even when they cannot take part personally, volunteer coordinators will want to make sure it is being done effectively, since it is through adequate training that students are kept involved and enthusiastic.

A well-trained service-learner will be knowledgeable about the program's objectives, will understand the role of students in the program, and will be equipped with the specific skills to make the assignment a positive and personally rewarding one. This competence is achieved through a sound training program, the objectives of which are to involve students in their placements quickly, sustain their interest, and develop their abilities prior to beginning their job assignments. Training takes time, but the time and effort invested in it are well spent.

The Training Process

In general, training students requires agency staff to do the following:

1. Assess the training needs of the students and confirm that they have the basic skills they claim to have; this will help avoid training them in skills they already possess.

2. Establish training goals by stating what the students are expected to be able to do at the end of the training. Make sure they understand these expectations.

3. Translate training goals into specific learning objectives that describe in detail what the students will be required to do and the level of accomplishment that will be required of them.

4. Select training methods and staff that are appropriate, utilizing trainers who are experienced in working with students. Many excellent training manuals are available and may be consulted for training procedures.

5. Set a realistic but flexible schedule for training sessions.

6. Plan training logistics carefully — physical facilities, required equipment, audio-visual and other materials, etc.

7. Invite the participants. Notify them of the time and place far enough in advance for them to adjust their schedules. Ask them to notify you if they cannot attend and schedule alternate sessions if necessary.

8. Conduct the training, keeping the activities practical and specific.

9. Evaluate the results of the training sessions and monitor the feedback you receive from participants. Be sure to find out how many of the trainees can actually do what you want them to do as a result of the training, and consider how you will deal with those who need more skills.

10. Avoid overtraining in order to set realistic expectations for students. Their role at the work site and the quality of work will be influenced by the expectations they develop during the training sessions.

Additional Training

Plan a second training session after the students have been on the job for 4-6 weeks. Remember that some may be overwhelmed by all the new information received at the first training session, while others will need and want more depth of training after becoming familiar with the people and procedures at the job site. This second stage of training may often be more important than the first in bringing student performance up to standards.

Training Criteria

A good training program not only teaches participants new skills; it also incorporates new knowledge and understanding into an increased awareness of self and others. Regardless of the specific skills to be imparted, successful training sessions may be characterized as:

- *Organized.* Training sessions are well planned while remaining flexible in allowing for expression of individual ideas on the part of trainers and participants.
- *Clear.* Trainers are direct in their presentations and articulate in stating objectives. Activities are efficient and educationally sound.
- *Challenging.* Successful training challenges participants with concepts, materials, and ideas but does not overwhelm them. Content and pedagogy are geared to the needs and experience level of participants.
- *Supportive.* Participants have ample opportunities to share experiences and to develop professional contacts. The environment encourages all present to ask questions, discuss problems and successes, and engage in problem-solving activities.
- *Diverse.* Presentations and other activities provide a variety of learning methods and changes of pace and location.
- *Respectful.* Trainers and participants work to build a sense of community and mutual respect which recognizes and utilizes individual differences.
- *Enjoyable.* Formal and informal activities allow for interaction, humor and enthusiasm.
- *Realistic.* Trainers present only the amount of material that can be thoroughly discussed and absorbed. They are vigilant in looking for signs of overload or burnout and adjust presentations accordingly.

- *Inclusive.* Trainers endeavor to involve all participants in training activities and to allow for individual differences in planning how this is to be done.
- *Timely.* Trainers begin and end sessions on time and negotiate schedule changes with participants.

Training Methods

The content of training sessions focuses on the specific skills, knowledge, and attitudes that students will need in order to do their specific jobs well. In selecting training methods, remember that people learn best through some kind of "doing" activity, and less well through lectures. Effective training methods for service-learners include:

1. *Skill-building:* simulations and other exercises that help students practice the skills they need.

2. *Problem-solving:* brainstorming and other techniques for reaching concensus or removing barriers to effective performance.

3. *Information-sharing:* lectures, media presentations, field trips, workshops, panel discussions, printed handouts, etc.

On-the-Job Training

Although many student needs can be met through pre-service training, on-the-job training remains an important part of many programs. Together, these two types of training allow students to continue to develop their skills over time and to take on added independence and responsibility as they demonstrate increased proficiency. On-the-job training has several benefits: it allows for a planned introduction and progression of training in relation to the specific work being done; involves students in self-assessment of their own skills and interests; legitimizes adult feedback and direction as important parts of the program; exposes students to work before requiring involvement or proficiency; provides models of good performance; provides a record of student growth and learning; allows new tasks and responsibilities to be added in response to changes in work plans or student interests and motivation.

Planning Steps

The following steps may be useful for developing on-the-job training programs:

1. Define tasks specifically by developing detailed job descriptions and service-learning agreements that specify what students hope to accomplish, activities to be carried out, and how student accomplishments are to be demonstrated.

2. Provide self-assessment tools with which students can assess their own readiness to perform each task.

3. Define the level of participation required or expected of each student. This can be determined mutually by the student and supervisor, using the student's self-assessment and other information about student motivation, skill, and interest.

- *Level 1: Observation Only.* Students observe others performing tasks, then discuss results and ask questions of the workers.
- *Level 2: Joint Performance of Tasks.* Students and supervisors or other staff members perform tasks as a team, then discuss student involvement and provide students with feedback on performance.
- *Level 3: Working Alone.* Students perform tasks independently. Supervisors or other staff members may observe students at work or review performance after tasks have been completed, then discuss work with students and provide feedback.

Training Resources

Coordinators of service-learning and volunteer programs can use a variety of training resources from the community and school. Experts in health, housing, literacy and many other fields may be excellent trainers, especially after being briefed on the special interests and needs of the students to be trained. High school and college faculty members may also provide training and assist in the design of training sessions. Students who have formerly been associated with community service programs may be willing to assist in training and to share their own experiences with new volunteers. The team approach to training, in which two or more persons with different but complementary experiences or skills make presentations to the group, can also be useful.

Other training resources include pencil-and-paper exercises, audio-visual materials, work simulations and handouts which provide background information or reflect desired attitudes, knowledge or skills. The many excellent training books and workbooks on the market may provide a rich source of materials to supplement those created especially for the specific training purposes of your program.

Training Checklist for Educators, Agency Personnel and Students

1. Does the training program provide the skills that students will need in order to be effective?

2. Does the training include a presentation of the students' role in relation to the professional staff of the agency and/or school? Is there adequate time for students to discuss and understand this relationship?

3. Will additional training be necessary once the project or placement has begun?

4. Are there special characteristics that the students should be aware of in working with the users of the agency's services? How are these needs addressed in the training program?

5. What is the total amount of time devoted to training? Are the students put to work soon after the training has been completed, so they will not forget what they have learned?

Supervising Students

The purpose of supervision is to provide guidance, encouragement, support, and occasional on-the-job training, while not unduly constraining or limiting the students' activities or imaginations. Supervision may be viewed as a process of defining and maintaining effective work relationships.

How Much is Required?

Students do not necessarily need either more or less supervision than do other volunteers. The amount required will depend, not primarily on age, but on the nature of the work being done and the particular skills of the individuals involved. Students usually work most effectively in an atmosphere of "unstructured structure," wherein the limits of their roles and responsibilities are carefully defined but a fair amount of flexibility is allowed.

Some volunteer jobs require little supervision, while others involve special situations in which more, and more consistent, supervision is needed. It is likely that students will need greater than average amounts of supervision in situations where:

1) volunteers do not have others nearby to work with or learn from;

2) supervisors are expected to evaluate the participants' performance;

3) placements are highly unstructured and thus require considerable personal judgment and minimum routine.

The Two Cycles

It is customary to think of supervision as a one-time-only process of explaining performance standards and overall job expectations before, or when, students begin an assignment. Equally important, however, is the second cycle of supervision, in which students receive feedback on their performance and progress. This type of communication usually takes place while the work is being done or after it has been completed, and may be as important, or even more important, to students than was the initial supervision — even if it is not particularly important to the organization for whom the students are working.

Who Provides Supervision

The responsibility for supervising students must be clearly established; otherwise they may receive too much, too little, or inconsistent supervision, all of which may produce confusion or anxiety on the job. If possible, students may be assigned supervisors at the beginning of their training period, who remain available to them in an advisory capacity throughout the placement. If students are working in your agency as part of a course, supervision should be the shared responsibility of the teacher or service-learning educator and the agency.

Various supervisory systems may be established to enable more experienced students to supervise less experienced ones. Sometimes, groups of students who work the same schedules can be supervised by a student "team leader." Whatever system is chosen, the basic goals of supervision are: (1) to meet the needs of those who use your agency's services, and (2) to affirm the value of the service-learning experience for the students.

Supervision Formats

Each of the following types of supervision has been frequently used in student community service programs and may be adopted to a variety of different situations, depending on the needs of the program and the students.

1. Group meetings. This form of supervision provides opportunities for students to meet with one another and with their supervisor. For best results it should begin within the first two weeks of the placement and continue at regular intervals throughout the placement period. Not all students will take advantage of such meetings, but most will appreciate the chance to talk with their supervisors as part of a group. Indeed, these meetings may be the single most important method of enabling students to make the most of their experiences and to stay involved with the agency or organization. Group meetings can also be used as regular training sessions, to introduce new materials, techniques and skills. This form of supervision works especially well if the supervisor cannot be at the work site, or if the students work on a one-to-one basis at widely scattered locations and thus seldom see one another or their supervisor.

2. On-site supervision. In this format, supervisors are physically present where the students work and can provide daily feedback, instruction and direction. This is the most time consuming form of supervision.

3. Pre-work meetings. Here, the supervisors and students meet early on each day. Expectations and assignments may be discussed, as well as problems and obstacles to the work, and questions may be raised and answered. This form of supervision can be used effectively with both individuals and groups, and can be combined with post-work debriefings (see below).

4. Post-work debriefings. This allows supervisors to meet with their students after each day's work has been completed to provide feedback, answer questions, and help them appraise what has occurred and plan for the future. This effective form of supervision is equally useful with individuals and with groups.

5. Daily reports. This is effective in conjunction with phone calls and/or regular meetings. Each student completes a daily written evaluation; the supervisor reviews these and uses them as the basis for future discussions. Daily reports are often a valuable resource for teachers or supervisors who must make formal evaluations of student learning, e.g., at the end of a course.

6. Phone calls. Supervisors who are unable to give personal supervision telephone students to provide direction and encouragement, and to assess student needs. Although telephone calls are not enough by themselves, they do provide immediate contact and can be combined effectively with weekly or monthly group meetings.

7. Student request. In this form of supervision, students operate relatively independently and may request supervision as needed. This type of supervision is appropriate only for very experienced people with good judgment, whose placements require minimal supervision.

8. ...*And one to avoid — Crisis intervention.* In this type of (non) supervision, students request a supervisor's help only when problems arise. This is seldom an effective form of supervision and is *not* recommended. If used as a last-resort method in the absence of supervisory staff, it should be replaced as soon as possible with one of the acceptable forms listed above.

Depending on the supervision needs of students, two or more of these supervision formats can be combined to provide the best possible guidance, encouragement and support. Faculty members may supervise students, either on site or from the vantage point of school or college. Experienced service-learners may help supervise less experienced ones. Agency staff members who work in close proximity to students may offer supervision and provide feedback.

A Supervision Checklist for Educators, Agency Personnel and Students

1. Does our method of supervision provide continuing feedback to and from students?
2. Are we in touch with both clients' and students' questions and problems as they arise?
3. Do the students feel restricted by their supervisors, or do they have an adequate sense of freedom and responsibility?
4. Do the students consider that they have too much supervision, too little, or about the right amount?
5. Do the supervisors relate well to the students? Have they been trained to work with students of the age and experience levels of those they supervise?

Supervision Forms

Supervision forms can help you keep track of supervision issues. A second reason for developing supervision forms is to provide uniform information on all students for school officials. Such forms will vary depending on the number and type of students involved, the type of placements, the methods of supervision, and the administrative needs of agencies and schools. It is important that schools receive copies of supervision forms promptly and that students are apprised of any information that may affect their progress. School officials also need to establish rules that guarantee students access to supervision records, since these may be important sources of information used in official recommendations and evaluations.

The Role of the Agency Supervisor

William R. Ramsay

Bill Ramsay examines the characteristics of students working in agencies and several structures for supervising them. He suggests functions and approaches that are part of effective supervision. The terms "internship" and "field experience" are used here as generic labels for students' learning through productive service experiences in public or private organizations. Reprinted with permission from Implementing Field Experience Education, *ed. John S. Duley, New Directions in Higher Education, Jossey-Bass, No. 6, Summer 1974, pp. 45-54.*

A FEW YEARS AGO, a law student completing his final report on an internship project in legal services remarked to his agency supervisor, "You know, the way I write this report will not just make a difference between an A and a B in a course, it will make a difference in the lives of people." This student was standing on the bridge between academic studies and the world of reality. Assisting him in crossing this bridge and seeing the view from its span was an agency supervisor. Supervisors of students in field experience situations are special kinds of educators. Typically, they are professionals in their fields and have other supervisory responsibilities.

This discussion is limited to specific opportunities for and methods of supervising students, rather than supervisory techniques in general. Certainly, basic tenets of good supervision apply to the use of students in work situations as well as to regular employees. Different objectives, however, and differences between students and nonstudents require special approaches in supervising field experience. This paper examines the characteristics of student workers; the types of structures for supervising student field experience are noted; supervisory functions are suggested; and the potentials of good supervision are summarized.

It is assumed for purposes of this discussion that productive work is a factor in the field experience situation. The amount of productive work will vary according to the structure used and the objectives of the particular program; however, implicit in a discussion of supervision is the expectation of some product or service. The characteristics of students, therefore, are discussed in terms of the possibilities and limitations of students as staff, an assumption which should be recognized by a supervisor both for effective staff utilization and for greatest learning.

Characteristics of Students

One rather obvious quality of students as staff is their short-term availability. Internships or other field experience situations generally range from one month to one year. This time factors has important implications for planning effective programs. It must be possible to accomplish the tasks assigned within the time limits of the arrangement. A schedule of progress must be concentrated in a much shorter period than would normally be the case with other employment. Furthermore, the student's short-term involvement and perception of time in general is important in terms of his or her own expectations and attitudes. What seems like a short time to a supervisor relative to other forms of employment seems often like a long time to the student who is used to thinking in much smaller increments of time. One of the problems resulting from these different perceptions is related to expected results. Students tend to think they can accomplish more in a short time than they can. Supervisors may err on the other side, thinking they can perform less than they can. If students are encouraged toward unrealistic expectations of accomplishment, their experience will end in frustration. On the other hand, if not enough expectation is built into the program, an opportunity for stretching the student to apply his utmost resources may have been lost.

Another characteristic of students is their orientation toward impact. Students desire a personal involvement and are very much concerned with being able to "make a difference." This desire for impact is a powerful motivating force and can be used by good supervision in place of the traditional motivating tools of salary, promise of advancement, benefits, and position. Students are concerned with compensation or other forms of support, but these may not be as major when the students as graduates are considering regular employment. It is therefore especially important for supervisors to encourage personal involvement and to help associate student efforts with results. Realistic goals against which achievement can be measured can be very helpful in meeting the student's needs to see the results of effort. Interpretation is also essential to help the student see the relationships between his effort and the efforts of others toward longer range goals of the agency or program.

An attitude often found among students, perhaps reflecting their orientation toward impact, is the feeling that "no one will really listen to me." Experience with many student work and service situations indicates that this is not nearly so often the case in reality as it may seem to the student. A student who thinks no one will listen may not speak up, or when she encounters first difficulties in suggesting what she considers new ideas, she retreats with the defense that she knew no one would listen. This issue of assumed or real barriers presents special problems with student workers, since their commitment is toward short-range objectives and they want a personal involvement in results.

Another characteristic of students as staff is their relative freedom. Partly because they are involved for short periods of time, they are free from the responsibilities of longer range interest. They can be used for short-term projects in many cases more effectively than can longer term employees because they can devote full time and attention to one task. Students are thus able to function at a great variety of levels in an organization and do not need to be restricted to the hierarchies of an organization chart. One supervisor observed that his students served as a form of media, carrying information from various levels of the organization to other levels, in a way which communication channels could not accomplish. Students are not restrained by experience. Lack of experience limits what they can do, but it also provides an opportunity for a fresh look and a new approach. As one student expressed, "I haven't learned yet what can't be done." Students can afford to make mistakes and therefore to take risks that persons with longer term employment could not or would not take. Because they are students they are excused for mistakes and the results can often be handled with a minimum of disruption. Recognition of this opens up a wider vista for potential assignments and may take students into areas that can be better served by this form of staff assistance than by any other.

Another important characteristic of good field experience programs is that students have educational goals as well as service goals. This dual purpose can add important dimensions to students' usefulness and affects supervision. Because of educational goals, they tend to undertake tasks with a questioning attitude rather than simply carrying out instructions. This approach can be considered a nuisance but also can be vital to certain types of assignments. Students may bring to their work situations a greater inquisitiveness and desire for understanding than is often present in other workers. Students are often concerned with meaning and have a broad interest in the implications of actions and programs. Students also represent potential channels for the agency's access to information, technical assistance, and other resources of the university, college or school with which they are associated. These can be used by a supervisor in enhancing both productivity and learning. All of these characteristics will not apply to all situations, but a recognition of the special circumstances of students can strengthen their value to the agency.

Structures

Agencies use a variety of structures for students who work with them as part of a field service experience. Several of these are mentioned briefly here to indicate some of the different supervisory situations which result. Perhaps the most often used structure for off-campus experiences is simply the traditional position in an organization. The student is "hired" as an employee and shows up on an organization chart as an intern, assistant, or some other such term. Supervision of students in such positions follows traditional methods, using job descriptions, office procedures, and the usual set of relationships with other employees. Berea College uses its 1400 students as its basic source of staff assistance, and every college department, academic and otherwise, is also a student work department utilizing students. Students work and learn in a great variety of assignments from typing to computer programming and from weaving to teaching adult literacy. Most colleges have some employment programs for students, but few are designed and supervised as field experience.

In a second type of structure the student might be termed an "honored guest." In these cases he is generally in a nonproducing situation where his main functions are to observe and prepare academic reports. Supervision in these cases is generally limited to arranging schedules for orientation and seeing that these are followed and that some information and understanding is in fact passed on.

Another internship structure gives the student the role of special assistant. He holds a position, but generally it is outside the usual personnel structures. A student may be an assistant to a city manager for a period or an aide to a legislator. Generally he receives highly personalized supervision, and the main benefit derived is his association with a professional of high caliber. If care is not taken in this situation, the student may end up being an errand runner with little planning or progress toward objectives.

A project is the basis of a fourth structure. In this case the student is given a task with specific objectives which can be accomplished within the time period of the experience. Supervision in the form of planning and direction is called for in the early stages of such an approach. A reporting system is important here, and some guidance is needed to see that time is not wasted and objectives are being met. In the most effective project arrangements, the student becomes largely self-supervised within the structure established.

Any one of these or other structures may be used effectively, depending on the particular situation of the agency involved and the educational relationships. In general, the project approach is considered superior in terms of actual accomplishment and learning and it requires less day to day supervision than the position approach. Careful planning is especially important. An example of this approach was used by the Training and Technology Project (TAT) of Oak Ridge Associated Universities. With the assistance of the universities a group of students were selected and assigned to seek out and collect information on graduates of the manpower training program of TAT. Students were trained in interview techniques and given assistance in locating graduates. They were dispatched to the points in the country where most graduates had found employment. Using a predeveloped system of forms, they collected information and sent them in to the central office. At the same time students pursued related study projects of their own on which they were required to report at the end of the period. In three months' time the students were able to collect a significant amount of data for an effective report on the status of graduates of this training program. In addition they prepared reports on their own individual studies and had seminars with university faculty assigned to each area. The nature of the supervision was different from that normally found in a typical supervisor-employee relationship. Once started, the initiative passed largely to the student rather than being retained by the supervisor.

Supervisor's Dual Role

Regardless of the structure used, the agency supervisor has a double role in relation to students engaged in field experience. He or she must see the student as both worker and learner. The supervisor's special contribution to the student's development is in helping the student relate through the service or work to the real world. This means holding the student to productive endeavor even when it is difficult and even when the results are imperfect. Supervisors know that they must deal with imperfect situations. They must often make decisions with lack of full information and choose among undesirable alternatives. Action is unavoidable and work must be tested against the criterion of usefulness, not simply satisfying an academic requirement. This special discipline is part of labor. The teaching function of the supervisor is primarily to interpret. The ability to relate actual individual experience to the experience of others and to models, theories, and information learned in the classroom does not develop automatically. The supervisor plays a critical role in helping the student bridge the distance between the world of action and the work of reflection. In general, supervisors are responsible for some output in terms of product or service. They must see that the objectives of the organization are met and that the work under their supervision is directed toward that end. However, the student is an end in himself, and success is measured in part by his or her development. The supervisor must, therefore, integrate the educational needs of the student and the production needs of the task for effective learning and service.

Steps in Supervision

Absolutely basic to all good field experience situations is effective *planning*. The position, project, or other form of assignment should be carefully defined, and all parties should have a clear understanding about what is expected in terms of both productivity and educational growth. The supervisor's job is to apply his or her knowledge of what is possible, given time constraints, resources, and the organization's purpose and scope. It is useful to define the intern's assignment in general terms and then in very specific terms with indications of steps to be taken, at least in its beginning stages. At the same time, it is important to keep from putting too tight a lid on the project or position before a student is directly involved.

Next, the supervisor should participate in the *recruitment* and *selection* of the students. At a minimum he or she should describe the qualifications necessary, and in the optimum situation he or she would actually conduct interviews and make the final selection. Many internships or field experience situations founder on the rocks of different perceptions of what is expected. This possibility can most effectively be cleared up by face-to-face contact between the agency supervisor, the academic representative, and the prospective student. Supervisory involvement in the selection process can also emphasize concern for standards. A professional personnel approach toward selecting the student lets him know that he is considered important and is expected to meet standards, and that he will play an important role in the organization.

Once an internship is planned and a prospective student identified, the supervisor must see that the necessary *supporting structures* are provided. Space will be needed, contact with other personnel, materials and supplies, equipment and basic information on how to get things done. This support structure is essential for the student to function quickly and effectively.

An *orientation* by the supervisor which gives the student information on resources and on the system in which she is to accomplish her objectives is essential. It is important for the student to be oriented to her specific work situation at the beginning of the program. The immediate questions of "Where do I fit? How do I get things done? What is expected of me here?" have first priority. Often the more general orientation relating the particular experience to the general goals of the field experience program is better accomplished after the student is somewhat secure in the field experience situation. If this broad approach is attempted in detail before placement it may seem to the student to be an academic exercise. But when the student is functioning and well grounded in his agency, it takes on real meaning and can be very helpful. The most important part of the agency orientation is an understanding of the objectives of the assignment and of the setting in which they are to be reached.

It is also important at the very beginning to establish a *schedule*. This is done with the student and should include reporting periods, time for consultation, dates for initial steps to be taken, and at least the indication of likely deadlines for different stages. The schedule may be revised from time to time, but no good project begins without a preliminary schedule.

During the student's assignment, *guidance and direction* are important, both at regularly scheduled periods and between times. Through this supervisory attention to the student's progress, standards of performance should be stressed and accomplishment of the work assigned measured. It is important to remind the student that what she is doing is important and is to be measured on the basis of usefulness as well as in terms of her own growth. Periodically, in addition to daily guidance, time should be set aside for a review of progress to date and for schedule revisions. Most effectively, such review should include representatives of the academic institution involved, and perhaps other people within the agency. A system of written reports also is important to direction, review, and the pursuit of objectives.

Interpretation. Throughout the assignment the supervisor helps the student interpret the experience he is having and the relationship between what he is doing and the work of the agency and of others. The supervisor cooperates with the academic institution's representatives in interpreting the student's experience in relation to broader concerns, academic studies, models and theories. Through interaction with the student and his academic representative, all parties can grow by learning from each other. Supervisor and student can relate as seekers of knowledge and workers toward common goals, each of whom has particular contributions to make. In cases where the student is assigned a specific project she may quickly become the expert in this area and know more about the particular situation than either her supervisor or her academic representative. This position can be very stimulating to the student, and if supervisors are not threatened the student's "expertise" can be very helpful to the organization.

If in spite of good planning and preparation problems develop to the point of impairing the effectiveness of the project or the well-being of the organization or student, termination should probably occur. The machinery for termination should be well established before the program begins and described in the orientation of the student. Close cooperation is necessary in such cases between the supervisor and the academic representative. Failure in an assignment may not mean failure in learning. Sometimes one learns most from negative experience.

Completion and evaluation. Toward the end of an assignment the supervisory role generally becomes more intense. Considerable assistance should be provided to the student to see that he recognizes the necessity of drawing his activities to a close rather than running up to the last minute and suddenly having to leave without having completed anything. A student who really gets interested in his task often has difficulty in stopping. An evaluation of the program should be made with the student, before she is gone, in terms of her progress individually and her contribution to the agency. The objectives of this evaluation are to assist the student in his or her growth, to improve the field experience program, and to help the agency and supervisor in their use of students. After the student leaves, a further evaluation of her contribution and growth is often helpful as a more objective review tempered by time.

Modeling

Often the interpersonal relations that develop between supervisors and students are among the most significant parts of the students' experience. Taking an interest in the students and their total activities and sharing with them feelings and interests beyond the work situation can be very helpful, particularly where the students are in a new environment. The supervisor, whether or not he or she wishes such a role, becomes part of the student's image of what it means to be a professional in the world of work. The supervisor is a model which the student may seek to emulate or to reject. This function places a special responsibility on those who supervise student programs to conduct themselves in ways which they would wish others to follow. A willingness to share oneself in this way can make a real difference in the kind of experience a student has and in his or her views of a profession and of his or her future service.

The supervisor's task includes maintaining effective interaction with the representatives of the educational institution involved. Contacts are maintained from the early planning stages through the assignment period and beyond for evaluation and follow-up. The relationships can be stimulating and very productive, both for the supervisor in the agency and the academic representative in the university. Good supervision in a field experience program or other program for student community service can assure that everybody gains. The supervisor uses the discipline of work with its demand for action and usefulness to motivate, to direct, and to measure progress towards both educational and organizational goals.

William R. Ramsay, past President of the National Association of Student Employment Administrators, has been Dean of Labor and Student Life at Berea College since 1970. Formerly he directed the Resource Development Program of the Southern Regional Educational Board and served with Oak Ridge Associated Universities from 1955 to 1967.

Assessing a Community Setting as a Context for Learning

Richard A. Couto

This chapter presents a model for assessing a community setting as a context for learning. The model is based on Couto's very useful concepts of the "community of need" and the "community of response," both of which are present in any community or public service experience. Couto uses a model of "balanced disequilibrium" that acknowledges the dynamic synergy between the community setting and the facilitation of learning. He also explores common pitfalls in service-learning which can lead to an imbalance in accountability, service, or learning. This paper was first commissioned by the Kettering Foundation in Dayton, Ohio, for the 16th Annual Conference of the National Society for Internships and Experiential Education held October 1987 in Smugglers' Notch, Vermont.

The frequent calls in the late 1980s to encourage public service among college and university students suggest a rare occurrence among officials in higher education: consensus. This consensual call for public service is in part an effort by educators to defend themselves from a double-barrelled peril present on all campuses: an obsession of students with grades, graduate or professional training, and high paying jobs; and a corresponding decline in altruism (Newman, 1985, pp. 31-40). Insofar as college education is intended to prepare a person for life and insofar as youth is a time of idealism, these are disturbing trends to many educators.

Some educators have responded to these trends. More than 100 presidents of colleges and universities belong to Campus Compact whose task it is to promote public service in higher education. In addition, students have organized new programs campus by campus in chapters of the Campus Outreach Opportunity League (COOL). COOL is not so much a reaction to the studies and reports as it is an indication that the case of declined altruism may be overstated. Certainly, the work of Campus Compact and COOL have helped to make us aware of the considerable amount of voluntarism on our campuses already.

The danger with consensus is that we may mistake it for action. We can often agree on what we all need to do and never get around to doing it. We can often agree on what others should do without seeing that it gets done. Frequently, consensus on a course of action is a tip that the prescribed action is relatively painless and probably does not go to the root of the problem. In the case of student attitudes and higher education, for example, those commentaries that discuss the worrisome student attitudes also suggest that students may be simply living down to the expectations of colleges and universities and reflecting the careerism and concerns of faculty and administrators (Levine, 1980, pp. 138-41; Astin, 1985). Our students may not have much altruism because it is not fostered on campuses and sometimes actually discouraged by what Astin has called the "competitive curriculum" (Astin, 1987). Consequently, as welcomed as the new consensus around public service is, it is still necessary to ask if we are doing enough to relate public service to the ordinary life of our colleges and universities, especially the curriculum.

The premise of this chapter is that the public service of students is a powerful learning experience which should be linked to the teaching mission of universities and colleges. The more effective public service is, the more learning it entails. Consequently, this discussion deals with characteristics of effective student-provided public service with provisions for the student's education as well. Its primary purpose is to share knowledge about assessing community settings as learning experiences, which is an important part of facilitating students' personal development, learning and effectiveness in service.

Public Service and Higher Education

Public service has a long but ambiguous relationship with higher education in the United States. Higher education began with colleges that trained clergy and professionals to serve American colonists and "assumed, from the first, that all of its graduates would participate fully in public affairs as well as their own careers" (Newman, 1985, p. 57). Land grant universities and the relation of

settlement houses to universities maintained the link between public service and American campuses. On the other hand, these links
were often tenuous, and settlement house staff were often adjunct
faculty — a status of recognition and courtesy but on the margins of
the universities' central concerns. Furthermore, these new links
reflected changes in higher education, such as compartmentaliza-
tion, which relegated public service to some marginal part of the
university or the college such as the chaplain's office. Likewise, as
universities became research centers, the research of their faculty
became their "public service." This sometimes introduced new
ambiguity as faculty and students sometimes took situations of
public need as opportunities to acquire or apply scholarship rather
than compassion.

The term public service in this discussion incorporates the idea
of training students as involved and committed citizens rather than
researchers. But public service does not assume a breach of academic study and compassion. Quite the contrary, my premise is
that we can teach students more effectively through public service if
we keep some basic principles and steps in mind. Public service is
the direct provision of a service which improves the quality of life or
addresses a need of an individual or a group. Research may be such
a service if it is conducted in a way that is accountable to individuals
and groups and if it attempts to make a service-type contribution to
them directly and not indirectly (Couto, 1987). In addition, public
service as used here intends to promote self-sufficiency and to avoid
constructing any dependence of those in need on those who respond
to that need. Thus, public service should promote the self-concept
and confidence of the people served and increase their competence
to address their needs or to enhance the quality of their own lives.
What follows is an examination of some steps to carry out effective
learning through public service.

The Community of Need and the Community of Response

There are at least two actors in public service: the community of
need and the community of response. We as educators have a
general awareness of the community of need although we tend to
lump those in need into large, undifferentiated categories that tell
us little about the root causes of their needs: "the poor," "the homeless," "the imprisoned," etc. We may have some awareness of the
issues that some people in the community of need confront, such as
stripmining, hunger, or illiteracy.

What we generally lack at the beginning of public service is knowledge about the second actor, the community of response. There is a community of response within every community of need. It may be as informal as a set of community leaders that others look to in all circumstances and needs. It may vary in effectiveness from issue to issue and from community to community, but the important point is that part of the community of response is local leaders. They continually address the needs of a particular community, and their response to a need does not begin with the arrival of "outsiders."

There is also a community of response from outside the community of need. It may be a varied set of voluntary associations and community organizations which depend for their staff and funding on resources outside of the community of need. A store-front ministry to the homeless is an example. These associations and organizations are generally private and non-profit. They generally have more financial and material resources than the leaders from within the community of need, although this is not to say that the resources are adequate. There may be private, profit-making services within the community of response as well, such as physicians and health centers. Finally, public agencies are another set of members in the community of response. They have a mandated and publicly financed role to respond to a community of need. Public health departments and some literacy campaigns are public members of the community of response.

Institutions of higher education are members of the community of response. Some have a voluntary role as part of the private, non-profit sector and others have a mandated role within the public sector. This distinction is blurred once examined closely, however. The large rates for overhead costs and for recovery of indirect costs available to institutions of higher education, private and public alike, are approved by public agencies. Similarly, foundations which are important to the support of higher education are the creatures of public law through state and federal tax codes. The public permits them to function because we understand that they promote the public good. Also, individuals and corporations have an incentive to make contributions to institutions of higher education because of tax deductions they may take. Without this funding, the finances of most private institutions of higher education would change drastically. Thus, Americans provide public support even to private institutions of higher education in many different ways because we understand that they have a public purpose. That public purpose may be public service in ways other than those defined here, but the membership of prominent private universities such as Brown, Georgetown, Harvard, and Stanford in Campus Compact suggests some recognition of at least the voluntary response of private universities and colleges to the community of need.

Whatever this voluntary response to social needs, the generally accepted public purpose of institutions of higher education is the production and dissemination of knowledge. The more clearly public service of various forms relates to learning, the more likely it is to be integrated into the explicit public role of universities and colleges. For this reason, we need to link the form of public service with which we are concerned to teaching and learning. The contribution of public service to learning depends in part on the correct assessment of the community of need and of the community setting as a learning context.

Assessing the Need of a Community

It is a common sense principle that we should ask for what we want, and this applies to asking others about the needs of a particular community which we seek to serve. The far more difficult questions are: ask whom? and ask what? We should, of course, ask members of the community of need what are appropriate forms of public service. But most especially, we should ask the community of response within that community, that is, local leaders. We may also ask members of the community of response who come from outside the community of need about appropriate forms of public service. In doing so, we should remember that students in the community of response ordinarily, at the time of their initial inquiry, share more in common with the voluntary sector than they do with either the private, for-profit sector or the public sector of the community of response.

Regardless of whom we ask about the needs of a particular community, there are important questions to keep in mind about all of the people we talk with if we are interested in a form of public service that promotes self-sufficiency among those being served. Are the people we talk with accountable to the community of need in some way? Do their services have boards of local residents? Are the boards broadly representative of the community? Do those representatives have formal and informal participation in decision making? Have the services of the agency reached all sectors of the community of need? Are some sectors ignored or unserved? Why?

Another set of questions deals with the ability of people with whom we speak to mobilize resources for existing or new services from within and from outside the community. Is there an effort to have local residents provide for their own services even if the effort is limited? Are local people being trained for new roles in the agency? Does the agency foster new links of local residents and outside resources, or does the staff control them exclusively? Can the agency's staff continue the work that students may start after they leave?

In addition to the questions we must ask about the people with whom we speak, we need to gain information from them about what students might do in a public service role. These questions focus on finding a specific task that addresses community needs and is within the abilities and limits of students. One measure of the relation of the task to a community's need is the effort the community of response has put into the task students might take up or the effort they are willing to make to continue on a task which students may initiate. The generosity of people in the community of response extends to giving students what they need, and they may promise to provide a task to students to satisfy their needs and not the needs of the community. *It is important that the task which students take on addresses a problem in the community and is not merely the community's solution to the students' need to find something to do.*

Assuming there is a need which students can help address effectively, time becomes an important limit in shaping a specific task for students related to the problem. Colleges measure time in quarters, semesters, semester breaks, and spring and summer vacations. These are very different measures of time than those of community organizations and most other organizations as well. The task also needs to be time-specific so that students can finish some tangible part of it that both they and the community can see and appreciate. Often the community of response has a need for technical skills. Students going to a rural, Appalachian community are sometimes surprised that rather than digging wells and outhouses, the community leaders ask them to design software for their computers to help with their management or fundraising. English majors may have the opportunity to edit newsletters and other publications or proposals. Health professions students, law students, architectural students, and environmental science students all may have technical skills which are very important but absent within the community of response. The use of skills which students have or are acquiring makes a rich learning context for them.

Often the community of response also has a need for manual labor or non-technical skills, and students can play an important part in this. The conduct of a recreation program, the provision of transportation, house repair or construction are examples of tasks in which students with few technical skills can make important contributions under the direction of local leaders. It is the work of educators, primarily, to fashion tasks appropriate for the level and forms of skills which students have — tasks which will benefit the community and which students can conduct successfully within the time they have. But educators cannot fashion these tasks without the leadership and perspective of those in the community of response and the community of need.

Assessing the Community Setting as a Learning Context

Relating public service to education requires that we not only devise good public service but that we also provide explicitly for the education of students. In practice, these go hand in hand. That is, the better the public service, the more learning goes on. The more we provide for reflection and learning, the better students are able to conduct their public service tasks. There are well-established principles of good practice in experiential education to promote learning such as small group exercises, journals, learning contracts and the like. Less well-established are the means to assess as a learning context the community organization in which students work. This section will outline some of the factors to consider.

It is important to know, for example, if the service of the organization is viewed primarily as the pursuit of justice for, by, or of the people of the community of need; a form of charity from the community of response to the community of need; a service exchanged for a fee; or an organizational output mandated by some legislative body. An organization which understands itself as pursuing justice is much more likely to come into conflict with authority than an organization that is trying to meet a specified number of outputs that authorities have established as its goal. The internal environments of organizations vary significantly depending upon the organization's view of its service. Different organizations will thus provide students with contexts for very different lessons.

Likewise, the size and nature of the staff of an organization is an important factor in the learning opportunity of public service. Whether a staff is full-time or part-time, paid or voluntary changes the character of an organization. An organization with a full-time, paid staff is more likely to have specific goals and a hierarchical structure with a division of labor than an organization with a part-time, voluntary staff. This will influence the amount of supervision available to students and the degree of responsibility provided them. Students working with a part-time, voluntary staff which understands the organization as pursuing some form of justice for its members, such as the halt to a pollution problem, are likely to give students a great deal of unsupervised responsibility. This may be as difficult for students as a situation in a very large, hierarchical organization where the supervision is very explicit but the responsibility is plainly "busy work."

A balance is needed between responsibility and supervision, and there are important steps to achieve this. First, the campus supervisor needs to be sure it is clear what degree of supervision and responsibility students will have in the organization. This should come from a set of discussions among the campus supervisor, the community organization and the students involved. It may be expressed in a formal manner such as a contract or in an informal manner such as a letter, but it needs to be in writing and shared with all parties to ensure that, as much as possible, there is an explicit understanding of the responsibility and supervision related to the task of public service.

In reaching this explicit understanding, it is most useful to impart to the community organization the school's expectation that the students are to be beneficiaries of services as well as the providers. In other words, the community organizations need to be aware of and accept their role as teachers and their responsibility to provide for the learning of students. Their role with students may be new and unique for them. It includes a teaching responsibility and may be different from their role with volunteers or paid staff in that they assume responsibility for the development and learning of a student apart from the needs of the organization. This means that the community organization must be willing to be accountable to the college or university program just as surely as the latter needs to be accountable to them.

Vectors of Learning: Accountability and Action Reflection

With this background I would like now to suggest several configurations which relate the settings of public service to education and delineate the risk of diminished learning involved in each configuration. On the one hand, we have community settings which may range from new and emerging to continuing and well-established. A continuing or well-established organizational setting would more likely offer clear lines of authority with many clear goals or a single goal. Such a setting may or may not be large. A student working in an organization with one full-time staff member working on a single clear goal may have as well-established a setting as a student working in an organization with hundreds of staff members and multiple clear goals. A public health clinic and a neighborhood soup kitchen may have very different staffing patterns and a different number of goals and programs but be equally established as a public service learning context for students. Staff in such settings are generally accustomed to students and other new people coming into the organization for short periods of time and for specific purposes.

A new or emerging community setting often entails unclear goals, multiple goals or confusing lines of authority. Such a setting is likely to be small and perhaps have a few part-time, voluntary staff who are relatively new to their tasks. But these characteristics might also apply to a large organization which is undertaking a new task or which depends primarily on a large number of informal arrangements to achieve goals which are often unstated. A public health clinic beginning a new program of health education in the community or a soup kitchen just getting started are examples of a new or emerging community setting. Staff in each setting may be accustomed to others acting in a relatively autonomous fashion and may be confused about their responsibility to a student. Supervision and direction may be serious problems for a student there.

On the other hand, we have the task of education. We may facilitate, monitor, and recognize the learning entailed in public service to different degrees. Direct public service may be part of the curriculum through many requirements or few. Public service may be part of a course and include reading, class discussion, faculty supervision and evaluation. On the other hand, public service may have only unfacilitated learning in the form of voluntarism with little or no orientation for student volunteers, little discussion among volunteers and no faculty or campus supervision and evaluation. In between these forms, we may facilitate learning through independent studies, class projects, and service projects of one to three weeks' duration. These provide varying degrees of orientation, group discussion, reflection, supervision and evaluation.

If we combine the community setting factor and the facilitated-learning factor as horizontal and vertical axes, we can divide the resulting quadrants by vectors of learning. At the end of each vector is a risk of diminished learning which results from a combination of an extreme of one factor over another. Importantly, there are risks in all directions just as there is promise for effective learning in all directions. Following is a discussion of two aspects of learning: accountability and the balance between action and reflection.

FIGURE 1

Vector of Learning - Accountability

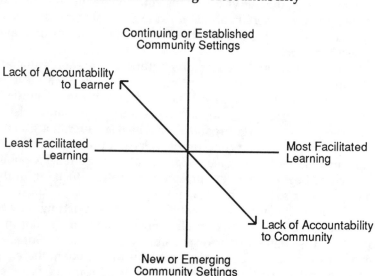

Figure 1 illustrates the risks of accountability which come with combining the factors of community setting and facilitated-learning in inverse proportions. There are risks of accountability both to the learner at one extreme and to the community organization at the other. For example, students with a semester-long internship of fifteen credits in community organizing placed in new or emerging community settings may soon get nervous that not much will be done during the semester to warrant their time or their grade. In the absence of specific, time-consuming tasks, students may work out tasks on their own or with faculty as to what "should be done" and begin working on this agenda to fulfill their academic requirement without the supervision or approval of the community organization. In some instances, students have actually worked to change the organization because of the dissatisfaction they have with the leadership and its inability to meet their expectations and requirements. The risk at this end of the vector is public disservice. The requirement for discussion and analysis in this example may exacerbate the problem if it results in "blaming the victim" organization for its shortcomings relative to the student's need.

At the other end of this vector is the risk of lack of accountability to the learner. Students in a well-established organization with little facilitated learning run this risk the most. Student volunteers working with incarcerated juveniles and adults exemplify this risk. The prison bureaucracy places the security of its internal environment far above the learning or service of students and may have few qualms about cancelling or changing arrangements with short notice or no notice. As another example, a community organization may give a student the task to "pose" as a student doing a term paper and to interview officials to acquire information that the staff has been unable to get directly. These examples can provide unintended lessons in institutional control and the ethics of inquiry. These are important lessons, of course, but the lack of facilitation of these students' learning means there is little chance for reflection on their public service experiences. Risks like these without facilitated learning are more likely to engender frustration without support and ethical dilemmas without resolution. These in turn are more likely to exhaust altruism than to encourage it.

FIGURE 2

Vector of Learning - Action-Reflection

Figure 2 illustrates the second vector of learning, the action-reflection vector. At both ends of the vector, the risk to learning is the same — action without reflection. The risk in a continuing or established setting with a lot of learning-facilitation is that students will simply be socialized to a professional role and will not examine the premises of that role. Medical students' rotations in hospitals or the internships of social work students in welfare agencies are examples of public service which entail this risk. At the other end of the vector is the risk of "do-goodism." Students volunteering in new or emerging settings for tasks that have little or no facilitated learning can easily fall into this. Settings which are examples of this risk include Big Brothers and Big Sisters and the charity work of fraternities and sororities. This is not to say that this type of public service is not to be encouraged or that learning and service do not occur in these settings. They can. But it is to say that the ends of each of these vectors represent settings where opportunities for effective learning or public service, as I have defined them, are potentially diminished.

The point is that to maximize learning and public service we have to promote forms of accountability and forms of action-reflection. In addition, we have to promote them in some proportion that prevents running a risk to either one. In doing this, it is useful to keep in mind Lawrence Kohlberg's concept of "structured disequilibrium" (Graham, 1973). As applied here this means providing something new and unfamiliar to students but in a way which allows them to make a contribution that utilizes their skills, which they feel is important, and upon which they can reflect with other students and with campus and site supervisors alike.

Figure 3 portrays a circle of structured disequilibrium and suggests the risks to learning in all directions. The task of the educator is to keep public service within this circle by assessing the community setting appropriately and establishing appropriate mechanisms for supervision and reflection.

Some specific steps that assist in making the appropriate links of community setting and facilitated learning include:

1.   establishing a specific task within the ability of students and their time limits;

2.   establishing a specific task which enhances the competencies of the community of need, individuals within it, or some part of the community of response;

3.   establishing explicit understandings with students, perhaps with learning contracts, that help foster realistic expectations; and

4.   establishing explicit understandings with community sponsors, in writing, for the supervision of students.

Balanced Disequilibrium

The concept of structured disequilibrium is an important but limited concept for establishing an initial link between public service and education. The problem with the model of structured disequilibrium is that it is static. While it does suggest movement along vectors, it also suggests that a fixed intersection can be established.

In practice, there are many other factors that make the interaction of public service and education much more dynamic. First, the curriculum varies from institution to institution, and the tradition of relating it to community needs will also vary from institution to institution. Some institutions have a long tradition of involving students in public service that pre-dates the renewal of interest in the 1980s. Others have a tradition of separating the curriculum from involvement in this and other reforms, treating them as fads. Second, community organizations' goals are not static. Agencies may formulate goals, displace them, and replace them. An organization may have the stated goal of empowering groups in the community of need but the operational goal of maintaining the dependence of

FIGURE 3

The Circle of Structured Disequilibrium

these groups to justify continued funding from outside resources. Where an organization stands in relation to the formulation and replacement of goals is as important as where the tradition of a college or university places its curriculum in relation to public service. Both factors affect the learning context for any particular student from a particular campus and within a particular organization. This suggests tremendous variation from case to case which Figure 3 conveys only partially.

In addition to the variation from case to case, each case will vary over time. Thus a community setting may be well-established one year but with a change in staff or goals, it may be far less established the next year. Likewise, a new administration or a curriculum change at a university or college may mean that the same institution adopts different policies towards public service and facilitated learning. More than that, as any experiential educator can testify, change occurs within the time a student is in a field setting. The staff of the community organization and the student make adjustments to each other with time which may require a new mix of accountability and action-reflection. Figure 4 is a schema of balanced disequilibrium which portrays facilitated-learning, community settings, accountability and action-reflection on overlapping orbits suggesting continual change. This atom-like model also suggests continual movement and a nucleus — some person or group of persons — that balances these factors in orbits that best guarantee both (1) the maximum learning for students, and (2) the form of public service that meets the needs of community residents and enhances their abilities and competencies.

The process of assessing a community setting as a learning context is dynamic and ever-changing from institution to institution, from community setting to community setting, from student to student, and within each instance over time. Thus, balanced disequilibrium may be an appropriate term because it acknowledges that readjustment and realignment are a continuing part of the process of integrating learning and public service.

Conclusion

Colleges and universities have a responsibility for the students they send into public service situations to see that their work is effective. This is especially important because students may have little or no experience in public service and little or no connection to the community of need. Equally important, universities and colleges have a responsibility for the students they send into public service situations to see that their service is educative. The assess-

FIGURE 4

Orbits of Balanced Disequilibrium

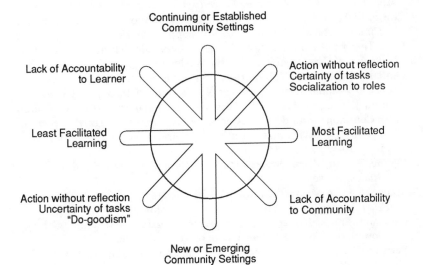

Continuing or Established
Community Settings

Lack of Accountability
to Learner

Action without reflection
Certainty of tasks
Socialization to roles

Least Facilitated
Learning

Most Facilitated
Learning

Action without reflection
Uncertainty of tasks
"Do-goodism"

Lack of Accountability
to Community

New or Emerging
Community Settings

ment of community settings as learning contexts and the concept of balanced disequilibrium may be useful tools in meeting those responsibilities.

Thanks to the Kettering Foundation, Dr. Jan Fritz, and the members of NSIEE for their help in the preparation of this paper.

Richard Couto is a political scientist who serves as the Director of Research at the Institute of Government at Tennessee State University. From 1972 to 1987 he directed the Center for Health Services at Vanderbilt University. He is the author of Streams of Idealism and Health Care Innovation: An Assessment of Service-Learning and Community Mobilization.

References

Astin, Alexander W., "Competition or Cooperation," *Change*, September/October 1987, pp. 12-19.

Astin, Alexander W., *Achieving Educational Excellence*, Jossey-Bass, 1985.

Couto, Richard A., "Participatory Research: Methodology and Critique," *Clinical Sociology Review*, 1987, Vol. 5, pp. 83-90.

Deal, Terrence E. and Allan A. Kennedy, *Corporate Cultures: The Rites and Rituals of Corporate Life*, Addison-Wesley Publishing Company, 1982.

Graham, Richard A., "Voluntary Action and Experiential Education," *Journal of Voluntary Action Research*, Vol. 2, October 1973, pp. 186-93.

Kendall, Jane C., "Values as the Core of Institutional Commitment: Finding a Common Ground," in *Making Sponsored Experiential Learning Standard Practice*, ed. by Thomas C. Little, New Directions in Experiential Learning, Jossey-Bass, 1983.

Levine, Arthur, *When Dreams and Heroes Died: A Portrait of Today's College Student*, Jossey-Bass, 1980.

Management Assistance Group, *Steering Nonprofits: Advice for Boards and Staff*, Management Assistance Group, Washington, D.C., 1984.

Newman, Frank, *Higher Education and the American Resurgence*, Carnegie Foundation for the Advancement of Teaching, 1985.

Perrow, Charles, *Complex Organizations*, third edition, Random House, 1986.

Also see "Assessing Community Needs," an excellent monograph edited by Marilyn Mecham of Lincoln, Nebraska, for ACTION. It includes sections on using existing assessments, conducting your own needs assessment, the advantages and disadvantages of various assessment techniques, determining overlapping needs, and monitoring changing needs. Available from the National Society for Internships and Experiential Education, 3509 Haworth Drive, Suite 207, Raleigh, NC 27609.

Community Impact Checklist

With resources scarce and requests plentiful, educators need written criteria for deciding where to place students. Reprinted from Synergist, *National Center for Service-Learning, AC-TION, Vol. 9, No. 3, pp. 27-28.*

RECOGNIZE THIS SCENE?   You've just returned from a workshop anxious to try out some of those recently acquired ideas. While you were gone, you had so many telephone calls and visitors that messages cover your desk like confetti.

After dealing with a few urgent calls, putting aside others to be handled next week, and delegating a heap of messages to your staff in the name of time management, you are left with a stack of notes and letters reflecting the deep-seated, too often ignored problems that sent you to the workshop.

Here is sampling from that stack:

- Urgent pleas from four agencies that heard about your program recently and want 10 students each. (And you can't even provide enough volunteers to the agencies you're currently working with!)

- The County Home wants five more students this year than they had last year, doing what they did last year. (And as far back as you can remember.)

- The students who work at the housing project are clamoring that they are "only being band-aids" and not working on the residents' "real problems." (Who's to say which problems are more real than others?)

Setting Criteria

Perhaps one way that some of these problems can be dealt with is to do an exercise used at the workshop. In the exercise, a small group developed a checklist of criteria for determining the agencies with which a service-learning program might work most closely.

The group listed qualities that an agency should have if a high school or university program is to agree to work with it. The exercise was based on the idea that a service-learning program has a finite number of resources — people, skills, budget, facilities — and that these should be used discriminately and effectively to meet both the service and learning goals.

Of course, not everyone agreed on what should be included in the lists. One workshop group decided to separate the criteria into two general categories — service (or community issues) and education (or student-centered issues). The final lists reflected only the criteria on which everyone agreed. Each item was worth a possible 5 points. The closer an organization complied with the criteria, the higher the score it would receive for that item. Organizations that consistently ranked high on both sets of criteria were the organizations that the service-learning program would work with most closely.

Using this assessment system probably means cutting down on the number of organizations in which a service-learning program places students or, to put it another way, it may mean decreasing the quantity in order to increase the quality. It also nudges a service-learning program to choose serving and learning areas to emphasize. The program no longer will try to respond to every social need; rather, the program will focus on a few community issues.

The workshop participants decided that this checklist system could offer several benefits, some administrative and others programmatic. Among them were the following:

• The entire staff could be involved in developing the checklist. This would give everyone a part in making program policy. It would standardize policy so that agency placements could be made more objectively.

• The criteria list can be evaluated and changed each year. If the criteria prove unrealistic, the staff can eliminate or modify the list.

• The list will help agencies understand your service and learning goals.

• The organizations with highest scores will be the ones to which you direct the most resources; their goals will be supporting your goals, and vice-versa.

• Organizations that scored low on the checklist can be included in a catalog of miscellaneous placement opportunities. You don't end up turning agencies completely away.

Limiting the numbers and types of organizations with which you work does not necessarily mean limiting the numbers and types of placements. If your staff members have decided to work on senior citizen issues and the Senior Center ranks high on your criteria checklists, many projects are possible within this one organization, e.g., drama club, continuing education courses, a handbook on bargains for people over 65, a beauty salon, an income tax service.

The Criteria

The workshop participants — all secondary and postsecondary educators — found it easier to come up with items in the education column than in the service column. They decided that in order for a service-learning program to devote a lot of its resources toward working with a particular agency, the agency had to support the students by: providing orientation and periodic training sessions; either making transportation available or reimbursing the students for public transportation; providing developmental placements, i.e., volunteers would have more responsibilities and more complex duties in their second term than in their first; completing an evaluation form or writing a letter of recommendation after the students finish their placements.

The service or community list took longer to develop and was more controversial. A few of the items decided upon are listed here, along with the reasons for including them.

Are those for whom the service is intended part of the decision making process? The participants unanimously agreed that the answer should be affirmative, yet they were able to name a dozen organizations that make decisions for other people. Deciding on the problems of and the solutions for others without involving them is, the educators felt, a bit paternalistic. Too often they had seen suburbanites making decisions for urban dwellers, whites making decisions for blacks, the young making decisions for the elderly, and the middle class making decisions for the poor.

To determine who takes part in the decision making, the educator may ask the following questions: Are community members part of the agency's staff? Are they on the organization's advisory board? Members of evaluation teams? Does the agency have citizens' committees or planning councils? Does it have public hearings or policy meetings? These are all indicators of how really community centered the organization is. High scores should go to agencies that can answer yes.

Is the organization addressing an issue your service-learning program is working on? If an organization isn't doing this, it probably won't be able to help you meet your goals. The group felt that a program

The group finally decided
that highest scores should go
to agencies providing both
direct service and advocacy
opportunities. The educators
agreed that it's important —
and cost effective — to attack
a problem; but it's also important
to meet immediate needs.

should beware of spreading its resources too thin. It's better to make a small impact in a few areas than flounder around in many. Again, many types of placements can be developed within one good agency.

Are the organization's mission, goals, and objectives clearly stated, and is it periodically evaluated on the basis of these goals and objectives? By developing your checklist (and *your* mission, goals, and objectives), you are being up front about your business. Are they? The workshop group complained about the time and effort it takes to write these up, but in the end agreed that they are necessary for a well run service-learning program or agency. Stated, measurable goals are easier to evaluate.

The following questions are relevant: Who evaluates the agency? Are previous evaluations available for you to look at? How were the goals and objectives chosen? (This goes back to who makes the decisions.) Do they have readily available descriptive material that clearly states their purpose? These are indicators of where they are going. Then you can decide whether or not you want to join them in going there.

Are the organization's services easily available to its target group? What good is an agency with excellent services if it requires five forms (in triplicate), a four-month waiting period, and approval by three other organizations? This is an indication of how responsive the agency is to the community's needs. You may want to check on whether the agency has bilingual services, materials written in large type, and well publicized, easily accessible services. Accessibility earns high scores.

How is the organization funded? One workshop participant told of a neighborhood clean-up campaign funded principally by a local factory — a factory that had more than 12 court injunctions pending against it for pollution violations. His service-learning program soon found out that the campaign was concerned with the trash in the neighborhood parks but not with the more important issues of trash in the neighborhood air and water supply. Participants noted that whosoever giveth the funds, controleth how this bounty is spent.

Is the organization working on both the causes and the symptoms of the community problems? The workshop participants discussed this point at length. Some felt that the best service-learning programs aim at changing the status quo, at making institutional changes. Others felt that a service-learning program should be a service provider, not a change agent. Emotionally charged arguments ranged from "Give people control over their lives" to "As outsiders we shouldn't meddle in their lives," from "We're just helping to build a dependency upon these agencies" to "Our students aren't sophisticated (or skilled) enough to deal with the sources of problems." The group finally decided that highest scores should go to agencies providing *both* direct service and advocacy opportunities. The educators agreed that it's important — and cost effective — to attack a problem; but it's also important to meet immediate needs.

Working with agencies that use both approaches allows a service-learning program a wider variety of placements for students with a range of interests and skills. Developmental placements can be designed for those students who wish to move into new areas within the same agency, much as a good organization has developmental positions for its paid staff.

These criteria and rationales were listed during one checklist exercise. The staff of every service-learning program will come up with a different set, but that's fine. Your final product will be a mutually agreed upon yardstick for measuring just how involved you will become with any organization. If you decide that an agency can receive up to five points for each item and you have listed 20 items, you may decide that you'll work with those organizations that have gotten at least 50 out of the possible 100. Or perhaps you'll decide to work with the top 10 scorers.

The important point to remember is that you have valuable resources to provide some organizations within your community. You and your staff have the responsibility for choosing the best agencies to receive them. The checklist is a tool for deciding how to distribute your resources objectively and equitably and to ensure that you are working toward your community service goals.

PART I

Practical Issues and Ideas for Programs and Courses that Combine Service and Learning:

Evaluation

Evaluating Student Volunteer and Service-Learning Programs

Michele Whitham

> *Michele Whitham spells out in simple, practical language the issues any program coordinator, faculty member, or agency director needs to consider in evaluating a program that combines service and learning.* Adapted from Evaluating Student Volunteer and Service-Learning Programs: A Casebook for Practitioners, *Michele Whitham, ed., National Center for Service-Learning, ACTION, 1983, pp. 17, 175-181.*

THERE ARE AS MANY APPROACHES to program evaluation as there are people conducting evaluation studies. And, while models of program evaluation can provide useful frameworks for thinking about the evaluation process, actual evaluations reflect the art of compromise with reality as well as the ideals of hypothetical models. It may thus be helpful, in thinking about how to apply the experiences described here to your own situation, to view evaluation as a *series of decisions* that you will make in order to discover information that could improve your program.

Why Evaluate?

Many service-learning programs are relatively young ventures. Most are still experimenting with approaches to student involvement in the community. In addition to being new, the programs are also fluid; they deal not only with predictable turnovers in their volunteer and client populations but also with administrative upheavals linked to fluctuating levels of institutional support. Finally, all of the programs are struggling with the complexities of bringing together diverse school and community constituencies. In response to these inherent uncertainties, service-learning educators speak unanimously of ongoing, honest self-appraisal as a key to informed decision-making and thus to the continuing health and success of their programs. A commitment to routine program evaluation activities can enable you to: 1) *demonstrate the continuing need* for your program, 2) *monitor the productivity and efficiency* of its administration, and 3) *assess the quality* of both the services provided and the learning of students.

But while many service-learning educators now argue the merits of systematic self-evaluation, many of them first entered into evaluation because they were faced with specific issues or problems that required objective information to solve. The needs assessment process used by the Youth in the Community Project of the Greater Birmingham Volunteer Information Center, for example, was born out of the frustrations that both prospective volunteers and placement agencies were experiencing in finding each other. The comprehensive formative evaluation process in UCLA's Field Studies Development office evolved over years of closely-monitored program development work aimed at answering faculty criticisms of experiential education. The CABLES program at Northwestern High School in Baltimore was faced from the day of its inception with implementing evaluation procedures mandated by the Maryland State Department of Education.

While many once-skeptical program administrators have come to appreciate the contribution of formal program evaluation to decision-making, the fact remains that many of us still engage in evaluation because we must answer a specific question for a specific audience. "Does the program reach whom we claim it reaches?" or "What does it actually do for these people?" our community sponsors want to know. "What's the unit cost of the program?" asks the governing board. "What are students learning and how does this contribute to their academic growth?" inquires the faculty. So many questions that could be answered; so many audiences to satisfy. It is thus important, before investing any of a program's precious resources in evaluation, to know exactly what and whom one is doing the evaluation for, and to be reasonably certain that the benefits of the program will outweigh the costs. Clarity of purpose is key. Know what general questions you need to answer and decide how to make the best use of those answers, *before* you even start to gather data.

Why Not to Evaluate?

Of equal importance to knowing why you are evaluating your program is knowing why *not* to evaluate. As a relatively new specialty of social science, program evaluation is currently enjoying a popularity that overlooks its limitations. It is a waste of time, money, and effort, for example, to gather evaluation data that will never be used because it provides information that no one was asking for or that does not contribute to the attainment of program goals. Nor is it necessary to gear up for an elaborate, formal evaluation if ordinary common sense readily provides the information you need. Remember, too, that you can be asked to evaluate the outcomes of your program too soon, before any results can reasonably be expected, as was the case with the Maryland State Department of Education's first study of the CABLES program. Or, you might not have access to the professional competence or material resources needed to insure that evaluation results will have merit. It is even possible that some requests for evaluation of your program will lead you into damaging dead-ends, requiring you to prove the unprovable or to correct program defects whose causes are beyond your control. As the USC Joint Educational Project's decision not to interview homebound senior citizens in the Senior Partners program so beautifully illustrates, it takes sensitivity to both the value and the limitations of evaluation strategies to make sensible decisions about how best to evaluate your service-learning program.

Note, too, the message of the research team from Ball State University's Center for Lifelong Learning: it is critical to have clear criteria that allow you to assess consciously whether the effort invested in the evaluation project will bear fruit *before* committing yourself to an evaluation effort. Before rushing into an elaborate data collection effort in response to some vague mandate to "evaluate" your program, be certain that you know *what you will be evaluating, for whom, using what resources.* While formal evaluation practices, routinely implemented, can contribute to your program's efficiency and effectiveness, it is important to keep evaluation in perspective and not over-invest in the process. The concept of "cost-effectiveness" applies as much to assessing evaluation options as it does to assessing service-program options themselves.

When to Evaluate?

A common misinterpretation of a program evaluation model is to see it as a neat, linear process in which each step leads to the next as a program builds from planning through program monitoring to summative evaluation. Nothing could be further from reality for most service-learning program directors, whose programs are usually well under way before they have a moment to stop, take a breath, and contemplate the possibility of initiating an evaluation effort. While having the luxury to approach the design and implementation of your program as systematically as a traditional evaluation model implies might be ideal, few of us have this opportunity. More often, like the Office of Service-Learning at Kent State, we are faced mid-stream with the press of events pushing us relentlessly toward evaluation and must scramble in the midst of our daily routines to put the pieces of formal evaluation in place.

Given such realities, when *should* you try to evaluate your program? The answer most often given by evaluation professionals is that concern with evaluation should begin in the planning stage, when you can project an evaluation based on a "best guess" of what you will eventually wish to know. The answer consistently given by service-learning directors is, quite simply, "all the time!" Pre-evaluation and evaluation activities will eventually be so completely integrated into your daily operations that they are often no longer even recognized as "evaluation." At Eastern Washington University's Center for Extended Learning, for example, conscious planning automatically suffuses every program undertaking. For CEL, planning is not something that occurred once, during the program's original developmental phase; it is a strategy for maintaining the day-to-day operation of the program. Similarly, the data-collecting instruments evolved by the Field Studies Development office at UCLA were consciously constructed to have multiple uses, thus serving today as both administrative and evaluative tools.

None of these programs developed such well-integrated, ongoing evaluations overnight. Instead, each started with a specific problem, devised an evaluation strategy that allowed them to focus on that specific need for information, then slowly absorbed the evaluation practices into the daily life of the program. This incremental development of evaluation practices sometimes takes place by making explicit things that are already done, often by constructing new procedures and instruments as needed, and always through trial and error. The programs mentioned here stand as examples of programs that evaluate routinely and comfortably, receiving a continuous flow of good information about their programs through data-collecting systems that complement the regular work priorities and responsibilities of staff members.

How to Evaluate?

The questions of what kinds of data to collect and what kinds of instruments to use are often the most vexing for program administrators called upon to evaluate for the first time. Indeed, inexperienced evaluators often let their anxiety rush them into worrying about data collection before they have defined whom the evaluation is for, what specific questions are to be asked, and what resources exist for undertaking the project. A review of the experiences of several programs lends some perspective to the often intimidating problems associated with data collection and analysis.

A. Fitting the Method to the Context

How programs gather evaluation data can differ markedly. To assess the impact of student volunteers on community agencies, for example, the Center for Lifelong Education at Ball State University relied exclusively on open-ended interviews. The CABLES program at Baltimore's Northwestern High School, on the other hand, used closed-ended questionnaires to measure student attitudes. By contrast, the Office of Service-Learning at Kent State employed many different techniques to collect information on every major aspect of its program.

An obvious, but important, conclusion can be drawn from these cases: the kinds of data you gather, and the methods used to collect it, should fit the context of the evaluation. Thus, Field Studies Development, faced with the coordination of a university-wide evaluation of all students participating in field studies offerings at UCLA, chose to work with standardized survey and record-keeping forms and to emphasize quantitative data analysis. The Joint Educational Project at the University of Southern California, on the other hand, concerned with participants' perceptions of their service-learning experiences, relied almost exclusively on face-to-face data collection methods, believing that the subjectivity of this method is its strength, given the purposes of the evaluation.

There is, in short, no single "right way" to gather, analyze, or interpret evaluation data. There are, to be sure, standardized statistical procedures for working with data, scientifically validated instruments for testing certain effects, and agreed-upon methods for developing reliable new procedures. Most of the program directors in the examples given, however, found themselves designing their own survey forms, interview schedules, or observation checklists to meet the particular information needs of their programs. The selection of instruments depends entirely upon the questions you need answers to, the kinds of information to be collected, and the resources available for conducting the evaluation.

B. Quantitative vs. Qualitative Methods

Despite the diversity of approaches reported here, many programs rely on face-to-face data collecting methods which yield, in the words of Richard Cone, "a few tallies, mountains of notes, and definite perceptions in the minds of the staff." Indeed, some program coordinators are openly skeptical of statistics as a way of analyzing or presenting information on their programs. The reasons for such reservations are important for you to consider in making decisions about how to conduct a program evaluation. Because service-learning programs are people-oriented, they place great emphasis on individualizing experiences for program participants. The typical program is thus very flexible, and no two individuals' experiences of it will be exactly the same. Under these circumstances, standardized measures that employ a single scale to measure effects are not likely to reveal significant individual changes. In addition, as we have said before, service-learning programs are complex partnerships that rely for their success on communication among the partners. Evaluation methods that are consistent with, and contribute to, promoting such dialogue are most easily woven into the fabric of these programs.

Because of the particular characteristics of service-learning programs, many evaluators have concluded that paper-and-pencil measures cannot adequately assess the effects of such experiences on students or community participants, effects which include the acquisition of skills, new perceptions, new understandings, and an increased ability to act in the world. Instead, these evaluators argue for a moratorium on questionnaires, surveys, and other paper-and-pencil tests, and a new emphasis on observations of actual behaviors over time. Such face-to-face approaches do allow you to look deeply into the behaviors and perceptions of program participants. However, observation, like all other approaches, has its own strengths and limitations; though very time-consuming for staff, it can be integrated unobtrusively into the daily operation of programs.

C. Using Multiple Measures

A final critical point about evaluation instruments is the value of using combinations of techniques (triangulation) to try to develop the clearest possible picture of a program's operations and effects. The needs assessment of Birmingham's Youth in Community Project, for example, actually consists of a whole collection of activities, from annual surveys to personal interviews with participants, aimed at gathering data to describe both individual and community needs. The UCLA's Field Studies Development office relies on no fewer than six different instruments, which yield both quantitative and qualitative data, to monitor program development. In its attempt to assess student learning and growth, the CABLES program in Baltimore combines classroom discussions and individual student project reports with pre- and post-tests of student attitudes using standardized instruments.

There are several benefits to using multiple measures:

1) In evaluating service-learning programs, we are sometimes faced with "measuring the unmeasurable." How, for example, are we ever to know whether a student's improved school attendance is directly attributable to his participation in the service-learning program? Or whether ten years of senior outreach programs have made a difference in the lives of elderly community residents? Often, the best we can do to demonstrate a program's effectiveness is to show, through a mass of data, that the evidence all points in the same, positive direction.

2) Because service-learning programs are not standardized, things happen that, despite all our careful planning, we did not anticipate. Using multiple measures increases the chances of discovering the unexpected outcomes of our programs.

3) Continuous data gathering, using every information source available, insures that we will have the fullest possible picture of the program, its ups and downs, when the time actually comes to undertake a conscious evaluation. "To leave no stone unturned in trying to determine how the program is working" is an appropriate goal for a service-learning evaluation.

How Much to Evaluate?

At this point, with all this talk of using multiple measures, you may be feeling overwhelmed. Take time, then, to consider the issue of how to limit the scope of your evaluation. In attempting to apply the approaches presented here to your own program, it is important to remember that the comprehensive evaluations at UCLA and Kent State evolved slowly over a number of years, building deliberately on the pieces that had been put in place at earlier times. While these are excellent examples of the kind of evaluation procedures you might strive for in the long run, the chances are that your initial evaluation efforts will begin much more modestly.

If you are a teacher, for example, understanding the impact of service-learning on your students may be your first evaluation priority. A program administrator faced with budget cuts, on the other hand, might choose a cost-effectiveness analysis, set in the context of careful program monitoring. As a general rule, it is better to begin with a focused study that is well designed and yields credible results than with a comprehensive evaluation which may be difficult to manage. When faced with hard choices about how much to try to accomplish, focus on getting critical, rather than comprehensive, information. By conducting several small evaluations (preferably ones that view the program from different perspectives), you reduce the risk of wasted time and poor results while opening up the possibility of benefiting from triangulation.

Who Evaluates?

Although the emphasis in this discussion has been on the value and feasibility of ongoing self-study, also consider the possibilities of external, as well as internal, evaluation. On the one hand, the USC Senior Partners program is an example of an internal evaluation conducted by the program's own staff in order to assess internal operations. The CABLES program at Baltimore's Northwestern High School, by contrast, provides an example of an external evaluation designed to test for certain outcomes that the program's funders had pre-determined to be significant. Most often, service-learning coordinators describe collaborative approaches to evaluation, in which all parties involved in the evaluation contributed to its conceptualization and design. In the case of Youth in the Community in Birmingham, for example, school and agency participants gather annually to discuss needs and to map out strategies for meeting them. In the case of Field Studies Development at UCLA, faculty involved in the program work together to develop, test, and refine the evaluation instruments. The Office of Service-Learning at Kent State developed a unique committee system for guaranteeing that all interested parties have input into the evaluation. Even the research team from Ball State's Center for Lifelong Learning, a professional group of external evaluators, developed their instruments and procedures by seeking feedback throughout the evaluation from the staff of the agencies they were studying.

Several factors must be considered in choosing between internal and external evaluation:

1) Resources

Does your program have the time and talent to conduct a self-evaluation? Although a self-study need not be expensive (a typical range might be $200 to $5,000 in annual cost), it can easily overtax your human resources, even when staff members have the required expertise. Despite the monetary costs, an external evaluation may be less costly than at investment of program resources in an internal project that yields shoddy results. (Centers such as the one at Ball State, which specialize in training program evaluators and which can thus barter evaluation resources in return for thesis projects for students, may provide high-quality, low-cost evaluations.)

2) Audience

The choice between internal and external evaluations may be a choice between objectivity and relevance. While self-study is likely to free you from the task of orienting outsiders to the program and the risk of their misunderstanding some critical aspects, external evaluations are generally considered to be less biased. Thus, the question of whom the evaluation is being done for is critical in deciding whether to undertake an internal or external evaluation. If your evaluation is to be a public one, designed to establish program credibility, the aura of objectivity lent by an external evaluation may be essential. But if your evaluation is a private affair, designed to improve day-to-day operations, an internal self-study may be entirely adequate.

Values, Bias, and Expectations

No discussion of evaluation issues would be complete without mention of the ethical and political questions involved. While we may agree that an evaluation should be as objective as possible, the fact remains that all evaluations are biased — in their choice of questions, their selection of data collection methods, their choice of methods to analyze data, and their interpretation of results. In this context, it is important to have realistic expectations of your program evaluation, to understand in advance that it may not accomplish what you imagined it would, and to be prepared to make as creative use of the experience as possible. It is also critical to remember that program evaluation, like all activities that affect people's lives, needs to be governed by your program's more general ethic of human service.

Attorney Michele Whitham has worked as a practitioner in the service-learning field for 20 years, directing programs at both the secondary and university levels. Since 1975, she has held a faculty appointment in the Field Study Office at the College of Human Ecology at Cornell University where she coordinates undergraduate field study programs in upstate New York. She has served as a trainer and curriculum consultant for the National Center for Service-Learning, where she designed NCSL's training seminar on program evaluation.

References

ACTION, *Evaluating Service-Learning: A Guide for Program Coordinators,* National Center for Service-Learning, 1978.

Anderson, S. B., ed., *New Directions in Program Evaluation,* Jossey-Bass, 1978.

Anderson, S. B., S. Ball, R. T. Murphy, and Associates, *Encyclopedia of Educational Evaluation,* Jossey-Bass, Inc., 1976.

Fink, A. and J. Kosecoff, *An Evaluation Primer and An Evaluation Primer Workbook,* Sage Publications, 1978.

Morris, L. *et al., Program Evaluation Kit* (8 small volumes), Sage Publications, 1978.

Rossi, P. H. and H. E. Freeman, *Evaluation: A Systematic Approach,* Sage Publications, 1982.

Smith, N. L., ed., *New Techniques for Evaluation,* Sage Publications, 1981.

Struening, E. L. and M. Guttentag, *Handbook of Evaluation Research,* Sage Publications, 1975.

Whitham, Michele, *Evaluating Student Volunteer and Service-Learning Programs: A Casebook for Practitioners,* National Center for Service-Learning, ACTION, 1983. Available from the National Society for Internships and Experiential Education, 3509 Haworth Drive, Suite 207, Raleigh, NC 27609.

Evaluation of Youth Programs and Individual Performance

Dan Conrad and Diane Hedin

Reprinted with permission from Youth Service: A Guidebook for Developing and Operating Effective Programs *by Dan Conrad and Diane Hedin, Independent Sector, 1987, pp. 46-49. The term "youth service" as used here includes an emphasis on combining service and learning.*

ADMINISTRATORS OF COMMUNITY SERVICE PROGRAMS often are required to evaluate some aspect of their program. First, school coordinators usually need to assess individual student performance in order to assign a grade or determine how much credit to give a student for volunteer work.

Second, all programs need to monitor such things as where students volunteer, how often they attend, the quality of their work, the kind of supervision the site provides, and whether the student volunteers are being given enough or too much responsibility. Having basic information about how your program is functioning is critical for its long-term health and success.

Finally, you may find yourself in a position where you must convince funders that their money is being spent wisely or convince a school board that the program is educationally sound and intellectually credible. In such cases, a different type of information is needed and you may need to conduct a formal program evaluation.

This section offers suggestions and tools for conducting all three types of evaluation. None will be treated in great depth here; rather, we offer a conceptual framework for thinking about evaluation, suggest alternative approaches to evaluating participants and programs, and share some specific evaluation tools.

Assessing Individual Student Performance

Assessing a student's accomplishments in any setting is a complex and chancy business that is more art than science. A volunteer service experience presents at least as great — and sometimes a greater — challenge to the evaluator as does traditional academic work in the classroom.

Among the complicating factors are the nature of the experience, the fact that it is not always performed under the watchful eye of a supervisor, the paradox that the greatest benefits of service often are the least tangible, and the fact that there is no pool of ready-made and valid test items to administer.

Some school programs assume that the relevant factors are so ambiguous and difficult to measure that they do not give letter grades at all, instead awarding credit for hours completed. (For example, a student completing 100 hours receives a credit regardless of the exact nature and quality of his or her performance.)

Some schools avoid grading service experiences out of principle, feeling that doing so may rob the participants of some important value of the experience.

Others, either by choice or necessity, do assign grades, assessing the quality of the student's performance on a variety of cognitive, social, and personal criteria. As in the assessment of any learning experience, the teacher must first specify what the student is expected to accomplish through volunteer work and at what level of achievement. The list of "Aims and Outcomes of Youth Service Programs" (pp. 517-518 in Volume I) is a good starting place.

Next, goals and expectations need to be communicated to the student (and possibly to the field supervisor, as well). A variety of assessment tools, based on the program goals, should be used to gain as complete a picture as possible of the student's performance. The teacher may use any combination of the following to arrive at a final assessment.

• *Written work by the student.* Under the section on "Learning from Service," techniques were suggested for helping students integrate their volunteer experiences with their academic

> *"A school's official transcript should include information on service work performed by the student."*

studies. They include keeping a journal or diary; completing observation reports and critical incident reports; preparing a research project chosen and developed by the student to reflect his expertise in his sphere of activity; writing an essay describing what the student gained personally and academically from the experience, and so forth. Any or all of these activities can be used in the evaluation process since judgments could be made about the quality, depth, and understanding conveyed by these written assignments.

- *Group discussions.* For some students, sharing experiences in a group discussion is easier and more natural than writing about them and they may tend to have deeper insights in such a forum. The student's level of participation could be part of the final assessment.

- *Individual conferences with students.* A private interview with a student may reveal knowledge, insights and skills that might not otherwise be forthcoming.

- *Evaluation by supervisor.* Rely on supervisors for information that only they can give you. Whenever possible, make their evaluation forms brief and easy to complete. Open-ended questions, though more time-consuming to complete than checklists, provide a more in-depth and complex understanding of the student's achievement.

- *Self assessment.* Students may be given a role in their own evaluation including suggesting the grade to be received, or evaluating the quality of the field placement and the supervision.

Monitoring the Program

Monitoring the community service program involves keeping track of what individual volunteers do. It includes gathering other information, as well, such as how effective the coordinator is in organizing, running, and publicizing the program; how successful the host agencies are in developing appropriate volunteer jobs for the students; how receptive the community is to youth volunteers, etc.

The primary purpose of monitoring is to give the program administrator some idea of how the total program and its sub-parts are functioning so that problems can be identified and corrected, and effective elements reinforced.

Another purpose simply is to document what is happening so information is available to parents, funders, boards of directors, principals, or whoever asks about the program.

A good monitoring plan should include a record-keeping system, visits to the project sites, regular telephone contacts, and written evaluation by volunteers, supervisors, parents, clients, etc.

A Record-Keeping System. The basic criterion in setting up such a system is that it not be too complicated to keep up-to-date. Records that are outdated or incomplete can be dangerous to the very existence of your program (for example, if a parent needs to get in touch with their child in an emergency and you can't locate him because you haven't updated your list of field sites). At best, incomplete or out-of-date records can be inconvenient (for example, to a substitute trying to oversee the program in the director's absence).

Some forms you may find it worthwhile to keep include:

• *Sign-in sheets* at the field sites or attendance cards for each participant to document hours of service. (These may be as informal as a blank sheet of paper or as formal as a time card to be punched when a volunteer checks in and out.)

Some programs are reluctant to impose a tight system of supervision on students because it seems to contradict the independence and autonomy encouraged through the program. Others think it essential to have an almost foolproof system of checking in and checking up on students.

• *Parent permission forms* on file indicating that parents are aware of and approve of their child's involvement. Note, however, that in terms of liability, these forms are not considered to be binding by the courts. Nevertheless they do help document an overall concern for the health and safety of the participants.

• *Student ID cards.* These can save confusion and embarrassment about the reason the students are out in the community. Student volunteers can show the cards to clients or anyone asking what they are doing. The card might read:

> **Mary Jones is a member of the community service class at Western High School from January to June 1988. Class members serve as volunteers in agencies across our community. If you wish further information, contact Mr. Goodturns, Western High School, Telephone 123-4567.**

• *A master chart* showing where volunteers are at any given moment. A wall map with colored dots showing your students all around the community is a good way to illustrate the scope of your program and impress visitors.

- *A record of each participant,* showing when and where he or she has worked, and the tasks performed. You may wish to keep a folder for each person that includes written work and associated materials such as supervisor reports. A school's official transcript should include information on service work performed by the student.

> *"A proposal that includes a reasonable evaluation plan may help convince funders that you are a good risk."*

- *A record of each agency* with which you are involved, giving brief details of current volunteer jobs, contact people's names and phone numbers, and, if desired, assessments of past involvement and suggestions for future activities. This might also include a volunteer job description, so that agencies can register their need for student volunteers and spell out exactly what they want volunteers to do.

- *A record of total hours of service provided* by the volunteer group, multiplied by some appropriate dollar amount (at *least* minimum wage). This yields an impressive and readily understood summary of how much the community has benefited from the program.

Similarly, a record of hours contributed by the site supervisors, trainers, etc., multiplied by a different dollar figure, yields useful information on the benefits (i.e., donated expertise) of the program to the sponsoring agency or school. Some programs print a list of these people and title them "adjunct faculty" to further emphasize the point.

Visits to Project Sites. There is no better way of getting a sense of the site — and of demonstrating to both supervisor and students that you think what they are doing is important — than to visit the placement. It usually is beneficial to get in touch with the supervisor beforehand and arrange a convenient time. However, unannounced informal visiting also can be very useful to give a truer idea of how effective the placement is for all concerned.

Telephone Monitoring. Regular site visits often are prohibitively time-consuming and telephone calls can supplement face-to-face contacts. It usually is difficult to develop a relationship by telephone alone, so try to visit the field site early in the program to establish rapport. Then use the telephone as a supplement.

Written Evaluations. Forms for supervisor assessment of student performance and student evaluation of the field site already have been described. In addition, asking parents to evaluate what their son or daughter has gained from the program can yield valuable information for measuring the program's performance, and also serves a public relations function.

Also, don't neglect the recipients of service themselves, who probably have the most detailed knowledge about the program's impact. Their evaluations sometimes can be gathered on a formal or informal basis.

Formal Program Evaluation

The need for a formal, written evaluation of a community service program is relatively rare, most often occurring when a program has received funding from a foundation or government agency.

Sometimes, offering to do a formal evaluation can help secure funding for a new program. A proposal that includes a reasonable evaluation plan may help convince funders that you are a good risk — a serious and thoughtful contender.

Moreover, an evaluation that shows positive results can be very helpful to friendly decision-makers (school board members, United Way allocation panels, legislators, city councils) to convince their critics to continue to support volunteer programs for youth.

Formal program evaluation is a process of systematically identifying, collecting, analyzing, and reporting information about an educational program or activity for the purpose of better understanding a program or making decisions about its future.

Since program evaluation is complex, technical, and not very enjoyable work, it's probably best to consult with or turn the task over to someone who has experience in the field. The disadvantages of using professional evaluators include expense and the difficulty of finding someone competent to evaluate a community service program. The advantages are that a good evaluator will bring a more objective view to the task than would the program's staff, and will be aware of a variety of evaluation techniques not readily available to most people.

If you can't afford a professional evaluator or can't find a competent one, you or someone in the program may be able to do the evaluation yourself. A manual, entitled "Instruments and Scoring Guides: Experiential Education Evaluation Project," contains instruments designed especially for evaluating community service programs. It is available from the Center for Youth Development and Research, University of Minnesota.

Dan Conrad directs community involvement programs at Hopkins High School in Minnesota. Diane Hedin is former Director of Community Relations at the Pillsbury Foundation and is now a professor at the Center for Youth Development and Research at the University of Minnesota. Over the past 17 years, Conrad and Hedin have co-directed several research and publications projects in experiential education, youth participation, and service-learning.

PART II

Profiles of Programs that Combine Service and Learning

Introduction to Program Profiles

This "book within a book" describes specific programs and courses that are working. It is written for those who are starting programs or planning new courses, those who want to refine or expand existing programs and courses, and those who just want to see how service and learning can be combined in actual programs.

The following chapters have two types of entries: (1) program profiles based on extensive questionnaires sent to the program staff or faculty, and (2) other articles describing particular programs and courses. In the questionnaire and in selecting the articles for inclusion, we asked questions about *why* and *how* people implemented particular programs and policies. We tried to help the reader get beyond basic descriptive information and get inside the thinking of those who direct these programs — inside the important decisions and challenges each faces. Because firsthand advice from experienced practitioners is invaluable, we have quoted directly their "lessons learned," "problems addressed," "biggest challenges," and "other advice" whenever possible.

These are not necessarily the best programs. They do not all fit the "Principles of Good Practice in Combining Service and Learning" outlined in this resource book. But they all have valuable models and lessons to pass on.

The programs and courses presented here are dynamic. They change continuously (some will by the time this reaches your hands), but their lessons are timeless. Some of the advice from programs in the 1970s is the still the wisest available, and it is included without reservation.

The profiles are divided into programs and courses based in: (1) Colleges and Universities; (2) K-12 Schools; and (3) Community-Based Organizations, Government, and Youth-Serving Agencies.

For many of the programs and courses profiled, sample materials — syllabi, brochures, newsletters, learning contracts, handbooks, videotapes — are available. Contact the individual indicated in each profile. The National Resource Center on Service-Learning, housed at the National Society for Internships and Experiential Education, also has available hundreds of program samples, syllabi, and resources for all settings and fields.

Many thanks to everyone who helped this "book within a book" become a reality — Sally Migliore for her assistance with the survey design; Barb Baker for her compilation and editing of the responses; Barbara Gomez of the Council of Chief State School Officers and Terry Modglin of the National Crime Prevention Council for their research and gracious reprint assistance; Lyn Baird, Jeanne Carney, and Carolyn Mulford for their work on *Synergist*, which provided valuable lessons from the recent past; the practitioners, faculty, and others who took the time to share their expertise by trudging through a six-page questionnaire; and Michelle Duggins, Annette Wofford, Carol Majors, Lacy Maddox, and Ann Farmer for their patient production assistance throughout draft after draft. This section in itself was a service-learning effort of many committed people.

— Jane Kendall

PART II

Profiles of Programs that Combine Service and Learning

Colleges and Universities

Boston College

PULSE Program, Boston College, Chestnut Hill, MA 02167, 617-552-3495. Richard Carroll Keeley, Director. Private, suburban college; 8200 students.

Participation: 185 undergraduates involved in the community during academic year for 26 weeks for average of 9 hours per week. Most effective publicity: word-of-mouth.

Overview: Began in 1970 through joint initiative of Student Government, Philosophy and Theology Departments. **Goals:** To provide students with supervised encounters with aspects of social injustice and suffering, to contextualize their encounters with reference to philosophical and theological traditions, and to foster the development of student leadership. Program supports students' intellectual, ethical, and moral development, and sense of social responsibility.

Structure: Based in Academic Affairs. Director reports to Philosophy Department Chair.

Budget: $64,000 from 100% school funds. Includes funds for administration, clerical support, long distance calls. **Staff:** 1 full-time, 1 part-time.

Faculty involvement: 6 are active.

Community involvement: Agencies define the role of students. Site supervisors are required to: attend meetings to discuss program and expectations, develop a work-learning agreement with students, hold periodic supervisory sessions, complete student and program evaluations. **Service sites:** Identified by program administrator, students. Criteria for selecting sites: congruence with program goals; meaningful tasks; good, available supervision; accessibility by public transportation; safety; neighborhood diversity. Most effective publicity: providing agencies with current catalogue/newsletter. **Compensation:** Students are reimbursed for transportation costs.

Preparation: Concurrent courses in Philosophy, Theology.

Learning: Structured opportunities for reflection and analysis include: philosophy and theology course "Person and Social Responsibility," several elective courses. Students spend average of 4 hours/week in structured reflection activities. Learning monitored and supported by teachers, student coordinators, site supervisors.

Academic credit: Yes; can be used toward electives, general education requirements.

Monitoring of service: Done by supervisors. Quality of service is evaluated by supervisors in conjunction with students.

Recognition: Faculty: Involvement is recognized as part of regular work load. *Site supervisors:* Developing program for site supervisors to receive graduate course tuition vouchers.

Program evaluation: Year-end evaluations are completed by students, student coordinators, supervisors.

Bronx Community College — City University of New York

SHARE, South Hall 112, Bronx Community College, Bronx, NY 10453, 212-220-6420. Michael Steuerman, Director. Public, urban college; 7000 students.

Participation: 25 freshmen and sophomores participate in the community for entire year for average of 8 hours/week. Most students recruited through Human Service and Community Health faculty and videotape at College Work-Study Fair.

Overview: Established in 1987 with grant from Fund for the Improvement of Postsecondary Education. **Goals:** To train core group of students to organize and run a food program for students and community residents, to reduce student indebtedness by paying students through work-study, to improve academic retention. Program supports students' intellectual, ethical, moral, career, civic, and personal development, and sense of social responsibility.

Structure: Based in Community Service Department. Director reports to President. Advisory Committee composed of 40% faculty, 10% students, 10% community representatives, 40% administrators.

Budget: $65,000 from 30% school funds, 70% federal. Includes funds for administration, site visits, clerical support, long-distance calls. **Staff:** 5 part-time.

Faculty involvement: 4 of 150 are active. They are required to review student papers.

Community involvement: Sites identified by program administrator. SHARE contract used. Most effective publicity: flyers, brochures, committed speakers.

Learning: Students required to take a pre-service course and weekly 2-hour seminar. Reflection and analysis encouraged through seminars and weekly reflection papers reviewed by program trainer. Learning is also supported through personal and academic counseling. **Academic credit:** Yes; can be used toward the major, electives.

Recognition: Students: Student government award. *Faculty:* Through overload compensation or as part of regular work load.

Program evaluation: By Advisory Committee and students through periodic questionnaires and seminar discussions.

Institutional benefits: Provides a community service and supports students' academic progress.

Problem addressed: "Developing student leadership — we have resisted making the program a faculty/administration-run project. Our seminars and informal meetings are used to heighten awareness of and address this issue."

Lesson learned: "Don't rely on media and brochures to publicize and enroll students. Meaningful, powerful conversations by committed speakers work."

Calvin College

Student Volunteer Service, Calvin College, 3201 Burton SE, Grand Rapids, MI 49506, 616-957-6455. Rhonda Berg, Director. Private, suburban college; 4250 students.

Participation: 425 undergrad and grad students, alumni, faculty, and staff involved in the community during academic year for 10 weeks for 3 hours/week. Most effective publicity: posters, recruitment by student staff.

Overview: Began in 1964 as student initiative with backing of Education Department to address high dropout rate among public high school students. Program started with 35 students tutoring in 5 schools. **Goals:** To provide opportunities for students to meet human and community needs, to help students mature in their understanding of the complex social, economic, political, and fundamental religious issues in life. Program supports students' ethical, moral, and personal development, and sense of social responsibility.

Structure: Based in Student Affairs. Director reports to Dean of Student Life. Advisory Board of 9% faculty, 36% students, 36% community representatives, 18% administrators.

Budget: $74,200 from 81% school funds, 19% funds raised for specific projects or programs. Includes funds for administration, clerical support, long distance calls, site visits, professional/faculty development. **Staff:** 1 full-time, 13 student coordinators.

Faculty involvement: 5-10 of 240 are active each year. Faculty participate in short-term, one-time activities such as mentoring a spring break service project or sitting on Advisory Board.

Community involvement: Agency representatives help develop program policies and procedures through representation on Advisory Board. Site supervisors are required to: submit a position description; interview, screen, orient, train and supervise students. College encourages supervisors to recognize student contributions and to keep a permanent record of their work. Students make independent agreements with agencies. **Service sites:** Identified by Director. Criteria for selecting sites: student benefits, placement benefits, community needs (priority on serving "underprivileged"), located within 6 miles of campus, ability to meet supervisory requirements, history of working relationship. Most effective publicity: word-of-mouth, contacts through volunteer managers' association. **Compensation:** Transportation or mileage reimbursement.

Preparation: Individual meetings with student coordinator to help students find sites. Students receive self-instructional materials and information about their roles and responsibilities as volunteers. Agencies responsible for training students.

Learning: Structured opportunities for reflection and analysis include: Round Table Devotions — informal discussions with faculty where faith and learning are brought together; Poverty Awareness Retreat — students spend 3 days working on a service project and reflecting on and learning about poverty; Spring Break Service Projects — faculty mentor accompanies small group of students on service project and helps facilitate discussion and analysis. **Academic credit:** Not in this program, but there are a few courses which require a service component.

Monitoring of service: Done primarily by agencies. College also requests feedback from supervisors each term. Sites use their own mechanisms to get input about program from ultimate service recipients.

Recognition: Students: Alumni Association provides annual recognition event. Students' service records are primary consideration for alumni scholarships. Letters of appreciation listing a student's involvement to date are sent each term. *Faculty:* Receive some institutional recognition but no reduction in other responsibilities. *Site supervisors:* Thank-you letters. Alumni Association recognizes one agency each year for its partnership with the College in providing service opportunities for students.

Program evaluation: Advisory Board evaluates how program can improve service to agencies and students every other year. Staff examines feedback forms from students and agencies and meets with focus groups.

Institutional benefits: Enhances students' educational experience.

Problem addressed: "Our program was originally part of student government. In addition to having no ties to colleagues, this system promoted tension between the Director and students. Through a year-long strategic planning process, the students and Director agreed it would be better for program to be incorporated into Student Affairs. Now student involvement is channeled more productively, and the Director has stronger ties to the rest of the College."

Lesson learned: "When starting our strategic planning process, I gave the major responsibility for making recommendations to a student group. I think the task was too large and undefined for them. From this experience, I learned to pay attention to students' developmental levels when giving assignments and to provide more structure, especially to students who are new to tasks."

Biggest challenge: "To formalize and strengthen the learning component of our program."

Other advice: "Understand your campus environment. Spend time listening to everyone: faculty, students, administration. Take risks. Be willing to accept responsibility for failures and give credit to students for successes."

Cornell University

New York City Field Study Program, Cornell University, 45 John Street, Suite 803, New York, NY 10038, 212-619-6392. Kenneth Reardon, Director. Urban program of a private, rural university of 12,000 students.

Participation: 40 juniors and seniors involved full-time during the academic year for 16 weeks. Participants spend 3 days/week in field experiences in corporate settings and 1 day/week working on a community project. During the last 2 weeks of the term students spend approximately 60 hours completing the community project. (Remainder of profile focuses on community projects part of program.) Most effective publicity: word-of-mouth, faculty advisor referrals. **Prerequisites:** Completion of fieldwork preparation course which provides introduction to experiential education, qualitative research, and critical thinking, and an opportunity to be involved in a community research study.

Overview: Began as internship program for juniors and seniors. **Goals:** To enhance self-directed learning skills, to deepen understanding of organizational behavior, to increase understanding of urban problems and civic responsibility. Program supports students' intellectual, ethical, moral, career, civic, and personal development, and sense of social responsibility. **Philosophy:** Students do fieldwork on critical problems facing people with low incomes in urban settings. The work always involves intimate contact with people with low incomes and those working with them in community settings. Students are expected to produce high-quality research of use to community sponsors and are *fully responsible* for managing their class as a consulting team. Faculty members go into the field with them to model research techniques, provide feedback on performance, offer moral support, and challenge students to think critically. An intensive orientation is organized during which bona fide community leaders help students understand the history of the community and the real meaning of the social problem being examined in the lives of those in the community.

Structure: Sponsored by 1 of 7 colleges at Cornell as an academic program. Director reports to Dean of College of Human Ecology.

Budget: $150,000 for NYC program; $400,000 overall for Field and International Study Program; from 100% school funds. Includes funds for administration, clerical support, long distance calls, site visits, professional/faculty development. **Staff:** 11 full-time, 6 part-time in overall program in Ithaca plus NYC.

Faculty involvement: Two faculty are centrally involved. Required of faculty: interest in students, experience with experiential education, strong research methods training, excellent community organization skills, patience, and endurance.

Community involvement: Faculty assist community organizations in formulating a 4-6 page statement of their need which is presented to the student class in the form of a Request For Proposal. Students respond to this request with a research proposal and work-plan. Organizations then review students' proposal. Community representatives are deeply involved in intensive student orientation to the community and to the issue. Additionally, they review all research instruments and receive a draft of final research reports prior to distribution. All copies of students' research reports are given to the organization, which controls the distribution and use of research results. Site supervisors are required to: have an interest in students and their development, be able to meet with faculty and students as needed. **Service sites:** Identified by faculty. Criteria for selection of sites: importance of issue, ability of student researchers to impact project, proximity to student work sites, fit with college mission statement, and faculty knowledge of issue addressed. Most effective publicity: program has developed a reputation for solid community research; interested groups seeking assistance call us. **Compensation:** Students are not paid, but some firms where students do their corporate field experiences cover basic expenses.

Preparation: Students complete a 4-credit fieldwork preparation course and spend 2 days in New York City the previous semester to preview the program. Former participants also operate a peer counseling program which assists students before and during their participation.

Learning: Required structured opportunities for reflection and analysis include: spending 1 day/week doing fieldwork related to community research project and 2+ hours/week in faculty-facilitated discussion group. Students work on their own for an additional 1-2 hours/week. Reflective seminar topics include: experiential education, organizational behavior, and urban ecology. Faculty also assist students in formulating learning plans. Students' learning evaluated through: self-evaluation based on learning plan, faculty and site supervisor observations, student papers, portfolios, class research report, and oral presentation of community research project. **Academic credit:** Yes.

Monitoring of service: Done by students, faculty, and community project sponsors periodically and at term's end using project goals agreed upon at start of project. Agency representatives talk with faculty weekly and meet with students monthly.

> *"For these programs to work, they must be carefully designed by experienced faculty. If inadequate faculty time is provided, the program may do more harm than good for students and community members. Some community involvement may not be better than none if the contact is minimal and superficial, and reflection is not structured. Such experiences may result in students' confirming stereotypes and understandings of the community which are simply wrong."*

Recognition: Students: Receive a "Big Apple" pin at program's completion. *Faculty:* Involvement is recognized as part of regular work load. *Site supervisors:* Receive plaques, publicity in local press.

Program evaluation: By faculty, students, and site supervisors through discussions of progress and process as part of project and at end. Students and faculty also complete written evaluations.

Institutional benefits: "It provides a very powerful learning experience for students, faculty, and community sponsors. It stimulates faculty to explore urban research topics."

Problem addressed: "Initially, students saw the community research project as another mandatory requirement of the university, and they resented it. They were also anxious about entering communities with which they were unfamiliar and whose residents differed from them in ethnicity, class, and religion. We addressed these problems by developing intensive orientation programs to the community with long-time residents, community leaders, human service workers, and academics showing them the community and sharing their observations. If students understand the social history of a community and meet people on a one-to-one basis, they develop real insight into a community and empathy for its people. This results in a tremendous commitment to the projects and more thoughtful research."

Lesson learned: "We tried to have students do individual projects on community issues in which they were interested on a less intensive basis. Students tended to do library research and very superficial studies of community problems."

Biggest challenge: "Students and faculty experience overload because of the scope and depth of the program. So many new experiences take place during the students' internship placements, community research activities, and their daily social lives in New York City. We are concerned that they may not be able to reflect adequately upon these experiences during 16 weeks. Perhaps students would get more out of a less active program which would provide more space and time for reflection."

Other advice: "For these programs to work, they must be carefully designed by experienced faculty. If inadequate faculty time is provided, the program may do more harm than good for students and community members. Some community involvement may not be better than none if the contact is minimal and superficial, and reflection is not structured. Such experiences may result in students' confirming stereotypes and understandings of the community which are simply wrong."

Dalhousie University

President's Leadership Class, Dalhousie University, 6136 University Avenue, Halifax, Nova Scotia, Canada B3H 452, 902-424-1315. Jim Neale, Coordinator.

Participation: 150 undergrad and grad students involved in the community during the academic year. Most effective publicity: personal contact while students are in high school, promotional literature passed on by guidance counselors. **Prerequisites:** Students must be committed and willing to serve others and to complete a 4-year degree in 5 years. (One year is spent working in a developing country.) Participants are required to submit a cover letter, resume, application, and transcript.

Overview: Program began in 1983 as a high school-based program. President's Leadership Class was developed in 1987 to address the needs of college students. **Goals:** To develop practical understanding of how to link personal learning with community service, to develop a service ethic among participants, to raise awareness among educators of the potential for enhanced learning that can occur in the context of serving others. Program supports students' intellectual, ethical, moral, career, civic, and personal development, and sense of social responsibility.

Structure: Coordinator reports to the President. Advisory Board of 75% faculty, 25% students.

Budget: $66,000 from 100% federal funds. Office space is provided by the University. **Staff: 3.**

Service sites: Program holds an orientation and training workshop for host organizations, groups, or communities and consults with project coordinators in the community. Criteria for selecting projects: must directly benefit community, must be work/projects that would not otherwise be done (i.e. not take work from others), must contribute to student's development with a particular focus on leadership and academic development.

Preparation: Five-year process including: a credit-bearing course "Introduction to Service-Learning," a group living experience for one academic year, group support meetings, group and individual service projects, leadership development activities, service in a developing country, participation in a 5-day orientation workshop on leadership and service.

Learning: Structured opportunities for reflection and analysis include: classwork, weekly group support/planning meetings, journals, individual consultations with Coordinator. **Academic credit:** Yes, but not automatic. Students are encouraged to fulfill academic requirements (assignments, projects) in ways that benefit the community (i.e. engineering students constructing ramps to make a library wheelchair accessible as a means of learning theoretical principles).

Monitoring of service: Quality of service is assessed by students, Coordinator, and site supervisors through performance appraisals.

Recognition: Students: Media coverage, recognition by University President, group meetings at which goals and achievements are identified. *Staff:* Involvement is recognized as part of regular work load.

Institutional benefits: Program promotes positive community relations and adds to the University's reputation for being innovative.

Problem addressed: "Recruiting appropriate students and service placements. We began by being discriminating and small to build a reputation for quality. Then we expanded. It is a mistake not to be selective for fear of being considered elitist. No one gains from poor-quality service."

Lesson learned: "The importance of holding orientation sessions for host organizations."

Biggest challenge: "Obtaining funding on an ongoing basis."

Other advice: "Become a part of a local and/or national network as soon as possible. Networking is crucial to discovering suitable placements."

Earlham College

Service Learning Program, Earlham College, #86 Student Development, National Road West, Richmond, IN 47374, 317-983-1317. Nancy Wood, Director. Private, suburban college; 1100 students.

Participation: 337 undergrad and grad students are involved in the community during the academic year for 10 weeks for 2-10 hours/week. Most effective publicity: staff recruitment, agency representatives coming to campus.

Overview: Program started through efforts of College President and student leader. Received ACTION grant in 1987. **Goals:** To involve 50% of student body; to involve more men; to provide incentives for and involve more students of color and students with low incomes. Program supports students' intellectual, ethical, moral, career, civic, and personal development, and sense of social responsibility.

Structure: Student-run, college-sponsored program based in Student Development. Director reports to Dean of Students. Advisory Board of 40% faculty, 20% students, 30% community representatives, 10% administrators. Faculty Research Committee has been established to explore possibility of required community service. Director is responsible for most communication between groups.

Budget: $25,000 plus administration from 60% school funds, 30% federal, 5% foundations, and 5% special developmental funds from school. Includes funds for administration, clerical support, site visits, long-distance calls, professional/faculty development. **Staff:** 2 full-time, 1 part-time.

Faculty involvement: 20 of 139 are active. Requirements of faculty vary.

Community involvement: Supervisors are required to train and orient students, provide oral and written feedback, return time sheets, and attend recognition banquet. **Service sites:** Identified by students and program administrator. Most effective publicity: media, mail, and Information and Referral Bureau. Sites selected on basis of training, supervision, and feedback provided for students; and need for and appreciation of student assistance. **Transportation:** Provided to sites by school, or students are reimbursed for travel costs by Earlham.

Learning: Preparation and opportunities for reflection and analysis include orientation to community service and Richmond community; tutoring leadership workshops; self-instructional tutoring tapes; seminars on poverty and other topical workshops such as "Working with the Elderly," "Working with Physically Disabled Persons," and "Family Violence and Working with Victims." Earlham offers counseling, advising, and process and evaluation seminars. Most agencies also offer in-house training and orientation. Some departments require a certain number of hours of workshops for a particular major. Time spent in structured reflection activities varies. Program Director available to counsel students about learning goals. Students are asked about what they are learning about poverty and if agencies are providing adequate support, training and opportunities for growth. Learning is evaluated through journals, workshop and seminar evaluations, and process seminar feedback. Learning is assessed by the Service Advisory Board, site supervisors, and student participants. **Academic credit:** Yes; can be used toward the major or general education requirements.

Monitoring of service: Quality of the service provided is monitored and evaluated through site visits by Program director and questionnaires completed by supervisors, parents of tutored children, and elderly participants. Evaluations are sent and analyzed by the Service Advisory Board.

Recognition: Students: Receive certificates at a recognition ceremony such as a pizza party or banquet held each term. Those volunteering over 50 hours receive t-shirts; student staff receive mugs. *Site supervisors:* Recognized at a banquet. *Faculty:* Receive some institutional recognition but no reduction in other responsibilities. Faculty who serve in the community themselves are honored at an annual concert for the community and in Service Learning Program newsletters.

Program evaluation: Service Advisory Board and ACTION evaluate the program. All participants and supervisors complete evaluations. Impact of program on school is measured regarding admissions, retention, student satisfaction with institution, alumni participation and giving.

Institutional benefits: "Alums love it! We're getting more capital gifts through our capital campaign."

Problem addressed: "The need for more local awareness of justice and poverty issues. Our students coordinated a 'Justice For All Day' and involved community leaders in their plans. It brought the community together to 'join hands around the county courthouse' in a symbolic effort to raise awareness. The group then came back on campus for a panel discussion on local problems. As a result, a Justice For All Coalition was established with task forces working on child care, church mobilization, empowerment issues and a workshop on how to bring about social change peacefully. A community that couldn't talk is now working together."

Lesson learned: "I try to give my student staff as much opportunity to grow and do responsible tasks as I can. Many things I could do more efficiently, but I have to allow them to try and even fail. I try to train them to manage their own areas. Sometimes the student flies with the responsibility and really grows. At other times seemingly capable youth can't handle the responsibility. I continually look for new training ideas. As Director, you work very hard on your program but are rather at the mercy of student whim. It's a risky place to be, but worth the success of those who soar. The greatest challenge is dusting yourself off to take chances on new students in hopes that they meet the responsibilities."

Biggest challenge: "We have successfully involved more males in our program but are still seeking ways to involve more students with financial need and more students from all the various ethnic groups on campus."

Other advice: "It has been especially helpful to have the college provide transportation for students to and from community sites."

"If you can win the College President's support, *things happen*! Our President is so committed to service that the excitement has spilled over into every area of the campus."

Georgetown University

Volunteer and Public Service Center, Georgetown University, P.O. Box 2255, Washington, DC 22057, 202-687-3703. Cecilia Delve, Director. Private, urban university; 12,000 students.

Participation: 700+ undergraduates and high school juniors involved in the community during academic year, summer, and spring break. Programs generally require involvement for at least 1 semester for average of 5-7 hours/week. Most effective publicity: students recruiting students, summer mailing to new students.

Overview: Developed by Student Affairs Department in 1978, a year after the Community Action Coalition, a student group, was formed. **Goals:** To expose students to issues of social justice, to develop leaders at Georgetown who look beyond monetary or personal gain, to encourage students to give a year or more of service after graduating and to consider careers in non-profits, to help faculty and staff integrate experiential education into classroom experiences. Program supports students' intellectual, ethical, moral, career, civic, and personal development, and sense of social responsibility. **Philosophy:** "We seek to expose students to opportunities which address social justice issues on the local, national, and international levels. With full respect for the diversity of faith and philosophy on campus, the VPS Center continues to uphold the distinctiveness of the Jesuit service tradition at Georgetown. As the President of Georgetown has said, 'We at Georgetown will work no miracles, nor expect to remake human relations within the city. For our little part we can, however, strive to make understanding grow, and we can care.'"

Structure: Based in Student Affairs. Director reports to Director of Student Programs. Advisory Committee of 57% faculty/43% students.

Budget: $164,000 from 80% school funds, 10% federal, 10% special developmental funds from school. Includes funds for administration, clerical support, long distance calls, site visits, professional/faculty development, student organization budgets. **Staff:** 4 full-time, 2 part-time, 2 work-study, graduate school interns.

Faculty involvement: 50 of 600 are active. The University's 4th Credit Option Program allows a student to receive 1 extra credit for learning gained through service which relates to their coursework. In this program, faculty are required to develop learning contracts with students and to monitor students work in the community.

Community involvement: Site supervisors are required to: fill out volunteer request form, be willing to meet with VPS Center staff, provide orientation and training for students. Feedback and evaluation comments from community organizations are taken seriously in the development of program policies and procedures. **Service sites:** Identified by Director, students. Criteria for selecting sites: agency reputation, completion of volunteer request form. Most effective publicity: Agencies generally contact program first, so publicity to community is not a problem. **Compensation:** Students are reimbursed by University for transportation expenses.

Preparation: Depends on program. Initial orientation and ongoing training are provided. Spring retreat for student leadership. Preparation programs have been established for "Freshman Orientation to Community Involvement (FOCI)" and for the High School Juniors Program. Peru/South Africa Programs have ongoing orientation during preceding semester and week-long training session.

Learning: Structured opportunities for reflection and analysis include: required weekly reflection/discussion groups for participants in District Action Project, a residence hall program; VPS Roundtable monthly meetings and leadership retreat (required for leadership of community service organizations); regular meetings between participants and student leaders; FOCI speakers and meditations (required for FOCI participants). Average hours/week spent in structured reflection activities depends on program. Learning is monitored and supported by: faculty for students taking 4th credit option, mid-semester evaluations for District Action Project participants, discussions while traveling to and from sites for high school juniors, and written evaluation for most programs at end of term. Learning assessed by: depends on program; sometimes faculty, agencies, administrators, and students. **Academic credit:** Sometimes yes; can be used toward the major, for electives, for general education requirements, for graduation.

Monitoring of service: Agency volunteer coordinator monitors service through feedback and evaluation. Program relies on agencies to get input from ultimate service recipients. In the case of Adult Literacy Programs, students and staff attend Tenants' Association meetings.

Recognition: Students: Office of Student Programs presents a yearly "Outstanding Student in Community Service Award."

Program evaluation: Impact of Program evaluated by VPS Advisory Board, student leaders, participants, and agency supervisors. Director and VPS staff prepare annual reports.

Institutional benefits: "Fulfils the Jesuit philosophy of service, and as a result, makes students more aware of their responsibility to their community. Georgetown is known for its commitment to community service. Many students are attracted to Georgetown for that reason."

Problem addressed: "To encourage and develop student leadership, we began monthly VPS leadership meetings, established a Spring Leadership Retreat, and meet with leaders individually once a month."

Lesson learned: "We need to rethink our 4th Credit Option Program and provide more support to students wanting to receive credit for the learning they gain through their work in the community. No one will graduate from Georgetown based on one extra credit, and currently there is a financial disincentive in that students must pay for the additional credit."

Biggest challenges: "We have experienced such rapid growth in the last three years that it feels as though we are playing 'catch-up' to ourselves. We are still working on identity issues as well as name recognition on campus."

How to encourage greater faculty participation and suggest ways to include service as part of the tenure process.

Other advice: "Initially, focus on being an educator to your students, *then* branch out to the community and agencies."

Goshen College

Study Service Term, Goshen College, Goshen, IN 46526. Ruth Gunden, Director of International Education. Private, rural college; 1100 students.

Participation: 200 students (mostly sophomores, some seniors) participate for 14 weeks during academic year. Participants live with a family in another country for 6 weeks. 12 international hours are required for graduation, but students may take an on-campus alternative. **Prerequisites:** 1 year of language; students must also have attended Goshen at least one term.

Overview: Program began in 1968 as part of major curriculum review. **Goals:** To promote: (1) intercultural awareness, the ability to function effectively with people of other world views, (2) the ability to communicate effectively in another culture, (3) the ability to think actively and strategically, emphasizing action-reflection learning, and (4) a healthy understanding of self and others. Program supports students' intellectual, ethical, moral, career, civic and personal development, sense of social responsibility, and expands their world view. **Philosophy:** Living in a developing country is beneficial to our program for several reasons: (1) students have to "break out of the shell" of their own culture; (2) they are exposed to human need and, it is hoped, are motivated to understand and work at coming to grips with this reality; (3) they are forced to live in another culture in such a way that they cannot be insulated from it; and (4) they have a chance to see that Christian servanthood in situations of need involves fully utilizing available resources.

Structure: Based in General Education Department. Director reports to the Academic Dean. Program Committee of 4 faculty, 1 student, 1 program administrator, and 1 student dean.

Budget: $600,000 from 99% school funds, 1% foundations. Includes funds for administration, clerical support, site visits, long-distance calls, professional/faculty development. **Staff:** 2 full-time.

Faculty involvement: 5-6 of 75 are active each year. Faculty sponsors are required to live in host country and coordinate entire Study-Service program (e.g. arrange housing, field trips, lectures, and service assignments for 23 students).

Community involvement: Community organizations are at the center of developing program policies and procedures. Requirements of site supervisors: written correspondence and at least one on-site visit, or more as needed. **Service sites:** Identified by program administrator and advisory group. Criteria used to select sites: must be a developing nation; service assignment must relate to student's interest and abilities. Program publicized through host contacts.

Preparation: Short orientation in addition to spending first 6 weeks in country studying language, listening to lectures by nationals, taking field trips, and living with a host family.

Learning: Required reflection and analysis activities include journals, language classes, field trips, reflections papers, and classes held by nationals. Students spend 25-30 hours per week on these activities. Learning is supported and monitored through reading and comments on journal, individual interviews, reading of reflective papers, and group discussions. Learning is assessed by both the faculty and student and evaluated through a 3-5 page evaluation. **Academic Credit:** Yes; can be used for general education requirements.

"The most important piece of general education — changes more lives than any other program."

Monitoring of service: The quality of service is monitored by director and faculty leader in each country, and by students. Additionally, there is regular dialogue with recipients of the service. "This is the heart of the Program."

Recognition: Site supervisors: Receive recognition letters and gifts. *Faculty:* Involvement is recognized as part of regular work load.

Program evaluation: Impact of program is evaluated through periodic faculty evaluations, student journals and evaluation forms at program's end, verbal and written evaluations by site supervisors, and periodic evaluations by administration. Impact of program on institution is measured regarding admissions, retention, student satisfaction with institution, alumni participation and giving.

Institutional benefits: "The most important piece of general education — changes more lives than any other program."

Biggest challenge: "Finding a French location that is not as expensive as Guadeloupe."

Metro State University

Community Service Internship Program, Metro State University, Suite 121, Metro Square, St. Paul, MN 55101, 612-296-8965. Jane Rauenhorst, Faculty. Public, urban university; 6000 students.

Participation: 200-300 juniors and seniors involved during academic year and summer for 10-52 weeks for 10-20 hours/week. Most effective publicity: announcements in student newsletter, class presentations, word-of-mouth.

Overview: Began in 1987 through grant from Fund for the Improvement of Postsecondary Education (FIPSE). **Goals:** To encourage student involvement in community service, to reduce student indebtedness, to develop and place students in internships. Program supports students' intellectual, ethical, moral, career, civic, and personal development, and sense of social responsibility. **Philosophy:** The needs, talents and priorities of adult college students are changing and becoming more diverse. Programs must plan for these changes.

Structure: Based in Curriculum and Assessment. Director reports to Dean of Curriculum and Assessment.

Budget: $54,000 from 100% school funds. Includes funds for administration, clerical support, long distance calls, site visits, professional/faculty development. **Staff:** 1 full-time, 1 part-time.

Faculty involvement: 7 of 40 are active. Faculty are resources to Coordinator, students, and site supervisors. Internship must be approved by a resident faculty member prior to registration.

Community involvement: Agencies develop internship opportunities and negotiate an internship agreement directly with the student to determine internship responsibilities, roles, and commitment. Site supervisors are required to: negotiate terms of internship with student, supervise intern, complete narrative student evaluation. **Service sites:** Identified by students and Coordinator. Criteria used to select sites: potential for credit-generating learning experience which meets FIPSE's definition of community service. Most effective publicity: direct contacts, community newsletters, media. **Compensation:** Some paid positions, tuition reimbursement program and Community Service Internship Scholarship Program provide $500 awards.

Preparation: Students receive guidance and advising from Internship Coordinator and academic advisor. Many sponsors offer on-site training.

Learning: Students and supervisors receive materials and guidance on reflection and analysis of internship experience from coordinator. Students are encouraged to keep journals. Supervisors are required to meet with interns on a regular basis. Average hours/week spent in structured reflection activities varies. Site supervisor is the evaluator and "instructor" for the intern. Coordinator supports supervisor and provides University guidelines and standards. Methods used to evaluate student learning: situational observation, simulation exercises, interviews. **Academic credit:** Yes; can be used toward the major, for electives, general education requirements, graduation requirements. Internship tasks and responsibilities must be worthy of upper division credit and contain theoretical as well as practical components.

Monitoring of service: Service recipients provide feedback to interns, sites.

Recognition: Students: Approximately 7 Community Service Internship Awards of $500 are offered each quarter. *Faculty:* Involvement is recognized as part of regular work load. *Site supervisors:* Supervisors are paid $100 per competence (4 quarter credits) that a student earns for the internship.

Program evaluation: Involves faculty, students, site supervisors, and administration. Includes assessment of: academic soundness of internships, quality of students' work and benefit to their agency, quantity of students served, and quality of experience.

Institutional benefits: Community-based learning opportunities enhance students' education.

Problem addressed: "Metro State serves adult students, many of whom work and have families. We have worked to develop opportunities that will be interesting to adults and flexible enough for them to be able to participate. Internships can begin or end as agreed upon by students and agencies. The weekly time commitment and length of the internship varies a great deal. The student and agency dictate these aspects, not the University. Because of this, more students and agencies participate."

Biggest challenge: "Increasing student involvement. Students are so busy, and many have not had previous community service experience. It is an educational process to inform and interest them in available opportunities."

Stanford University

Public Service Center, Stanford University, P.O. Box Q, Stanford, CA 94309, 415-725-2859. Tim Stanton, Associate Director. Private, suburban university; 13,000 students.

Participation: 1500-2000 participants including undergrad and grad students, alumni, faculty, and staff involved in the community for 1 day to 52 weeks during the academic year and summer for 1-45 hours/week. Most effective publicity to students: word-of-mouth, notices in student newspaper. **Prerequisites:** Some programs require application and certain background criteria.

Overview: Program initiated by President who thought the values of service and citizenship were not emphasized enough. He appointed an assistant to conduct a year-long inventory. A recommendation was made to establish the program in 1984-85. **Goals:** (1) to promote, organize, and support effective public and community service by members of Stanford community, especially students; (2) to promote and support a life-long commitment to public service; (3) to provide opportunities for students to increase their effectiveness in public service work whether as leaders or followers; and (4) to enhance the quality of campus academic programs and intellectual debate related to public service issues. Program supports students' intellectual, ethical, career, civic, and personal development, and sense of social responsibility. **Philosophy:** "As a multipurpose, centralized, campus center for public service, we take a broad view of public service and its place in the university. We are interested in all forms of social involvement, at all levels of intensity. We take students where they are and help them gain increasingly challenging and rewarding opportunities to participate in public space. Through Center-sponsored or -supported activities, we hope students develop and practice the leadership, management, experiential learning and collaborative team-building skills necessary for effective public service."

Structure: Director reports to Provost. Center has Faculty Steering Committee composed of 80% faculty/20% students and a Community Advisory Board of 100% community members. Structure of individual programs varies. Tutoring program has a campus/community coordinating group, school partnership has a contract, fellowships for summer projects require community organization sponsorship, Gardner Fellows are placed by staff, students in academic internship courses use contracts/learning plans.

Budget: $700,000 from 43.5% school funds, 1.5% federal, 30% foundations, 4% student fees, 12% from individuals, and 9% President's discretionary fund. Includes funds for administration, site visits, long-distance calls, clerical support, computers, professional/faculty development. **Staff:** 7 full-time, 6 part-time, 20-30 students.

Faculty involvement: 25-35 of 1200 are active. Faculty sponsors are required to facilitate and evaluate learning.

Community involvement: Varies by agency. Tutoring program is administered with continual consultation with affected school personnel. Requirements for site supervisors: depends on program, minimally required to provide feedback on student and Center performance. **Service sites:** Identified by program administrator.

Sites selected for their identified needs and ability to utilize and supervise students effectively. Most effective publicity: direct mail, word-of-mouth. **Compensation:** Some students receive stipends or work-study wage; some are reimbursed for travel and incidental expenses.

Preparation: 3 pre-field courses are offered for public policy interns covering local, state and federal governments. Tutoring program requires 1 day orientation and offers supervision and training seminars for credit through Education School. Many projects provide short orientations (in dorms for service projects, over 5 days for Latin American internships).

Learning: Structured opportunities for reflection and analysis include seminars offered by departments or center staff, reflective/focus groups offered through clearinghouse for non-credit programs, speakers series for all students, retreats for student leaders and staff, and an annual "You Can Make a Difference" conference. Learning requirements depend on program. Academic internships require seminar or other reflective activity. Average hours/week spent in structured reflection activities: 0-15. Support and facilitation of learning depends on program: varies from none to very extensive and structured with most extreme being Stanford-in-Washington, a residential, full-time fall quarter academic internship program. Faculty assess learning through journals, research papers, and exams. **Academic credit:** Yes; can be used toward the major, electives, general education requirements, graduation requirements.

Monitoring of service: Primary responsibility lies with community sites. Depending on program, Center takes little to much responsibility as well. Evaluation research is used to assess quality in tutoring program — pre- and post-tests of tutees; statements from teachers, families and tutors; and tutor self-evaluations are examples of our most extensive evaluation efforts. Service recipients are consulted regularly. In the Tutoring Program, tutees, teachers, school principals, the district superintendent and school board are consulted. "We don't send students unless they are invited in."

Recognition: Students: Campus Compact Robinson Award; Public Service Fellowship from Center for summer project expenses; John Gardner Fellowship given to 6 graduating seniors at Stanford and UC Berkeley; and Deans Service Awards given by Dean of Students to nominees across campus. *Site supervisors:* Thank-you letters, receptions on campus and letters from University President. *Fac-*

ulty: Some institutional recognition but no reduction in other responsibilities.

Program evaluation: Grad student evaluation coordinator works with students and Center and program staffs to produce a variety of evaluation reports. Faculty Committee and site supervisors are included in program evaluation as well. Several questions related to the Center and service involvement are included in senior survey.

Institutional benefits: "Contributes to both curricular and co-curricular undergraduate program; provides good public relations for University; provides focal point, visibility, and strength to University's public service efforts."

Problems addressed: "We looked at two questions: (1) whether and how to centralize and consolidate service activity (both student- and university-sponsored activity), and (2) whether to integrate local, policy-oriented, human service, social change-oriented, and international programs under one roof. We've done both."

"We are proud of our ability to support and strengthen student-initiated public service projects. Student-initiated projects are often high on idealism, however, and low on consultation with community groups, and on administrative strength and continuity. We have learned the art of giving both autonomy and independence to our affiliated groups, as well as advice, criticism, and necessary resources. In a short time the student groups have become dynamic forces on campus and in the community."

Biggest challenge: "Gaining an institutionalized position and budgetary support beyond the term of the current President and Provost. This means raising endowment funds, working out with University leadership the level of continuing support they can provide, and working out with faculty and deans our relationship (and that of service learning) to them."

Syracuse University

Community Service in an Educational Context Project

(CSEC), Syracuse University, Honors Program, H.L. 307, Syracuse, NY 13244-1170, 315-443-2780. Mary Stanley, Project Director. Private, urban university; 12,000 undergraduates.

Participation: 50 sophomores, juniors and seniors in Honors Program involved in practicum and seminar. Students participate in the community for 10 hours/week for 11 weeks during seminar/ practicum. Most effective publicity: sophomore seminar, Honors newsletter, former students. **Prerequisites:** Sophomore honors seminar and a clear interest in the seminar and practicum topic.

Overview: Honors Program moved toward an emphasis on civic education in 1986. Required sophomore seminar focused on civic education and political philosophy. The original Community Leadership Practicum was supported by a joint project of the Exxon and Kettering Foundations. That seminar has been expanded to the CSEC project with funding from the Fund for the Improvement of Postsecondary Education (FIPSE). **Goals:** (1) to give students the intellectual concepts, historical background, and guided experience to help them make informed, reflective and critical judgments regarding public life; (2) to introduce students to the actual practice of civic life through work with a mentor in a service/public institution; (3) to introduce students to an area of public life that is problematic and contentious, and to help them reach insight regarding the facts and values at issue; (4) to encourage students to perform important community service by relieving them of their work-study or work obligations while involved in the seminar/practicum. Program supports students' intellectual, moral, ethical, civic, and personal development, and sense of social responsibility. **Philosophy:** We strive to help create reflective, compassionate, and rational citizens. We assume that to be civically educated is to recognize there is a plurality of meanings of democracy and citizenship and to be able to inquire into the possibility of justice and common grounds despite this. We ask students to take seriously the historical evolution of a public issue, to reflect upon its history in a concrete community, and to recognize that there are multiple and often competing ways of conceptualizing public problems and their solutions. In public service we witness the doing of democracy. Conversation and self-reflection about this action can bring clarity, compassion, and more accurate and adequate grounds for future public action."

Structure: Based in the All University Honors Program. Director reports to Director of the Honors Program and confers with a faculty/student Honors Council.

Budget: $56,000 for the first year from FIPSE. Includes funds for administration, faculty/staff salary, clerical support, long-distance calls, transportation, evaluation. The University provides up to $45,000 in student grants to free students from work obligations while enrolled in a seminar/practicum. **Staff:** Full-time Project Director, 1 part-time Project Assistant.

Faculty involvement: 2 faculty members and the Project Director develop and teach 3 seminar/practicums each year. Project staff recruits mentors and students, organizes mentor meetings, and develops research/evaluation project components. Other faculty are involved through the Honors Council.

Community involvement: Relationships among community mentors, students, and faculty are informal. Seminar facilitates opportunities for all involved to reflect and talk openly. Mentors are invited to group meetings to help faculty develop seminars, to discuss student progress, and to share their understanding of service-learning. Mentors are involved in the issue on which the seminar/practicum focuses (architectrual preservation, the environment, or homelessness and housing) and are invited to the seminar during the last 4 weeks. After the seminar, they are asked to complete an evaluation. Mentors are encouraged to view students as apprentices engaged in learning the skills and judgment necessary for democratic life. **Service sites:** Identified by project staff, faculty, and former mentors. Sites selected for their relevance to issues studied, staff interest in the mentor/apprentice concept and in the problems and possibilities of experience-based civic education. Most effective publicity: personal contact, public meetings, faculty knowledge, former mentor recommendation. **Compensation:** Students are reimbursed for expenses incurred to attend relevant conferences or public meetings. They also are relieved from work obligations so they are free to contribute 10 hours of service each week for the semester.

Preparation: Students take the honors sophomore seminar, which deals with problems related to civic education in a pluralistic, democratic political culture. As part of that seminar, students attend public meetings in Syracuse and inquire about how civic life is accomplished.

Learning: Required structured opportunities for reflection and analysis include: a 3-hour weekly seminar, assigned readings, oral presentations, and a written final project integrating readings, experience, and reflections. "In the seminar, tensions between theory and practice are explored through questions raised about the ambiguous role of the university, and of knowledge in general, in the life of a democratic political community. The seminar on homelessness was the prototype for CSEC project. The seminar on the environment asks students to consider the possible roles of scientific experts, citizens, and policy makers when confronted with an issue which seems to demand technical expertise. The seminar on architectural preservation asks students to explore the value of history and esthetics in the life of a community. The overarching question which organizes all seminars is, 'How should the young be prepared for democratic citizenship in the late twentieth century?'" Learning is supported and monitored through journals, oral reports, class discussion, and final project outlines. Because learning is also, in part, ethical and political, the seminar explores the importance of emotion and passion in learning and the use of rational judgment in public life. **Academic credit:** Yes; can be used for electives outside the major, for general education requirements, and to fulfill upper-level honors requirements.

Monitoring of service: Students work closely with a mentor who guides them in their experience and reflection upon it. Quality of service is evaluated by mentors.

Recognition: Students: Students' participation is highlighted in Honors Program newsletter and local newspaper. They are also invited to attend conferences at other schools. Students also conduct a university-wide "teach-in" on what they have learned from involvement in the Project. *Faculty:* Involvement is recognized as part of regular work load and through overload compensation. *Site supervisors:* Thank-you letters and public recognition at relevant community meetings (e.g. Syracuse Task Force on Homelessness).

Program evaluation: Students complete Honors Program evaluation. Mentors complete written evaluations. Director provides written and oral reports to Honors Director and a yearly report to FIPSE. Project staff and faculty are designing an evaluation/research process for participating mentors and students to explore the evolution of the public self through thought and action.

Institutional benefits: "It contributes to the conversation regarding what an undergraduate education entails and what the role of the university in a democracy is."

Problem addressed: "One problem in democratic life is the difficulty in compassionately understanding the life circumstances of strangers. Our project addresses this problem by inviting students to take seriously the world and citizenship of homeless persons. Students try to internalize the voices, experiences, and visions of homeless persons, their advocates, and those who attempt to meet their needs. Although students do not always agree with each other, mentors, or theorists regarding the causes or assumptions used to explain homelessness, they do come to see homeless people as persons and citizens."

Lesson learned: "Integrating theory and practice in the context of the practices of a real community is not easy. Students seemed to find it difficult to be both passionate and 'rational' about an issue. They were able to integrate theory, history and emotion in their written work, but it seemed difficult to do the same in conversation. I think this was problematic because I did not take seriously my own recognition that theory is often encased in stories. In short, justice, the common good, and human nature are often present in the stories people tell regarding their experiences. We will continue to expore how to understand narrative as a form of theorizing."

Biggest challenges: "How to institutionalize and expand the program after FIPSE support ends; how to bring a civic dimension to other experience-based learning opportunities at the University; and how to design an evaluation process sensitive to how students, mentors, and faculty use theory and practice to make sense of the public world."

Trinity College of Vermont

Community Service Learning, Trinity College of Vermont, 208 Colchester Avenue, Burlington, VT 05401, 802-658-0337. Ron Chesbrough, Director. Private, urban college; 1200 students.

Participation: 200 undergraduates involved in the community during academic year for 20 weeks for 3-5 hours/week. Most effective publicity: class lists, dorm visits. **Prerequisites:** Time, interests, skills.

Overview: Began in 1987 with ACTION grant. **Goals:** To involve students in community service, to encourage civic and social responsibility, to provide out-of-classroom learning opportunities. Program also supports students' ethical, moral, and career development. **Philosophy:** "Our program is geared toward the interests, skills, and schedule of the individual student. It is based on a student leadership model, with students as coordinators of areas of the program. Services are based on community need, as perceived by community representatives."

Structure: Based in Student Life. Director reports to Associate Dean of Students. Advisory Board of 20% faculty/60% community representatives/20% administrators.

Budget: $20,000 plus salaries from 50% school funds, 50% federal. Includes funds for administration, clerical support, long distance calls, site visits, professional/faculty development, space and equipment. **Staff:** 1 full-time, 1 part-time.

Faculty involvement: 4 of 75 are active. Time, effort and commitment to program is required of faculty.

Community involvement: Regular input of community representatives sought through Advisory Board, phone calls, meetings. Site supervisors are required to train, support, and evaluate students. **Service sites:** Identified by Director, students, faculty. Criteria for selecting sites: training and support provided, student interest. Most effective publicity: brochures, phone calls, visits, on-campus recruitment days. **Compensation:** Students are reimbursed for travel expenses.

Preparation: Pre-service training, agency orientation.

Learning: Structured opportunities for reflection and analysis include weekly meetings with student leaders. Working to do more. **Academic credit:** No.

Monitoring of service: By agency supervisors and student leaders. Discussions are held regularly with the ultimate service recipients.

Recognition: Students: T-shirts upon completion of 40 hours of service; ongoing recognition in campus and community publications; annual recognition dinner for leaders. *Faculty:* Some institutional recognition but no reduction in other responsibilities. *Site supervisors:* Informal thank-you's.

Institutional benefits: "Helps foster a sense of community and purpose."

Problem addressed: "Working collaboratively with other campuses. We meet regularly to discuss program services relevant to community needs to avoid duplication or gaps in services."

Lessons learned: "Work hard and keep at it."

Biggest challenge: "Securing future funding."

University of California — Los Angeles

Service-Learning Courses/Programs, UCLA, Field Studies Development, 405 Hilgard Avenue, Los Angeles, CA 90024-1514, 213-825-7867. Jane Permaul, Director; Rob Shumer, Associate Director. Public, urban university; 35,000 students.

Participation: 500+ undergrads involved in the community during academic year for 10-11 weeks for 6 hours/week in addition to enrollment in concurrent course/program. Most effective publicity: direct information to selected student groups, academic/career counseling, direct mail. **Prerequisites:** varies depending on course/program.

Overview: Began in 1973. **Goals:** To teach specific academic subjects and skills, to provide students with firsthand experience related to course objectives, to enable students to make a substantive contribution to their community. Program supports students' intellectual, ethical, and moral development, and sense of social responsibility. **Philosophy:** "At UCLA, service-learning is a special form of experiential learning. We encourage students to learn in an academic context with reading, discussion, and active participation in the classroom and the community at large. Through these activities, students perform community service. As part of their fieldwork, students assist community members in a variety of ways: tutoring youth, spending time with elderly adults, developing plans for agencies, and writing public service announcements. The service is always connected to the educational purpose of a service-learning course. By preparing students academically for the service in which they are involved, students are more proficient in giving service. As a result, *all* parties benefit."

Structure: Based in academic departments with support from Field Studies Development. Instructors report to their respective department chairs and deans. Director of Field Studies Development reports to Director of Instructional Development. Several committees are involved with these programs: Department Executive Committees, College Executive Committee, UCLA Senate Committee on Undergraduate Courses and Curriculum, UCLA Human Corps Task Force, and ACTION Advisory Council. When all are combined, approximate composition is 85% faculty, 5% students, 5% community representatives, 5% administrators.

Budget: $6000 per course offering for approximately 30-40 students. Program funded by a combination of state instructional and development funds and other university funds with occasional grant support. Includes funds for administration; clerical support; site visits; instructor, student, and site supervisor support. **Staff:** Varies. For each course, 1/4 FTE Instructor, 1/4 FTE Graduate Assistant, plus miscellaneous support from Field Studies Development.

Faculty involvement: Varies. Average of 25 faculty teach a field studies course each year as part of their regular teaching load.

Community involvement: Agencies are involved in the development of program policies and procedures through regular program evaluations and/or discussions with university. Requirements of site supervisors vary. **Service sites:** Identified by program administrator, students, faculty. Criteria for selecting sites vary for each course, but all sites must provide mutual learning and service opportunities for students that relate to specific course objectives and be willing to host students with limited time. Most effective publicity: "We have more requests than we can ever fill. We do contact selected sites to invite them to participate from time to time." **Compensation:** Varies. Most students receive no compensation. Some courses/programs provide stipends, some assist with transportation, others are considered in financial aid awards.

Preparation: Varies. Some courses/programs require students to complete certain courses, others have orientations and/or site visitations.

Learning: Structured opportunities for reflection and analysis vary for each course/program. All require regular meetings with instructor and field studies coordinator on individual and/or group basis supplemented by reading and specific course assignments. For 4 quarter units of credit, students spend an average of 4-6 hours of class time and another 6-12 hours on assignment preparation each week. Evaluation of student learning is based on student performance, class participation, and quality of assignments. Learning is assessed by instructors with assistance from field studies coordinators. **Academic credit:** Yes; can be used toward the major, for electives, for general education requirements in some cases and for units toward degree attainment. Students can receive credit with or without grade.

Monitoring of service: Done by community sponsors.

Recognition: Students: Students receive certificates of appreciation and can obtain reference letters. *Faculty:* Involvement is recognized as part of regular work load. *Site supervisors:* Certificates of appreciation.

Program evaluation: Each course/field study project is reviewed periodically. Impact of program is evaluated by faculty when negotiating for next offering, by students through program/course and instructor evaluations, by site supervisors through evaluations, and by the administration through the Field Studies Coordinator's Quarterly Report. The integration of service-learning into the undergraduate curriculum and its contribution to undergraduates' educational experience is also evaluated.

Institutional benefits: Improved quality of undergraduate education.

Problem addressed: "We are successfully dealing with institutionalization by involving the academic departments and faculty, enabling their interests to be realized as well as our concerns for service and learning."

Lesson learned: "Trying to work under Student Affairs with the academic sector of UCLA did not work well for us. If you want service-learning to be academically integrated, then it must be a part of the academic structure."

Biggest challenges: "Student enrollment. Getting more service-learning courses into general education requirements will help increase enrollment. Transportation to field sites is also a major challenge."

Other advice: "Do not single out service-learning as a 'program.' Instead, develop courses or a sequence of courses which are service-learning in nature and put them in the established academic structures."

University of Michigan

Project Community, University of Michigan, 2205 Michigan Union, Ann Arbor, MI 48109-1349, 313-763-3548. Jeffrey Howard, Director. Public, urban university; 35,000 students.

Participation: 720 undergrad and grad students involved in the community during academic year for 12 weeks for 4-6 hours/week. Most effective publicity: word-of-mouth, advisors.

Overview: Begun in 1961 by a group of students who started a breakfast program at local schools for children from families with low incomes. **Goals:** (1) To help students learn about human service institutions (schools, prisons, health care facilities) through field experience, readings, and comparing theory with reality; (2) to encourage development of student values, ethics, self-knowledge, and problem-solving skills; (3) to provide service to persons and groups experiencing social inequities. Program encourages students to question traditional learning norms and supports students' intellectual, ethical, moral, and personal development, and sense of social responsibility. **Philosophy:** "We work hard to provide an internally consistent philosophy of education in all aspects of our program. The training program for our project coordinators prepares them to 'de-socialize' both themselves and their students around classroom norms that are productive for experiential learning. The seminars are small, participatory, and value opinion, values, and personal knowledge more than knowing another person's 'expert' theory. In papers, students are required to bridge theory, experience, and their own values. All staff understand their role to be educators (even though the University perceives them as administrators)."

Structure: Based in the Office of Student Services with institutional links to the Sociology Department and the School of Education. Director reports to the Director of the Michigan Union/Student Programs.

Budget: $136,000 from 90% school funds, 10% student lab fees. Includes funds for administration, clerical support, long distance calls, site visits, professional/faculty development. Also received a 1-year University grant of $32,000 for start-up for diversifying our service-learning program and promoting the general message to serve. **Staff:** 4 full-time, 35 part-time.

Faculty involvement: 2 of 1500 are active. Faculty collaborate with staff in developing course readings, assignments.

Community involvement: Supervisors determine what students will do at their agencies. Site supervisors are required to: engage students directly with the service receivers, provide support and feedback to students, provide feedback about students' work to staff supervisors, and provide feedback about the program in general. **Service sites:** Identified by program administrator, agencies. Criteria for selecting sites: direct service with consumer of agency, learning potential from a sociological or educational perspective, geographic accessibility (within reasonable driving distance). **Transportation:** Program provides vehicles for students to drive to the placements.

Preparation: Students are oriented to site by agency or program staff. An orientation to service-learning is provided through readings and structured experiences in the first 2 seminars prior to the start of the field experiences.

Learning: Structured opportunities for reflection and analysis include: required weekly meetings to compare theory and practice, writing of reflection and critical analysis papers, journal. Students spend an average of 4 hours/week in structured reflection activities. Learning monitored and supported through weekly seminars which bring students in like placements together to discuss issues, examine relevant values, and bridge readings with experiences. One-to-one conversations may be arranged by students with their project coordinator (usually a graduate student). Learning is evaluated through: participation at site, seminar, quality of journal and paper. Evaluation is based on "mastery" program that yields a credit/no credit notation on the student's transcript. Teaching Assistants review student papers which bridge theory with experience to determine if students have mastered the subject of their choice. If not, they are asked to improve the paper until they demonstrate mastery of the topic. **Academic credit:** Yes; can be used for general education, graduation requirements.

Monitoring of service: We do not evaluate the quality of service, but rather the quality of the commitment to service. Site supervisors provide evaluation that helps project coordinators monitor the student's commitment to the agency's consumers. There is not a formal mechanism through which the ultimate service receivers determine the service. It is usually the agency staff who determine this. In adult facilities there is often dialogue about the specific agenda for each visit (e.g., determining discussion topic in a prisoner rap group).

Recognition: Students: Some agencies give students certificates. *Faculty:* Involvement is recognized as part of regular work load. *Site supervisors:* Thank-you letters from program directors.

Program evaluation: Students complete comprehensive evaluations of all facets of program. Site supervisors also evaluate the program. The Director reviews the program annually with supervisor. Placement sites are reviewed using student and site evaluations. Currently exploring how to measure the impact of program on admissions, retention, student satisfaction with the University, alumni participation and giving.

Institutional benefits: "Many students are interested in learning in the community, so it satisfies a consumer (student) demand."

Problem addressed: "Because students perceived participation in our program as a lower priority than their other courses (because this is an elective and graded credit/no credit), attendance was a problem. We instituted an attendance policy and attendance has improved significantly."

Lesson learned: "We thought about a recognition effort for the top service providers, but the project coordinators pointed out that doing so might move service provided by students from an internally to an externally driven matter."

Biggest challenge: "Expansion. Our program purview had remained fairly consistent for many years. Though we have received a 1-year grant to diversify our program, we need to secure funding to continue these efforts."

University of Minnesota

Special Learning Opportunities, University of Minnesota, 220 Johnston Hall, 101 Pleasant Street SE, Minneapolis, MN 55455, 612-624-7577. Emma Freeman, Coordinator. Public, urban university; 55,924 students.

Participation: 1500 undergrad and grad students involved in the community during academic year and summer for 10-20 weeks for 10-20 hours/week. Most effective publicity: student newspaper, faculty and advisor referrals, word-of-mouth.

Overview: Began in mid-60s as part of the Living Learning Center. **Goals:** To enrich the academic program for students by bringing community resources to bear upon their educational experience, to assist faculty to teach by using resources of the community in the curriculum and as extra-curricular activities, to provide needed services to the community in ways that achieve mutually desirable goals and connect the campus to the Twin Cities and greater Minnesota. Program supports the University's mission of service and students' intellectual, ethical, moral, career, civic, and personal development, and sense of social responsibility. **Philosophy:** "The hallmark of the University's field learning program is that it is centered in the curriculum. It brings faculty, students, and community together in a vigorous climate of learning that also provides needed services to individuals and organizations in the greater community beyond the campus. This not only enriches academic programs, but it establishes important ties between the education of our students and the needs of the community."

Structure: Based in the College of Liberal Arts. Director reports to Associate Dean for Curriculum. Advisory Board of 40% faculty, 20% students, 40% community representatives.

Budget: $73,413 from 75% school funds, 25% special developmental funds from the University. **Staff:** 1 full-time, 1.75 part-time.

Faculty involvement: Department policies determine faculty responsibilities.

Community involvement: A Community Advisory Board meets regularly to advise program. Staff also consults regularly with individuals in the community. Requirements of site supervisors are determined by the academic department's requirements and the needs of individual students. **Service sites:** Identified by program administrator. All legitimate organizations have access to program. Most effective publicity: calls, letters, and referrals (e.g., by United Way, government offices). **Compensation:** Most positions are not paid, but some agencies pay students, some offer work-study, and the University awards some grants to assist students.

Preparation: Classes are offered in some majors, and some students work with faculty on independent study projects. Advising takes place when students select the experience. Most agencies have orientation and training programs.

Learning: Students conducting independent study projects complete contracts with faculty. Structured opportunities for reflection and analysis are facilitated through faculty-directed studies or individualized study projects. Students spend an average of 4-8 hours/week in structured reflection/analysis activities. **Academic credit:** Yes, sometimes; can be used toward the academic major, for electives, for graduation requirements. Varies by college and department. To receive credit for learning, a "product" is required, usually a paper, but it can be a work of art, a photographic presentation, or other project agreed upon by the faculty member and student.

Monitoring of service: Quality of service is monitored, and usually evaluated by, site supervisors. Would like to see more evaluation of the service by the individuals who receive it.

Recognition: Students: Student service awards are given each year to recognize leadership. Through alumni contributions, 20-30 grants are awarded each year. *Faculty:* Appreciation for their involvement is voiced in informal ways, but there is no institutional recognition through overload compensation. *Site supervisors:* individual thank-you's, certificates of appreciation signed by the Dean for exceptional contributions.

Program evaluation: Impact of program is evaluated informally by faculty, students, and site supervisors. If a student receives a grant, there is a formal evaluation process. The program is also evaluated annually by the Dean of the College.

Institutional benefits: "We help faculty to teach, students to learn, and the community and campus to realize increased communication and mutual support."

Problem addressed: "Making volunteer work affordable for those who must work to support educational expenses is a continuing problem. We implemented an annual drive to raise funds from alumni contributions and are now able to offer grants to 20-30 students a year to help them carry out unpaid internships. Most of these internships involve community service activities."

Biggest challenge: "Keeping the funding and staffing ratio in balance with student participation. The program keeps growing — 15-35% increases each year in student interest — but the number of advisers remains constant."

Other advice: "Working with the community as well as the faculty is very important. We must respond to the needs that the *community* identifies. We must also keep the needs of students as our *first* consideration."

University of Southern California

Joint Educational Project, University of Southern California, Los Angeles, CA 90089-0471, 213-743-7698. Richard Cone, Director. Private, urban university; 30,800 students.

Participation: 1,400 undergrads involved in the community during academic year for 8 weeks for 1-6 hours/week. Most effective publicity: faculty; class presentations by student staff. **Prerequisites:** In two programs, previous experience is required.

Overview: Began in 1972 as a tutoring project with local elementary schools. **Goals:** To offer students opportunities to apply information, concepts, and techniques learned in classes in the "real world"; to offer community residents, schools, and agencies needed assistance; to foster better communication between the university and community. Program supports students' intellectual, ethical, moral, career, civic, and personal development, and sense of social responsibility. **Philosophy:** "JEP stresses the importance of mutuality with both the community and students learning from each other. USC is a private, predominantly Anglo institution of students from upper middle to wealthy backgrounds. Many students have never interacted with people of differing ethnic, religious, or social groups. Students tend to have an attitude of superiority when they see, talk with, or think about the community residents around USC. At first, many students do not see the mutual benefits of their JEP work. Getting involved in the community, making new friends, and testing career options, however, assists in students' personal and educational development."

Structure: Based in College of Letters, Arts and Sciences. Director reports to Dean of College. An Advisory Board of students, faculty, and community representatives helped launch JEP and served the Project for its first 8 years. The Board was discontinued as the project was institutionalized.

Budget: $390,000 from 90% school funds, 10% foundations. Includes funds for administration, clerical support, long distance calls, site visits, professional/faculty development. **Staff:** 5 full-time, 14-18 part-time.

Faculty involvement: 70 of 500 are active. Faculty can be as involved in the program as they wish. Minimum involvement includes offering partial credit. Some faculty are actively involved in training and integrating learning opportunities.

Community involvement: Site representatives are involved in the development of program policies and procedures through meetings with JEP staff to review the program each term. All community placements are in response to needs perceived by local agencies. Site supervisors are required to: make requests; act as supervisor, advisor, teacher; complete student evaluations; and in some instances, conduct orientations. Ongoing communication is an important aspect of the program. JEP staff uses an advocacy system with staff members serving as advocates for each participating group. Advocates communicate with the group they represent and speak on behalf of that group at decision-making meetings. **Service sites:** Identified by program administrators. Criteria for selecting sites: learning opportunities available to students; site's need; atmosphere conducive to learning; supervisors' willingness to teach, supervise, advise students; location.   Most effective publicity: word-of-mouth.

Preparation: Students are required to attend 2 training sessions (3 for non-school assignments). Student staff conduct sessions using training package developed during 16-year history.

Learning: All participants are required to submit weekly journals describing their work in the community and how they feel about it. Students receiving credit for learning answer academic questions each week to help them relate their experience with classwork. They also write an analytical paper at the term's end. Students spend an average of 1 hour/week in structured reflection activities. Learning is monitored and supported by student staff who read journals, communicate with and train students. JEP staff also observe over 60% of participants in the field. Learning is assessed by faculty and JEP staff through site supervisor evaluation and papers. **Academic credit:** Yes, as part of existing courses.

Monitoring of service: Done by JEP staff through site visits, discussions with students, and regular meetings with professionals at sites.

Recognition: Students: Students receive thank-you letters from the Vice-President of Student Affairs. *Faculty:* Involvement is recognized as part of regular work load. *Site supervisors:* Annual letters, reports are sent thanking them for their support and involvement.

Program evaluation: Impact of program is evaluated by faculty, students, site supervisors, and the administration. "We measure the impact of student learning and service to the community and have secured solid institutional support by proving to the University our academic credibility and our ability to enhance university-community relations."

Institutional benefits: "Promotes a positive image to the community-city in which the institution is located. Demonstrates how a university can work in an urban setting."

Problem addressed: "Each semester, JEP sends out 700-1000 students into the community. At one time, all students came to the office on a specified day to pick up their assignments. This caused much confusion, but also gave students the opportunity to by-pass the training sessions facilitated by our staff. We then decided to hand out student assignments at our trainings. This insures that there is communication between staff and participants and guarantees all students are trained."

Lessons learned: "A few years ago, we sent a group of pre-health majors to teach a mini-course on health and nutrition at a nearby senior center. We thought sharing health information with seniors would be a great idea. Students were welcomed the first week, but subsequently found their audience dwindling. After checking with some seniors, we found that they lead busy lives (Bingo was at the same time, trips came up each month, doctors appointments were scheduled). This taught us to plan more with the seniors and not just on our own. We have also learned that the most critical ingredient in programmatic success is training."

Biggest challenge: "Faculty development — while many faculty are involved, few actively integrate student experiences in the community with their classroom lectures. As a result, students are not always sure of the connection between their course work and their community experience."

Other advice: "Stay in touch with other experiential education programs on campus and elsewhere."

University of Vermont

Center for Service-Learning, University of Vermont, 41 South Prospect Street, Burlington, VT 05405, 802-656-2062. Hal Woods, Director. Public university; 8000+ students.

Participation: 600 undergrad, grad, and continuing education students involved in the community during the summer and academic year for 14-52 weeks for average of 12 hours/week. Most effective publicity: mailings, word-of-mouth. **Prerequisites:** Motivation for service-learning, skills and interests which match community needs, commitment to complete projects.

Overview: In 1970-71 as part of the student volunteer movement, the University Year for Action Program developed links to academics. Now the Vermont Internship Program has comprehensive service-learning options. **Goals:** To increase student involvement in community service, to link community service to the curriculum, to increase financial support to sustain program and student involvement. Program supports students' intellectual, ethical, moral, career, civic, and personal development, spiritual growth, and sense of social responsibility. **Philosophy:** "We have successfully linked the positive energy of student involvement in the community with the growthful life of the individual through a well recognized curriculum that fosters and motivates both deeper participation and commitment to service and rigorous reflection on the meaning and outcome of the service experience."

Structure: Based in Student Affairs. Director reports to Dean of Students.

Budget: $204,000 from 62% school funds, 33% federal, 5% agency fees. Includes funds for administration, clerical support, long distance calls, local site visits, professional/faculty development. Staff: 5 full-time, 1 part-time.

Faculty involvement: CS-L staff are faculty; an additional 20-30 other faculty out of 1500 are active. Faculty requirements vary by department.

Community involvement: Involved in the development of program policies and procedures through feedback given to CS-L staff on a regular basis or at annual meeting with agencies. Site supervisors are required to: complete a work plan and Sponsor's Agreement; explore work-study or agency funding; interview students; provide support, space, materials, funds for student projects; supervise students; participate in evaluation process. **Service sites:** Identified by program administrator, community. Criteria for selecting sites: Understanding of service-learning dynamics, a work plan developed, and willingness to sign a Sponsor's Agreement to provide support, resources, and complete an evaluation. Most effective publicity: mailings, agency meetings, student contacts. **Compensation:** Intensive Internships may carry a stipend, some students are paid by agencies, some earn work-study wages. Also setting up a John Dewey Fund for Public and Community Service to provide support.

Preparation: Provided through previous experience, application process, interviews with CS-L staff, and orientation and training by sponsoring organizations.

Learning: Students spend an average of 3 hours/week in structured reflection and analysis activities. The Vermont Internship Program has a specific curriculum for the Intensive, the Semester, and Field Studies components of the program. These involve a combination of reading, writing, seminars, and journal assignments designed to deepen the students' participation in an action/reflection process. Learning is monitored and supported through: dialogue and feedback from agency supervisors, CS-L staff, faculty, other students; papers; and professional portfolio of experience for Intensive Interns. Methods of evaluation include: observation of performance, degree of completion of learning tasks, quality of written materials, grasp of dynamics of service-learning experience, level of engagement and participation in service-learning processes, readings, and final papers. "All of this is designed to deepen a student's contribution to the community as well as learning. The learning is drawn from the service. Service is primary." Learning is assessed by the CS-L staff/faculty or by faculty in major department. **Academic credit:** Yes; can be used toward the major, for electives, for general education requirements.

Monitoring of service: Done by community organizations. Quality of service is evaluated by site supervisors, other agency staff, and ultimate service recipients through interactive or formal procedures at each agency.

Recognition: Students: Annual Recognition event. *Faculty:* Involvement is recognized as part of regular work load in some cases but with no institutional recognition in others. *Site supervisors:* Feedback from students.

Program evaluation: CS-L faculty evaluate performance and achievement of learning goals. Faculty in student's major department determine when credit is earned for learning. Students evaluate progress with site organizations and faculty. Self-assessment procedures are built into the program. Site supervisors meet weekly with students. Dean of Students Office reviews program annually.

Institutional benefits: Links University to community through positive student effort and helps fulfill institution's community service mission.

Problem addressed: "We are working hard to solve the problem of information coordination by establishing a network-based information system using a program called Resource Match, published by Volunteer. This system, once completely up, will give us excellent access to placement and follow-up information on both community needs and volunteer resources. We built the system over 5 years and did a lot of fund-raising to get it installed."

Lesson learned: "We are still working hard to counter rampant careerism that exists among students. We are seeing signs of increased interest, but it is not a ground swell yet. Service-learning is not yet a burning issue. Best advice is to stay with it. It is worth the effort. Persistence yields very positive outcomes for students and community."

Biggest challenge: "Our biggest problem is institutionalization of our program, and sustaining program staffing to continue and strengthen high-quality performance. We are very dependent on grants and are working hard to find a way to keep the pieces together."

Other advice: "Hire staff with profound commitment to the values of service-learning and encourage administrative creativity to support and sustain a program. [Despite a 25-year history,] this is still a very new idea in higher education and needs a lot of development."

Westmont College

Westmont Urban Program, Westmont College, 3016 Jackson Street, San Francisco, CA 94115, 415-931-2460. Steven Schultz, Director. Private, suburban college; 1200 students.

Participation: 50 sophomores, juniors, and seniors involved in the community during the academic year for 15 weeks for 24 hours/week. Most effective publicity: word-of-mouth, student assemblies each term. **Prerequisites:** Sophomore status and 2.2 g.p.a.

Overview: Program was begun by Sociology faculty in 1972. This urban program in San Francisco is about 300 miles from the home campus in Santa Barbara. **Goals:** To inform students about contemporary social issues and ways they can become involved, now and in the future, based on their religious faith; to help students develop a vocational direction; to serve area organizations. Program supports students' intellectual, moral, ethical, career, civic, and personal development, and sense of social responsibility. **Philosophy:** "We attempt to integrate all aspects of our program (internship, coursework, life in community) to help students think about life-long service goals that go beyond present experiences. We attempt to help students learn about social needs which exist out there, and about skills and interests they have to meet those needs."

Structure: Program is an academic department. Director reports to Academic Dean. Advisory Committee of community supervisors and agency staff.

Budget: $250,000 from 100% school funds. Includes funds for administration, site visits, clerical support, long-distance calls, faculty/professional development. **Staff:** 2 full-time, 2 part-time.

Faculty involvement: 2 1/2 faculty members are full-time in San Francisco. 30-40 of 70 faculty have been active in granting departmental credit, grading, and advising students. Home campus faculty roles vary depending upon their interests. On-site faculty advise students in developing a learning contract, read student logs, meet with students and site supervisors, monitor service, assess learning, and teach a required urban studies course.

Community involvement: Advisory Committee meets at least once a semester. Supervisors required to: read a comprehensive guidebook describing the program, the college, and expectations of supervisors; interview prospective interns; meet weekly with interns; help monitor service and assess learning. Supervisors are included in process of developing a student's learning contract. **Service sites:** Identified by students and faculty. No standard approach of outreach is used. Organizations become involved as students interview and choose to intern there. Criteria for selecting sites: an effective match between students' educational goals and organizations' needs, and the commitment and skills to facilitate students' learning. **Compensation:** Students may receive a stipend on rare occasions.

Preparation: There is an extensive orientation process once students arrive in San Francisco before selecting sites. Forums with presentations by a range of community organizations are held each term to help students in choosing a site.

Learning: Students and site supervisors, with advice from faculty, develop a contract with learning objectives. Interns are required to: write weekly journal entries, write weekly log describing activity of previous week, read books assigned by supervisor, compile a portfolio of work, complete a mid-term and final evaluation with their supervisor. Students also spend 6 hours/week in an urban studies course which focuses on social concern as it relates to different urban issues. The student, faculty, and site supervisor meet together twice/term. Several classes focus on topics such as "learning under supervision" and "assertiveness." A student's main grade is provided by the supervisor and confirmed by the faculty. Work submitted directly to a faculty member may raise or lower that grade. **Academic credit:** Yes; can be used toward the academic major and graduation requirements, and for electives and general education requirements.

Monitoring of service: Each site has its own mechanism for getting input about the program from the ultimate service recipients.

Recognition: Faculty: Involvement is recognized as part of their regular work load. *Supervisors:* A reception is held each term to honor them.

Evaluation: Students complete a mid-term and final self-evaluation. They also evaluate the site, the faculty, and overall program. Faculty evaluate the program informally with students and by visiting the program in San Francisco. The President or a member of the President's staff visits the program frequently. A report is made to the Academic Dean bi-annually.

> *"The more an academic dimension is built into a program, and the more you are able to obtain academic credit for students who participate, the higher student participation will be, and the more you'll be able to involve faculty."*

Institutional benefits: "Program provides a unique opportunity for direct engagement by students with the intellectual, personal, and moral implications of contemporary social issues."

Problems addressed: "To develop and maintain a high level of faculty involvement, we regularly invite faculty to visit the program, publish a newsletter, and encourage students to convey the meaning of their experience to faculty."

"When encountering resistance by some campus faculty to seminar topics and approaches, we maintained a dialogue through the Academic Dean, provided clear information about what our goals were to those who were critical, and maintained strong administrative support."

Lesson learned: "We have not been as successful as we would like in getting some faculty who follow a more classical model to support our program. Perhaps we did not lay enough groundwork in advance. Work through others whom very traditional faculty respect, and expect *slow* progress."

Other advice: "The more an academic dimension is built into a program, and the more you are able to obtain academic credit for students who participate, the higher student participation will be, and the more you'll be able to involve faculty."

MULTI-CAMPUS PROGRAMS

Partnership for Service-Learning

Service-Learning — Kingston, Jamaica, Partnership for Service-Learning, 815 Second Avenue, Suite 315, New York, NY 10017, 212-986-0989. Howard Berry/Linda Chisholm, Co-Directors. The Partnership for Service-Learning is a consortium for 40 colleges and universities.

Participation: 100 undergrad and grad students involved in all programs, 30 in Jamaica per year for 10-13 weeks for 20-30 hours/ week during the academic year and summer. Participation is required in some cases where participating colleges use the program as part of honors studies. Most effective publicity: word-of-mouth from previous students, active campus faculty/program directors, notices in national experiential education publications. **Prerequisites:** maturity, responsibility, participation in learning whether or not credit is received, recommendations from home campus and other sources, sophomore standing or higher (freshmen are accepted with careful interviewing).

Overview: Jamaican Program began in 1985 with an on-site visit by the Co-Directors in cooperation with a Jamaican familiar with the culture; 12 in-country colleges were visited before identifying one for affiliation. Agencies and agency networks were visited before identifying a central organization for placement services. **Goals:** To foster international/intercultural learning, understanding, and sensitivity of students and those in other countries; to promote student and faculty awareness of the pedagogy of linking the service experience to learning, disciplines, and critical thinking; to foster personal growth and to develop identity and values through service. Program also supports students' ethical, moral, career, and civic development, and sense of social responsibility. **Philosophy:** "Because of the international/intercultural dimension of the Partnership's service-learning programs, the ideas of 'mutuality,' and 'parity of respect' are important. Mutuality means both the student and community served benefit from the experience. Parity of respect means the structured intercultural learning results in sensitivity to diversity and different values. Additionally, the Partnership places great emphasis on the importance of the pedagogy which links learning to service, believing that the two together result in a synergy larger than either academic studies or volunteerism alone."

Structure: Administrative base varies at participating colleges. The Partnership works with deans, departments, and directors of international education programs.

Budget: Program is funded from 10% regular school funds, 70% student fees, 20% financial aid.

Faculty involvement: 3 in-country faculty. Faculty are required to: understand the nature, goals, and purposes of service-learning in international/intercultural settings; have some experience in screening students they might recommend to the program; provide students with accurate information about programs. On-site seminars are held to introduce faculty to programs.

Community involvement: Initially, agencies are informed of the program design and agree to participate based on acceptance of that design. Agency suggestions about program policies and procedures are taken on an ongoing basis for subsequent programs. Site supervisors are required to: accept concept of linking learning and service, accept basic program design of alternating service and reflection, be active in promoting student-learning, submit regular evaluations and a final estimation of the value of the student's service. **Service sites:** Identified by the Partnership, faculty, administrators. Criteria for selecting sites: that sites are genuinely helping a human community, will be active in students' learning and service, and are willing to evaluate students' contribution; that the service is meaningful and useful to both students and the community. Most effective publicity: Program emphasizes the value of working with a student engaged in structured studies versus working with "just a volunteer." The intercultural dimension of U.S. students learning about other countries also has much appeal.

Preparation: Students receive materials on the country and service-learning. An orientation is held in-country 2-3 weeks before service begins. Continuing reflection is done through regular meetings with in-country supervisors and faculty. Some participating colleges have established special preparation courses for the program.

Learning: Required structured opportunities for reflection and analysis include: History/Political Science course which covers historical and political aspects of the country, a Literature/Humanities course which uses the literature of the country to examine cultural values, and an "Institutions in Society" course which uses the agency as a case study of the culture. Students keep journals and write a "critical issue" paper on a topic affecting the society as reflected in the agency. Participants are able to individualize studies to meet home campus needs and student interests by the choice of topic or emphasis in papers. Students spend an average of 15 hours/week in classes, seminars, and tutorials. They spend additional time recording critical incidents and personal reactions to their experiences in journals. Learning is monitored and supported through regular meetings with faculty, seminars, tutorials, quizzes, journals, critiques of papers, regular meetings with supervisors. Learning is evaluated through grades received for academic work according to U.S. standards and narrative evaluations by faculty which include aspects such as general cultural behavior, attendance, discussion, and understanding which may not appear in written work. Academic credit: Yes; used on home campus toward the major, electives, general education requirements, graduation requirements, co-op credit.

Monitoring of service: The quality of service is monitored primarily by agency supervisors and staff in cooperation with faculty liaisons. The quality of service is evaluated primarily by the agency staff person assigned to work with a student. Weekly reports and a final comprehensive evaluation are done by the agency. How ultimate service recipients are involved depends on the agency and persons they serve. Some are emotionally/mentally disabled and their response can be difficult to obtain, but supervisor's evaluation includes staff and service recipients.

Recognition: Students: Some students receive recognition by being part of the preparation of the next group. Others receive awards from their college or community groups. Faculty: Varies by school. *Site supervisors:* In some programs agencies are given a symbolic gift of money (usually used for the agency's work) to recognize the extra time and effort required to work with a student. Plaques or certificates are also given.

Program evaluation: Students evaluate all components of the program at end of term and in a post-program survey after 3-6 months. Site supervisors and faculty also complete evaluations. Administrators make regular on-site visits for discussions with all involved.

Institutional benefits: "Participation of the affiliated colleges and universities allows the Partnership to reach a wider audience with service-learning opportunities, and to develop new programs and directions which a single institution would find difficult to do."

Problem addressed: "The Partnership is able to provide opportunities to more students than can a single college program and reduces administrative costs. Student cost is also kept low, which allows students with limited financial resources to participate. Additionally, we have been successful in demonstrating that service and learning are not incompatible, and that international/intercultural literacy including the Third World, can be accomplished through the union of the two. We've also seen that bringing students together from two- and four-year, public and private colleges, can be done within the same program and provides an added dimension of students learning from each other as well as from the program."

Lesson learned: The balance between learning and service needs to be monitored as students have a tendency to let the academic work slide in favor of an exciting service experience. The Partnership has also seen the need to strengthen post-program follow-up and processing of the student's experience and to explore ways of linking the program experience even more closely to the student's curriculum.

Biggest challenge: "Recruitment. Many students welcome a service experience, but opportunities are often not visible on their campuses."

Other advice: "We recommend an emphasis on the active alliance of colleges and service agencies in creating programs based on the idea of mutuality and sensitivity to the needs and purposes of each, whether the program be local or international. The world is not a plaything for U.S. students to take from."

Washington Center for Internships and Academic Seminars

Internships in the Independent Sector, Washington Center for Internships and Academic Seminars, 514 Tenth Street NW, Suite 600, Washington, DC 20004, 202-624-8073. Mary Stewart, Program Manager. Non-profit urban organization.

Participation: 75 sophomores, juniors, and seniors involved in internships in the nonprofit sector during the academic year or summer for 10-15 weeks for 35 hours/week. Most effective publicity: direct mail, campus liaisons (faculty representatives at 600+ campuses nationwide). **Prerequisites:** Participants must have previous community service experience.

Overview: Program began in 1987 through funding from Aetna Life and Casualty Foundation and the Exxon Education Foundation in response to a growing need within the independent sector for better prepared leaders. **Goals:** To prepare students for leadership roles in the independent sector, to encourage students to consider careers in the independent sector, to provide a service to the Independent Sector. Program also supports students' intellectual, ethical, moral, and personal development, and sense of social responsibility. **Philosophy:** "The Washington Center's Internship in the independent sector is not just another entry-level job. It is an internship with today's senior management within the independent sector, designed to teach, at a senior level, the issues, problems, pressures, and rewards associated with nonprofit management. It is our goal to prepare students to assume leadership positions upon completion of the program."

Structure: Program manager reports to the Director of Internships at the Washington Center, an independent nonprofit organization that serves colleges and universities across the country. Program Advisory Board of 25% faculty, 25% community representatives, 20% program administrators, and 30% foundation representatives.

Budget: $85,000 from 85% fees paid by students or their schools, 15% corporate contributions. Includes funds for administration, clerical support, long distance calls, site visits, professional/faculty development, marketing. **Staff:** 1 full-time.

Faculty involvement: Faculty teach weekly course and help assess learning. Campus faculty liaisons are responsible, in part, for recruiting students and assisting them with credit arrangements.

Community involvement: Organizations are involved in the development of program policies and procedures through participation on the Program Advisory Board. Site supervisors are required to: provide substantial projects and work, participate in the daily management of the students' activities, and provide evaluation. **Service sites:** Identified by Program Manager. Criteria for selecting sites: senior-level manager must be willing to supervise student, organization must be a nonprofit organization, must be willing to pay $1000 stipend. Most effective publicity: through articles in professional newsletters and journals (e.g., *Nonprofit Times*), direct mail to development directors. **Compensation:** Students receive a $1000 stipend.

Preparation: One-day orientation session. A learning contract is used which states student's goals and expectations.

Learning: Required structured opportunities for reflection and analysis include: weekly course on "Philanthropy, Volunteerism and Public Policy in America," and guidance from the Program Manager throughout the internship process. Students spend an average of 5-7 hours/week in structured reflection and analysis. Learning monitored and supported by Program Manager and the site supervisor. Student learning evaluated through learning contract, participation in small group discussions, academic course evaluation, performance evaluation by supervisor, mid-term and final evaluations. Learning is assessed by Program Manager, site supervisor, faculty leader and the student. Program Manager reviews grades and evaluations submitted by faculty leader and site supervisor and recommends final grade. Academic credit: Yes; used at home campus toward the major, electives, general education requirements, graduation requirements.

Recognition: *Students:* Students have been featured in newspaper articles. Press releases are sent to their hometown and college newspapers. *Faculty:* On-site faculty receive compensation for involvement.

Program evaluation: The impact of the program is measured by student learning and satisfaction with their internship placement.

Institutional benefits: "It gives The Washington Center the opportunity to give something back to the community in return for their support."

Problem addressed: "It was difficult to find appropriate faculty to teach the course. We asked the Association for American Colleges for recommendations of faculty who have received grants for course development in this field."

Biggest challenge: "Gaining credibility and recognition within the academic community."

The Service-Learning Dimensions of Field Study:
Cornell's Human Ecology Field Study Program

Dwight E. Giles, Jr. and Jamille B. Freed

This paper presents four dimensions of service-learning and applies them to field study as a method of education. They are: direct service to individual clients; service to an organization sponsoring student internships; service to groups or coalitions of organizations through special projects; and service to a locality or geographic area through ongoing field study efforts. These four dimensions are analyzed using the field study program of a large university as a case study. Concluding discussion considers the implications of this analysis for designing service-learning programs. These ideas were first presented at the March 1985 conference of the Partnership for Service-Learning and were revised in November 1985.

THAT CLUSTER OF EDUCATIONAL METHODS known as "off-campus" education includes service-learning[1] field study, cooperative education, experiential learning, and internships (Borzak, 1981). Although they share some common elements, they also differ in several important ways, making it difficult to define and differentiate them. For example, the term "service-learning" is often used to refer to a range of voluntary action and experiential education programs (Sigmon, 1979).

The purposes of this paper are: 1) to operationalize the concept of service-learning, and 2) to apply the concept in the context of undergraduate education programs. The potential contribution of a refined notion of service-learning is the provision of some guidelines and models for developing new service-learning programs or for expanding existing ones. This contribution is needed at this stage of the development of service-learning as educators turn their attention from developing the rationale, methods, and criteria for service-learning (Stanton and Howard, 1981; National Center for Service-Learning, 1980) to applying service-learning in international and intercultural contexts and to developing structured curricula that link service to the core learning activities of secondary and post-secondary education (Dickson, 1982). Accompanying this evolution of methods is the shift from "pure" or single models of service-learning, where the emphasis is solely on learning through helping individuals, to "mixed" or more complex models of service-learning. In these mixed models, the complexity arises from different dimensions of service and from different learning agendas. Thus service-learning activities may be part of a pre-professional internship program, a college of international studies, a discipline-based academic department, or interdisciplinary fieldwork courses.

Factors affecting the evolution of mixed service-learning programs might include decreasing student demand for "pure" service-learning programs, increasing career and vocational pressures on institutions of higher education, and instructional agendas of colleges and universities that are less likely to include the emphases of the late 1960s and early 1970s on relevance and application of knowledge, and of the 1980s on community service. What all of this means for service-learning is that it will probably compete with other methods of off-campus education and that where it is institutionalized in undergraduate curricula it will be one of several ideological and pedagogical elements. The need to analyze and develop mixed models of service-learning appears, then, to be a crucial one if the service dimension of service-learning is to be preserved and enhanced.

Dimensions of Service

A review of the articles published in *Synergist*, the primary forum for discussion of service-learning from 1971-1981 (National Center for Service-Learning, 1981), indicates that most of the service components of the service-learning programs presented involved the provision of direct services to the individual clients of agencies or to individuals connected with community projects. Tutoring, counseling, information and referral, and recreation are among the

Figure 1. Dimensions of Service in Service-Learning Programs

Dimension	Predominant Type of Service	Examples
Individual	Helping through provisions of resources or assistance	Tutoring Counseling
Organizational	Volunteer staff services	Program interns Administrative assistants Special project
Interorganizational	Generating and/or applying knowledge	Field research Needs assessment Technical assistance Community organization Project development
Locality	General problem-solving	Action research Consulting Provision of problem-solving resources. Identifying other service opportunities Community development

"pure" models of service-learning. Types of service mentioned less frequently include serving organizations, communities, or interorganizational coalitions. In order to develop mixed models of service-learning, however, it is necessary to consider all the dimensions of service.

By delineating the *recipients* of services and the concomitant *types* of services, it is possible to identify four separate but related dimensions of service that are components of service-learning[2] programs (see Figure 1). While in practice, more than one dimension may be involved, the important determinants of the dimension are the *primary recipient* of service and the *predominant type* of service rendered. It is also likely that several of these dimensions may be present in a service-learning program but in separate program aspects or over different periods of time.

The individual dimension will often be linked to the organizational dimension in that those served are clients of the organization. In this case the organizational dimension is secondary because the organization is the indirect recipient of service. This is in contrast to the situation where the service is provided directly to the organization, with either little or no direct emphasis on the organization's clients or customers. Similarly the other dimensions may be combined so that different types of service are provided simultaneously but a primary type of service can be identified. As the case study presented below indicates, one aspect of a mixed model service-learning program is the mix of dimensions of service.

The Pedagogy of Experience

As Eskow (1980) observed, in order for the learning component of service-learning to be academically credible, a pedagogy of experience is needed that will design experiences and provide the tools for establishing evidence of learning. This pedagogy of experience, apart from service-learning, has been developing for at least the past 50 years (see Dewey, 1943) and has generated a considerable body of practice and literature in recent years (Fry and Kolb, 1979; Keeton and Associates, 1976). The central task that experiential educators have undertaken is designing, monitoring, and evaluating experience for its learning potential. On the surface this pedagogical endeavor seems to be identical to the learning goal of service-learning, namely, to learn from the experience of service. The two are not identical, however, because experiential education does not dictate that the experience be service-oriented. Similarly, service-learning may be more narrowly focused on learning *how* to serve and less concerned with the larger pedagogy of experience. In actuality then, the relationship between the two may range from complete compatibility to bi-polar opposition due to different emphases on service and learning.

In the broad and evolving field of experiential education, one can identify different learning emphases such as personal development of the learner, application of a disciplinary knowledge base, preprofessional training, practice of skills and methods, and applied interdisciplinary studies such as urban studies or community studies. Thus the curricular emphases across or even within programs will vary due to educational goals, student needs, and institutional contexts. Common to all is some sort of off-campus or field-based study that focuses on the learner's experience. "Field study" as used here then covers this range; it is both learner-centered and experience-centered (Borzak, 1981).

Service-Learning & Field Study: The Cornell Experience

Because the Cornell Field Study Program has existed long enough to have undergone some of the changes noted above, and because it has developed as a "mixed model," it is useful to analyze it in terms of the four dimensions of service.

The New York State College of Human Ecology at Cornell University established its Field Study Office in 1972 to "develop and implement interdepartmental field study programs that emphasize multi-disciplinary, human ecological approaches to social problems" (Field Study Office, 1984). The two unique aspects of this program in the first eight years of its existence were a New York City field study course (Howard, 1979; Holzer, 1983) and a pre-field preparation course (Whitham and Stanton, 1979). As the program has evolved during the past five years, it has developed a generic, field-based curriculum on "The Ecology of Human Organizations" (Stanton, 1981) that forms the pedagogical framework for students doing field study in locations across the United States.[3] Regardless of the degree of service focus in their field placements, all students are encouraged and assisted "to develop frameworks for thinking more critically about social systems and to appreciate the variety of disciplines necessary to solve complex human problems" (Field Study Office, 1984).

Included in this curriculum are a required pre-field preparation course, three internship or field placement courses and a special projects course. Two of the field courses are campus-based in Ithaca, New York, one is located in New York City, and the third is campus-based but with field placements located all over the United States (except for New York City and the Ithaca area). The field project component of the pre-field preparation course takes place in the local communities surrounding the campus. All courses are offered within the College of Human Ecology but are open to students from all colleges in the University and bear an interdepartmental (ID) designation. The analysis below presents a brief description of each course and then analyzes the mix of service dimensions present in each.

Pre-Field Preparation

The pre-field preparation course (ID 200) is a 4-credit course designed to provide pre-field students with instruction and practice in field learning skills that will enable them to enhance their learning from field study, internships, and other experiential learning courses. These skills include: analysis of assumptions, perceptions, and biases; field data gathering methods such as participant observation and interviewing; analysis of non-verbal communication; self-directed learning skills such as critical reflection and setting learning objectives; and effective communication and interaction in small groups.

The heart of the course is a field project that serves as the vehicle for the application of skills in gathering field data. Using these skills, students apply ethnographic methods to produce reports that are designed to contribute to the solution of community problems. The *interorganizational* dimension of service is the primary one here in that most field projects are developed and sponsored by coalitions of organizations. In a secondary way the *locality* dimension is also served because of the continuity of involvement by students and faculty in local issues and problems. Examples of these projects include a survey for downtown small businesses, assessment of the quality of life in a neighborhood for a neighborhood council, and a transportation feasibility study. Working with a community agency committed to providing better housing for the rural poor in upstate New York, the students in ID 200 have completed a housing survey that also served the Town Board by allowing it to apply for and receive Community Development Block Grant monies. This field project illustrates well the *interorganizational* dimension of service.

Urban Field Study

"The Ecology of Urban Organizations: New York City" (ID 408) involves a semester of working and learning in New York City. The major focus of the course is the development of students as independent learners who can think critically about themselves, others, their work organizations, and the urban environment.

ID 408 students work in a wide variety of organizations that provide information (e.g., marketing, research, advertising or communications), plan or make policy, provide direct services to clients and/or consumers, or design apparel or living/working environ-ments. In addition, students spend time in a reflective seminar and time doing special assignments or field visits. The course is taught and administered by a Human Ecology faculty member based in New York City. The primary service dimension of this course is the *organizational* one in that students usually provide staff services. The *secondary* dimension is that of individual service, which has declined in recent years. Many of the organizations served are in the private sector and would not traditionally be considered true recipients for service-learning. (This question is discussed further in the conclusion.) The *interorganizational* dimension is an occa-sional dimension of this course in that special field research projects sometimes serve several organizations. A recent example is the assessment of the effects of development on a neighborhood in Brooklyn. This study was designed collaboratively with a variety of neighborhood groups and city planning agencies.

Local, Campus-Based Field Study

"Field Experience in Community Problem Solving" (ID 407) is a course designed in the service-learning tradition, with equal em-phasis on service to the Ithaca area and students' educational objec-tives. Working in interdisciplinary teams, students from several departments of the College serve as special projects staff to commu-nity organizations that arrange for their services. The central focus of the course is to develop students' skills as problem solvers who are able to approach the analysis of complex community problems ecologically and to design solutions that reflect this ecological per-spective. Contributing substantive, enduring results to the commu-nity is a major priority of the course.

Because the projects have usually been large and fairly complex, they have often involved an *interorganizational* dimension of service. The breadth of projects has often been of a community-wide scope, thus emphasizing the *locality* dimension. In only a few cases have the projects focused on the *organizational* dimension. Examples include developing a pesticide education curriculum for children of migrant farm workers, producing videotaped documentaries for the local cable TV channel, and surveying the voters of a downtown ward. The projects are designed so that students can balance service and learning.

The second campus-based field course is, "The Ecology of Or-ganizations in the Upstate Region" (ID 409), which is designed for students who wish to work in a field setting within a 55-mile radius of Ithaca, while simultaneously studying the social ecology of the upstate region of New York State. The course is organized around the dual objectives of teaching students to "think ecologically" about human organizations and to "become self-directed" as independent learners able to think critically and systematically about themselves, their colleagues, their work organizations and the regional environment. ID 409 also emphasizes developing a sensitivity to community concerns, requiring students to balance objective, critical inquiry with committed action in the public arena.

The service dimensions of this course are an equal mix of the *individual* and *organizational* as the primary dimension, followed by the *locality* dimension as secondary. Historically this course utilized mostly human service agency placements in which students provided direct services to clients. As the course has evolved, it has taken on the organizational dimension whereby students provide staff services to the organization through in-house projects and activities. The locality dimension is served by the continuity of placements and by faculty and student involvement in the ongoing community needs addressed by various organizations. This dimension is strengthened by the linkages between this course and the pre-field and community project courses. Together the three courses act as a catalyst for community development by creating placements and projects that contribute to solving general community problems.

Off-Campus Sponsored Field Learning and Internships

"Sponsored Field Learning/Internships" (ID 406) serves as the College of Human Ecology's sponsorship of and curriculum for students' participation in off-campus field experiences or internships that they arrange independently away from campus and outside New York City. Sponsored off-campus field programs are administered by non-credit granting institutions such as the New York State Assembly Internship Program, the Philadelphia Center, and the Washington Center. Because participating students carry out their field studies in a variety of locations, supervision is given through regular, structured assignments which are mailed each week to the course instructor on campus. Where necessary and possible, the instructor makes site visits. The primary recipients of service in this course are *organizations*. The predominant types of organizations served are public policy and regulatory, but students are placed in the same wide variety of placements as in the other courses. In only a small number of cases do students in this course provide the *individual* dimension of service.

Because of the wide variety of locations used as placements in this course and because of the distance from campus, the *locality* and *interorganizational* dimensions of service are not emphasized.

Discussion

The above analysis indicates that in this "mixed model" program of service-learning, the service dimension that appears most frequently is the organizational one; the individual dimension appears less frequently and is often a secondary dimension. However, the interorganizational and locality dimensions occur to some degree in the three field courses and in the pre-field preparation course. All of these service-learning dimensions operate in a curricular context that emphasizes field data gathering skills, applied problem solving skills, and learning about organizational and community settings through participant observation. The service-learning dimensions are supported by the College of Human Ecology's mission to apply knowledge to solve human problems and a history of personal and professional commitment by Field Study Office faculty to the value of service-learning. This mixed model program has evolved in ways that operationally expand the definition of service-learning to include dimensions of service other than direct help to individuals. The emphasis throughout the curriculum that students can and should learn through the provision of service in field settings has allowed the program to be creative in balancing service and learning needs.

However, this expansion of the dimensions of service in service-learning raises some questions. For example, should service to organizations that are profit-oriented be considered service in the sense of service for the public good, or is it more of a form of social exchange? Do the non-individual dimensions of service promote a service ethic in ways similar to the individual dimension of service? Is it possible or desirable to develop a mixed model service-learning program where service-learning may be absent from some aspects of the program? Shaping the answers to these questions are the values of field study educators, the needs of the students who choose to do field study, and the institutional contexts in which service-learning occurs.

One programmatic area not analyzed in this case study is how to apply this mixed model in international settings. The Cornell program is presently a domestic program, although discussions about expanding to international settings are now taking place. Given the strong emphases on ethnographic methods and on viewing field study settings as "cultural scenes" (Spradley and McCurdy, 1972), it seems likely that this model would translate well to international settings. The service emphasis, which seeks to prevent "academic voyeurism" (Goodlad, 1976) in domestic intercultural settings by requiring students to be sensitive as both participants and observers in different cultures, could be expanded for international settings. [Editor's Note: The Cornell program has now expanded to international settings.]

Considerations for Program Development

In order for the model developed by the Field Study Office of the College of Human Ecology at Cornell University to be useful for service-learning educators in other institutional and geographic contexts, it is necessary to assess the four dimensions separately. In building a program it may be necessary to concentrate on one or two of these dimensions in the beginning, recognizing that the four dimensions presented above evolved over a 12-year period. Service settings need to consider whether a field study model where students have a curriculum of social ecology and field methods would fit with their service needs. Educational institutions need to determine if an ethnographic approach to learning about organizational and community settings would fit with the curricular emphases, or if other curricula would need to be developed for field study. Because service-learning can be used for teaching generic skills in pre-field preparation courses, it is a model that is easily adapted to a wide range of disciplinary, pre-professional and subject areas. Indeed, these pre-field courses may be the starting point for developing institutionally unique field study curricula that include one or more of the four service-learning dimensions outlined here.

Dwight Giles is Senior Lecturer for the Field and International Study Program at Cornell University, where he teaches service-based field courses and conducts research on international service-learning. He also serves as a consultant to other institutions through the National Society for Internships and Experiential Education. Jamille Freed is a graduate candidate in social work at Boston University. She was a Teaching Assistant and Program Associate for Cornell's Field and International Study Program and has worked for a variety of human service agencies.

Footnotes

[1] This paper uses the American term, "service-learning" with full recognition of the British use of "study-service."

[2] It is possible that a fifth dimension could be added that would include larger units of social organization. For example, a service-learning program in a smaller country that provided service projects aimed at national needs and goals could legitimately be considered a national dimension. Similarly this could be identified as an international dimension if the service and learning included more than one country.

[3] Historically the program has focused on domestic field study. However, in recent years a few students have done field study outside of the United States. See the concluding section for discussion of expanding the model to international settings.

References

Borzak, Lenore, ed., *Field Study: A Sourcebook for Experiential Learning*, Sage Publications, 1981.

Dewey, John, *The School and Society*, University of Chicago Press, 1943.

Dickson, Sir Alec, "A Service-Learning Retrospective," *Synergist*, National Center for Service-Learning, Spring 1982, pp. 40-43.

Eskow, Seymour, "Views from the Top," *Synergist*, National Center for Service-Learning, Spring 1980, pp. 19-25.

Field Study Office, "Orientation to Field Study in the College of Human Ecology," Unpublished Handbook, Cornell University, 1984.

Fry, Ronald and David Kolb, "Experiential Learning Theory and Learning Experiences in Liberal Arts Education," in *New Directions for Experiential Learning: Enriching the Liberal Arts Through Experiential Learning*, Jossey-Bass, 1979, pp. 79-92.

Goodlad, Sinclair, "Academic Voyeurism," *Synergist*, National Center for Service-Learning, Fall 1976.

Holzer, Madeleine Fuchs, "The Value of Students in the Workplace," *Human Ecology Forum*, Cornell University, Vol. 113, No. 3.

Howard, Catherine Pratt, "In the Field, In the City," *Synergist*, National Center for Service-Learning, Winter 1979, pp. 19-21.

Keeton, Morris T. and Associates, *Experiential Learning: Rationale, Characteristics, and Assessment*, Jossey-Bass, 1976.

National Center for Service-Learning, *Building Support for Your College Program: A Service-Learning Package*, ACTION, 1980.

National Center for Service-Learning, *Index 1971 to 1982*, ACTION, 1982. Available from National Society for Internships and Experiential Education, Raleigh, North Carolina.

Sigmon, Robert L., "Service-Learning: Three Principles," *Synergist*, National Center for Service-Learning, Spring 1979, pp. 9-11.

Spradley, James P. and David W. McCurdy, *The Cultural Experience: Ethnography in Complex Society*, Science Research Associates, 1972.

Stanton, Timothy K., "Discovering the Ecology of Human Organizations: Exercises for Field Study Students," in Lenore Borzak, *Field Study*, Sage Publications, 1981, pp. 208-225.

Stanton, Timothy K. and Catherine Pratt Howard, "Principles of Good Practice in Postsecondary Education," *Synergist*, Winter 1981, pp. 16-18.

Whitham, Michele A. and Timothy K. Stanton, "Pre-Field Preparation: What, Why and How," in *New Directions for Experiential Learning: Enriching the Liberal Arts Through Experiential Learning*, Jossey-Bass, 1979, pp. 23-34.

Motivated to Serve: A Student Perspective and a Student-Led Seminar

John G. Farr

Stanford University student John Farr describes a seminar developed by a group of students. Reprinted with permission from Experiential Education, *National Society for Internships and Experiential Education, Vol. 14, No. 4, September-October 1989, pp. 6-7.*

IN 1988, SEVERAL STANFORD STUDENTS and I started "Motivated to Serve: Public Service Theories and Practice," a student-led seminar in which participants come to a personal philosophy of service through both practice and critical reflection. Participants meet for weekly discussions, complete readings, keep a structured journal, participate in a concurrent experiential learning/public service experience, and write an 8-12 page final paper exploring an issue related to service of particular importance in our own lives. The class is supported by Stanford's Haas Center For Public Service, with which many students in the class are involved.

Our inspiration for initiating the class stemmed from a concern that the education we pursue is divided sharply into two seemingly unrelated halves. On the one side are our majors, our academic lives, the education which most students expect to receive. Like most students, we know what it is that we study, but are less sure what we study for.

On the other side, we are involved in various projects designed to have a beneficial impact in communities about which we care. We do public service work. We recognize such projects as important educational opportunities, but we have difficulty articulating exactly what we learn.

We wished to develop an academic seminar through which students could develop a personal philosophy of service. Such an approach seemed logical. Public service and academic study offer each other a great deal. Nowhere else in our college experience do we as students find what we are doing so directly applicable to the needs of society as in public service. Critically considering issues of public service can enhance academic study by making it more relevant to issues about which students care.

This reflection also helps students confront the ideas and values implicit in their service projects. How someone chooses to serve depends on her/his particular view of what is in the public interest, and how such interests are best accomplished. One person might limit her/his concept of service to direct service work while another might see the need for more fundamental structural change. Understanding each other's views helps students to consider their own goals and methods more carefully and, consequently, improves the quality of their service.

Efforts to build support for the class within the university met with barriers. Initially, the class was rejected by a university committee for having an "all-good" notion of service and not being sufficiently critical. We found faculty members busy and full of assumptions about what we meant by a class addressing service. Eventually, we gathered a faculty advisory board which helped refine the syllabus. This led to the "directed individual study" arrangement by which students now earn credit for the class.

As the class developed, we discovered deeper implications to our new approach than we had envisioned. We involved ourselves in an entirely different epistemology. In previous academic experiences, a detached analytical approach encouraged us to treat what we study as something separate from ourselves. Yet, in this class, we did not pose service as a bloodless abstraction, as a body of material to be identified, isolated, and analyzed. We discovered that we could not study service separate from ourselves. We learned things about the world, but even more, we learned things about our relationship within the world.

In class we dealt with issues which concerned us: homelessness, international development, drug abuse, and others. We asked "Why is this something that concerns me?" and "What impact do I or can I have on this issue?" Participating in concurrent public service projects concerning homelessness, development and drug abuse reinforced such questioning because we were personally involved in the issues we studied.

The process of creating the class forced us to face another epistomelogical challenge. Recognizing the separation between our academic learning and service-learning experiences was easy.

True to our academic training, we had analyzed the situation and recognized a problem. Having exposed the problem, we thought we were nearing the end of the process. In reality, however, the ensuing effort to create opportunities to integrate academic and service learning proved most difficult. We had to overcome our own passive notions of education. Engaging faculty in discussions about service helped us realize that we can actively shape our education, and not be recipients only.

That we chose a different way of knowing and learning is significant. The way we come to know the world will have real consequences for the way we come to interact with it. (See *Change*, September/October 1987, "Community, Conflict, and Ways of Knowing" by Parker J. Palmer, reprinted in this resource book, for more discussion.) Developing a personal philosophy of service meant we worked to come to a more coherent understanding of our relationship with the world. More than just a benevolent extracurricular activity, public service can be a powerful tool by which students develop their social and political world view.

This kind of opportunity is sorely lacking in education. Our detached ways of knowing lead to a way of living which views our own fate as separate from the rest of society. We fail to recognize the communal nature of society and our interdependence. We are excessively concerned with preparing to have responsible positions in society; we are unconcerned with the impact we in responsible positions will have on that society.

Much as the study of service means considering how we as individuals affect and shape the world, participation in "Motivated to Serve" means students must consider how they affect and shape their own education. Future participants in the seminar must discover this different epistemology in order to constantly regenerate the course content and structure to match their educational needs.

John Farr, Stanford Class of '88, first facilitated "Motivated to Serve" during the 1988-89 academic year.

International Profile of Post-Secondary Study-Services

Irene Pinkau

Irene Pinkau, author of "Service for Development: An Evaluation of Development Services and their Cooperative Relationships," evaluated more than 30 development services, including post-secondary study-services, in 14 countries (Benin, Canada, Costa Rica, Denmark, Germany, Indonesia, Israel, Kenya, Malaysia, Nigeria, Panama, Thailand, the United Kingdom, and the United States. The United Nations Volunteers were also included.) Here Dr. Pinkau summarizes some of her findings about post-secondary study-services, offering an interesting international and historical perspective. Reprinted from Synergist, *ACTION, Vol. 6, No. 1, Spring 1977, pp. 25-27.*

DURING THE 1950s and 1960s, four categories of development services emerged in most countries around the world. They were created to facilitate learning and to aid the disadvantaged and poor through community-oriented service activities and employment. Study-services is one category within this family of development services, which also includes training and employment schemes for early school leavers, social and technical development services, and overseas or "export" volunteer programs.

While service-learning is a feature of all four categories of development services, the term "study-service" suggests that the program is unique because it is an intentional educational effort, linked to educational institutions at various levels, and it is oriented to development and to service. Although the involvement of students in service activities is nothing new, study-service links the curricula of educational institutions with development services.

For the purpose of this discussion, development is defined as "mobilization and advancement of people to achieve and maintain an adequate livelihood and self-reliance, in contrast to improvement of institutions and growth of profit." Service is defined as "work performed for the benefit of others, in response to causes and needs, that does not entail financial gain for those who serve."

The roles of study-service schemes, and of all development services, are determined by the conditions or problems which brought them into being. Three major problems can be identified. These are: (1) limitations of the higher education system; (2) lack of services for the poor and other disenfranchised groups; and (3) social, racial, and cultural gaps among people of one nation and the need to learn to cooperate for purposes of national development.

Post-secondary study-services usually define their objectives in general terms, such as "to provide experiential learning opportunities to students," "to train students to sacrifice and work for the public benefit," or "to help communities in their development efforts." The Nigerian National Youth Service Corps adds to its objectives: "to encourage career employment all over the country for free movement of labor" and "to enable Nigerian youth to acquire self-reliance." Relating their objectives to the problems which brought about the creation of study-service, the Indonesian KKN, Nepal's National Development Service, and the U.S. University Year for ACTION emphasize changes in higher education itself.

Post-secondary study-service schemes involve students ranging in age from 18 to 25, primarily during or at the end of the undergraduate studies. The duration of service ranges from six months to a year, on a full-time basis. Part-time service for credit normally requires a long-term commitment on the part of the volunteers. Young women fill from 16 to 53 percent of the total study-service assignments, and women are not necessarily restricted to traditional female roles.

Most post-secondary study-service schemes in Africa and Asia are governmental and obligatory. They are considered as compulsory credit courses. Those in Latin America, Thailand, and the Philippines are nongovernmental and voluntary. In industrialized countries, only U.S.' University Year for ACTION is a government-sponsored program, and all study-services are voluntary.

Organization and Management

There are three approaches to the organization and management of study-services. One is the government-centered approach in which government agencies recruit volunteers and administer the program. A second is centered at a university or college, either under a national policy (Indonesia, U.S.A.) or as a locally initiated

service (Thailand). A third approach is centered around a development service. In this system, the development service assumes the
role of a facilitator, making the services of students available to meet
local community needs on behalf of educational institutions (Costa
Rica, Panama, United Kingdom).

These three approaches differ with respect to the delegation of
authority and degree of citizen participation, and therefore they
result in different levels of effectiveness. Research has indicated
that a study-service scheme that is university or college-centered,
and based on national educational policy, with governmental coordination, can embrace many or all universities in the country. This
combination ensures decentralization of authority, leadership, and
program management — by delegating it to the individual university — and at the same time it brings about changes in the entire
system of higher education.

A study-service scheme that is university-centered but has no
national coordination is a local effort, with limited impact. A
scheme in which a development service facilitates study-service
directly with the students, does not work with the faculty or the
educational institution. As a result, this approach also has a limited
impact.

Study-services are scheduled at different phases of the academic course of study, depending on the country (Fussell and
Quarmby, 1974). One system, called "intervening," schedules the
period of service between academic semesters. This system is used
in Indonesia, Ethiopia, and the U.S. A second system, called "interwoven," schedules part- or full-time service concurrently with
course work. This system is used in the United Kingdom, and in a
large number of college-sponsored student volunteer projects. A
third system, called "subsequent," schedules service after academic
studies have been completed but prior to graduation. This system is
used in Nigeria and Thailand.

Volunteer Training

Volunteer training and preparation for field work are arranged
by the universities, and lack of trainers with practical field experience has frequently been reported. An exception is the University
Year for ACTION program in the U.S., which distinguishes between
pre-service training, on-the-job preparation, and in-service training
as a continuous parallel to work programs. Community organizations or other technical institutions provide necessary skill training
for the student volunteer to improve his or her job performance.

Work projects include formal and nonformal education, assistance to farmers, craftsmen, small industry, work with young offenders, etc. With the exception of the Nigerian National Youth Service Corps, which assigns corpsmembers primarily to regional or district governmental development agencies, all other study-services are community-centered, i.e., local citizens supervise the projects and work along with student volunteers.

Credit for service is a requirement of most study-services but is not easily achieved. There is usually no problem in awarding credit for training or the writing of papers — the academic part of study-service. More difficult, and not yet satisfactorily resolved, is the assessment and accreditation of education derived from field experience. The Nepal National Development Service has devised a comprehensive 10 point system of crediting performance during service, including grades for teaching school; conservation or construction work; attendance at training; presence in village; relationship with villagers; adaptation to village life; discipline, and moral behavior. [*Fortunately, the assessment of experience-based learning has come a long way since 1977! See* Assessing Learning *by Urban Whitaker, 1989, summarized in this resource book.*]

Problems

Problem areas of post-secondary study-service operations include that of convincing administrators and educators that study-services can make a difference in higher education. A pilot study-service project is often the best way to change the thinking of university educators. Another problem is the training of student volunteers, which requires bringing in professional people in lieu of faculty, who do not have the "how to" techniques needed in the field. A third problem is that of integrating field service and academic learning, and developing a standardized system for giving academic credit.

A fourth problem is that of setting up an administrative structure and procedure that will permit study-service to have a broader impact on both the educational system and the community. University-centered administration of a study-service scheme, with national policy coordination, appears to be the optimal solution. A fifth problem is that of gaining local community participation in a field project with an academic approach to work plans. Experience has shown that, when the skills and knowledge of the student volunteers are supportive of the villagers' interests, cooperation and a high level of satisfaction resulted.

Performance

Study-services are effective if they are able to bring about educational change and at the same time to help eliminate the problems which brought about their establishment. These problems are: (1) limitations of higher education in terms of experiential learning, employment, and development orientation; (2) need for skilled labor, especially in rural and poverty areas; and (3) need to bridge cultural and societal gaps between tribes, the educated and uneducated, the urban and rural, and to develop a common identity as a self-reliant nation.

Research indicates that an effective study-service scheme has the following characteristics:

1. University-oriented management that facilitates linkages between academic and field work, thus changing the limits of higher education.

2. National policy that ensures participation of a large portion of that student population and outreach to all geographic areas.

3. Institutionalization of work/service as a learning program of higher education characterized by:

    a. Official educational policy

    b. Policy for faculty participation and allocation of adequate faculty time for involvement

    c. Citizen participation in the training of students

    d. Establishment of an administrative unit, within the educational institution, to manage the program

    e. Accreditation of both the training and the field work components

    f. Integration of study-service into the regular higher education budget.

4. Institutionalization of study-service within the local community or provision of skilled staff to mobilize citizens, indicated by:

    a. Citizen participation in all program areas in advisory and planning roles, as trainers, supervisors, or participants

    b. Provision of professional services, such as education, health, legal, community development

    c. Continuation of requests for student assignments.

5. Linkage of study-services with other private and governmental institutions which ensure resources (financial, planning, program support) and use of the students in areas where they are needed.

6. Training and field program design that facilitates not only technical or social services, but also cultural learning by integrating

the student into the local community and providing him or her with a means to analyze his or her reactions to different ways of life, social patterns, and values.

The efficiency of study-services is indicated by the costs per volunteer year, month, or hour. To arrive at this figure, divide the total program costs by the number of volunteers who serve full-time for one year, month, or hour. The costs per volunteer year in study-service worldwide vary from U.S. $650 to $4,600 (including a portion of administrative overhead). High unit costs are usually the result of high allowances to volunteers, high faculty/volunteer ratio, and high administrative costs of institutionalizing study-service in the university.

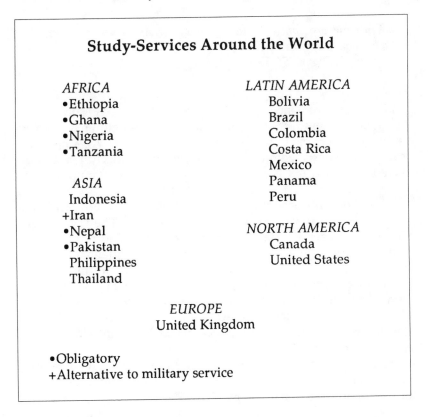

Study-Services Around the World

AFRICA
- Ethiopia
- Ghana
- Nigeria
- Tanzania

ASIA
Indonesia
+Iran
- Nepal
- Pakistan
Philippines
Thailand

LATIN AMERICA
Bolivia
Brazil
Colombia
Costa Rica
Mexico
Panama
Peru

NORTH AMERICA
Canada
United States

EUROPE
United Kingdom

- Obligatory
+Alternative to military service

Irene Pinkau was Director of the Development Services Cooperation Project in Washington, D.C., when this article was written.

Graduate Students Serve as Resource Persons to Elderly Volunteer Advisers

A unique program in which graduate students assist senior advisers. Reprinted from Synergist, ACTION, Vol. 9, No. 1, Spring 1980, pp. 54-55.

Each semester since fall 1977, a graduate student in social work and a law student from the University of Washington have served as resource persons to Senior Rights Assistance (SRA), a program that trains elderly volunteers to advise other elderly persons on such diverse matters as coping with Medicare and planning funerals.

The first two graduate students worked as interns with the program while it was in its formative stages. The social work student, Kathleen Kendziorski, helped organize and run meetings of the elderly volunteers in order that they might identify the areas in which older people are in greatest need of information and counseling. Following that, she served as a contact person with the community and organized training sessions for the advisers. She also persuaded the local Medicare and Social Security offices to develop pilot training courses. SRA chose this former intern to be the new director of Senior Rights Assistance.

The law student acts as a resource to the program when legal advice is necessary. Since SRA often serves as an advocacy group in such matters as tenancy rights and Social Security, the law students have been instrumental in interpreting relevant legislation.

SRA is the Seattle branch of a program called Volunteers Intervening for Equity, which was funded for a three-year demonstration period in nine cities by the Edna McConnell Clark Foundation in New York.

PART III

Profiles of Programs that Combine Service and Learning

K-12 Schools

Champlain Valley Union High School

DUO (DO UNTO OTHERS), Champlain Valley Union High School, RR 2 Box 160, Hinesburg, VT 05461, 802-482-2101. Joan Braun, Director. Public, rural high school; 800 students.

Participation: 185 students in grades 9-12 involved in the community during the day, after school, on weekends, and in the summer for average of 3-5 hours/week. Most effective publicity: word-of-mouth, daily announcements. **Scheduling:** Students participate during free class periods for in-school programs and are excused from classes 1 day/week for out-of-school programs.

Overview: In 1971, 2 teachers expressed a need for school-sponsored, community-based experiences for students. The State Department of Education simultaneously proposed DUO as a high school service-learning program. **Goals:** To provide community-based learning experiences for students, to enable students to understand the need for concern and caring within their own community, to expose students to new thoughts and ideas through contact with community members and their resources. Program supports students' intellectual, ethical/moral, career, civic, and personal development, and sense of social responsibility. *Philosophy:* "DUO provides students with the opportunity to design their own learning. They control what they learn, when they learn, and where they learn. DUO provides opportunities for students to realize that they are responsible for important choices in their lives. As they become involved, they discover they have something to contribute to the adult community, and that they *can* make a difference."

Structure: Director reports to Principal.

Budget: $4500 plus salaries from 100% school funds. Includes funds for administration, clerical support, long distance calls, site visits, students' travel to service sites, professional/teacher development, library, insurance. **Staff:** 2 full-time, 1 part-time.

Teacher involvement: 5-10 of 80 are active. Teachers serve as "agency supervisors." They also develop class community service projects outside the program such as tree planting, peer counseling, and tutoring.

Community involvement: Community organizations are involved in the development of program policies and procedures through evaluations and conversations with DUO staff. Site supervisors are required to: plan students' activities, supervise students, evaluate students' work. **Service sites:** Identified by program administrator. Criteria for selecting sites: opportunity for high-quality experiences, sensitivity of supervisor to students, accessibility to transportation. Most effective publicity: phone calls followed by letter and brochure.

Transportation: Vocational buses, public buses, students' cars.

Liability insurance: CIMA Volunteer Insurance — accident and liability.

Contract: An application is signed by all parties including parents.

Preparation: Interviews with DUO staff and agency.

"Providing students with an opportunity to learn that they each have something special to offer another human being is one of the most powerful forces in education."

Learning: Structured opportunities for reflection and analysis include: journals, required workshops, written evaluations. Students spend an average of 1 hour every 3 weeks in structured reflection and analysis activities. Learning is monitored, supported, and evaluated through: appointment during 3rd week with DUO staff, call to supervisor, written evaluations, conversations. DUO staff assesses learning. **Academic credit:** Yes; used for electives.

Monitoring of service: Quality of service monitored by site supervisor, conversations with students, DUO staff, written evaluations.

Recognition: Students: Recognition evening for students, parents, and agencies; certificates of appreciation. *Teachers:* Involvement is recognized as part of regular work load. *Site supervisors:* Thank-you letters, annual reception held in their honor, certificates of appreciation.

Program evaluation: Entire program is evaluated twice a year. Teachers are involved informally, students and site supervisors through written evaluations. Director submits annual evaluation to administration.

Benefits to school: "DUO is a program that is equally beneficial to *all* students at CVHS."

Problems addressed: "DUO often has more service opportunities than students. Historically, projects had been set up for individuals, but we changed our 'advertising' and asked peer-conscious teens to join a *group* involved in service. Same opportunities, but with 2-3 group meetings a year. Program's first effort at this saw the number of participants almost quadruple."

Lesson learned: "DUO tried to involve students with elderly persons using announcements and posters. Only one student responded. Most students have little experience with older adults and couldn't picture themselves in activities with them. Having presentations by agency staff, arranging 1-day group activities (concerts, etc.), then trying one-to-one projects works better."

Biggest challenge: Maintaining program enrollment as graduation requirements increase.

Other advice: "Providing students with an opportunity to learn that they each have something special to offer another human being is one of the most powerful forces in education. DUO's success is due, in part, to the designers who built in a flexibility which enables it to respond to changing times and changing student needs."

Charlotte-Mecklenburg Schools

Academic Internship Program, Charlotte-Mecklenburg Schools, 428 West Boulevard, Charlotte, NC 28203, 704-343-5400. Joyce McSpadden, Lead Coordinator; Evelyn Blackwell and Linda Stephens, Coordinators. Public, urban high schools; 15,554 students in 11 schools.

Participation: 500-600 students in grades 10-12 involved each year in the community after school and during the summer for 9-30 weeks for average of 6 hours/week. Most effective publicity: classroom presentations, high school curriculum guide, student handbook, school newspaper articles, word-of-mouth by students and teachers. **Prerequisites:** Second semester sophomore status, approval from parent and teacher sponsor. Some internships require certain classes as prerequisites.

Overview: Began in 1975 with a 3-year federal grant in the open school at West Charlotte High School. Students from 3 high schools were soon involved and within 5 years, the program was established in all 10 high schools. **Goals:** To provide opportunities for students to explore academic, career, or service interests through internships with local government, civic agencies, businesses, industries, and individuals; to establish positive school-community relationships. Program also supports students' ethical/moral and personal development, and sense of social responsibility. **Philosophy:** "AIP believes the ultimate goal of education is to help students develop a 'whole brain' and put it to use for self-development, personal aesthetics, and service to society. Students have better opportunities to bring together knowledge and understandings acquired in the classroom when they can apply that learning in the work-world where interactions are more diverse than those in schools alone. AIP provides such opportunities."

Structure: Based in Staff Development Center. Internship Coordinators report to Director of Staff Development. Advisory Board of 10% teachers, 17% students, 50% community representatives, 18% administrators, 5% parents.

Budget: $154,000 from 100% school funds. Includes funds for salaries, administration, clerical support, long distance calls, site visits, professional/teacher development, conferences. **Staff:** 4 full-time.

Teacher involvement: 175 teachers are active. Teachers are required to: confer with students regularly, guide students to help them get the most they can from the program, assume responsibility for evaluating and assigning credit for students' performance. Some teachers visit sites, attend Advisory Board meetings, and provide opportunities in class for interns to share their experiences.

Community involvement: Community organizations are involved in the development of program policies and procedures through the Advisory Board and discussions with internship coordinators. Site supervisors are required to: orient students to the agency and to internship responsibilities, supervise students, facilitate learning, and serve as a resource for students. **Service sites:** Identified by program administrators, students, teachers, Advisory Board, prospective community sponsors. Criteria for selecting sites: student interest, site staff's willingness to participate, quality of learning experience, safety. Most effective publicity: word-of-mouth, brochures, phone calls, personal visits.

Transportation: Students are responsible for their own arrangements.

Liability insurance: School has liability insurance on its employees in case of negligence, but none on students. Students may opt for school insurance in case of accident or are covered by parent's insurance.

Contracts: In initial interview, community sponsor and student discuss expectations of the internship and the student's goals and objectives. The Internship Coordinator and teacher sponsor are responsible for seeing that the requirements of a good learning experience are met. Interns sign an Internship Commitment, and all parties receive a copy. Goals and activities may be adjusted any time during the internship with agreement from all parties.

Preparation: Students are counseled individually by internship coordinator. Each site orients intern. Many give students reading materials prior to start of internship. Teacher sponsors help students set goals and objectives.

Learning: Required structured opportunities for reflection and analysis include: journals, self-evaluations, discussion. Students are also encouraged to develop projects which use knowledge acquired through their internships. Time spent in structured reflection and analysis varies. Learning is monitored, supported, and evaluated by teachers and community sponsors and internship coordinators through conferences, informal conversations, and feedback on students' journals, projects, and internship activities; community sponsor evaluations; and student self-evaluations. Internship progress is reviewed at least every 2 weeks. At the midpoint and end of the internship, students' journals are reviewed and signed by involved parties. Teachers assess learning and assign grades and credit. **Academic credit:** Yes; used toward graduation requirements, as electives.

Monitoring of service: Quality of service is monitored by internship coordinator, teacher, and community sponsors. Ultimate service recipients provide feedback to community sponsors.

Recognition: Students: Occasional recognition in their schools' Awards Day Programs for outstanding service. *Teachers:* Receive some school recognition but no reduction in teaching load or other responsibilities. Involvement meets one of the career development program expectations for teachers. *Site supervisors:* written or verbal thanks from program coordinators; sometimes certificates of appreciation or letters from school superintendent.

Program evaluation: Program coordinators review all evaluations, journals, and student projects and confer with students and community sponsors to determine success of program.

Benefits to schools: Provides an opportunity for students to participate in the community in meaningful ways. Good public relations for the school system.

Problems addressed: "How to become more institutionalized. We have realized that it is a slow, gradual process and that there are benefits to remaining somewhat marginal. Another problem we have addressed is office space. Until 1985 the 3 program coordinators did not share a central office. This made it difficult to share ideas and to work together as closely as we should have. Since obtaining space in the school system's Staff Development Center, there is more team spirit, it is much easier to plan together, and our secretary is readily accessible to each of us."

Lesson learned: "Assisting students with transportation has been a challenge as some schools are not located on city bus lines and school buses don't follow routes close to major internship sites. We have also learned that to be successful, programs must appeal to students. This is especially important when student participation is optional. Without their interest and input, a program is not likely to succeed."

Biggest challenge: "Even though interest in the program and the number of high schools are increasing, we have not been successful in our efforts to obtain any additional staff."

Hopkins High School

Community Involvement, Hopkins High School, 2400 Lindbergh Drive, Minnetonka, MN 55343, 612-541-7150. Dan Conrad, Coordinator/Teacher. Public high school; 2000 students.

Participation: 150 seniors involved in the community during the day and after school for 18 weeks for an average of 7-8 hours/week. Most effective publicity: word-of-mouth, program video. **Scheduling:** Community Involvement class is scheduled as a 2-period class each day.

Overview: Program includes community service class in Social Studies Department, field work for regular social studies classes, English as a Second Language Peer Tutoring, Community Service

Internships, "and anything else we can invent as we go." (Most of this program profile will focus on the community involvement class in the Social Studies Department because it involves the most students, is unique, and has a clearer structure.) Began in 1972 as pilot social studies class. **Goals:** Service to community, personal development, academic learning. Program also supports students' ethical/moral, career, and civic development. **Philosophy:** "In the current wave of enthusiasm for service by high school students, the emphasis seems to be on personal/social rehabilitation — when the impetus for ours was to improve education, enliven it, make it real and lasting. It seems the academic power of learning through service is being neglected by many. We try not to do the same."

"There's no more enjoyable and satisfying way to teach."

Structure: Program is a regular 12th grade Social Studies offering. Director reports to Principal.

Budget: Resources provided for teacher/coordinator, clerical support, long distance calls. **Staff:** 1 full-time.

Teacher involvement: 2 for this social studies course, 10-20 of 80 are active in other programs.

Community involvement: Site supervisors are required to: work out contract with student, delegate as much responsibility as they can to students, discuss students' performance on regular and quarterly basis, complete a checksheet for each student. **Service sites:** Identified by teachers and students. Criteria for selecting sites: significant work involving direct service to others. Most effective publicity: visits by teachers and students, a "guide for supervisors."

Transportation: Students walk, drive, or ride with other students.

Liability insurance: Covered under same policy as work-study students.

Preparation: 2-3 week orientation at beginning of year — run as a kind of "workshop in human service."

Learning: Structured opportunities for reflection and analysis include: journal, final paper, and required weekly seminar which provides a forum to discuss immediate issues and has a theoretical focus, which is basis for an analytical essay. Students spend an average of 2 hours/week in structured reflection and analysis activities. Learning monitored, supported, and evaluated through: group and individual discussions, papers, journals, essays. Teachers assess learning. **Academic credit:** Yes; used to fulfill 12th grade social studies requirement.

Monitoring of service: Site supervisor monitors and evaluates quality of service with student throughout term and through a formal evaluation at term's end.

Recognition: Students: General service award open to all students (not just program participants). *Teachers:* Involvement is recognized as part of regular work load. *Site supervisors:* Thank-you's and letters at end of program.

Program evaluation: Teachers evaluate impact of program through grades based on field work, journals and papers. Sometimes a pre- and post-test is administered on students' personal, social, and intellectual development. Students evaluate program verbally and through questionnaires. The administration evaluates program informally through comments from students, teachers, and the community.

Benefits to school: "Student satisfaction, enthusiasm; broadens options; good publicity (via TV and newspaper)."

Problem addressed: "We have involved a broad range of students by making it a regular course meeting a social studies requirement."

Biggest challenge/lesson learned: "The hardest part is to make the seminar component work effectively and engagingly. Haven't solved the problem, but it helps to divide into smaller groups, meet in non-classroom settings, and keep focus as close as possible to the field work."

Other advice: "There's no more enjoyable and satisfying way to teach."

Los Angeles Unified School District

See the "Community Program Profiles" section of this resource book for a description of the service programs sponsored by the Constitutional Rights Foundation in the Los Angeles Unified School District.

Maryland State Department of Education: Community Education

This profile is used as an example of the many community education programs through which adults and young people provide instructional and non-instructional services in public schools across the country. For more information on this program, contact Darla Strouse, Maryland State Department of Education, 200 W. Baltimore Street, Baltimore, MD 21201-2595, 301-333-2304.

Overview: Since 1975, the Maryland State Department of Education has had a community education staff person assigned to school volunteer program support. Today, that specialist works with student and adult volunteer programs as well as "partnership" programs in Maryland. The state provides coordination services by bringing together local volunteer administrators twice a year for updates and briefings. Conferences on current subjects and for staff development are also provided by the state. The Department of Education also provides outstanding volunteer recognition awards to qualifying schools and individuals and disseminates information and awards on behalf of the Governor's Office on Volunteerism. Each of the 24 local school districts in Maryland designates a person to coordinate its volunteer program. In addition, some school systems designate an additional person to develop school-business and other partnerships. Local volunteer coordinators' salaries are supported entirely by local funds. Although adults make up the largest segment of volunteers in the schools, a growing number of public school and university students are volunteering in instructional and non-instructional programs. Some of the peer or cross-age volunteer programs are non-credit, and in some the students tutor or assist teachers as an elective course. In 1986-87, 1,810 college and university students instructed students in schools across the state. Also in that year, the number of student volunteers in the schools increased by 95% over the previous year with 29,975 youth and teens providing instructional and non-instructional support services. Youth and teens represent 20% of the total number of volunteers in the public schools. **New directions:** Some of the new areas targeted for assistance by youth and adults include: dropout prevention mentoring programs, literacy instruction and teen reading projects, citizenship tutoring programs, the Teen Literacy Corps, student counseling projects, and career exploration opportunities.

Maryland State Department of Education: Student Literacy Corps

Maryland Student Literacy Corps (SLC), Maryland State Department of Education, Office of Communications and Special Projects, 200 W. Baltimore Street, Baltimore, MD 21201-2595, 301-333-2304.

Overview: **Students:** The core of this literacy program is a "shared experience" among students. Students may either volunteer to become members of SLC or may be nominated by school faculty. Every participant both serves and benefits from the program, each is equal, and none is identified as receiving services from others. SLC members participate in paired or group activities designed in some way to promote enthusiasm about reading. Participants will not always be peers; relationships may also include friendships, older students working with younger students, or students who share interests. The actual membership of any local SLC chapter depends on how the program is expected to complement its school education program or adapt to existing activities. **Adults:** Any interested school-based adult can serve as the Facilitator for a school Student Literacy Corps. Facilitator provides support for SLC members and helps them work among their peers, both younger and older, to promote enjoyment of reading. To make the program run smoothly, the Facilitator must understand the philosophy and goals of the SLC and assure that they are reflected in every aspect of the program. Once the logistical details are in operation, the Facilitator works to: encourage potential participants; enroll SLC members; orient students, parents, and community support groups; provide day-to-day support; evaluate the program; and give feedback to participants. Most effective publicity: youth press conferences; celebrity endorsements; sponsorship by school organizations; and recognition for membership and commitment to the program. **Staff:** 1 part-time Facilitator per school. **Philosophy:** "The SLC focuses on youth helping youth. Young people in school can be our best resource in building a literate nation. Getting our youth to accept an invitation to read begins with a book, with friends, and with pleasure. The first book must be followed by another and another. Only then will reading become a valued and treasured activity. Peers play a crucial role in this process, by setting the standards and forming a community of readers. The SLC is open to all, centers on literacy, motivates, supports, builds friendships, and is non-remedial."

Community involvement: "An aggressive campaign aimed at parents and the business community is vital for a sustained SLC. Parents must be made aware of the benefits to and responsibilities of their children. Their support can result in needed volunteers as well as word-of mouth promotion. Every member of the business community will not be actively involved in the program. However, because their fiscal support is necessary, they are invited to attend activities and in other ways reminded of the advantages the community is receiving."

Academic credit: Varies by school; used for community service credit, elective credit for graduation.

Program evaluation: "Many schools' programs aim to raise levels of achievement first and hope to affect attitudes only as a by-product of learning. Such programs may measure success with test scores, but while a SLC has the potential to raise achievement in youth, test scores are not the primary focus of its evaluation. The school facilitators look at participation levels, quality of activities, and traces of attitudinal change in participants. This information can come from unusual sources — library circulation changes, attendance, or possibly even discipline referral rates. Information also comes from interviewing students or teachers. Since flexibility is one of the most important features of the SLC design, facilitators are encouraged to change the Corps Program when evaluation points to a better path to success."

Maryland State Department of Education: Student Service Alliance

Maryland Student Service Alliance, Maryland State Department of Education, 200 W. Baltimore Street, Baltimore MD 21201-2595, 301-333-2427. Kathleen Kennedy Townsend and Margaret O'Neill.

Overview: "The unique aspect of service-learning in Maryland is the bylaw passed by the Board of Education in 1985. School systems in Maryland are required to offer students elective credit for service. David Hornbeck, then Superintendent of Schools, felt that a period of service during high school was a critical part of a well-rounded education. The outcome of this process would be people who are able to think, to care about one another, and be knowledgeable in the skills of citizenship. Students with these skills would then better contribute to society, both in the work force and by participating in the democratic process. Since many other graduation requirements were passed at the same time, little happened in the way of service. A couple of jurisdictions wrote guidelines for programs, but no course or credit-bearing extracurricular programs were established. In 1988, two staff were hired for two years to help the school systems get their programs off the ground. The goals of this two-year pilot program are: (1) At least 12 school systems will have a coordinator of community service for the school system, 1 or 2 of whom will be full-time coordinators; (2) 1000 students will be actively engaged in community service that provides credit towards graduation (or its equivalent); (3) an additional 5000 students will be engaged in community service as an extracurricular activity; (4) 6 secondary schools will have community service programs that are an identifiable part of the programs they consider outstanding; (5) 5000 students will be actively engaged in community service activities during the summer; (6) appropriate recognition/publicity about community service activities will be provided to the educational community and to the general public; (7) appropriate connections will be made with business, industry, and other organizations to promote community service; (8) proper supervision of the community service activities, including training for supervisors, and program/curriculum development will be provided; and (9) promotion of the Student Literacy Corps, as one meaningful option for community service, will be provided.

"Through a series of visits to superintendents, high schools, and service agencies we have begun to address the concerns which hindered LEAs implementing the bylaw. We are working with our advisory board, the Maryland Student Service Alliance, to define the appropriate stance of the state on the fine line between providing flexibility and autonomy to LEAs and providing sufficient guidance to develop quality programs.

"Discussions with superintendents around the state reveal that they are basically supportive of the idea of school-sanctioned community service but are stymied by many factors. Most are not precisely sure what service-learning is, and do not realize that, to some degree, service is already occurring in many schools, nor do they know how to harness its educational potential. Further LEA personnel express concerns about liability issues, confusion over criteria for awarding credit, and sources of revenue to finance faculty positions and to obtain course materials. The lack of information and understanding crippled the LEAs until the State Department took the initiative to establish the Maryland Student Service Alliance. It is clear from this experience that there need to be individuals and an office identified with student service in order for it to develop on a statewide basis.

"The programs we are helping develop have three common characteristics: preparation, action and reflection. To incorporate these elements, it is often necessary to develop a class. This conforms with the letter of the bylaw. To fulfill the spirit of the bylaw, we encourage principals to enrich existing school service projects with preparation and reflection activities.

"The programs at schools around the state vary to meet specific needs in the school and community. Some students are working on individual projects, others are working in small groups. Most projects involve students in relationships with people who are different from themselves. Some students are doing advocacy projects. In some places the students do service primarily to the school community. This is especially true in places where the school needs lots of help. Elsewhere, students are working in the community, usually at service agencies. We are encouraging opportunities for students to develop their own projects to meet needs they see."

Pittsburgh Middle Schools

Project OASES (Occupational & Academic Skills for the Employment of Students), Pittsburgh Middle Schools, 850 Boggs Avenue, Pittsburgh, PA 15211, 412-488-2531. Al Markowski, Supervisor. Public middle schools.

Participation: 150 8th graders involved in the community during the school day for 36 weeks for average of 5 hours/week. Most effective publicity: school faculty/administrators identify eligible students. **Prerequisites:** Participants must be considered at-risk. **Scheduling:** Students are assigned in the OASES Laboratory for 2 hours/day. Students assigned to math, reading, language arts, and physical education have reduced academic schedules.

Overview: Program began in 1982 at 4 schools and is now in all 8 middle schools. **Goals:** To increase attendance, improve academic achievement, increase motivation to stay in school, provide service to community. Program supports students' intellectual, ethical/moral, career, civic, and personal development, and sense of social responsibility. **Philosophy:** "The OASES Program is designed to make education relevant to students, not only by teaching them skills for future employment, but also by allowing them to apply what they learn to an immediate work situation in a community service setting. Many students are not motivated by today's educational practices because so much does not apply to their life situations. It is the school system's responsibility to prepare students for the future and to provide them with basic skills, both academically and occupationally. Many students need to apply what they learn immediately and to witness results in order to reinforce the learning experience and make it meaningful."

Structure: Based in individual schools. Director reports to Supervisor of Career Occupational and Vocational Training (COVT).

Budget: $370,000 from 90% school funds, 10% foundation grants. Includes funds for administration, site visits, students' travel to service sites, professional/teacher development. **Staff:** 16 full-time.

Teacher involvement: 1 teacher/school is active. Required of teachers: commitment to carry out program goals and objectives, full-time teaching position. OASES teaching staff has written the curriculum and participates in a 2-hour monthly in-service used for planning and evaluation.

Community involvement: Community organizations are involved in the development of program policies and procedures through local PTAs, which identify school and community service projects and provide feedback to school principals and OASES teachers. Considering establishment of an Advisory Board. Site supervisors are required to: oversee initial placement, review student performance with teachers, forward secondary placement to COVT Director, and follow up. **Service sites:** Identified by program administrator, teachers, principal, community leaders. Criteria for selecting sites: nonprofit organizations and community members with greatest need. Most effective publicity: through PTAs, principals, agencies.

Transportation: Each school has its own van.

Liability insurance: Through School District.

Preparation: OASES teachers prepare students. Jobs are pre-planned with necessary skills orientation provided in the school laboratory prior to service experience. Orientations for community organizations, the PTA, and parents are provided by the OASES teacher in each school.

Learning: Structured opportunities for reflection and analysis include: required OASES laboratory experience to provide daily counseling and reflection on students' progress in meeting program goals. Problem-solving and critical thinking is an ongoing process used in planning service projects. Students spend average of 10 hours/week in structured reflection and analysis activities. Learning is supported by OASES teacher and academic staff who closely monitor academic achievements. Academic skills that support contracted services are identified by OASES teacher and monitored at the work site. Recognition for a job well done is reinforced by school staff and community leaders. Academic/OASES teachers assess learning. **Academic credit:** No.

Monitoring of service: Quality of service is monitored and evaluated by contracting agency.

Recognition: Students: Perfect attendance and honor roll awards are provided each report period, including recognition from teachers and community leaders regarding service in the community. *Teachers:* Involvement is recognized as part of regular work load. *Site supervisors:* Supervisors are recognized by OASES teaching staff, school-based administration, and COVT Director.

Program evaluation: Every 9 weeks teachers evaluate academic achievement, attendance, and work completed in school and the community. Students monitor their progress in these areas as well. Program supervisor observes on-site activities and conducts monthly in-service with staff to evaluate program goals and objectives. Conferences are conducted to improve performance. Principals observe and confer with teachers and provide feedback to Program Supervisor and COVT Director.

Benefits to schools: Motivates 8th grade students who are potential drop-outs to remain in school.

Problem addressed: "To prepare students to work as a team rather than as individuals in the community, teachers moved students from individualized projects to small team projects to larger community projects."

Lesson learned: "We have experienced problems with service projects that do not require all students' participation at the same time. We resolved this by being more selective in choosing projects and grouping students into specialized working teams such as painters, carpenters, etc."

Biggest challenge: "Program's success has created a great interest by students who could benefit from the program, and there is a need for space to accommodate additional participants."

St. Ignatius College Prep

Community Service, St. Ignatius College Prep, 2001 37th Avenue, San Francisco, CA 94116, 415-731-7500. David Mezzera, Program Director. Private, urban high school; 1175 students.

Participation: 800 students in grades 10-12 involved in the community during the academic year or summer. Participation is required for graduation. Most effective publicity: information fair, word-of-mouth. **Prerequisites:** Students must attend an orientation session before choosing a service site.

Overview: Began in 1975 as an elective course combining aspects of religion and sociology. Participation became a school-wide requirement. Students serve 100 hours in the community and participate in reflection activities. **Goals:** "To allow students to serve others in need in order to come to an appreciation of their need for respect, justice, and love; to allow students to experience the relationship between their traditional faith and the call to live the message of the gospels; to allow students to seek new experiences which will help them grow in self-esteem and learn how to accept themselves, both their talents and limitations; to have students begin to appreciate the satisfaction of giving in service for other people; to enable students to articulate feelings of growth and maturation during the reflection process." Program also supports students' ethical/moral, and civic development.

Structure: Program is a separate academic unit. Director reports to Dean of Instruction.

Budget: $425 plus salary from regular school funds. Includes funds for administration, long distance calls, site visits, professional/teacher development. **Staff:** 1 part-time.

Teacher involvement: Teacher directs program. Indirect support of the program is provided by teachers through particular classes.

Community involvement: Agency supervisors attend yearly information and orientation sessions with potential student participants and attend a debriefing session with the Director. Site supervisors are required to provide on-site orientation, establish a work schedule, record and verify students' hours, and provide an evaluation of the student's progress. **Service sites:** Identified by Director. Criteria for selecting sites: Program generally works with nonprofit organizations and projects in which students work directly with people; proper supervision must also be provided. Most effective publicity: word-of-mouth by other agency volunteer coordinators, brochures.

Contract: Students complete a registration form for each agency with whom they work indicating what they will do and who their supervisor will be.

Preparation: Class presentations are made to groups of 30 students on the philosophy of service and ministry. A large group presentation is made to all students entering program to explain logistics. Additionally, an Information Fair allows students to meet with 25-30 agency representatives. Each agency then conducts its own individualized training.

Learning: Structured opportunities for reflection and analysis include a reflection paper and a project of the student's choosing. Learning is monitored and supported through progress reports from agencies. Learning is evaluated through student's reflection paper. Program Director assesses learning. **Academic credit:** Yes: used toward graduation requirements.

Monitoring of service: Quality of service is monitored through reports submitted by site supervisors.

Recognition: Students: Letters of appreciation and recognition; many agencies also provide thank-you luncheons or dinners for students. The School provides community service awards to selected seniors.

Program evaluation: Impact of program is evaluated by students, site supervisors, and program administrator. Impact of program as it relates to the School's stated goals and philosophy is measured for W.A.S.C. accreditation, admissions, and parent satisfaction.

Benefits to school: "A wonderful tool for admissions! We are a private institution and have to compete with other private and public schools. Our service program is seen by many parents as an advantage to our school."

Problem addressed: "I initiated a full-day orientation and information session to allow students who have not yet begun their service to meet with agency representatives to learn about different opportunities and to be guided through the early stages of service. Prior to this, the philosophic and pragmatic orientation of our students was hit-and-miss."

Lesson learned: "Requests from the community often out-number the students who are available and willing to get involved. I try my best to publicize events and activities, but warn agencies up-front that we may not have students who volunteer for service to their program."

Biggest challenges: "Maintaining better and closer communication between the School and agencies. This may require us to reduce the number of agencies we try to serve and to visit sites more frequently. Another challenge the Program faces is that it does not have a centrally located office. Finding effective ways to disseminate information to students has been difficult."

San Francisco University High School

Community Service Learning, San Francisco University High School, 3065 Jackson Street, San Francisco, CA 94115, 415-346-8400. Debbie Genzer, Director of Community Service Learning. Private, urban high school; 380 students.

Participation: 380 students in grades 9-12 are involved. Students in the Service Learning Program are in the community during the day for 16 weeks. Twenty Hours Program requires 20 hours of service after school. Most effective publicity: students recruiting students to a project they have initiated and designed or to a project they enjoyed in the past. Program is required for all students. **Scheduling:** Service Learning Program is scheduled during the school day one day per week for 2 and 1/4 hours for 9th and 10th graders and for 1 and 1/2 hours for 11th and 12th graders.

Overview: Since School's founding in 1973, students have been required to provide 20 hours of service to the school or broader community each year. This mandate comes from the school's philosophy which emphasizes using the city as a classroom and helping students learn to use their education in responsible ways. The program has grown to include more emphasis on learning through and about service experiences; the semester-long Service Learning Program has been added as a result. **Goals:** To help students learn that they can make a difference, to develop a sense of social responsibility within students, to give students a multi-cultural perspective, and to help students think critically and sensitively about social issues. Program also supports students' intellectual, ethical/moral, civic, and personal development. **Philosophy:** "Student leadership is a major component of our program. Our School Council Vice-President for Community Service, our Student Community Service Counselors, and our Junior and Senior Liaisons are all involved in designing service projects, setting program policy, and helping other students find worthwhile service activities. Students who were not leaders previously are encouraged to assume these positions. Through this leadership, other students are often inspired, and the leaders themselves frequently become committed to service and are more thoughtful about its meaning."

Structure: Director reports to Academic Dean. Advisory Board of 30% teachers, 30% students, 30% administrators.

Budget: Funds are available as needed from regular schools funds. Resources provided for administration, limited clerical support, long distance calls, site visits, students' travel to service sites, professional/teacher development, and speakers. **Staff:** 1 full-time, 1 part-time.

Teacher involvement: All teachers are involved to varying degrees. Advisors must discuss the experience with students and visit the site once a semester. Class deans help design the program. 9th and 11th grade teachers assign coursework related to the service. The role of 10th grade teachers is currently being reviewed by a 10th grade curriculum committee. The School's educational philosophy was a major topic at a recent faculty retreat. Faculty were asked to consider case studies of the School's service programs and how teachers could better facilitate learning from these experiences.

Community involvement: "Community organizations help develop program policies and procedures through year-end evaluations in which they are asked for their opinions and recommendations. Their responses are a primary source of ideas for changes. An agency visit is required before students are sent to a site, and we ask that 9th and 10th grade students work directly with people rather than doing clerical work. Site supervisors are required to check attendance and, if a student does not arrive on time, to call the school." **Service sites:** Identified by program administrator and students. Criteria for selecting sites: accessible from school by bus in 1/2 hour (for Service Learning Program), supervisor's commitment and availability to supervise, positive rating by former students at that site, student interest, agency's need for assistance.

Most effective publicity: letter to agency introducing program with
follow-up site visit by program administrator. Parents, teachers,
and participating agencies refer others.

Transportation: Students usually use city buses. Some students
are driven in a school van by a teacher or parent. On rare occasions,
students drive.

Liability insurance: Through regular school insurance policy.

Contract: Students and agencies are made aware of each other's
goals and needs during orientation and the agency visit. The Director represents the needs of each group to the school. This is all done
in writing and reviewed verbally.

Preparation: Service Learning Program: In each grade students
are prepared for service with an orientation in which students from
last year's placements discuss their experiences. Professionals from
various service fields are guest speakers during the term. 9th and
11th grade teachers have students write and read about related
subject matter. Advisors at all grade levels counsel students about
service. 20 Hours Program: Student Community Service Counselors help students select placements.

Learning: Service Learning Program: In 9th and 11th grade curricula, students are required to write, research, and discuss their
service in relation to skills and concepts in their courses (especially
English and History). In all grades, time is set aside during weekly
advising cluster meetings to discuss community service. 20 Hours
Program: Students can discuss issues in advising cluster and with
their student community service counselor. In both programs,
students spend average of 1/2 hour per week in structured reflection and analysis activities. Teachers and program administrator
assess learning. Assignment form is usually graded. Usually students are given written comments. Students also evaluate their own
learning through reflection in journals and evaluations. **Academic
credit:** Service Learning is part of the regular curriculum. 20 hours
of service are required for graduation, but no specific academic
credit is given. Students can also do an internship in community
service and receive 1 elective credit.

Monitoring of service: Quality of service is monitored by Director
through agency visits, phone conversations with supervisors, written and verbal evaluation by students, and comments from teachers.
Program is considering ways to ask ultimate service recipients for
input about the value of services provided.

Recognition: Students: The Student Community Service Committee is philosophically against giving awards or recognition for service, except to educate and inspire other students. This year profiles of student activities which did this were posted in the hallways. *Teachers:* Involvement is recognized as part of regular work load. *Site supervisors:* Program tried hosting a reception for supervisors, but attendance was low. Now thank-you notes are sent each year. Students also bring handmade gifts during holidays.

Program evaluation: Director reviews program with agencies each semester. Sites complete written evaluations. Students meet with advisors and complete mid-semester and year-end evaluations. Teachers evaluate the program in committee meetings. Questions addressed in evaluation include: Did students complete required hours? What did students learn? Were students needed, helpful, enthusiastic? Were the experiences enjoyable and worthwhile? Program is still grappling with a way to measure specific outcomes.

Benefits to school: Program helps school fulfill its mission.

Problem addressed: "It was difficult for the Director to facilitate a high-quality 20-hour service experience for 380 students. A Student Community Service Counselor Program was designed which trains students to help their classmates find worthwhile service experiences and to follow up with them once they are placed."

Lesson learned: "Ninth graders were asked to write in journals about their service experience. This did not work well, and the quality of reflection was poor. Because the journals were evaluated by the Director, not the teacher, there seemed to be no real consequences for not doing it or not doing it well. Advice: Emphasize the importance of reflection from the beginning and integrate this with other dimensions of the students' coursework. Have teachers evaluate journals."

Biggest challenge: "Getting teachers to be committed to helping students learn from and about their service experiences and doing it well."

SerVermont

SerVermont, P.O. Box 516, Chester, VT 05143, 802-875-2278. Cynthia Parsons, Coordinator. Public, rural/urban/suburban schools; 60,000 students.

Participation: 10,000 students in grades 1-12 involved in the community during the day, after school, and during summer. Most effective publicity: a clear community need, teacher/principal involvement. **Scheduling:** Varies with each project (e.g., peer tutoring during a free period, repair of elderly person's electrical equipment in shop, typing for nonprofit in a practice assignment). Some students are exempted from class to participate in program. One school exempts interns for 1 day/week and provides make-up material.

Overview: Began in 1986. **Goals:** To encourage all students to serve in their community, to integrate student service with classroom teaching, to foster concept of U.S. as a participatory democracy. Program also supports students' ethical/moral, career, and personal development. **Philosophy:** SerVermont emphasizes *voluntary* service and believes that the best service is done when recipients are involved in the planning and the service is integrated with academics.

Structure: SerVermont is privately funded and run. Coordinator reports to the Governor and Education Commissioner.

Budget: $20,000 from 100% foundations grants. Includes funds for administration, clerical support, long distance calls, site visits, professional/teacher development, and mini-grants for teachers and student groups. **Staff:** 1 part-time.

Teacher involvement: 30 teachers have received direct grants. Teachers are required to integrate service with academics, using journals, seminars, and discussions. Program encourages teachers to team-teach and work together on service projects.

Community involvement: Community organizations must be involved in the development of program policies and procedures in order for student groups or teachers to be eligible to receive a mini-grant. Requirements of site supervisors vary. **Service sites:** Identified by teachers, students. Criteria for selecting sites: need; projects working with seniors, the environment, and those that are based in SerVermont towns. Most effective publicity: direct mail.

Preparation: Varies with project, but service is integrated as part of a course. Coordinator holds workshops regionally to teach teachers how to do this. Program has also developed a book, *SerVermont and the U.S.A.*, on how to do this.

Learning: Learning monitored, supported, and evaluated through recall, reflection, and community recognition. **Academic credit:** In some cases; used toward graduation requirements, electives.

Monitoring of service: Quality of service is monitored locally and by SerVermont Coordinator. Quality of service is evaluated by Coordinator through discussion with students and those with whom they work in the community. Ultimate service recipients must be represented on planning team for teachers and students to qualify for a mini-grant.

Recognition: *Students:* SerVermont Annual Student Service Awards to 5-10 student groups nominated by state legislators and judges. *Teachers:* Recognition for involvement varies with each school. SerVermont provides recognition in media. *Site supervisors:* Varies for each site, but SerVermont seeks media recognition for all supervisors.

Program evaluation: Informally done by teachers, students, site supervisors, and SerVermont Board.

Benefits to schools: Program makes voluntary service a part of a growing number of students' lives.

Problem addressed: "Principals and teachers are not sure how to include service in a student's already crowded schedule. School visits, workshops, and our book have helped."

Lesson learned: "We tried to get all schools to do a 'Help Needed' listing of all available service opportunities and contacts and got little response. We need to spend more time with agencies."

Biggest challenge: "Avoiding public funding and bureaucratic control."

Other advice: "For a state-wide effort, it's helpful to be outside government, but to have full backing from the top down."

Sidwell Friends School

Internship-Senior Credit/Community Service, Sidwell Friends School, 3825 Wisconsin Avenue NW, Washington, DC 20016, 202-537-8180. Carla Gelband, Director of Community Involvement. Private, urban high school; 420 students.

Participation: 4 students in 12th grade involved in internships for an average of 8 hours/week for 1 semester or year. In addition, every Upper School student is expected to perform significant community service as a requirement for graduation. Students serve in the community for average of 30 hours. Most effective publicity: word-of-mouth, special announcements. **Scheduling:** Students participate in Internships during the day and during evenings and weekends. Students work in the community during free periods in school, after school, on weekends, during school vacations and the summer. **Prerequisites:** For the internship: demonstrated ability to do independent work.

Overview: Internship began in 1976 as an outgrowth of a political problems seminar. **Goals:** To provide experiential learning opportunities for students within an academic context. Program also supports students' ethical/moral, career, civic, and personal development, and sense of social responsibility. **Philosophy:** There is a strong Quaker belief of God being in every person, that all can equally serve, and be served. The program is egalitarian in that it depends on no talent — academic, athletic, artistic — for a student to be successful.

Structure: Director is an administrator on the Upper School staff. Director reports to Principal. Advisory Committee of 25% teachers, 75% students.

Budget: $1500 plus salary from school funds. Includes funds for administration, long distance calls, professional/teacher development, field trips, special projects. **Staff:** 1 full-time.

Teacher involvement: Director and students' advisors are active. Teachers also serve on the Community Action Committee.

Community involvement: Community organizations are involved in the development of program policies and procedures through conversations with Director. Site supervisors are required to sign student's community service contract and complete a student evaluation. **Service sites:** Identified by Director, students, teachers. Criteria for selecting sites: students will work directly with people, no office or a lab work. Most effective publicity: newsletters (e.g., senior citizen's group advertised our "Student Fixit Service").

Contract: Negotiated between student and supervisor; must also be signed by parent/guardian, advisor, and Director.

Transportation: Students go on their own; parents sign waivers.

Preparation: All 9th graders take a required course in community awareness.

Learning: Interns are required to meet weekly with supervisor, keep a journal, and write a term paper; students involved in service activities complete an evaluation. Interns average 1 hour/week in structured reflection and analysis activities. Learning monitored, supported, and evaluated through: weekly meeting with supervisor, contract. Director assesses learning through: conferences, journals, term papers. **Academic credit:** Yes for interns; used for electives.

"Start small! Begin with a pilot project you know will work, so it will be received enthusiastically — then expand!"

Monitoring of service: Quality of service is monitored and evaluated by site supervisors. How ultimate service recipients are involved in determining the value of service depends on the nature of the program (e.g., people are vocal at a soup kitchen, less so at a day care center).

Recognition: Students: Council for Religion in Independent Schools Award, awards from community organizations. *Teachers:* Some involvement is recognized as part of regular work load; others receive some school recognition but no reduction in other responsibilities. *Site supervisors:* Thank-you letters from Director.

Program evaluation: Students and supervisors complete evaluations.

Benefits to school: Students become more responsible and sensitive as a result of service and more independent through internships.

Problem addressed: Students are better prepared for service and make better choices in selecting service sites because of the preparation course the Program developed.

Lesson learned: "Allowing students to have unlimited opportunities in placements makes quality control more difficult as there is limited time in which to visit sites and to get to know supervisors."

Biggest challenge: "Involving more males and others beyond what is required.

Other advice: Start small! Begin with a pilot project you know will work, so it will be received enthusiastically — then expand!"

Suitland High School

Student Support/Service Program, Suitland High School, 5200 Silver Hill Road, Forestville, MD 20747, 301-568-7770. Camille McCann, Community Service Coordinator. Public, urban high school; 2400 students.

Participation: 60 students in grades 9-12 involved weekly, 100 students involved in special projects per year. Students involved in the community during the day, after school, and during the summer for average of 3 hours/week. Most effective publicity: students recruiting students, videotape on program. **Scheduling:** For day projects, student leave from student government class (last period of day) and continue service after school.

Overview: Began in 1987. Students serve in the community and assist their peers in school. Specific projects include: visiting nursing home residents; tutoring elementary students; assisting students with learning disabilities and physically disabled adults; working at a summer camp; and participating in the PEP (Peers Encouraging Punctuality), AIM (Academic Improvement Measure), Peer Tutoring, and CHAT (Community to Help Alleviate Troubles) programs. **Goals:** To promote responsible participation in the community, to serve the community of which students are a part, to develop students' sense of self-worth. Program also supports students' intellectual, ethical/moral, and career development.

Structure: Program is part of student government. Director reports to the Coordinator of Instruction.

Budget: Funds provided for administration, long distance calls, and drivers. **Staff:** 1 part-time.

Teacher involvement: Teacher coordinates program. Coordinator must be willing to work after school, transport students, volunteer on weekends, and work during the summer.

Community involvement: Students develop and implement programs with approval of agencies. Students are self-directed in projects, but community service coordinator is on site if students have questions or problems. **Service sites:** Identified by students, teachers. Criteria for selecting sites: student interest, location, need. Most effective publicity: most agencies contact the school.

Transportation: Student drivers, county school bus.

Preparation: Students complete a 2-week training program in student government class which covers problem-solving, communication skills, and assertive versus aggressive behavior. Students are trained after school for special projects.

Learning: Students meet with their service group after each week's activity. They discuss successes and problems, make needed revisions in plans, and complete a journal entry. Students also update student government class on projects for feedback. Students spend average of 1 hour/week in structured reflection and analysis activities. Learning monitored and supported by school coordinator, site supervisors, and peers. Learning is evaluated and assessed by self-evaluation, peer-group evaluation, teacher and supervisor evaluations. **Academic credit:** No.

Monitoring of service: Quality of service is monitored by teacher, site supervisors, students, and persons served by the program through formal evaluations and informal discussions.

Recognition: Coordinator has one 45-minute period each day to coordinate program. *Site supervisors:* Videotape recognition; students also make gifts.

Program evaluation: Program is evaluated and revised annually by students, supervisors, and community service director.

Benefits to school: Positive school relations with the community and county.

Problem addressed: Coordinator worked with the county school transportation department to arrange a free bus to transport students to service sites.

Lesson learned: Requesting parent drivers did not work well.

Biggest challenges: Transportation, funding, adequate release time for Coordinator.

> *Thanks to Barbara Gomez of the Council of Chief State School Officers (CCSSO) for researching the information in the following entries through a CCSSO project.*

Atlanta Public Schools

Community Service, Atlanta Public Schools, 2960 Forrest Hill Drive, SW, Atlanta, GA 30315, 404-827-8608. Barbara Whitaker.

Overview: Began in 1984. Required course for graduation. Students give 75 hours of unpaid service during non-school hours in agencies approved by the Atlanta Public Schools and receive 1/2 Carnegie unit of credit. Advisors certify students, completion of required hours. "Students acquire coping skills and learn about the significance of giving to their communities. They gain a sense of worth and pride as they understand and appreciate the function of community organizations."

Participation: Required, 5000 students in grades 9-12.

Staff: Each school has a contact person for whom this course is an additional duty.

Resource materials: Course guide, brochures for parents and students, catalogue of approved agencies.

Baltimore City Schools and the
National Institute for Citizen Education in the Law

Teens, Crime and the Community, National Institute for Citizen Education in the Law (NICEL), 25 E Street, Suite 400, Washington, DC 20001, 202-662-9620. Judith Zimmer.

Overview: Began in 1985 in Baltimore. Program combines education and action to help teens understand how crime affects them, their family, friends, and community, and how they can prevent it and make their schools and communities safer and more vital. It couples classroom lessons with opportunities to work in school and the community to reduce or eliminate a specific problem. Program assumes that high school students can understand crime's effects and costs, and that they can take responsible action against crime. Local partnerships between schools and crime prevention or victims' service programs enrich the curriculum and support teen projects.

Budget: Funding sources: Citizenship/Law-Related Education Program for the Schools of Maryland, Baltimore City Schools, NICEL, and the National Crime Prevention Council.

Resource Materials: Teens, Crime and the Community textbook provides a basis for understanding the nature, impact, and prevention of crime as well as the needs of victims and the dynamics of community and crime.

Burbank High School

Burbank Community Service, Burbank High School, 903 North 3rd Street, Burbank, CA 91502, 818-843-2150. Toni Cannon.

Overview: Began in 1980. Community Service is a voluntary, one-semester class designed to provide field work experiences in a variety of community agencies. Students are asked to work at least 60 hours in the community. 5 credits for completion of independent study assignments may be applied toward career knowledge or senior studies requirement. Students choose a site based on personal interest and schedule. Participants work with several tutoring programs, seniors, and children with developmental and physical disabilities and as hospital aides and at local animal shelters.

Participation: 63 students in grades 11-12. Demographics: 9% Asian/African American/Native American/Filipino, 32% Hispanic, 59% Caucasian.

Budget: Part of regular curriculum budget. **Staff:** 1.

Resource materials: Volunteer packet, slides taken at sites.

Center for Advanced Study in Education (CASE)

Early Adolescent Helper Program, CASE/Helper Program, Graduate School and University Center of the City University of New York, 25 West 43rd Street, New York, NY 10036, 212-719-9066. Joan Schine. See the chapter on this program in this resource book.

Overview: Began in 1983. Program is part of curriculum in some schools, part of extracurriculum in others. Where program is part of the Attendance Improvement/Dropout Prevention Program, it is a required career exploration experience. Training covers topics of human development, developmental traits of children, communication, problem-solving, and "how-to" information related to specific programs with which students will work. Pre-employment skills, workplace habits and attitudes, and the meaning of responsibility are also explored. Students discuss their experiences, feelings, aspirations, and learning with skilled adult leaders.

Participation: 200+ students in grades 6-9 serve up to 4 hours/week during or after school. Demographics: Students are from inner-city schools with large ethnic populations.

Budget: $120,000. Funding source: foundations. **Staff:** 1 full-time, 1 part-time plus part-time consultants and field associates.

Resource materials: Program guides, Helper Program brochure, "You and Your Helper" leaflet for child care staff, newsletter.

Community Leadership Seminars

Youth Leadership Project, Community Leadership Seminars, 530 Walnut Street, 14th Floor, Philadelphia, PA 19106, 215-928-9999. Arthur Schwartz.

Overview: Began in 1987. Extracurricular program, but Project is part of curriculum in some schools. Project places a strong emphasis on volunteerism and the social responsibility of citizenship. A 6-week training curriculum, designed to develop student leadership skills, addresses topics of communication, problem-solving, motivation, decision-making, conflict resolution, and advocacy. Students design and implement community projects and enlist the participation of other students with guidance and support from an adult community mentor.

Participation: 15 students in grades 9-12. Demographics: Urban Philadelphia, African American students.

Budget: $28,500. Funding sources: Cigna Foundation, Bell of Pennsylvania, Samuel S. Fels Fund, Aetna Foundation. **Staff:** 1.

Resource materials: Student-written newsletter describing reasons for developing various projects.

Facing History and Ourselves

Choosing to Participate, Facing History and Ourselves, 25 Kennard Road, Brookline, MA 02146, 617-232-1595. Alan Stoskopf and Margot Strom.

Overview: Began in 1985. Encourages teachers and students to examine critically what it means to be a responsible citizen in a democracy. Through a 5-chapter resource book and videotapes, students explore case studies of people who have tried to make a difference in American history. Readings concentrate on individuals and groups who have often been left out of textbooks but have been essential in shaping our democratic heritage. Lessons encourage students to think about questions of motivation, choice and responsibility and apply them to their lives today. Program encourages teachers to infuse parts of the resource book into their curricula.

Participation: Teachers and students from grades 8-12. Demographics: School systems across the country can participate — suburban, inner city, public, parochial, and private.

Budget: $175,000. **Staff:** 1 full-time project coordinator, 2 part-time program staff consultants, 1 part-time secretary.

Resource materials: Resource book.

Fallston High School

Student Activities Club, Fallston High School, 2301 Carrs Mill Road, Fallston, MD 21047, 301-877-7400. Jim O'Toole.

Overview: Began in 1982. Extracurricular program. Student Activities Club consists of 38 committees which serve the school, community, and state. As needs are identified, a new committee is formed. The organization's leadership is provided by a supportive administration, a teacher sponsor, 4 student officers, and a chairperson for each committee. Projects include: maintaining school grounds, cleaning school showcases, assisting at Red Cross blood drives, visiting nursing homes, sponsoring wheelchair basketball games, assisting Fuel Fund drives, working at soup kitchens. All work is done on students' own time, usually after school and on weekends.

Participation: 300+ students in grades 9-12. Demographics: Middle/upper middle class, rural/suburban bedroom community; 97% Caucasian, 1% African American, 1% Asian, 1% other.

Budget: Sponsor volunteers time and carries full teaching load; all funds are secured through fundraisers.

Hudson High School

Hudson High School Student Volunteers, Hudson High School, 77 Oviatt Street, Hudson, OH 44236, 216-653-3371. Dee Phillips.

Overview: Began in 1985. Extracurricular program. Students serve Hudson School and the local community. Students strengthen their values while learning to care about others.

Participation: 100 students in grades 9-12. Demographics: Students are primarily from a suburban/high income area.

Staff: 1 volunteer teacher.

Resource materials: Tape, slides, booklets.

Minneapolis Public Schools, Mayor's Office of Minneapolis, and United Way of Minneapolis Area

Fresh Force, University YMCA, 1901 University Avenue SE, Minneapolis, MN 55414, 612-625-3800. Tim Gusk.

Overview: Began in 1985. Most of Program is extracurricular, but is integrated in the curriculum in some schools. The main purpose of Fresh Force is to engage junior high students in community betterment projects. Recruitment is facilitated through school liaisons and university student "service leaders" who manage training and recognition and other program activities. Participants earn t-shirts and job reference letters from the Mayor. In one year, approximately 50 projects are completed, with an average of 5500 service hours provided.

Participation: 250 7th and 8th graders from 12 Minneapolis schools, 20 university student "service leaders." Demographics: Multicultural, 75% female, 63% from families with low incomes, 56% from families with only 1 parent at home.

Budget: $53,000. Funding sources: United Way, Pillsbury Company, Jostens. **Staff:** 1 full-time.

Resource materials: 1-page program description, forms packet, 2 program reports.

National Youth Leadership Council

National Youth Leadership Projects, 386 McNeal Hall, University of Minnesota, St. Paul, MN 55108, 612-624-2719. Rick Nelson.

Overview: First project began in 1982. Extracurricular program offered during the summer. Some schools have integrated the training program into their curriculum. Training programs run 8-10 days and are based in residential camp settings. Programs have been developed for the Upper Midwest, the Santa Fe Mountain Center in New Mexico, Bradford Woods in Indiana, Leadership Experience in Alaska, and the National Indian Youth Leadership Project in New Mexico (see chapter on this in this resource book). Program includes multi-cultural participation, exploration of leadership styles, experiential learning, exploration of social issues, and service. The staff is multi-cultural with diverse experience. Groups of students represent youth organizations or schools and are expected to complete a service project upon returning home. Activities range from high ropes courses to theater, from exploring issues to performing a vaudeville show at a nursing home, from working in a soup kitchen in downtown Indianapolis to white water rafting in New Mexico. Program focuses on personal development and social responsibility and on empowering young people to become valuable and active producers, not just consumers of information and goods. Students become part of a multi-cultural community that is presented with a variety of physical, intellectual and social challenges. The National Youth Leadership Council's ultimate mission is to develop servant-oriented youth leaders.

Participation: 50-150 students per site in grades 10-12. Demographics: Multi-cultural.

Budget/Staff: Depends on site.

Resource materials: Slide show, brochures, videos.

Plainview-Old Bethpage School District

Community Studies Corps, Project Outreach, John F. Kennedy High School, Kennedy Drive, Plainview, NY 11803, 516-937-6377. Richard Koubek.

Overview: Began in 1983. Program is both extracurricular and part of curriculum. It will soon be part of a mandatory 12th grade social studies course. Students are placed in service programs (e.g., student government, school newspaper, public library, YMCA) where they serve 15 hours/semester and observe how decisions are made in the organization. Students attend 4 classes/week in which a "Participation in Government" curriculum is used. The course explores themes of power and politics in organizational decision-making, leadership and democratic theory within organizations, and organization and public policy analyses.

Participation: 10 students in grades 11-12. Demographics: Middle-class suburban students.

Budget: New York State Division of Criminal Justice Services provides funding.

Resource materials: Curriculum guide, sample materials.

Princeton Regional Schools

Learning in the Community, Princeton High School, 151 Moore Street, Princeton, NJ 08540, 609-683-4480 ext. 47. Ron Horowitz, Coordinator.

Overview: Began in 1980. Part of curriculum. Provides students with an opportunity to work with community members who share their career interests. Students are exposed to community resources, provide a community service, explore possible careers, and improve communication skills. Students sign up for 1 or 2 semesters for 1 or more periods. Participants are required to complete a project (a paper, slide show, film, model, extended log, portfolio, or exhibit) demonstrating what they have learned. Credit is granted based on participation and quality of project reports. Students participate on an individual or small group basis.

Participation: 200 students in grades 10-12. Demographics: Relatively affluent suburban school located midway between New York and Philadelphia.

Budget: 1 full-time coordinator and 1 full-time assistant funded by the school district, 1 part-time Intergenerational Director funded by independent sources.

Resource materials: Brochure, descriptive materials.

Rainier Beach High School

Leadership Development Program, Rainier Beach High School, 8815 Seward Park Avenue South, Seattle, WA 98118, 206-281-6090. Kathi Lehr.

Overview: Began in 1986. "Leadership I" and "Leadership II" are elective courses. Program was established to prepare young people to become involved in the community after graduation. Students take Leadership courses to improve their communication skills, learn to work with others, and become more involved in school. Program includes community service, student exchanges with other high schools, and meeting with civic mentors. Community leaders participate in the class, and students assume leadership responsibilities as part of the school-based management project.

Participation: 40 students in grades 10-12. Demographics: Urban school of 1150 students; multi-cultural.

Budget: Regular school funding. **Staff:** Quarter-time teacher for the 2 classes.

Resource materials: Course outlines, videotape on the program produced by the Economic Development Council, and students who will make program presentations.

Riverside-University High School

Education and Human Services, Riverside-University High School, 1615 E. Locust, Milwaukee, WI 53211, 414-964-5900 ext. 5125. Judy Skurnick, Implementor.

Overview: Began in 1983. Education and Human Services Program consists of 3 elective courses for sophomores, juniors, and seniors who want to learn how to work with, teach, and help people. Sophomores take an "Introduction to Education and Human Services" class and are required to serve 2-3 hours/week in a community agency. Community service is built into the curriculum to help students learn to be productive through helping others. Juniors take "Introduction to Psychology." Seniors take a seminar course. Seniors can also explore career interests through an internship and receive academic credit for the learning they gain. They are allowed to work at internship sites during the last 2 class periods each day. The program is based on a pre-university curriculum. It also serves students in technical programs.

Participation: 350 students in grades 10-12. Demographics: City-wide school, 47% African American, 36% Caucasian, 13% Hispanic, 3% Asian, 1% other.

Staff: 4 teachers.

Resource materials: Catalog, program summary sheet, handbook.

St. Paul Open School

Community Service, St. Paul Open School, 1023 Osceola, St. Paul, MN 55101, 612-293-8680. Dorothy LeGualt.

Overview: Began in 1971 with inception of school. Program is part of an alternative public school for grades K-12. Each student must complete a service activity to graduate. Hours required depend on the student and project.

Participation: Currently 28 students in grades 10-12. Demographics: School serves entire city; multi-cultural.

Resource materials: Brochures.

Tucson High Magnet School

Intergenerational Program Pilot "Generations Together," Tucson High Magnet School, 400 N. 2nd Avenue, Tucson, AZ 85705, 602-882-2481. Chuck Holman, Assistant Principal for Activities.

Overview: Began in 1987.

Participation: 35 students in grades 9-12. Participation is voluntary for individual students and mandatory for the Student Council as total classes (e.g., 9th, 10th, 11th, and 12th grade community service projects). Demographics: Hispanic, Native American, African American, Asian, Caucasian.

Budget: $330 from Tucson Education Enrichment Fund.

Community Service at a Middle School

A middle school demonstrates that community service is a viable option for younger students — and a valuable part of the curriculum. Reprinted with permission from Reaching Out: School-Based Community Service Programs, *National Crime Prevention Council, 1988, pp. 44-45. For more information about this program, contact Winifred Pardo, Community Service, Shoreham-Wading Middle School, Randall Road, Shoreham, NY 11786, (516) 929-8500.*

SINCE ITS INCEPTION IN 1973, thousands of students at the Shoreham-Wading River Middle School have had the option of performing community service as part of their curriculum. "Community Service" was initiated by a teacher and backed by the principal and the district. The program has benefited from a gradual increase in non-instructional staff and additional means of transportation. Four groups are served on a regular basis: children in neighboring day care centers, nursery schools, Head Starts, district kindergartens, and Story Hours at the Shoreham-Wading Public Library; elementary school classes where the volunteers team up with the younger students to lead a variety of learning activities; children with disabilities at nearby hospitals and Special Education sites; elderly residents of the community.

Community service is an integral part of a six- to ten-week unit of study with either one class, or a team of two classes, participating. The class includes a one-hour visit each week to work at a field site. Much classroom work revolves around each project: orientation sessions using speakers, films, and discussions; reading; journals and other writing; planning for work at the field sites; and evaluation. The primary focus in the classroom is learning the "caring" functions, learning about the groups and ages served, learning cross-age teaching, how to plan, and how to take on responsibility.

Many other service opportunities are offered: hosting young children or children with disabilities and the elderly at the Middle School and its farm; taking puppet shows, the band, or the chorus into the community; and running a Thanksgiving Food Drive for migrant farm workers.

Each year several hundred students do community service. Some among them are mainstreamed students with disabilities. In a study about these students, Joanne Urgese, currently the Community Service Director, noted: "Handicapped students experience success and receive positive reinforcement, which together strongly enhance their self-esteem. The similarities between students with disabilities and the rest of the student population are emphasized while the differences are minimized."

Students share the teachers' and administration's strong belief in community service. As one seventh grader explained: "I really don't like Community Service. I love it! It's much more interesting than sitting in a classroom all day. It's better going out and getting a real life experience ... you deal with other people and how they act and feel and are." Another student added: "One thing I've learned from going to the nursing home is, you have to experience some things yourself. You'll never know the true meaning of something unless you are there to witness it. To see the people's faces light up as you talk to them is really a happy sight. It makes me feel good all over."

Early Adolescent Helper Program

edited by Diane Harrington

Early adolescents are too often a forgotten population. At an in-between age, they require more guidance than older teenagers and more independence than children. Their need for hands-on learning, for opportunities to develop and test new roles and skills, is acute. This article describes a program model for this age group. Reprinted with permission from Community Roles for Youth, *the newsletter of the early adolescent helper program, Center for Advanced Study in Education, Graduate School and University Center for the City University of New York, and the* Journal of Experiential Education, *Association for Experiential Education, Vol. 9, No. 2, Summer 1986, pp. 26-29.*

SCHOOL-BASED PROGRAMS IN WHICH young people take active, responsible, "grown-up" roles — as tutors, counselors, helpers, or interns — have become more common in recent years, and the benefits, for the young people involved and for those they help, are generally acknowledged. But these programs are usually aimed at high school youth; the early adolescent, aged eleven to fourteen, is excluded.

Early adolescents are too often a forgotten population. At an in-between age, they require more guidance than older teenagers and more independence than children. Their need for hands-on learning, for opportunities to develop and test new roles and skills, is acute. These opportunities are rarely offered to early adolescents, at home, in school, or in the community.

After-school activities for eleven to fourteen year olds are also virtually nonexistent. In New York City, where well over half of the mothers with school-aged children work and the number of single-parent families continues to multiply, tens of thousands of children are unsupervised after school. Research on this group is scarce, but it does suggest that these children often exhibit academic or behavior problems in school. In addition, concern about their safety is growing.

Recognizing the need for more active learning experiences and for appropriate after-school activities, the Early Adolescent Helper Program has designed and tested a program model for this age group. Students serve as interns (Helpers) in child care or senior citizen centers after school at least twice a week. In school, they participate in a seminar that combines relevant knowledge and information (about topics like human development) with problem-solving, decision-making, and work readiness skills. It also guides them in reflecting on and evaluating their experiences as Helpers.

Making Placements

The Helper Program began with child care placements because past experience showed that eleven to fourteen year olds relate well to young children; both age groups experience a similar tug between independence and the need for support. In addition, learning that human development proceeds through predictable stages can help some adolescents to understand and accept themselves. Senior citizens and early adolescents share a common bond, too. Society relegates both to passive roles as receivers rather than givers. The energy and inquisitiveness of eleven to fourteen year olds, like the senior citizen's perspective gained by a lifetime's accumulated experiences, are valuable resources all too often minimized or ignored.

Child care and senior centers are attractive choices for Helper placements, but students can also be Helpers by tutoring their peers or younger students, by serving as guides at a local museum, by reading stories at the public library, by assisting at a playground, and in many, many other ways.

Scheduling

The Helper Program's basic model includes an in-school seminar once a week and after-school internships at least twice a week. Ingenuity is sometimes needed to design a schedule that enables the program to work that is compatible with the needs of both school and work site.

At the school, the ideal approach is to make the program part of an existing course. One participating school has done this by scheduling the seminar as part of a home economics class; in another, the program comprises a one-semester credit-bearing course called "Parenting." A number of other options make sense, too. Keeping a journal or log can bring a new dimension to a language arts class. Community service placements can be part of a career exploration course.

If this approach doesn't work in a particular school, other ways can be found to schedule the seminar. In some schools, students miss one period a week of non-academic electives to attend the seminar. In one or two others, the seminar is held during lunch period.

Although scheduling is simplified by incorporating the Helper Program into an existing course, thought should also be given to when that course meets. The best arrangement is to schedule it during the last period of the day at least three times a week.

Since scheduling and curriculum flexibility vary from school to school, all of the approaches described here have been tried in one school or another. The "right" arrangement can be found (or invented) for any setting. When administration, students, staff, and placement site share a commitment, and the Helper Program is perceived not as an "add-on" but as an important part of the school's offerings, obstacles are overcome and a workable schedule emerges.

Role of the Program Leader

Usually the Program Leader is a teacher or counselor in the school, although in one participating school a volunteer fills this role. The Program Leader is responsible for recruiting students, placing them in community sites, leading the seminar, and, in general, coordinating the program at the school.

No other role in the Helper Program is more demanding or important than that of Program Leader. In leading the seminar, he or she must be flexible and student-centered: able to elicit and react to students' immediate concerns or problems, guide them through the needed training, help them assess their internships, and, above all, relate classroom learning to experiences outside the school.

This role is often quite different from "traditional" teaching. It demands the ability to provide the structure and support needed by young adolescents while still allowing them to act responsibly and creatively.

On top of this, the coordinating functions of the Program Leader can easily consume whatever free or preparation time he or she might have during the day. Balancing the schedules and procedures of the school and community site is not easy, nor is finding the time and energy to wear all these hats in addition to regular classroom teaching or counseling duties.

Role of Staff at the Placement Site

First, child care teachers (or the staff at another kind of placement) must be *willing* to work with eleven to fourteen year olds. No matter how interested an agency director might be in the Helper Program — and this is essential — young adolescents will not have a good experience unless the staff wants to work with them and recognizes that they can indeed bring benefits to the program. It is important, too, that the placement site present a positive model for the helpers.

Even willing staff members might not understand *how* to work with early adolescents. They need to meet with the Program Leader, attend orientation sessions or workshops, and visit the school if possible. Common mistakes during the Helper Program's first two years fall into one of two extremes: either the site staff expected too much of students or they expected too little. Young adolescents need clear limits and structure. They're unlikely to initiate a project and carry it to completion entirely on their own, as older teenagers will. But, within defined parameters, they can be very responsible. In a child care center, for example, they can be asked to choose and read a story every day, design and lead simple crafts activities, or help with disruptive children. But, in the beginning at least, they do need to be asked.

Recruitment of Students

The Helper Program is designed for a cross-section of students. Students of varying intellectual achievement levels, students with handicapping conditions, students who have failed in school, as well as "achievers," can all benefit from participating. Since the skills needed to be a good Helper are different from those usually called on in school, some students will succeed in this program although struggling in other academic work.

Preparation of Students

Young adolescents are not automatically responsible or knowledgeable about how to care for young children. Just out of childhood themselves, they're sometimes more inclined to play than to discipline. At other times, they may be over-zealous disciplinarians. They may also not understand such "job protocol" as calling the center when they can't be there or will be late.

Eleven to fourteen year olds (like most of us) often have misconceptions about people different from themselves, whether members of another culture or another age group. In the Helper Program, many speak initially of young children as "cute," unaware of how strong-willed or individual little ones can be. They may see young children as either "good" or "bratty," and need help in understanding the meaning of children's behavior. A similar lack of awareness colors their view of the elderly. Many early adolescents have little patience at first with forgetfulness or a pace slower than their own, or are afraid of and even disgusted by aging.

The preparation of Helpers must deal with all of this. Actually, the term "preparation" is a misnomer in the sense that it implies an end. Preparation must be ongoing, helping students ask questions and solve problems. For example, the seminar might encourage students to figure out when to intervene in a quarrel among three year olds and when not to. Or it might include a discussion of how to deal with the prejudice shown by white, immigrant seniors toward Black and Hispanic Helpers.

The Helper Program has developed, tested, and revised a curriculum guide for the seminar. This guide contains several suggested lessons to precede students' work at their placements, and others with useful problem-solving and discussion techniques. Program Leaders have used the guide as a model, adapting it to their particular students, and agree that it can be very helpful in the ongoing process of preparation.

Working with Early Adolescents

Eleven to fourteen year olds can be restless, unpredictable, and contrary. They can also be cooperative, creative, and loving. They experience wild mood swings, and are often uncompromising, certain of their own righteousness. Their development is inconsistent, and their abilities can change from day to day. Those who work and live with young adolescents must be honest, patient, and firm, but no one, of course, is able to do this all the time. Conflicts and crises are bound to occur, as the adult's patience wears thin and the adolescent's vulnerable self-image is wounded.

The fun and rewards of working with early adolescents are at least equal to the difficulties. Young people at this age are very energetic and laugh a lot. When an adult earns their trust, a special connection is made forever. They can be touchingly honest about their feelings and about their unique perspectives. As they search for new role models, their growth in response to attention and appreciation is visible — and absolutely unmatchable.

In structuring a program for this age group, all of this must be taken into account. Rules and limits, as well as consequences, must be spelled out. New responsibilities and skills must be developed and tested gradually. Specific assignments must be flexible, and there must be support for failure. And there will be failure. But, as those who have participated in the Early Adolescent Helper Program's first three years will affirm, progress will also happen — as self-confidence and competence grow.

If you are interested in introducing the Helper Program in your school or agency, or in adding the Helper role to an existing class or program, call or write the Early Adolescent Helper Program, CASE, CUNY Graduate Center, 33 West 42nd Street, New York, NY 10033, (212) 719-9066.

Eighth Graders Write to Elderly Before First Visit

A simple idea helps break the ice and prepare eighth graders for community service. Reprinted from Synergist, *ACTION, Vol. 9, No. 3, Winter 1981, p. 55.*

FOR THE FIRST TWO YEARS that eighth graders came from St. Catherine's School's community service program to the Beth Sholom nursing home in Richmond, Virginia, they accomplished little. The students from the private school for girls either roamed the building aimlessly or bunched together and talked to each other, too inhibited to interact with the elderly residents in what was supposed to be a friendly visitor program.

In the third year, the nursing home's volunteer coordinator, Rae Cumbie, developed a more structured — and far more effective — program. First she went to the school to orient the students to the needs of elderly people and life in a nursing home. Then she matched up pairs of students with groups of four senior citizens. The key new element was the letters that the coordinator told each girl to write to her elderly companions prior to the first trip to the home. The volunteer coordinator suggested that each girl write informal, personal notes telling a little about herself and saying that she was looking forward to visiting.

Cumbie said, "The residents were delighted to get the letters. When the students came, there was already the beginnings of a rapport. Instead of the girls coming in and saying, 'Hi, I'm so-and-so, and I'm going to be visiting you,' they could say, 'I'm the one who wrote you that letter.' The residents already felt that they *knew* the students, and were excited about meeting the ones who had already written to them."

"Young volunteers don't have a lot of confidence," Cumbie pointed out, "and in eighth grade, you have a problem because some of them are already fairly mature while others are still basically children. It's hard for them at that age to take the lead and introduce themselves to older people about whom they may have real inhibitions. Putting it on a personal basis — by matching them up and using the letters of introduction — really breaks the ice."

Consumer Action Service Teaches High School Students Rights and Responsibilities

High school students assist low-income residents with consumer problems while learning a wide range of academic and practical lessons. A good example of service-learning as advocacy. Reprinted from Synergist, *National Center for Service-Learning, ACTION, Vol. 6, No. 3, Winter 1978, p. 17.*

"PROTECT YOUR RIGHTS AND MONEY," a class at the St. Paul Open School, offers a consumer action service to residents of St. Paul and Minneapolis. Under the leadership of coordinator Joe Nathan, students who sign up for the class combine experiential learning and community service. They take on consumer complaints ranging from disputes with auto repair and insurance companies to landlord-tenant disputes. The class has resolved — to the satisfaction of the consumer — about 75 percent of the cases it has handled.

St. Paul is an alternative school, and Nathan's students, some of whom have dyslexia or other learning disabilities, gain self-confidence because (1) the classroom work is goal oriented, (2) they apply traditional academic skills to real life situations, (3) they can see the results of their efforts, and (4) they help people with low incomes. A project with visible results gives students satisfaction that increases their academic motivation.

The students published a 24-page booklet, "Consumer Action Service: How You Can Do It," and a promotional flier, "Are You Getting Ripped Off? If So — Write Us." They distribute the flier at area libraries, stores, and neighborhood centers. The flier advises consumers that the students offer a free service; that clients must refer their complaints to the class by letter (in order not to overuse the school telephone); and that the students cannot offer legal advice, but they can refer clients to legal aid. Each letter the class receives is logged in and then discussed. Students decide if they need more information and, if so, a team of two or three students solicits additional facts from the consumer. Next, they set a goal and develop a strategy for achieving it. One step in solving the problem is to find out the business' version of the dispute. Students write or call the company. They learn how to write effective business letters as part of their classroom work. They role play telephone conversations in class before calling the business. The team handling the case reports back to the entire class. Then the goal and strategy are reevaluated and sometimes revised in the light of the new information. Students ask clients to keep them informed of new developments in the case, and each case is fully documented by the students with copies of correspondence plus a summary giving the final disposition.

Students learn the importance of keeping receipts for purchases, of reading contracts and insurance policies carefully before signing, of understanding warranties. At a nearby law library they perform legal research in the consumer protection field. Most important, they learn to hear all sides of a dispute before referring it to a governmental consumer protection agency as a last resort. The consumer division of the Attorney General's Office, for example, advised the class that it should hear several different views of a case before referring it. "The kids learn that you cannot jump to conclusions on the basis of hearsay evidence," said Nathan.

Nathan got the idea for the consumer action service when he was teaching ecology to St. Paul students. The students noticed heavy industrial air pollution near the school and traced it to four industrial plants. The class researched the state air pollution standards. After interviewing industry spokespersons, the students called for plant inspections by the city's pollution control agency. They petitioned residents and other businesses near the school, testified at a public hearing, and launched a media campaign to bring public pressure to bear on the problem. Finally, after three years, the pollution control agency ordered schedules of compliance from each offender. Nathan cites a study by the American College Testing Service showing there is little, if any, correlation between students' grades in school and their success later in life, but there *is* a correlation between achievements in nonclassroom activities and later success. Subsequent research reinforces this finding. [*Editor's note: Author of* Free to Teach: Achieving Equity and Excellence in Schools, *Joe Nathan went on to work for the National Governors' Association, Public School Incentives in St. Paul, and the Regional Issues Forum at Spring Hill.*]

Starting Young

Alice B. Pierson

Children as young as four prove themselves valuable service-learners in an Ohio school for children with developmental disabilities. Reprinted from Synergist, ACTION, Vol. 10, No. 3, *Winter 1982, pp. 3-7.*

THE FIRST GRADER raised his hand. "What should I do if he hits me?"

The teacher answered, "Look him in the eye and say, 'Don't hit me. That hurts.'"

"What if he keeps on hitting me?" persisted the small boy.

"Well, you could walk off, or push him away. Treat him just as you would anybody else."

This was part of the question-and-answer period during the orientation of first graders to prepare them to be special friends to preschool children with developmental disabilities. As a matter of fact, when the special friends go to the preschool classroom, there isn't any hitting. The children are so delighted to see each other and they keep so busy on their projects for the day that there aren't any behavior problems.

But the first graders don't know this for sure before they go. They worry a little. "What if he throws things or won't sit down?" The answer is the same. "Treat him just like you'd treat anybody else. You don't have to put up with bad behavior just because he's developmentally disabled."

These children are taking part in one of the four programs sponsored by Weaver School in Tallmadge, Ohio, using students from kindergarten through eighth grade. Weaver provides education for all children in Summit County with moderate, severe, or profound developmental disabilities — and in doing so uses the services of hundreds of volunteers of all ages. Programs involving elementary and junior high students are the most recent and have been particularly successful.

Project Special Friend

The first graders are at Newberry Elementary School, where Weaver uses several classrooms for its preschool program. Initially teachers and parents were concerned about what the interaction might be between the Newberry students and the newly arrived children with developmental disabilities. Having had little exposure to youngsters who were different, the Newberry students had a tendency to avoid or possibly even ridicule the newcomers. An enterprising first grade teacher, Polly Tucker, said, "Let's get involved."

The first graders started with reading about developmental disabilities. They discussed disabilities and how it feels to be different. The teacher emphasized *likenesses* rather than differences. They went on to talk of how they could help. All were eager to visit the special children.

The great day came — amid apprehension, curiosity, excitement, even pity. The first graders edged into the special preschoolers' room and lined up against the wall uncertainly. The teachers introduced the students to each other and, after assigning each first grader to a preschooler, gave each pair a Halloween art project to work on. This was followed by an action record for the whole group.

From this small start three years ago, Project Special Friend has grown into a permanent program. The classes visit about twice a month on special occasions for seasonal projects, film strips, and games.

"The hardest lesson the first graders had to learn," the teacher reports, "was self-control. They want to do *everything* for their special friend. It's much harder to let him do it for himself. The more experienced second graders are better at this.

"These kids will always accept people who have developmental disabilities. Their ideas have changed a lot about differentness in other people," she continued, "and they've learned to treat them normally."

The first graders are proud of successes achieved by their special friends, and they tell their other friends, "Hey, you should try it, too!"

The Weaver teachers cite gains among the preschoolers also. Preschool Department head Carol Mitchner said, "They pick up normal behavior patterns; they learn concepts we're trying to teach them much more quickly from another child; they love to watch them and imitate them; they pick up language patterns faster and want to participate more in group activities. The one-to-one attention is especially good for them."

Though Project Special Friend officially involves only first and second graders, the third graders — the first group of special friends — still wander down to visit informally and still help their special friends as needed when they meet in the restrooms.

Siblings as Volunteers

Rilla White, a Weaver preschool teacher, grew up with a younger brother who was developmentally disabled. She felt responsible for him; she felt the effects of family decisions made about him without her participation. She says that older siblings feel left out and that they need to be able to verbalize their feelings and know they're not alone. So she invited all the siblings of her preschoolers (three-year-olds) to come and volunteer in her room during the Weaver summer session.

These siblings ranged in age from four through the teens. All the younger ones stayed in the preschool room, usually spending half a day a week in structured play activities. Some of the older siblings, who worked one, two, or even three days a week, assisted in other classrooms. All but the youngest had the regular volunteer orientation, which consists of a slide show on the causes and degrees of developmental disabilities and how Weaver School works with disabled youngsters, going over a handbook that explains what volunteers do (and don't do), and an interview with the director of volunteers to ascertain with which developmental level the volunteer would prefer to work. Rilla White supplemented this with after-school inservice training, which included general discussion of problems, one day a week. She covered such topics as the causes and effects of developmental disabilities; dealing with other people's reactions to the disabled sibling; ways of dealing with inappropriate behavior; how parents feel and how siblings can improve communication with them; what can be done about changing the public's attitude. During the sessions the siblings did role playing, simulated physical handicaps, and learned sign language, the use of which often helps children with disabilities to communicate.

Junior High Students

Holy Family in Stow, Ohio, is a K-8 parochial school that stresses community service. After teachers and eighth graders discussed possible service projects, they invited the Weaver volunteer director to talk about the Weaver program and its needs. The teacher, students, and volunteer director developed a plan whereby the eighth graders were divided into four groups of ten students. Each group took a turn in going to Weaver every Monday morning for four consecutive weeks to work in classrooms with students with developmental disabilities ranging in age from very early teens to preschool. (Weaver usually does not place volunteers with those chronologically older than they are.)

The eighth graders' orientation started with classroom discussions about community service and finished with specific training about people with developmental disabilities and ways of working with them. Slide shows, special handbooks, and personal interviews were part of the training.

Each eighth grader in a group went to a different classroom and participated in the regular classroom activities. During the two-hour period (Weaver has found that to be an excellent span of time for volunteers), an eighth grader usually would help with both group and individual activities. These might range from helping a severely disabled child alternate feet to go up a stairway to using flash cards with two or three moderately disabled youngsters. Each Weaver teacher provided whatever inservice training and supervision was needed. Weaver teachers also forwarded their evaluation (which they do on every volunteer) to the Holy Family teacher.

Not surprisingly, it developed later that no matter how painstaking the orientation, some of these adolescents were still pretty apprehensive about working with children with developmental disabilities.

"To me," said Marty in the report he wrote on his work at Weaver, "this was an eye-opening experience. I was scared and nervous at first. But this fear was dissipated when I saw what people with developmental disabilities were like. They are special people."

Shelley wrote, "The first two weeks I hated it! It was so hard to keep my patience. But now I'm glad I went. The smiles on their faces were enough to keep me happy all day."

Pat Reigler, their teacher at Holy Family, said that some of the greatest benefits of the program accrued to students who did poorly academically or had disabilities themselves. "It was a fantastic experience for them because they were successful — they got recognition and were suddenly appreciated by the other kids."

Chris, for instance, has orthopedic disabilities and was able to empathize with the children. He was one of the most successful volunteers and had a new sense of achievement and self-respect. He wrote: "There was one special person in the room. His name was Keith. He could not talk but made a lot of noise trying. Keith was very ornery. He wouldn't do what he was told and ignored you when you called him. Keith as far as the teachers were concerned wouldn't listen to anyone, but after my third day in the room he started following me and my orders only. Keith wasn't the only special person there. There was Dennis who couldn't walk or talk and Patrick who couldn't see very well. I really wish I could go back."

The teacher was enthusiastic about carrying on this program even though it took class time from several academic subjects. She said, "The other teachers feel the sacrifice of half a day's academics each week has been worthwhile because of the growth and change of attitudes they see in these children."

Other junior high schools also have been pleased with the results of service-learning programs, though theirs have operated in different ways. Tallmadge Junior High initiated a program in which the students could choose any one of a number of activities, including serving at Weaver, to do on Thursday afternoons. Though the activities included such draws as swimming, cross-country skiing, and photography, so many students signed up to volunteer at Weaver that they couldn't all be used at once.

Bolich Junior High has a student-initiated program in which interested students may be excused during their free periods (as many as three a week) to volunteer in the Weaver classrooms at Newberry Elementary School, which is next door to Bolich. Usually they work with one child on a special project.

Summer Programs

Weaver conducts both school and recreation programs involving approximately 150 volunteers during the summer. More than half of them have not yet entered high school.

News of these programs has spread mainly by word of mouth. Both parents and teachers are pleasantly surprised to find a service-learning program available to students during the otherwise idle summer months — and the teachers at Weaver say that the younger volunteers seem to have easier rapport with the special children than do many older volunteers.

A half-day orientation for volunteers of all ages each June includes an overview of the total program, facts about developmental disabilities, and information about the characteristics of the different classroom or recreation sites. The volunteer director then interviews each prospective volunteer and matches each with the classroom or program fitting the student's interests and age level.

The summer school program is for those with severe and profound developmental disabilities, and the activities are much the same as during the regular academic year. The major added element is recreational activities, particularly field trips. These sometimes require a volunteer for every class member.

The recreation program, which serves moderately disabled children, has five sites scattered around the county. Volunteers help with such activities as arts and crafts, music, swimming, hiking, and various games.

Most of the young volunteers worked one, two, or three full days a week. The volunteer office notified the administrators of the children's presence and urged them to advise the volunteer director if any complaints about the young volunteers came in. The plan was to treat any complaints on an individual basis and not jeopardize the use of children as volunteers if one or two didn't work out. The precaution proved unnecessary. The K-8 volunteers made valuable contributions to both school and recreation programs. The youngsters logged in more than 6,000 hours in one summer, approximately half of all volunteer time.

Many schools are like islands set apart from the mainland of life by a deep moat of convention and tradition. A drawbridge is lowered at certain periods during the day in order that the part-time inhabitants may cross over to the island in the morning and back to the mainland at night.

Why do these young people go out to the island? To learn how to live on the mainland. When they reach the island, they are provided with excellent books that tell about life on the mainland....

One evening a year the island's lights burn late for an event called graduation. Then the islanders depart never to set foot on the island again.

After the graduates leave the island for the last time, they are bombarded by problems of life on the mainland. Sometimes one of the graduates may mutter, "On the island I read something about that in a book."

— William G. Carr to the
National Congress of
Parents and Teachers, 1942

All students receive personal notes of thanks from the director of volunteers for their involvement in Weaver School and are awarded certificates of merit in school assemblies at the end and beginning of each school year.

A New Horizon

What have we found so far? Certainly that children down to the lowest elementary grades can, with proper training and supervision, become very effective partners in enhancing the educational and socialization processes in children with developmental disabilities. Experience has yielded strong evidence that these children can achieve desired levels of improvement more rapidly with the one-on-one aid of children near their own age than they can without that aid. The teachers saw widespread indications that most of the children, after having overcome an initial apprehension about the assignment, enthusiastically participated in the experience and were more than willing to continue beyond the first year. In fact, their own socialization and maturing processes seemed accelerated by the special friend roles.

The universal opinion of teachers in both the K-8 schools and at Weaver is that this pairing with children with developmental disabilities is opening up a new vista in education, and merits much wider evaluation. It is hoped that these initial efforts can provide useful guideposts in designing more elaborate programs in Summit County and across the country.

Alice B. Pierson is the director of Volunteer Services of Weaver School, Tallmadge, Ohio.

PART IV

Profiles of Programs that Combine Service and Learning

Community-Based Organizations, Government, and Youth-Serving Agencies

BOCES Geneseo Migrant Center

Farmworker Arts, Culture, and Education with Students (FACES), BOCES Geneseo Migrant Center, Holcomb Building 210, Geneseo, NY 14454, 716-245-5681. Robert Lynch, Project Director. Rural, nonprofit program serving migrant farmworkers.

Participation: 7-10 college juniors and seniors involved as interns during fall, winter, and summer for average of 14 weeks. Most effective publicity: Letters of invitation to students identified as eligible, formal and informal communications with academic department chairpersons and internship coordinators in the SUNY Geneseo community.

Qualifications: Students' eligibility is determined by SUNY Geneseo Internship Program guidelines. Interns must have junior status, an overall g.p.a. of 2.75, 3.0 g.p.a. in major prerequisites, and department chairperson's approval.

Participant responsibilities: Students work on in-camp teaching teams providing remedial educational services to migrant farmworkers, and with the Center's CAMPS/Folk Arts Program developing and mounting interpreted exhibitions of farmworker arts and culture. Placements are flexible and are adjusted to the transient nature of migrant farm labor.

Screening: In-depth, in-person interview; transcript; faculty recommendations. Criteria used to determine roles filled by participants: Previous experience and training, professional goals, needs of farmworkers.

Overview: Began in 1987 with a grant from the Fund for the Improvement of Postsecondary Education. **Goals:** To recruit, train, and place students in internships providing needed services to migrant farmworkers; to provide students with professionally relevant skills and experience; to assist in relieving student indebtedness through honoraria for services. Program supports students' intellectual, ethical/moral, career, and personal development, and sense of social responsibility. **Philosophy:** "Our program's philosophy and policies are consistent with the following commitments made by our agency to its migrant farmworker clients: Services should be comprehensive, meeting a wide range of migrant needs; available to all members of migrant families and camps; delivered wherever possible in migrant camp settings and in combination with community awareness alerting host communities to the contributions and skills of migrant workers as well as to their needs; and finally, the migrants come first."

Structure: Part of the BOCES Geneseo Migrant Center. Program Director reports to Migrant Center Director.

Budget: $30,136 from 100% federal funds. The Migrant Center supplies substantial in-kind support for staff time beyond what is funded. The Center also provides additional office supplies, materials, and transportation for interns to field sites. **Staff:** 4 of 39 are involved.

Compensation: Interns receive honorarium; transportation is provided or interns are reimbursed for transportation costs.

Agreement: The contract specifies placements, the supervision to be provided, field responsibilities, academic requirements, and what percentage of the grade will be determined by each part of the field and academic work. Contract is developed in consultation between the field supervisor, faculty director, and student; it is signed by these parties, the department chairperson, and the Dean for Continuing Education and Public Service.

Preparation: Faculty determine standards for academic preparation. A 2-hour pre-service orientation followed by individualized training using Center training materials is provided for all interns. Interns also attend biweekly seminars on migrant farmworker needs and socio-economic conditions. These seminars also provide opportunities for in-service training and evaluation of interns' progress.

Supervision: Interns receive direct field supervision from a Migrant Center staff member. Faculty director sets academic requirements, supervises academic aspects, and observes the intern on-site at least once. Interns submit detailed, biweekly journals to the field supervisor and faculty.

Evaluation of service: At least 50% of a student's grade is based on field performance which is evaluated by the field supervisor.

Learning: Structured opportunities for reflection and analysis include journals, seminars, and pre- and post-service inventories on life goals and attitudes toward migrant farmworkers. Learning is supported and monitored through close communication with field supervisors and other Center staff, direct observation, supportive feedback in the field, extensive comments on journals, and candid discussions in biweekly seminars. **Academic credit:** Interns receive 3-6 hours of credit for successful completion of learning goals.

Recognition: Students: Recognition ceremony at annual All-Camp Day (get-together for all migrant farmworkers served by the Center). *Site supervisors:* Involvement is recognized as part of regular work load.

"Look closely and candidly at your organization's strengths and at all of the experiential opportunities which you can offer."

Program evaluation: Students complete an extensive evaluation that requires them to present critical and candid assessments of the program and to make specific recommendations for change. Field supervisors provide ongoing feedback about the effectiveness of the program in meeting farmworker and student needs. The Internship Coordinator and Project Director maintain detailed records of student contact hours, evaluate student journals, and conduct a review of all evaluation data each year for reports to funding source. Faculty directors evaluate the Program's impact on the academic progress of interns and are asked to provide feedback.

Benefits to organization: "Program provides us a wider pool of adjunct staff with pre-professional training and high motivation. It also facilitates recruitment and retention of qualified in-camp staff."

Problem addressed: "Initially, recruiting interns was more difficult than anticipated because of insufficient lead time for announcements and over-reliance on academic department communications. We now work directly with student groups and internship coordinators. The Center also rethought the range of its needs and potential services and developed more placements for students from a wider range of academic backgrounds."

Lesson learned: "Advertising internships through mass mailings and letters to department chairpersons was not as effective as anticipated. We suspect service-learning is a lower priority than research and formal instruction in some departments. We now specify, very clearly, the skills and understandings students can gain through service-learning."

Biggest challenge: "We will be disseminating regionally and nationally our model for linkages between universities and migrant service agencies. This will require a thorough and candid assessment of our experience and what can be generalized from it as well as what should be modified for successful dissemination."

Other advice: "Look closely and candidly at your organization's strengths and at *all* of the experiential opportunities which you can offer; tailor your recruitment strategies to develop appealing and productive matches between what you can offer and what prospective interns can offer *and* what they want from a service-learning experience."

Common Cause

Intern Program, Common Cause, 2030 M Street NW, Washington, DC 20036, 202-833-1200. Michael Brogioli, Volunteer Coordinator. Urban, nonprofit, public interest group.

Participation: 50-70 undergrad, grad, and 11th and 12th grade students involved during fall, winter, spring, and summer for average of 9-12 weeks. Program publicity: Mass mailing to college career placement offices and government departments, local college advertising, *Common Cause Magazine* intern ad, listings in several intern guides. Most effective publicity: Word-of-mouth, college files on Common Cause.

Participant responsibilities: Students act as grassroots organizers, press office aides, issue development researchers, *Common Cause Magazine* research assistants, congressional monitors, and mail correspondents on specific issues.

Qualifications: Participants must have strong communications skills, be flexible, and demonstrate a commitment to the public interest.

Screening: Application, phone interview, writing sample, 2 recommendation letters. Criteria used to determine roles filled by participants: Match between student's stated needs and organizational needs.

Overview: Began in mid-1970s several years after Common Cause was founded. **Goals:** To provide students with an opportunity to see how a major public interest group works, to fill current needs and future positions at Common Cause. Program supports students' career, civic, and personal development, and sense of social responsibility. **Philosophy:** "Common Cause truly values its volunteers and interns, and goes out of its way to make this known and felt by each intern. We have created a genuinely dynamic spirit here where staff and interns mix easily and freely."

Structure: Coordinator reports to Director of Administration. Oversight committee of Common Cause staff members.

Budget: $60,000 from regular organizational funds. **Staff:** 20-25 are involved. **Compensation:** For transportation. "We are interested in knowing how many programs give stipends to interns and how big of an effect this has on the socio-economic makeup of intern groups. Most Common Cause interns, all of whom volunteer, come from wealthy families and attend prestigious universities."

Agreement: "Occasionally schools request that we sign a contract which typically states their desire for adequate supervision, and we oblige."

Preparation: Interns participate in a general orientation with staff members from various departments and a more detailed orientation pertaining to their particular position.

Supervision: Each department designates full-time staff to supervise interns.

Evaluation of service: Quality of service is evaluated by supervisor who works most closely with intern.

Learning: Structured opportunities for reflection and analysis include Volunteer Task Force meetings, Intern Evaluation form. Learning is supported and monitored by supervisors who meet with interns periodically. **Academic credit:** Students occasionally receive credit for learning.

Recognition: Students: Students are usually recognized at a full staff briefing early on, and later by the President of Common Cause. Interns receive a commemorative print, and each department is encouraged to do something unique. *Site supervisors:* Involvement is recognized as part of regular work load.

Program evaluation: Interns complete written evaluation. Volunteer Coordinator also seeks verbal feedback in informal settings. Supervisors and management evaluate program at staff and Volunteer Task Force meetings.

Benefits to organization: "It provides youthful, idealistic, enthusiastic workers who contribute thousands of hours advancing our issue agenda."

Problem addressed: "Burnout is a problem in some positions. We plan numerous extracurricular activities such as tours, guest speakers, and social hours to give interns a break."

Biggest challenge: "Attracting interns from a broader range of backgrounds."

Other advice: "Always remember to recognize students' hard work, but treat them as you would paid professionals — don't let them off easy; hold them accountable."

Constitutional Rights Foundation

Youth Community Service (YCS), Constitutional Rights Foundation (CRF), 601 S. Kingsley Drive, Los Angeles, CA 90005, 213-487-5590. Cathryn Berger Kaye, Program Director. Urban, nonprofit, school-based program serving teachers and students in 23 Los Angeles Unified School District high schools.

Participation: 1000 students in grades 9-12 directly involved during fall, winter, spring, and summer for 1-4 years. Over 20,000 students indirectly involved. Program is open to all, but is especially interested in involving a diverse group of students, students who have leadership potential not yet directed, new immigrants or students who are bused into another community, and students who have not established a personal connection with any aspect of a school. Most effective publicity: School site recruitment by students and program alumni, use of 19-minute YCS video documentary.

Responsibilities of participating schools: Initiating, planning, implementing, and evaluating service projects; contacting government and community agencies; recruiting non-YCS members as project volunteers.

Screening: Registration form required.

Overview: Began in 1984 with a grant from the Ford Foundation. **Goals:** To bring students from diverse backgrounds together to build positive bonds between youth, institutions, and traditions in society; to strengthen students' self-esteem and interest in academics; to develop students' organizational and leadership skills; to empower students to make responsible decisions and affect change, encouraging a life-long service ethic. Program supports students' sense of social responsibility, and their intellectual, ethical/moral, civic, and career development within the public service sector. **Philosophy:** "High school students are often denied vehicles to extend their education beyond the walls of academic institutions. Through community service, students frequently discover a link with the world at-large that enhances their desire to learn, thereby motivating academic achievement. Community mobility also instills a sense of personal power in youth. They understand the machinations of society, access adults in new ways, and increase their confidence of expression and action. All of this magnifies the potential of young people and makes them more open to careers in the public service sector."

Structure: Program Director reports to Education Director. A community advisory board is being formed.

Budget: $185,000 from 75% foundations, 25% federal funds. Additional in-kind staff time is provided by the Constitutional Rights Foundation. **Staff:** 3 1/2 of 35 at CRF are involved.

Compensation: Training is provided.

Agreement: A note on student applications explains that participation in all aspects of program is required for those accepted. Program staff meet with principals and other school administrators to clarify program philosophy and expectations.

Preparation: Students attend overnight leadership training retreat, conferences, and meet twice a week to plan and implement service projects.

Supervision: Students receive ongoing support from CRF staff and teacher sponsors. Teacher sponsors attend a 2-day training and monthly meetings.

Evaluation of service: Quality of service is evaluated on an ongoing basis at each school by members and teacher sponsor. CRF staff also meet with the school administrator and teacher sponsor at the end of each year.

Learning: Structured opportunities for reflection and analysis include retreats, conferences, articles, evaluations, weekly school meetings. Learning is supported through peer teamwork and relationships with adult role models. Learning is monitored by teacher and staff observation. **Academic credit:** Students occasionally receive credit for learning. Los Angeles Unified School District offers a credit option, but only 3 of 22 schools have used this option so far. Three schools are piloting a 1-semester YCS elective course.

Recognition: Students: Certificates. In some cases, schools and CRF recognize participants and nominate them for scholarships and other awards. *Teachers:* Involvement is recognized through overload compensation.

Program evaluation: Students evaluate impact of program verbally and through written reflection after each event. Supervisors evaluate program monthly with CRF staff. School administrators meet at least once a year with CRF staff to evaluate program. A staff review is also done. Also, UCLA's Center for the Study of Evaluation completed a 1-year study of YCS in 1988 (available upon request).

Benefits to organization: "Establishes a strong community link with other community and government agencies. People are generally more aware of CRF and the variety of our programs."

Problems addressed: "One school site was struggling with poor meetings, low student motivation, and no projects. A CRF staff member began attending weekly meetings guiding the group and modeling for the teacher sponsor how to move the group forward. The teacher appreciated this and was able to pick up and keep the ball rolling."

Lesson learned: "We established a community mentor component to the program linking an adult in the community with each YCS school group. Mentors were to assist students and teachers with all program aspects. It didn't work. We changed the design and now call them community resource volunteers and allow a wider range of possible interactions."

Biggest challenge: "Continued funding that secures the life of the program as it now exists and allows for expansion to more schools in L.A."

Other advice: "Make contact with other experienced programs to make use of their experiences, materials, and staff expertise. Why reinvent the wheel? Then, share what you do with others — including the old-timers and newcomers. We all have much to learn in this growing field!"

Resources available: Program has also developed a YCS video documentary, "Making a Difference," a guide to establishing student-initiated community service programs and projects, "Six Skill Builders" workbooks to strengthen specific skills to be effective community service leaders. CRF is currently writing a comprehensive program and curriculum guide and publishes *School Youth Service Network*, a newsletter for educators, policymakers, and community agencies which includes articles, program profiles, curriculum ideas and examples, and reviews of literature and resources.

Generations Together

Youth in Service to Elders (YISTE) — Generations Together, University of Pittsburgh, 811 William Pitt Union, Pittsburgh, PA 15260, 412-648-7155. Sally Newman, Executive Director. Urban nonprofit serving homebound, frail, elderly persons and nursing home residents.

Participation: 250 college and high school students (grades 9-12) participate during fall, winter, spring, and summer for average of 15 weeks for 2-4 hours/week. Most effective publicity: Through teachers and involved students, face-to-face presentations.

Qualifications: Participants must be 14-22 years old (under 18 requires parental permission), have acceptable application and character reference, attend two 2-hour training sessions.

Participant responsibilities: Visiting frail homebound elderly, facilitating and enabling other students' participation by sharing their experiences, making telephone calls, filing, co-leading training sessions, writing newsletter articles. Criteria to determine eligibility of students: Interest, commitment, reliability, honesty, ability to maintain confidentiality, communication skills, positive reference from an adult.

Screening: Application, character reference, in-person interview.

Overview: Began in 1982 with grant from ACTION's Young Volunteers in Action program. Students work with the elderly alone and in groups. **Goals:** To promote intergenerational exchange, to serve the elderly, to educate students about aging. Program supports students' intellectual, ethical/moral, career, civic, and personal development, and sense of social responsibility. **Philosophy:** "As students engage in experiences that are mutually gratifying, they develop meaningful relationships with the elderly that contribute to their well-being. Students learn through service and gain work experience, a broader sense of career options, and a sense of responsibility."

Structure: Program Coordinators report to Executive Director. Advisory Board of 10% agency staff, 20% students, 30% faculty/ school staff, 20% community representatives, 10% agency clients, 10% politicians and public relations personnel.

Budget: $50,000 from 10% agency funds, 15% federal, 10% foundations, 25% state, 20% corporate, 10% fees from participating organizations, 10% other. Release time for teachers and computer time are provided. **Staff:** 2 professional, 1 secretarial, 1-2 student interns.

Compensation: Accident and liability insurance and transportation are provided.

Agreement: Students write a learning contract stating learning goals and objectives.

Preparation: Two 2-hour training sessions. First session focuses on students and their previous experience with elderly persons, and educates them more about older adults. Second session covers communication and problem-solving skills. Students also select the projects with which they will work at this session.

"Personal satisfaction and feedback are important to students. They are grateful for clear, honest feedback and supervision."

Supervision: Students meet weekly with their supervisor for an hour, receive direct supervision of their tasks, and attend staff meetings. Some are also required to keep a journal.

Evaluation of service: Quality of service is evaluated by site supervisor and student separately and then jointly based on the student's learning goals and objectives.

Learning: Structured opportunities for reflection and analysis include group debriefing sessions. Students are encouraged to talk with staff, ask questions, and "shadow" staff. Student learning is also monitored through weekly meetings. **Academic credit:** Students occasionally receive credit for learning.

Recognition: *Students:* Certificates, recognition dinner, reference letter from site supervisor. *Site supervisors:* Involvement is recognized as regular part of work load in some cases; in others, there is some recognition but no reduction in other responsibilities.

Program evaluation: Students complete extensive evaluation forms.

Benefits to organization: "YISTE is part of Generations Together where young people are service providers."

Problem addressed: "Since 14-year-olds are limited to working at sites in which there is close supervision, they are given an opportunity to choose from a variety of sites."

Lesson learned: "Though recruiting through flyers, posters, and newspaper articles has resulted in limited numbers of volunteers, it is important to use many strategies in the recruitment process. Most students are recruited through 1-to-1 or small group presentations."

Biggest challenge: "Maintaining consistent funding."

Other advice: "Personal satisfaction and feedback are important to students. They are grateful for clear, honest feedback and supervision."

State of Illinois

Illinois Government Internship, 1900 W. Monroe, Springfield, IL 62704, 217-525-3016. Donald Davis, Coordinator. Urban, government program.

Participation: 60-65 high school seniors involved during the school day for average of 36 hours/week for 16-17 weeks. Most effective publicity: Student-to-student, presentations at professional meetings.

Qualifications: Above average maturity, demonstrated leadership, good communication skills.

Screening: In-person interview, teacher recommendations, resume, application, transcript, writing sample. Criteria for selecting agencies for interns: That they provide challenging, hands-on experiences which interest youth; that intern role is substantive.

Overview: Began in 1975 as a local program in Springfield. A pilot program with other school districts was begun in 1977. In 1979 the

General Assembly funded a statewide program. **Goals:** To develop students' understanding of government, to help them explore career interests, to increase confidence and awareness of their skills and abilities. Program supports students' intellectual, ethical/moral, career, and personal development.

Structure: Coordinator reports to the Superintendent.

Budget: $130,000 from 75% state funds, 25% local district (in-kind). Includes resources for clerical support, funds for student transportation, student housing. **Staff:** 2 full-time, 1 part-time.

Teacher involvement: 1 teacher is active.

Contract: Memorandum of understanding is used.

Transportation: Mass transit (see below under "Compensation").

Liability insurance: Provided through local district policy.

Compensation: Food, housing, and transportation costs are paid by a grant from the State Board of Education appropriated by the General Assembly. Housing is arranged with local families, and bus passes or a stipend is provided for transportation to and from internship.

Scheduling: Program is scheduled during the day. Participants are exempted from class and/or extracurricular activities.

Preparation: Orientation, seminars, handbooks.

Learning: Learning is monitored and supported through debriefing sessions, logs, and drop-in visits. Students spend average of 6 hours/week in structured reflection/analysis activities. Coordinator and Student Adviser evaluate student learning through written and oral exams, portfolios, self-assessments, and debriefing. **Academic credit:** Yes; used toward graduation requirements, electives.

Evaluation of service: Quality of service is monitored and evaluated by program staff and through logs and site visits.

Recognition: Students: Certificates of Achievement. *Teacher:* Involvement is recognized through extended contract. *Site supervisors:* Recognition luncheon.

Program evaluation: Students and site supervisors evaluate program verbally and in writing. Teachers and administrators evaluate program verbally.

Problem addressed: "We were able to document learning outcomes successfully when we implemented several different assessment techniques."

Biggest challenge: "Funding."

New York City Volunteer Corps

New York City Volunteer Corps (CVC), 838 Broadway, 3rd Floor, New York, NY 10003, 212-475-6444. Michael Bosnick, Director, Planning and External Affairs. Urban, nonprofit program serving youth ages 16-20.

Participation: 770 young people involved each year. Participants include young people not in school as well as high school and college students. Corps members participate full-time for 1 year or full-time in the summer and part-time during academic year for up to 2 years. Most effective publicity: Newspaper ads, subway and bus advertising, public service announcements, word-of-mouth.

Qualifications: Participants must be 16-20 years old, demonstrate at 1-week CVC training that they can work cooperatively as a team-member, test negative for drug use, have no history of several categories of felonies.

Participant responsibilities: Work on teams of 10-15 supervised by a CVC staff person. Teams provide services to the institutionalized, homebound elderly, and persons with disabilities; tutor young people in the public schools; conduct public surveys and education campaigns; and work on environmental conservation projects.

Screening: Application, in-person interview, phone interview, successful completion of week-long training program. Criteria used to determine roles filled by participants: Must be services that would not otherwise be provided, must be substantive and expose young people to social issues and careers, must be balanced mix of services in all five boroughs of New York City, and a balance between human service and physical work.

Overview: Begun in 1984 by the Mayor using NYC tax levy. **Goals:** To enroll New Yorkers aged 16-20 to provide full- and part-time community service to New York through work with government and nonprofits, to promote volunteers. Personal development through exposure to service systems and careers and through education classes. (Once enrolled in CVC, volunteers enroll in education classes available through the program.) Program supports students' intellectual, career, civic, and personal development, and sense of social responsibility. **Philosophy:** "CVC emphasizes the ability of young people from many ethnic, cultural, economic, and academic backgrounds to work as a team to make basic, substantive contributions to the community. Through this work, coupled with education classes, volunteers significantly enhance their ability to contribute as successful, civic-minded adults."

Structure: Program is the sole work of CVC. Board of 100% community representatives. Director reports to Chair of the CVC Board of Directors and to the First Deputy Mayor.

Budget: $6.2 million from 97% regular organizational funds, 3% foundations. **Staff:** 85.

Compensation: Participants receive a salary or stipend, health insurance, and cash or scholarships upon completing program.

Agreement: Volunteers agree to meet attendance requirements in the field and in education classes and to perform as productive team members. For high school and college students working part-time, CVC agrees to keep the schools informed of their progress and to avoid conflicts with the school schedule.

Preparation: Volunteers receive a 3-hour orientation, and then go to a residential camp for a week of team-building exercises and sessions on values, communications, and CVC operations and programming.

Supervision: Each team is supervised in the field by a CVC team leader. Sponsoring agencies also assign supervisors to work with team leaders.

Evaluation of service: Quality of service is monitored by the team leader who conducts a monthly evaluation.

Learning: Structured opportunities for reflection and analysis include weekly team meeting with Team Leader, and Corps Member Development Program — a weekly program where volunteers' service is related to topics such as national service, the political process, etc. Learning is supported and monitored through above activities and required education classes (ESL, ABE, GED, college prep, college course). **Academic credit:** Yes, for GED and college education classes; students occasionally receive school credit for learning achieved.

Recognition: Participants: Stripes are added to uniform to recognize longevity; selected volunteers assist at training; election to Volunteer Advisory Committee; selection to attend conferences and exchanges with other programs.

Program evaluation: Volunteers complete an evaluation for each project lasting at least 4 weeks. Supervisors assess volunteers, performance and complete bits on projects. Management assesses the program by reviewing supervisors' reports and participant evaluations, by measuring volunteers' gains in education, and by studying the effects of CVC on participants through a 3 1/2 year foundation-sponsored study currently underway.

North Carolina Youth Advocacy and Involvement Office

North Carolina State Government Internship Program,

Youth Advocacy and Involvement Office (YAIO), North Carolina Department of Administration, 121 West Jones Street, Raleigh, NC 27603, 919-733-9296. Kit Tanzi, Internship Coordinator. Government program serving state agencies across the state.

Participation: 100 college sophomores, juniors, seniors, law, and graduate students involved during the summer for average of 10 weeks; 25 students involved in spring and fall for average of 12 weeks. Program publicity: Annual list of projects is submitted to all post-secondary schools in October. Campus and community media are alerted regarding application deadline. Most effective publicity: Contacting career planning and cooperative education offices at post-secondary schools; on-campus recruiting by Internship Coordinator.

Qualifications: Must be a N.C. resident attending in-state or out-of-state college or university. Students at 4-year schools must have completed 2 years: student in 2-year technical programs must have completed 1 year. Applicants must have at least a 2.5 g.p.a. on 4.0 scale.

Participant responsibilities: Varies in each department.

Screening: In-person interview, phone interview, cover letter, application, transcript. Criteria used to determine roles filled by participants: projects must be challenging to interns with a reasonable chance for successful completion in 10 weeks; project objectives and outcomes and intern's tasks must be outlined; a specific, qualified employee must be identified to supervise intern.

Overview: Began in 1969 when the Southern Regional Education Board initiated service-learning internships in North Carolina as a special pilot project. **Goals:** To provide experiential learning opportunities for N.C. post-secondary students, to provide service to participating state agencies, and to encourage students to consider public service careers. Program supports students' intellectual, career, civic, and personal development. **Philosophy:** "The Program's primary purpose is to provide college students with an educational experience that will bridge the gap between their classroom learning and intended career. Service to the agencies of state government is important and valued, but the focus is on providing the student with a high-quality project which adds real-world flavor to their theoretical background."

Structure: Director reports to Executive Director of YAIO. Advisory board of 75% faculty/school staff, 25% students.

Budget: $230,870 from state funds. **Staff:** 2 are involved.

Compensation: Summer interns are paid.

Preparation: 1-day orientation and telephone interviews with supervisors.

Supervision: Each student has a daily supervisor; Department Coordinators act as liaisons between YAIO and the agencies.

Evaluation of service: Quality of service is evaluated by site supervisor and through site visits by Internship Coordinator.

Learning: Learning is supported and monitored through daily contact with supervisor and periodic contact with Internship Coordinator. **Academic credit:** Students occasionally receive credit for learning.

Recognition: Students: Governor's certificate presented at a picnic with the Governor.

Program evaluation: Students and supervisors complete questionnaire at program's conclusion.

Benefits to organization: "Infusion of new ideas and enthusiasm from students."

Problem addressed: "We revised the process for telephone interviews between supervisors and students. We allow more time now and also provide students with names and numbers of supervisors so each can initiate calls."

Lesson learned: "We attempted to set up a 1-day interview conference for supervisors and law students. Supervisors only interviewed a select few students. It did not work because we relied on supervisors to interview more students than time allowed."

Rhode Island State Government Internship Program

Rhode Island State Government Internship Program, Room 14B, State Capitol Building, Providence, RI 02903, 401-277-6782. Robert Gemma, Executive Secretary. Urban, government program.

Participation: 210-240 college juniors and seniors, graduate students, and law and pre-med students involved during spring and summer for average of 8-14 weeks. Program publicity through school career development offices, college newspapers, posters on campus, academic advisors. Most effective publicity: Word-of-mouth from previous students; college newspaper.

Qualifications: College junior or senior, minimum g.p.a., interest in state government.

Participant responsibilities: Research, writing, communications; varies with each placement.

Screening: In-person interview, cover letter, resume, application; law students also submit writing sample. Criteria used to determine roles filled by participants: year in school, g.p.a., major, career objectives.

Overview: Spring program was begun in 1968 by a legislative act. **Goals:** To help students have high-quality experiences in state government, to meet their career objectives through government placements, to strengthen their confidence and responsibility as future members of the work force. Program supports students' intellectual, career, civic, and personal development, and sense of social responsibility. **Philosophy:** "We make every possible effort to produce a high-quality experience for every student."

Structure: Program is part of Legislative Services. Director reports to Speaker of the House of Representatives. Board of 10% faculty/school staff, 10% community representatives, 80% legislative commissioners.

Budget: $8000 for spring program from 100% state funds. **Staff:** 3 are involved.

Compensation: Stipend, transportation, work-study.

Preparation: Intern staff, with the help of faculty, conducts orientation for interns. Some departments also conduct orientations specific to their areas.

Supervision: Intern Placement Supervisor is responsible for collecting time sheets and evaluations and periodically reports to the intern staff on each student's progress.

Evaluation of service: Quality of service is monitored by intern progress reports.

Learning: Supported and monitored through phone and written contacts. **Academic credit:** Yes, most students receive credit for learning.

Recognition: Students: Interns completing program receive stipends and certificates of achievement. *Site supervisors:* Involvement is recognized as part of regular work load.

Program evaluation: Impact of program is evaluated by students, site supervisors, faculty members. Their input helps staff determine what are high-quality placements, and how best to match students with placements.

Benefits to organization: "Nationwide exposure."

Biggest challenge: "School vacations are a major problem for our spring program. We work with several different schools which have assorted vacation schedules. This creates a problem during our 14-week lecture series."

Rock Creek Foundation

Rock Creek Foundation, 1107 Spring Street, B1, Silver Spring, MD 20910, 301-589-6675. Beth Albaneze, Director. Urban, non-profit program serving individuals with chronic mental illness and/or developmental and intellectual impairments.

Participation: 60 undergrad and grad students, adults 19-60, and retired seniors involved during fall, winter, spring, and summer for average of 1 or 2 semesters. Most effective publicity: University contacts.

Qualifications: Participants must be committed, responsible, and have some knowledge of program and its goals.

Participant responsibilities: All staff positions are supplemented by students/volunteers.

Screening: In-person interview, application, references. Criteria used to determine roles filled by participants: School's requirements.

Overview: Began in 1972 as state-regulated program to keep individuals with chronic mental and/or developmental impairments in least restrictive environments with support. Agency provides comprehensive service delivery to meet the needs of clients for daily living skills, pre-vocational and vocational skills, therapeutic recreation, and outpatient and residential services. **Goals:** To provide on-going education programs for the community; to enhance participants' education; to provide experiential and didactic experiences through direct care, supervision, in-service trainings, and evaluations; to provide opportunities to expand participants' job prospects based on acquired skills. Program supports students' intellectual, ethical/moral, career, civic, and personal development, and sense of social responsibility. **Philosophy:** "We see each intern as an individual with unique life experiences and contributions to make, and we work to empower him or her to be a contributing member of our team."

Structure: Students supervised by program staff who report to Director of Student Volunteers.

Budget: From 90% state funds, 10% foundations. **Staff:** 80 are involved.

Compensation: Some stipends provided on an individual basis, some transportation supplement.

Agreement: Contracts, job descriptions.

Preparation: Individual orientation, training, and supervision.

Supervision: Each participant has a supervisor, attends staff meetings, and has a clear job description.

Evaluation of service: Quality of service is evaluated by Student/Volunteer Director with feedback from department staff.

Learning: Structured opportunities for reflection and analysis include surveys and meetings with faculty and department supervisors. Learning is supported and monitored through role modeling, hand-outs, in-service training. **Academic credit:** Yes.

Recognition: Students: Governor's Award and Agency Award, luncheons, dedication of rooms. *Site supervisors:* Receive some organizational recognition but no reduction in other responsibilities.

Program evaluation: Impact of program is evaluated by students, supervisors, management, and faculty/school administrators.

Benefits to organization: "Supplements agency staff."

Problem addressed: "Our philosophy of working with students and volunteers is now similar in all departments."

Lesson learned: "Group orientations did not work well for us. We now orient students individually to recognize their unique experience and the special contributions they can make."

Biggest challenge: "Budget constraints."

St. Paul Parks and Recreation

Internship Development, St. Paul Parks and Recreation, 17 W. 4th Street, St. Paul, MN 55102, 612-292-7430. Pat Moynagh, Volunteer Services Supervisor. Urban government program serving the general public.

Participation: 28 college sophomores, juniors, seniors, graduate students, and adults not in school involved each year during fall, winter, spring, and summer for average of 10 weeks. Most effective publicity: Urban Corps Program, job descriptions mailed to local college advisors.

Qualifications: Must have genuine interest in general program as well as specific area in which they wish to work.

Participant responsibilities: Special projects as well as some day-to-day operations.

Screening: In-person interview, phone interview, resume. Criteria used to determine roles filled by participants: Projects must be finite, able to be completed within a specified time, and provide a good learning experience for an intern.

Overview: Began in 1985. Agency needed additional staff, so it drew up job descriptions for potential internships and then contacted the Urban Corps Program and local colleges. **Goals:** To provide a high-quality learning experience for interns, to provide an expanded work force for the agency. Program supports students' intellectual, career, and personal development.

Structure: Director reports to Manager of Support Services.

Budget: Undetermined. Supplies and training are supplied by St. Paul Parks and Recreation. **Staff:** 6 are involved.

Compensation: Interns receive salary or stipend through St. Paul's Urban Corps Program.

Agreement: Program uses Urban Corps' or local schools' standard contracts.

Preparation: Informal orientation.

Supervision: Done by staff in specific department in which intern is working.

Evaluation of service: Quality of service is monitored by site supervisors, who also complete evaluation forms for participating schools and Urban Corps Program.

Learning: Structured opportunities for reflection and analysis include daily meetings between interns and supervisors and required evaluations. Learning is supported and monitored through periodic review of progress in meeting goals and objectives. **Academic credit:** Yes.

Recognition: Students: Interns receive a letter of recommendation. *Site supervisors:* Involvement is recognized as part of regular work load.

Program evaluation: Impact of program is evaluated by interns and supervisors through formal evaluations and by management when planning the budget.

Benefits to organization: "Provides additional high-quality work force at little cost."

Problem addressed: "The quarterly intern schedule does not coincide with our work load. An intern may begin a project which overlaps into the next intern's schedule. Occasionally, an intern is not able to complete a project, thus the intern's experience is not as complete as it should be. We try to reschedule projects. When that is not possible, we adjust the intern's hours."

Biggest challenge: "To get a chance to speak personally with interns and sell them our program. Most of our recruitment is done by mail."

Quebec-Labrador Foundation

Atlantic Center for the Environment, Quebec-Labrador Foundation, 39 South Main Street, Ipswich, MA 01938, 508-356-0038. Julie Early, Program Operations Director. Rural, nonprofit, environmental organization serving residents of the Atlantic region.

Participation: 50 college juniors and seniors and graduate students involved during fall, winter, spring, and summer for average of 8-10 weeks. Program publicity: Alumnae, field contacts, university personnel, environmental organizations, professional societies. Most effective publicity: Alumnae and staff contacts, university contacts.

Qualifications: Enthusiasm, interest in the regions in which Program works, ability to work with others.

Participant responsibilities: Conservation education, research and natural history work, development of publications, resource assessments.

Screening: In-person interview, phone interview, cover letter, resume, application, transcript, sometimes a writing sample. Criteria used to determine roles filled by participants: Educational background, experience, personality, interests.

Overview: Atlantic Center began in 1975 in response to growing environmental concerns in the region. **Goals:** To educate people in the Atlantic region, Appalachia, and the Caribbean about natural history and resource management; to give Center constituents the information and skills needed to make informed choices affecting their environment; to provide interns with valuable hands-on opportunities to use skills they have learned through pre-professional experiences. Program supports students' intellectual, career, and personal development, and sense of social responsibility.

Staff: 12 are involved.

Compensation: Salary or stipend, housing, transportation.

Preparation: 2-3 day orientation.

Supervision: Site visits, reports from field contacts, periodic calls from interns to program office.

Evaluation of service: Quality of service is monitored by project directors and permanent staff.

Learning: Learning is supported and monitored through conversations, written reports, mid-program evaluations. **Academic credit:** Students occasionally receive credit for learning.

Recognition: Students: Alumni Achievement Awards.

Program evaluation: Through student program reports, supervisor evaluations of students' work, and feedback from community contacts.

U.S. Public Health Service

Commissioned Officer Student Training Extern Program (COSTEP), U.S. Public Health Service (PHS), 5600 Fishers Lane, Room 7A-23, Rockville, MD 29857, 301-443-1470. Ivana Williams, Program Coordinator. Urban, government program serving U.S. health care recipients.

Participation: 500 college sophomores, juniors, seniors, and graduate students involved during fall, winter, spring, and summer for average of 4-17 weeks. Program publicity: Through student and professional health journals; at health professional conferences (exhibits and presentations); letters to students, deans, and clinical program directors; site visits to colleges and universities. Most effective publicity: Site visits to colleges and universities, letters and word-of-mouth by former COSTEPs.

Qualifications: Participants must have completed 1 year of medical, dental or veterinary school; 2 years of a professionally accredited program in dietetics, engineering, nursing, pharmacy, therapy, sanitary science, medical records, or computer science at the baccalaureate level; or health care administration, psychology, or sociology at the masters or Ph.D. level. Participants are expected to return to school after completing assignment. Applicants must be U.S. citizens under 44, in good physical condition and have no prior obligation or responsibility conflicting with active duty status.

Participant responsibilities: Clinical, regulatory, research, public health and administration, depending on the agency and assignment.

Screening: Application, transcript, phone interview, references, medical history. Criteria used to determine roles filled by participants: Year in school, background and experience, geographic location in which student wishes to work.

Overview: Began in 1948 as a summer employment program for medical students. In 1955, educational disciplines were extended and summer employment further developed. In 1956 students began to be commissioned as officers. The PHS promotes and advances health in the U.S. and offers a wide choice of training opportunities. **Goals:** To further the professional knowledge and experience of students in health-related fields, to expose them to new career opportunities, to provide a viable pool of potential candidates for future assignment. Program supports students' intellectual, career, and personal development, and sense of social responsibility.

Structure: Program is under the direction of the Chief of State. Program director reports to Director of the PHS Recruitment Program.

Budget: $300,000 from federal funds. **Staff:** 10 of 5,600 are involved.

Compensation: Salary, housing allowance, military health insurance, transportation, meals (subsistence allowance), uniform allowance, paid leave.

Agreement: Contracts with students include application, Statement of Duties, Oath of Office, Personnel Order, Call to Active Duty Order, payroll documentation.

Preparation: PHS-wide orientation plus agency-specific orientations. Conferences, meetings, social activities held to encourage exchange of career and agency information.

Supervision: Each intern is assigned to a Professional Preceptor or Mentor who is responsible for providing a rewarding and educational assignment. Many students are given specific projects to initiate and complete during their assignments. Whatever the assignment, students are closely supervised and given personalized guidance and training.

Evaluation of service: Quality of service is monitored by students' preceptors.

Learning: Learning is supported and monitored through preceptor, agency representative, and the COSTEP program. **Academic credit:** Students occasionally receive credit for learning.

Recognition: Students: As COSTEP is a uniformed service program, students can receive military medals and awards. Work-related projects can also be submitted to COSTEP incentive program. *Site supervisors:* Some involvement is recognized as part of regular work load; for others, there is some recognition but no reduction in other responsibilities.

Program evaluation: By students on standardized form. Preceptors evaluate students' performance and the program. "Student, preceptor and program comments and evaluations are constantly reviewed and changes made accordingly."

Benefits to organization: "It provides an avenue for recruitment and retention of career health professionals in the PHS."

Problem addressed: "Low percentage of applicants and officers from various ethnic groups. The PHS has begun an initiative targeted towards historically Black colleges and universities as well as Hispanics and Native Americans."

Biggest challenge: "Revitalization. We are reorganizing and improving the Program."

Urban Corps Expansion Project

In an attempt to meet the growing demand for research and evaluation detailing effects on volunteers and on the community, Public/Private Ventures and the National Association of Service and Conservation Corps will use a $2 million, five-year grant to operate the Urban Corps Expansion Project (UCEP) and to evaluate its impact. By 1992, UCEP will establish 15 experimental urban corps, provide them with technical assistance, and encourage them to take advantage of the success stories in the field. Such successes include the San Francisco Conservation Corps, which emphasizes physical rehabilitation projects, and New York's City Volunteer Corps, which pioneered the use of corps members in human service work.

UCEP will stress the personal development of corps members. Work must provide marketable skills such as those developed by the competency-based curricula found in the East Bay Conservation Corps. Also, counseling, support services, and a strong job placement component will be incorporated to help youth develop job-seeking and interviewing skills. A major objective is to demonstrate the cost-effectiveness of building capacity, maintaining program quality, and disseminating research findings in a carefully staged progression from concept, to pilot project, to limited demonstration, to larger replication, and, finally, to widespread dissemination. *Reprinted with permission from* Community Service: A Resource Guide for States, *National Governors' Association, 1989, p. 5.*

Volunteer Clearinghouse of D.C.

Volunteer Opportunity Program, Volunteer Clearinghouse of the District of Columbia, 1313 New York Avenue NW, Washington, DC 20005, 202-638-2664. James Lindsay, Executive Director. Urban, nonprofit program serving volunteers and agencies.

Participation: 4 students in-house (most of profile will focus on this program as most aspects vary at each agency); 1000 high school and college students referred each year to the community during fall, winter, spring, and summer for average of 12 weeks. Program publicity: Brochures to schools and agencies, monthly meetings with networks of high school and university community service directors, bi-weekly student network meetings. Most effective publicity: Word-of-mouth, school recruitment.

Qualifications: Open to all young people ages 13-22.

Participant responsibilities: Program development, peer counseling, public speaking, school technical assistance, program evaluation.

Screening: In-person interview, application. Criteria used to determine roles filled by participants: Compatibility of program needs and students' learning goals and objectives.

Overview: Began in 1984 with Young Volunteers in Action grant of $20,000 from ACTION. The Volunteer Clearinghouse has produced a videotape and discussion guide about the art of making a service-learning program work (inquire about "Growing Through Giving"). **Goals:** Student leadership development, school technical assistance, agency job development. Program supports students' intellectual, ethical/moral, career, and personal development, and sense of social responsibility. **Philosophy:** "A key factor in our success is that we value student participation in designing projects to meet community needs. Our Student Community Action Network enables students to examine community issues and put a plan into action to involve their peers in community service."

Structure: Program is 1 of 3 programs at the Volunteer Clearinghouse. Program director reports to the Executive Director. Board of 20% faculty/school staff, 80% community representatives.

Budget: $25,000 from 50% federal funds, 30% foundations, 20% fees from schools, 1% in-kind corporate donations (e.g., printing, graphics). Clearinghouse provides space, office equipment, administrative support. **Staff:** 1 of 4 1/2 are involved.

Compensation: Salary or stipend, transportation costs reimbursed.

Agreement: Clearinghouse uses a service-learning agreement signed by student and Youth Services Director.

Preparation: Students are oriented individually.

Supervision: Clearinghouse has open-door policy for students to ask questions and receive guidance as needed.

Evaluation of service: Through verbal mid-term and verbal and written final evaluations by the Youth Services Director.

Learning: Learning is supported and monitored through close contact with Youth Services Director. **Academic credit:** Students occasionally receive credit for learning.

Recognition: Students: Clearinghouse writes letters of recommendation and serves as a reference for future employment. *Site supervisors:* Involvement is recognized as part of regular work load in some cases; in others, there is some organizational recognition but no reduction in other responsibilities.

Program evaluation: Program evaluated by students verbally and in writing, by site supervisors verbally, by management through annual Board review.

Benefits to organization: "Program provides visibility to agency and adds to its reputation."

Problems addressed: "We learned to accomplish all the demands of running this program by delegating specific projects to students that fit with their learning goals. We have also developed higher-quality placements through workshops for agencies and allowing students to develop their own projects."

Lesson learned: "Our Community Advisory Council was useful in the beginning, but continued monthly meetings were not needed to enhance the Program. Sending quarterly written updates and calling on them for their particular skills and expertise have worked better."

Biggest challenge: "Getting more faculty involved."

Other advice: "Get faculty behind your program."

For information on over 600 other organizations' programs, see The National Directory of Internships, *edited by Amy Butterworth and Sally Migliore, available from the National Society for Internships and Experiential Education, 3509 Haworth Drive Suite 207, Raleigh, NC 27609.*

Fact Sheet: The California Human Corps

Pamela Spratlen

A summary of the Human Corps legislation and concept enacted in California. Provided by Pamela Spratlen of the Ways and Means Committee of the California Assembly, (916) 445-7082.

The Human Corps: What is It?

THE HUMAN CORPS IS a statewide program of student public service in California public colleges and universities. Created in January, 1988 by AB 1820 (Vasconcellos, Chapter 1245/87), the program is underway on all 19 campuses of the California State University (CSU) and all eight general campuses of the University of California (UC). Community colleges and private colleges and universities are encouraged to participate.

What is the purpose of the program? The Human Corps gives renewed and expanded priority to the tradition of public service on university and college campuses. It creates linkages between the university and the community, between academic instruction and experiential learning, between the private goals of students and the social needs of the state. The challenges facing the state require an investment of talent and resources from a variety of sources. The purpose of the Human Corps is to build this commitment to the community as part of a university education.

What Does the Law Require?

For the 350,000 CSU students and 150,000 UC students, the Human Corps legislation states that every student, with specified exceptions, shall be "encouraged and expected, although not required, to participate in 30 hours of service per year" during his or her college career. The goal of the Human Corps is 100 percent participation by 1993. Service includes work on a wide array of social issues from illiteracy to environmental contamination, to the hunger and nutrition needs of the elderly and others.

For the university systems, the legislative intent is for the universities to become the home bases for Human Corps programs. The universities convene task forces to plan and set policy and assign staff to train students, coordinate, and monitor campus and community programs.

For the faculty, the law recommends participation on campus Human Corps task forces and consideration of how and whether students should get academic credit for the learning gained through the service performed.

For the community, the Human Corps provides a new resource for volunteer talent and innovative projects with universities.

For the state, the legislation provides for monitoring of the overall progress of the Human Corps by the California Postsecondary Education Commission, which is responsible for periodic reports to the Legislature.

What about Funding?

The original Human Corps legislation appropriated $240,000 in planning funds to the UC ($70,000) and CSU ($180,000) systems. The governor vetoed this appropriation as well as a request for $500,000 in 1988. Private corporations and foundations have provided some support for the Human Corps, but campuses have used their own resources for all activities to date.

Progress: What's Happening?

In 1988, all campuses of the California State University and the University of California instituted planning task forces. In addition, a new coalition of 40 campuses across California have come together to form the California Compact to promote the development of university public service.

We also intend to consider ways in which the Human Corps might expand to high schools. The California Compact will continue to grow and attract new members. The UC and CSU systems will pursue refinements to existing programs, as well as ways to fund new programs. All of these initiatives are an integral part of California's role in a nationwide trend toward building a commitment to public service in the nation's high schools and colleges.

The Cherokee Nation's Approach to Leadership

McClellan Hall and James Kielsmeier

A Cherokee leader and the President of the National Youth Leadership Council describe the evolution of the Indian Youth Leadership Conference, which engages high school students with 7th and 8th graders. This article is adapted from an article in New Designs for Youth Development, *Association for Youth Development, May/June, 1985, and is reprinted with permission. It has also been reprinted in the journal of the Association for Experiential Education.*

"An Indian leader is very important in these times."

"An Indian leader should help in taking care of our environment and be a leader for non-Indians as well as Indians."
— Cherokee 8th Graders

THE EDUCATION DEPARTMENT OF THE CHEROKEE NATION of Oklahoma had its hands full in early 1984. The second 30-member class of the high school Youth Leadership Program concluded its year-long series of meetings and projects, while a new group was recruited for the 10-day National Leadership Conference in Minnesota. Fifteen graduates of last year's Leadership Program prepared for a 1,500-mile bike trip retracing the Trail-of-Tears from North Carolina to Oklahoma, at the same time that a team of high school and college students planned for the Second Annual Indian Youth Leadership Conference for one hundred 7th and 8th graders in June.

From modest beginnings a spark is brightening into a flame in Oklahoma — some would say analogous to the sacred Cherokee fire that has burned throughout the history of the people. Not only is there heated activity emanating from this unusual youth program, but illumination on the issue of modern Indian leadership as it affects both Indian and non-Indian people and how it can be nurtured in tribally-controlled settings. Our purpose here is to tell the story of the Cherokee Nation Youth Leadership Program, emphasizing how this experience relates to a more general understanding of Indian leadership.

Background

In 1982, discussions at the Cherokee Nation Education Department centered on the dysfunctional relationship between Indian young people and the Oklahoma public schools. In Adair County, which has the highest concentration of Cherokee youth in the tribal area, 70% drop out before high school graduation. The development of a program to deal with the school failure rate would require a bold undertaking.

In addition to geographical separation (the Cherokee Nation in Oklahoma today includes all or part of 14 counties), the tribe has been factionalized by religious conflict (Christian versus Traditional), and cultural loss brought about by intermarriage with non-Indians. A constitution which provides for election of 15 council members at large, rather than as representatives of geographical districts adds further political dissensions. Finally, for nearly 50 years, from 1907 to the 1950s, they were without formal tribal leadership. These factors have combined to fragment and disperse the tribe to the point where a tribal community spirit is difficult to recognize, and programs that effectively engage Cherokees from all 14 counties are rare.

Cherokee Nation Youth Leadership Program (CNYLP) began with the vision of drawing elements of the tribe together through an innovative youth program. Initially, thirty high school students were selected from within the 14-county area and spent one year in a program designed to instill self-confidence, positive regard for Cherokee identity, and a sense of community spirit through service to others. From this first step other directions and programs have developed to bring the vision closer to a reality. The program marks the first attempt since Oklahoma statehood in 1907 to bring young Cherokee people from the entire Nation together to work and learn as a group, addressing directly the issue of leadership. The service-oriented approach to leadership has proved to be the catalyst that unified the group, and it has had a profound impact on individual young people:

"I feel great about being one of the Cherokee Nation's first leadership students. I consider it a privilege and success in itself. I felt successful because I was looked up to by the kids this week. I hope I was a good example to them."

— Cherokee High School Student Staff Member
Indian Youth Leadership Conference

Program Development

Before they could train and educate the young, the staff needed to be clear themselves about what they were educating for, and what the curriculum of the program would be. Borrowing from another group's cultural experience was not appropriate, nor were there clear outlines available in other Indian programs. There was, however, a multicultural youth leadership development program created by the National Youth Leadership Council (NYLC) that held promise as a foundation on which to develop a distinctively Cherokee model. In broad outline, the program involved training selected Cherokee Nation high school youth in a challenging multicultural setting — the National Leadership Conferences — and then creating ways of "bringing back" the high motivation generated there and applying it to useful service projects in home communities.

Cherokee traditional religion teaches that the creator made the four races of people and gave them their original instructions. The Cherokee once believed that all races are to be respected equally, and all are mentioned in some of the ancient songs of prayer and healing. However, most Cherokee people today, especially the younger ones, are products of the broader American culture in which they have grown up and have strong racial attitudes, often borrowed from their non-Indian neighbors. There is a certain amount of distrust and uncertainty regarding whites and a great deal of prejudice toward blacks held by Cherokee people. The Cherokee students who attended the first NYLC experience were apprehensive about spending 10 days in close contact with complete strangers, many from other racial groups. Further contributing to their anxiety, was the uncertain self-image the Cherokee young people had of themselves.

The multicultural experience had positive consequences for individual Indian youth and the Cherokees as a whole. The insecurity experienced by the Cherokee students rapidly gave way to a feeling of new-found importance. For the majority of the non-Indian participants, this was their first contact with contemporary Indian people and they were very respectful. As the students experienced challenges together and became better acquainted, the racial barriers dissolved and good friendships developed.

During the six-hour drive to the camp, the Cherokee leadership students had plotted ways to stay in the same cabins and to stick together as much as possible, since they had heard that they would be separated once they reached the camp. But the separation of the group and contact with other people of different races, in spite of initial apprehension, proved a key element in the success of the camp. It was important to Indian youth to know that there were members of the Cherokee Nation staff nearby to provide support but also to know that they would have to deal with many of their problems personally.

It was clear to the Cherokee staff that a significant change in self-image occurred as a result of the camp experience. (This was borne out by the evaluation data to be discussed later.) Not only did students feel better about themselves as individuals, but a distinct pride in being Cherokee developed as well. For example, during many hours spent preparing for a cultural presentation to the entire camp, the Cherokee youth came to realize how little they really knew about their heritage, and they needed to work hard to pull it together. Their presentation on contemporary Cherokee life in Oklahoma received a long standing ovation.

The NLC Design: Creating a Multicultural Community

The National Leadership Conference (NLC) by design includes participants from a diversity of cultures (50% of the students have been people of color). The program is planned to create a neutral setting for every group represented. Activities, therefore, are geared not to a single culture nor just to the outdoor or athletically inclined, but also to young people more comfortable in artistic or other less physically demanding settings.

From its base in a semi-primitive residential camp, the NLC uses the wilderness, but also nearby cities and towns as its campus. Combining action and reflection, outdoor adventure challenges with formal lectures and discussions, the curriculum focuses on a unifying theme, such as justice or youth participation. It emphasizes a particular model of leadership, the "servant leader": one who leads by serving and empowering others.

Participants are initially thrown together in highly intensive Seminar experiences which combine physical, intellectual and moral challenges. These are followed by experiences, both on and off ground, called Pursuits of Excellence, in which smaller groups develop and apply the concepts and skills introduced in the seminars. Following these, the participants reunite to reflect on and to synthesize these experiences. Together, each sub-group forms the compact through which they will apply their new and strengthened leadership skills in their home schools and community.

All of this takes place within the crucible of community-building, the very real and difficult task of developing a multicultural community of love, respect, trust and caring by young people who had not experienced such diversity before. As one student commented: "It was the working together of 200 people from all cultures and races that really made it work — and us work. This was 'real world' democracy and equality." Another summarized what they had learned most clearly: "Wow, this is feasible! All races of people can get along, trust each other and be great friends no matter if they're Black, White, Indian or Mexican-American. We must bring this message to others — no matter if it takes 10, 20, 50 or 100 years" (Conrad, 1982, i,ii).

Increasing Self-Esteem at the NLC

Dominant groups in American society have been slow in recognizing the achievements of ethnic minorities. Typically, this has left the minority group with a sense of collective inadequacy which is translated into low self-esteem for the individual young person growing up in such a group. It is one of the aims of the NLC to break into this destructive cycle to raise the self-esteem of the individual participants, and further, to help them apply their new perspectives on themselves to the groups with which they identify.

The NLC finds the raw materials of raised self-esteem in building positive relationships with others, and in carrying through challenges successfully. When the various groups arrive at camp, their baggage generally includes many cultural stereotypes — both about themselves and about the other groups. As they move through the program, the young people are confronted with a series of demands which carry a certain amount of risk — whether it be interpersonal, social, intellectual, or physical. It is hoped that as they proceed through these activities, they will come to see themselves as capable risk-takers — as able as any of the others to undertake and meet a variety of challenges. This sense of accomplishment, of being on a par with others whom they may have either held in awe, or have disparaged, is a key factor in the strong sense of community which develops in the course of the 10-day experience. In the surmounting of obstacles, including their stereotypes of themselves and others, and in the building of a trusting and caring community, more positive self-images emerge. The data from evaluation studies conducted in 1982 and 1983 indicate that this is indeed happening.

The evaluation data are consistent with the informal assessment made by Cherokee Nation staff who felt that the young people returned to Oklahoma with a stronger collective sense of self. They left Oklahoma as individual representatives from the 14-county area, but after excelling in an intense experience with people of many other backgrounds were able to return home with new pride in themselves and their Cherokee heritage.

"A good leader is not marked with a sign that says 'leader.' Anyone can be one if they really want to. A leader, though, has to be willing to help others and to serve."

— Cherokee Nation 8th Grader

Leadership in Oklahoma

In the two years of the program there has been activity in Oklahoma which is more indicative of actual leadership development than test scores can show. Returning home after the summer, the Cherokee Nation Youth Leadership Program focuses attention on home communities. During the year following the camp experience, monthly sessions are planned and conducted with a great deal of input from youth participants. A "curriculum" of applied leadership development is being built — staff and students defining together what it means to be an Indian leader through the projects and programs created. Actual accomplishments speak loudly to the substance of the dormant leadership that is now blooming:
- Renovation of the Cherokee Artists' Association building
- Service projects with senior citizens and nursing homes
- A nearly 70% participation rate in the follow-up programs by high school students
- Creation of a ropes-challenge course that can be used by young people from throughout the tribal area
- Creation of a leadership training camp in Oklahoma for 7th and 8th graders
- A 1,500 mile bike expedition along the route of the Trail-of-Tears completed in 1984 and repeated in 1985
- In addition, there have been numerous individual accomplishments by the high school students beyond previous expectations, such as improved grades and a higher rate of college entrance.

Direct results include a significant number of parents and school personnel who have rediscovered the concept and the value of the experiential approach to education. The traditional Native American educational model has always been experientially based. Traditionally, Indian young people become adults through a natural process of working with and emulating adults, gradually assuming their roles within tribal societies. The idea of bringing young people into direct contact with the subject matter to be learned — experiential education — is the heart of the teaching method at the National Leadership Conferences and its back-home programs. Enlarging the classroom to include the rivers, hills, forests, towns, and cities, brings life to learning. In the case of the leadership training, people learn leadership by "doing leadership." Realizing the benefits of this approach, the Cherokee Nation staff structured their entire program in order to place participants in responsible, decision-making activities. Young people not only wielded paint brushes at the renovation of the Artists' Association building, but helped organize the project. They play key roles in the operation of the 7th and 8th grade leadership camps and have been asked to provide leadership in other community projects initiated through the program.

Service-learning — engaging young people in community service projects for the purpose of developing responsible citizens — is a method of experiential education used extensively by the CNYLP. It is based on the premise that one develops elements of character such as honesty, a sense of fairness, and compassion by doing acts that call on these capacities. The open demonstration of the service ideal through the many projects operated by staff and students has had an important impact on participants and community alike.

Indian Youth Leadership Conference: A New Model

The Cherokee Nation Education Department had a dual concern: they needed more creative outlets for the able young high-school leaders finishing their training, and they wished to design a program for 7th and 8th grade youth. School retention studies have identified this age as a critical period. The decision was made to operate a leadership camp in Oklahoma using elements of the NLC model but directed specifically towards the needs of Indian youth. The junior-high level camp would be staffed in part by the high school leadership students after they received intensive training in small group skills and experiential education methods.

Funded by the Johnson-O'Malley program, the camp focused on the theme, "Today's Indian Youth — Living in Two Worlds."

Sixty-five 7th and 8th graders attended the first Indian Youth Leadership Conference at Camp Lutherhoma on the banks of the Illinois River. Student leaders and younger students worked together on service projects, were engaged in seminars related to self-worth and environmental education, and were exposed regularly to elders who spoke to the group. Dan Conrad from the University of Minnesota served as the external evaluator and summarized the major outcomes of the camp as follows:

> ... For the young participants (there) were, first of all, a new sense of personal confidence and competence, and, secondly and relatedly, increased pride in being Indian and stronger identification as such. Other outcomes reported by participants were a resolve and a commitment to try harder in life, to persevere in the face of difficulty; a strong belief in the power of cooperative effort and the value of sharing; and new ideas about what it means to be a leader — particularly that a leader is one who serves his/her followers. Not the least of the outcomes was the very real accomplishment of saving the life of a drowning man on the Illinois River. The major outcomes for adult staff members were gaining insight into and skill in working with junior high youth; development and testing of a leadership training model; and building their own skills in leading the same." (Conrad, 1983, p. 2)

Key to the success of the week was the effectiveness of the high school leaders. They were assigned significant responsibility and worked very hard serving as teachers, counselors, role models and friends to the 7th and 8th graders.

Cultural rootedness, confidence in a multicultural world, ideals of compassion and service to others combined with a strong sense of self and personal competence are the key aims of the Cherokee Nation Youth Leadership Program. They are the personal characteristics that many Cherokee Nation young people have already begun to demonstrate with their behavior. We believe they are important characteristics of the effective Indian leader — for today and for the next generation.

Note: *The model described here is now being used as a community development model by four tribal groups in New Mexico. McClellan Hall is directing the project in cooperation with the Santa Fe Mountain Center. This study was made possible in part by a grant from the Lilly Endowment.*

McClellan Hall, Cherokee, is former director of Stillwell Academy, Cherokee Nation's alternative school in Stillwater, Oklahoma. He also served on the staff of the Cherokee Nation Youth Leadership Program where he helped organize the first Indian Youth Leadership Conference in 1983. In his current position in Ramah, New Mexico, he initiated the first Navaho Youth Leadership Program. James Kielsmeier is President of the National Youth Leadership Council and has served as consultant to the Cherokee Nation Education Department.

References

Allen, Richard and Jerry Bread, *Johnson-O'Malley Program: Youth Leadership Conference Curriculum Design*, 1983.

Conrad, Dan, *Evaluation Report of the National Leadership Conference, Camp Pin Oak, Missouri and Camp Miniwanca, Michigan*, Center for Youth Development and Research, University of Minnesota, October 1982.

Conrad, Dan, *Evaluation Report of the National Leadership Conference, Bradford Woods, Indiana and Lake of the Ozarks, Missouri*, Center for Youth Development and Research, University of Minnesota, November 1983.

Conrad, Dan, *Evaluation Report of the Indian Youth Leadership Conference, Camp Lutherhoma, Tahlequah, Oklahoma*, Center for Youth Development and Research, University of Minnesota, August 1983.

LaClair, Marlene, *Developing Student Leadership Skills*, Indian Education Act Resource and Evaluation Center Five, Tulsa, Oklahoma, 1984.

An Agency Initiative
The BOCES Geneseo Migrant Center

Sue Roark-Calnek and Jane F. Hogan

A longstanding joint program of a university and a center for migrant farmworkers shows how a creative partnership can recognize and respect the needs of all parties involved in a service-learning exchange. Reprinted with permission from Experiential Education, *NSIEE, Vol. 14, No. 4, September-October 1989, pp. 5, 16-17.*

FACES (FARMWORKER ARTS, CULTURE AND EDUCATION WITH STUDENTS) is an internship program developed by the BOCES Geneseo (NY) Migrant Center with an Innovative Projects for Student Community Service grant from the Fund for the Improvement of Postsecondary Education (FIPSE). FACES recruits, trains, and places SUNY Geneseo students in internships serving an ethnically diverse population of migrant farmworkers in several counties of western New York. Interns have enabled the agency to expand and upgrade the level of service to migrant farmworkers, and provide a cost-effective solution to the recruitment and retention of part-time staff.

Intern placements to date include: teaching English as a second language, secondary school re-entry curriculum, Adult Basic Education, preschool readiness, and art in the migrant camps; mounting interpreted exhibitions of traditional migrant arts and culture; documentary photography; oral history research; needs assessment, advocacy and referral for social services; on-campus and community recruitment of volunteers; public relations for other Center initiatives, among them a national scholarship fund for migrant youth; production of informational resources including the Center's nationally distributed newsletters for migrants and service providers; and management tasks for the local affiliate of Literacy Volunteers of America.

Background. FACES builds on earlier service-learning initiatives developed by the Center's founder, Gloria Mattera, and on close relations with SUNY Geneseo. The center is now admini-stered by the Livingston-Steuben-Wyoming Board of Cooperative Educational Services (BOCES). It is administratively and fiscally in-dependent of the college, but its accessible, on-campus location facilitates student and faculty involvement. The internship pro-gram operates within the guidelines of the SUNY Geneseo College-Wide Internship Program and is coordinated by a SUNY Geneseo faculty member. The college is exploring the possibility of released time or other institutional support for internship coordination be-yond the period of FIPSE funding. In summer-fall 1989, FACES accounted for one-third of SUNY Geneseo's internship placements and was the only multiple-placement off-campus field site.

A dissemination model under development will link academic internship programs with migrant service providers in target areas where the use of migrant farm labor is significant, and will encour-age other agencies to initiate service-learning programs. The grant is being evaluated using Naturalistic Response Evaluation, an eth-nographic approach using qualitative as well as quantitative meas-ures and assessing project outcomes for all interested "stakehold-ers" — migrants, agency staff, faculty, and students. Some prelimi-nary lessons learned from this agency initiative follow.

Characteristics of a Strong Program

A good internship experience in which the agency or other field site is actively involved enhances the *mutuality* and *reciprocity* of service-learning. All parties to the internship receive an experien-tial education. Students learn through direct application and field testing of strategies presented in college courses. Discipline-bound academics redefine and expand their knowledge through interac-tion with colleagues in other disciplines, the agency, and field visits. Agency staff are challenged to conduct systematic, ongoing assess-ment of how their organization actually works and what it really needs. The agency has clearly set goals for the interns, in contrast with an ad hoc "Where can we put this kid they've sent us?" mindset. Agency clients benefit from and contribute to the resultant rise in the quantity and quality of services delivered.

Facilitation of Outcomes. How can these outcomes be facilitated? The emphasis should be on process, not short-term product. Developing mutually instructive relations between agen-cies and academia takes time and may require a modest start. From the perspective of an agency-initiated program, the process should:

• *Start with a limited population.* FACES began with Edu-cation and Anthropology, two departments already attuned to the benefits of service-learning. The program then incorporated Communications, a less obvious but potentially productive field for migrant-service interns. Key people whose personal and professional priorities support service-learning can be found on both sides of the academia/agency relationship. Identifying these people can open doors.

• **Clarify expectations.** An agency-initiated internship may be discomforting at first to academics because of possible misunderstandings about constraints of the agency, its priorities, or its expectations of college faculty. Faculty may be reluctant to assume an active role. Students may be uneasy about how to respond both to agency personnel and to faculty in a more informal, non-classroom setting. Roles, responsibilities and joint sharing among faculty, students and agency personnel may be defined in seminars.

• **Capitalize on the diversity of participants' past experiences.** The FACES program designs encounters in which participants share and process experiences from different personal and professional perspectives. In reflection, the strange becomes familiar, or at least understandable. The learner begins to see alternative methods, courses of action, and value positions, and to view them non-judgmentally. The familiar becomes strange and subject to critical analysis.

• **Be prepared to deal with culture shock.** The interstate migrant farmworkers in the Center's service are African American, Algonquin Indian, Haitian, Mexican American and Puerto Rican. This living laboratory for multi-ethnic, multi-cultural awareness generates culture shock for some middle class Caucasian interns and faculty. Even those who have lived or visited abroad have little awareness of the culture of migrancy, the conditions in migrant camps, or the coping strategies migrants use to adapt to adverse situations. With careful field supervision and opportunities for reflection on their experience, learners begin to suspend judgments and see strength in diversity.

• **Provide ongoing reinforcement for interns.** New goals and new ways of meeting original goals may emerge in the internship. Recognizing and validating these changes can help interns cope with problems they encounter. An anthropology intern is unable to complete a case study because the subject abruptly leaves for Florida; an education intern cannot teach a carefully planned lesson because of an impromptu migrant camp party. Immediate frustrations may cloud interns' ability to recognize long-term learning. Nonetheless, they have gained valuable insights into migrant lifestyle and the need for flexibility. Most important, interns come to learn from the migrants as they teach. In the field, in seminars and through their journals, interns experience the shift from teacher/provider to learner/recipient.

Benefits to Those Involved

Through FACES, migrant farmworkers are exposed to groups with whom they seldom have contact, breaking down social isolation. The intern is a bridge to the college setting, facilitating a transition to post-secondary education for some migrant youth who might never have seen this as an option.

The agency receives additional staffing to complement and extend limited funding. It is able to tap into current research through the college faculty. The idealism and impatience of youth force the agency to rethink policies and procedures.

The interns gain the opportunity to "try on" a career. They set objectives, outline a task and implement it. They evaluate the product and the process. They chafe at the constraints of bureaucracy, but often for the first time they really experience the norms of a workplace culture. Their desire to work in this field is challenged or reaffirmed.

College professors learn to apply the methodologies of other disciplines and broaden personal areas of interest. Working with interns provides a stimulation different from classroom teaching. The field setting may provide new directions for research as well.

Developing an Agency-Initiated Internship

The FACES model of reciprocal teaching/learning among agency staff, college faculty, students and migrant farmworkers is adaptable to other human service agencies. To transfer the model, agency staff first need to brainstorm agency goals and student outcomes for the internship. Second, approach a college to discuss the mutual benefits. A clear statement of what interns will do is essential. The college will need to realize how experiential learning can complement the college curriculum.

Sue Roark-Calnek is Assistant Professor of Anthropology at SUNY Geneseo and has served as Folk Arts Consultant and Internship Coordinator at the BOCES Geneseo Migrant Center. Jane Hogan is Associate Professor of Reading at SUNY Geneseo and the current Internship Coordinator for the FACES program.

Feasible and Adaptable: Intergenerational Service-Learning

James P. Firman and Catherine A. Ventura

An evaluation of the Intergenerational Service-Learning Project shows the types of activities most likely to be effective. Reprinted from Synergist, *National Center for Service-Learning, ACTION, Vol. 10, No. 2, pp. 35-36.*

THE GRAYING OF OUR POPULATION portends major changes for virtually all societal institutions, including colleges and universities. With increasing frequency higher education will be called upon to train students to meet the changing social and economic needs of an aging population.

To what extent and in what ways is service-learning an appropriate and effective way for colleges to respond to the growing needs of older people? How can schools better train students from a wide variety of disciplines to work well with older people? What roles should faculty and students assume to help strengthen the programs and services available to the elderly?

In recognition of the growing significance of these questions, the National Council on the Aging (NCOA) initiated the Intergenerational Service-Learning Project (ISLP), a national demonstration effort involving 13 colleges and universities in seven states. Funded by the Community Services Administration, the Robert Wood Johnson Foundation, and the participating schools, the 30-month project had the following purposes:

• To develop adaptable models for involving students and faculty from a wide variety of disciplines in service-learning projects for and on behalf of older people;

• To test the feasibility and cost effectiveness of a campus-based intergenerational service-learning center as a mechanism for developing and supporting innovative projects;

- To identify feasible strategies for designing, marketing, and financing service-learning activities related to aging; and
- To identify and remove existing barriers to intergenerational service-learning.

To maximize the applicability and adaptability of the findings and models, NCOA selected a mix of six public and private, large and small colleges and universities and one consortium. Some had well developed gerontology programs; others had programs in the initial stages of development. NCOA gave each institution a $25,000-a-year grant to help establish and operate the model programs. During the first two years, 1,914 students from 40 disciplines took part in a wide variety of service-learning activities as part of their coursework, as volunteers, and as part-time employees. In the process, each institution developed several significant models.

Findings

NCOA conducted an extensive evaluation to determine the impact of specific projects on participating students, faculty, and community agencies. The data and major findings were published by NCOA in *Intergenerational Service-Learning: Strategies for Campus/Community Collaboration*. A summary follows.

Intergenerational service-learning is a concept that is feasible and adaptable to a multiplicity of disciplines. Colleges successfully developed and are likely to continue projects involving students in almost all disciplines except the natural sciences. For example, a French major provided orientation sessions to an elderly French immigrant; business students developed plans to help community agencies market their services more effectively; and veterinary students developed a Back-to-the-Farm reminiscence therapy project that involved taking animals to nursing homes.

There are significant differences in the duration and types of services rendered through course-related, volunteer, and employment projects and by different levels of students. The students participating in course-related projects provided an average of 62 hours each of service a year; volunteers averaged 15 hours each of service a year; and salaried students averaged 197 hours each of service a year.

Services aimed at improving individuals' functioning were the most prevalent type rendered by all projects. Services that help people remain at home (e.g., assisting with household chores) and assistance to agencies were provided effectively through course-related and employment projects, but not by volunteers. Services vital to everyday living (e.g., finding inexpensive housing) were not provided effectively by any of the service-learning projects.

An extensive analysis of feasible, adaptable service-learning projects showed that students at different levels have different capabilities in addressing and solving problems. For example, freshman and sophomores usually carry out small projects in response to predetermined needs while graduate students also can diagnose needs, search for solutions, and formulate new practices.

Community agency personnel reported that students were most effective in two roles: working directly with older persons on a one-to-one basis and developing and implementing special projects. Since many students, particularly undergraduates, have limited skills and work at an agency only a few hours each week, one-to-one involvements were particularly successful. Because agency staff are often extremely busy, intergenerational interaction was beneficial in addressing the needs of the elderly.

Special projects designed especially for and by students also were quite effective. In these projects students took the initiative in using their abilities, skills, and creativity for a specific activity, such as creative drama, that the staff had neither the time nor training to carry out.

The existence of a single contact person strengthened and, in some cases, significantly improved relationships between community agencies and the participating college. Prior to the initiation of ISLP, campus-community tension was evident in several of the participating communities. Many service providers felt that the university's academic orientation to serving the elderly sometimes conflicted with practical realities. Many community people reported that the ISLP coordinator bridged this gap by being the sole contact person within the university. Most participants reported an improved town-gown relationship and an increased sharing of resources and expertise.

The Future

The Intergenerational Service-Learning Project was an exploratory effort that examined the mutual implications of the emerging fields of service-learning and gerontology. The models developed should help to fuel future implementation and innovation. Among the more promising areas are interdisciplinary projects, intergenerational service-learning teams of students and older people, the use of retired faculty and agency personnel as field supervisors, and the involvement of older adults as service-learners.

James P. Firman was the project director and Catherine A. Ventura was a research assistant for the Intergenerational Service-Learning Project of the National Council on the Aging, Inc., Washington, D.C. For additional information write to the National Council on the Aging, Inc., 600 Maryland Avenue, S.W., West Wing #100, Washington, D.C. 20024.

Valued Youth Partnership Program

A San Antonio program addresses a school dropout problem creatively through service in a cross-age tutoring model. Reprinted with permission from Reaching Out: School-Based Community Service Programs, *National Crime Prevention Council, 1988, p. 49. For more information about the Valued Youth Partnership Program (VYP), contact Alicia Salinas Sosa, VYP, Intercultural Development Research Association, 5835 Callaghan, Suite 350, San Antonio, Texas 78228-1190, (512) 684-8180.*

IN RECENT YEARS, the dropout rate for students had risen from 32% to 44% in San Antonio. The Valued Youth Partnership Program, developed by the Intercultural Development Research Association, funded by Coca-Cola USA, was designed to prevent students from dropping out through cross-age tutoring. In 1988, eight campuses were involved in the program. Through personnel in area school districts, Hispanic students at high risk of dropping out are identified as valued youth and are given an opportunity to tutor younger children. Under this tutelage and care, the younger Hispanic students make gains in school. As the tutors care for and teach basic skills to the younger children, they reinforce their own knowledge of the skills, develop positive perceptions of self, and remain in school.

The student tutors take special classes to gain greater competence in communication, reading, and writing skills, as well as to gain a practical awareness of child growth and development theories, before and during their tutoring work. The students tutor the children between five and eight hours each week. In some schools, the tutoring is done after normal school hours. In others, the tutoring is done during the school day.

The students receive the federal minimum wage for their work. Students who are financially strapped often cite these problems as the reason for dropping out. The wage serves as a secondary, *not* a primary, incentive for students to join the program and relieves some of the financial pressure that they may experience.

Parents are involved in the program as much as possible. Before a student begins tutoring, the parents' understanding and support is sought and their child's involvement explained. Students involved in VYP go on field trips with their "tutees," a further chance to interact. Adults who are successful in their fields also speak to the tutors on various topics related to counseling and career development. These adults serve as role models and are often graduates of the tutors' school districts. The tutors are awarded recognition by Coca-Cola and their teachers in special ceremonies.

VYP has had a positive impact on Hispanics: in 1985-86, of 100 students identified as being at high risk of dropping out, 94 remained at school. This figure is well below the attrition rate that was the norm in this area. The participating schools have also witnessed a marked improvement in the tutors' grades, a decrease in their absences, and a decline in discipline referrals. The tutors' self-reported data also indicated quite clearly that "being the teacher" gave the students a glimpse of themselves as reluctant learners and that their success with the young children gave them the motivation needed to change.

Senior Citizens as Service-Learners

Reprinted from Synergist, *ACTION, Vol. 10, No. 2, Fall 1981, p. 27.*

At the University of Hawaii at Manoa's continuing education department about 30 elderly citizens train to work as counselors at intermediate and high schools or as consultants at senior centers.

After eight weeks (40 hours) of intensive classroom training in communication and interpersonal skills, the senior citizens (all of whom are 58 or older) receive specialized training for their specific placements. Those who are placed in schools having primarily low-income and minority students take a 15-hour school counselor course offered by the Department of Educational Foundations. The training includes role playing and reading and reporting on materials about the role of counselors and the troubles of youth today. The senior citizens then go to various school sites to work with students for five months either on an individual counseling basis or in group counseling sessions.

Other senior citizens are trained by the Hawaii State Senior Center to provide information about reorganization and development of senior centers throughout the state. They are paid a small stipend by the agency to help senior centers develop programs.

An agency or school supervisor and the senior citizens' instructors supervise the continuing education students.

The campus field coordinator for the Gerontology Center and the staff of the Department of Educational Foundations have conducted several pre- and post-tests to determine the success of the program and its meaning to the senior citizens. The tests showed great gains in self-esteem and interpersonal competencies. Most of the participants agreed that the work experience was the highlight of the program. Those who had been counselors at the school sites felt that they had been important and helpful to the students.

Recycling with an Educational Purpose: A Fifth Grade Project

Tom Gerth and David A. Wilson

An environmental educator and a high school student describe a recycling project that could work in any elementary school. High school or college students could help organize it. Reprinted with permission from Journal of Experiential Education, *Association for Experiential Education, Vol. 9, No. 2, Summer 1986.*

From Missouri Botanical Garden's Perspective

THE ECO-ACT ENVIRONMENTAL LEADERSHIP PROGRAM sponsored by Missouri Botanical Garden was selected by the National Science Teacher Association as an exemplary program in its 1983 Search for Excellence in Science Education. What follows is one example of a project conducted by students in that program.

Four high school students from St. Louis University High School taught environmental science once a week in Mrs. Velma McCall's fifth grade class at Buder Elementary School in St. Louis. In December, they encouraged their class to bring in aluminum and steel cans for recycling as part of their study of resources and resource management.

Students spent three weeks collecting 30 pounds of cans worth approximately $6. Based on this experience, the high school students involved the class in a program to establish a recycling competition throughout the school.

As the high school students met with teachers, the principal, and the custodian, and laid plans for the project, they gained practical experience as organizers and leaders and taught the fifth graders those skills as well.

The class was first divided into teams, with one group preparing speeches, the other posters. Students read contest announcements over the school PA, and subsequently students announced weekly contest winners in similar fashion.

As the collection campaign began, one crew went around to the rooms each day to pick up the bags of metal cans, another crew smashed cans, and all weighed and recorded results by classroom. The collection, weighing, and recording process took 40 minutes of class time each week. As they tallied each classroom's volume, they had an opportunity to use their mathematical skills. They prepared charts and graphs and weighed the cans by the metric system. Then they converted their figures to pounds to estimate the amount of cash they could expect to earn at the local recycling center.

In a five-week contest, the school collected over 500 pounds of aluminum and steel worth about $135. The winning class received a field trip to Missouri Botanical Garden. Then Mrs. McCall's class decided how to spend the money for the school.

This recycling project was conducted with the assistance of several high school students working in an elementary classroom. The fifth grade class became the true leaders in their school in the project. While every elementary teacher may not have some high school leaders to help, a project like this can be undertaken with minimum risk and maximum learning. It is an effective way of involving students in concrete action based on what they learn about the environment.

From a Student's Perspective

Project Description and Objectives. Our project was one that involved beautifying and cleaning up the environment, while at the same time saving energy and natural resources. The project consisted of three phases: (1) collecting the beverage cans, (2) saving and eventually recycling these cans, and (3) using the resulting cash to further beautify the environment — in our case, buying and planting trees.

The objectives of the project were many. Of course, the major thrust of the program was to allow the students to help improve their environment. By letting them take part in (and actually operate) the collection and recycling process, we taught them practical ways in which they can do their part, both in the project and eventually on their own. In addition the students also learn organizational, public relations, and money management skills.

Pre-Project: How did we prepare? The first thing we had to do was discuss our plan with the fifth grade teacher, Mrs. McCall, and the principal, Mr. Eckols. They were both very receptive to the plan, so we went ahead to plan a small-scale, trial can drive. This drive included only one fifth grade class and lasted a total of three weeks. To plan this small drive, the only necessary preparations were to explain the plan to the class, give a crash course on recycling and its importance, and ask for input. After three weeks, the class collected almost 30 pounds of cans, worth $6. With these statistics, we figured that a 19-classroom school like Buder would recycle a lot of metal and make a lot of money.

The next step was to plan for the drive and work out the logistics. We had to discuss our plans with the different teachers, find a place to store the metal, organize a "pick-up" crew, and plan trips to the recycling center. To get maximum results, we decided to operate in competition style. Each classroom competed for a prize: a field trip to the Missouri Botanical Garden.

With the logistical problems out of the way, the next step was to publicize the project. Since our fifth graders were the ones running the project, we divided them into two groups — the speech group and the poster group. The poster group made big colorful contest posters, while the speech group submitted speeches, one of which was chosen to be read by its creator over the school P.A. system (we continued to use the P.A. for publicity, later announcing the weekly and contest winners). We, the ECO-ACT students, also attended a teachers' meeting where we announced the project plans to the entire faculty.

The Project Itself. Once the project was underway, the work was still far from done. We divided the class into committees to cover all facets of the project. We had a collection crew (which went around to the rooms each day and picked up the metal), a smashing crew (to maximize space efficiency), a weighing crew, and a recording crew (to keep track of which room was winning the contest). Idealistically, we planned on spending the initial 10 minutes of class doing this. In reality, however, it took about 30-40 minutes.

After five weeks of collecting aluminum and steel, the whole school had collected over 500 pounds, worth about $135. And with the first two phases of the program over, we went into the final stage: spending the money to help beautify the Buder School environment. After a lengthy class meeting, we decided on buying and planting trees. These trees not only taught the students the practical art of planting, but also added beauty by providing two

living monuments to ECO-ACT, to the concept of conservation, and
to the Buder School.

An In-depth Look at Planting a Tree ...   When our fifth grade
class decided to use its project money to buy and plant trees, we had
to figure out the best ways for them to learn about planting a tree.
What did we do? First we brought the tree into the schoolyard,
placing it in a spot where the class would have to pass it on the way
to the planting site. When we brought the students out, we let them
examine the tree, showing them the parts, the function of the bur-
lap-wrapped base, and the size. We let them discover the elements
necessary to tree growth — sunlight, oxygen, rain. We then sat
around the tree and asked general discussion-type questions: What
do the trees need for growth? What purpose do the wood chips and
mulch serve? How big would the tree get? What good would it do
for Buder? We had a nice discussion before planting.

To plant the tree, each student helped. Some took turns digging,
others measuring the depth of the hole, others filling, watering, and
mulching. What did the students learn?

- practical art of planting a tree
- basic Biology – plant parts
- basic Earth Science – elements necessary for plant (andani-
  mal) growth
- mathematics – measuring
- working together
- satisfaction of getting a job well done.

Problems We Encountered. Surprisingly enough, we encountered very few problems. Just for the record, though, I'll relate the
ones we did have, and how we attempted to solve them:

- **Missing students!** Since some students would be busy
working with their committees, sometimes several students would
miss a class; and this can really throw off a lesson plan that relies on
the previous class. To overcome this problem, we taught self-
contained lessons — ones that taught a concept in one class.

- **Noise!** Several teachers complained about noise, both from
the students and from the crashing and smashing of cans. First, we
warned the students about their noise. Second, we got permission
for a new storage room, downstairs and away from the classrooms.

- **Bugs!** Towards the end of the project, the janitors complained about cockroaches that were attracted to the empty soda
and beer cans. The project was almost over, so we couldn't really do
anything to solve the problem, In the future, though, more frequent
pickups could help.

- **Assault!** Some of the kids threw cans at each other on the bus, and one of the drivers wouldn't allow cans on his bus anymore. What could we do? We had to take the loss.

Evaluation. In general, the project went exceptionally well. The students learned a lot about recycling, organizing a project, money management and use, and practical knowledge about improving the environment. More importantly, though, is the fact that the students did more than learn; they put their knowledge into use — they acted. And that's what ECO-ACT's all about.

Tom Gerth graduated recently from St. Louis University High School. David Wilson is Instructional Coordinator at Missouri Botanical Garden and manages the ECO-ACT Environmental Leadership Program.

Services and Publications of the National Society for Internships and Experiential Education

About the
The National Society for Internships and Experiential Education

THE NATIONAL SOCIETY FOR INTERNSHIPS AND EXPERIENTIAL EDUCATION is a national resource center and professional association that supports the use of *learning through experience* for civic and social responsibility, intellectual development, cross-cultural awareness, moral/ethical development, career exploration, and personal growth.

NSIEE's mission: As a community of individuals, institutions, and organizations, NSIEE is committed to fostering the effective use of experience as an integral part of education, in order to empower learners and promote the common good.

NSIEE's goals are:
- to advocate for the effective use of experiential learning throughout the educational system and the larger community;
- to disseminate information on principles of good practice and on innovations in the field;
- to enhance professional growth and leadership development in the field;
- to encourage the development and dissemination of related research and theory.

Experiential education includes community and public service when combined with learning, internships, field studies, intercultural programs, leadership development, cooperative education, experiential learning in the classroom, outdoor education, and all forms of active learning.

NSIEE's services include conferences, workshops, publications, newsletters, the National Resource Center on Service and Learning, professional network services, and in-depth consulting for program and institutional planning. See the following pages for membership information and a publications list.

NSIEE was founded in 1971 as the National Center for Public Service Internship Programs and the Society for Field Experience Education. NSIEE's national office is in Raleigh, North Carolina.

What are NSIEE's Services?

Experiential Education Newsletter – Current issues, new publications and programs, research results, legislation, opportunities for professional development, funding. Published bi-monthly.

National and Regional Conferences – Newcomers and advanced experiential educators gather for the exchange of ideas and materials, professional support and development, state-of-the-art discussions. Ask about dates for the next national and regional conferences.

Publications – Papers and books examining key issues and sound practices in experiential education, a three-volume resource book on service-learning, a directory of internships for learners of all ages, "how to" guides, sourcebooks for educational pacesetters. See order form on pages 492-495. NSIEE members get a 30-40% discount.

Information on Programs, Practices, Research and Policies – NSIEE houses the National Resource Center on Service and Learning, the comprehensive national clearinghouse for information on all aspects of combining learning with community and public service — history, rationales, policy issues, syllabi, research, design and administration of sound programs for particular fields and client groups, sample program materials and forms, and professional and faculty development.

Consulting Services – Assistance in assessing your needs and referrals to experienced consultants. Help available for program planning and evaluation, course development, institutional planning, faculty workshops, and other on-site needs.

National Talent Bank – NSIEE sponsors the national talent bank of faculty, administrators, and program directors knowledgeable about the practical and conceptual aspects of effectively combining service and learning. They volunteer their expertise to help you with your planning. The *NSIEE Membership Directory* also serves as a continuous source of contacts for members.

Special Interest Groups – Opportunities for professional leadership and support. These interest groups and committees provide forums for discussions about community and public service-learning, career development, cooperative education, cross-cultural learning, learning theories, arts and culture, human ecology and environmental studies, research, publications, conference planning and the special needs of faculty, internship coordinators, community colleges, high schools, and community and agency sponsors.

Services for Agencies and Community Sponsors – A special subscription service to help employers and field sponsors publicize their opportunities and recruit qualified students. Ask for details.

Who are NSIEE's Members?

NSIEE's membership is diverse. Members represent public and private colleges and universities, internship programs, school systems, deans' offices, community service programs, academic departments (liberal arts, professional, and technical fields), high schools, cooperative education programs, state and local governments, museums, international programs, counselors, career planning and placement offices, community-based organizations, corporations, consulting firms, and interested individuals from all fields.

What Benefits do NSIEE Members Receive?

EXPERIENTIAL EDUCATION **newsletter** — a one-year subscription.

Discounts — 30-40% off — on NSIEE publications, conference registration fees, consulting services.

Membership Directory— a complete directory with indexes by state, by individual name, by school or organization name, and by interest area. A handy reference book for your old and new professional contacts.

Opportunities for Professional Leadership and Contribution— NSIEE offers its members vehicles to contribute locally and nationally through conference presentations, publications, conference planning, research, the exchange of ideas and information, and outreach to other groups.

Eligibility to participate in NSIEE Committees and Special Interest Groups— publications, research, community and public service-learning, career development, secondary education, faculty, international and cross-cultural, learning theories, cooperative education, field sponsors, internship coordinators, human ecology and environmental studies, community colleges, arts and culture, conference planning, and nominations.

Full voting privileges; eligibility for the NSIEE Board of Directors.

Access to other NSIEE services (see list), including the NSIEE staff's time to select and recommend resource materials in response to your specific needs.

Special projects and services— NSIEE members are invited to participate in national and regional pilot projects and other services funded by grants to NSIEE for innovative activities.

Categories of NSIEE Membership

1. **Institutional, Organizational, or Departmental Membership ($225)** — for colleges, universities, departments, established programs, secondary schools and systems, nonprofit organizations, government agencies, and corporations. Covers full membership benefits for up to 5 individuals from one school, department, organization or agency. This is the membership category for presidents, deans, administrators, departmental coordinators, and directors of established programs. On the initial membership form, one person is designated as the primary NSIEE liaison; up to 4 other people can then be added to receive the full benefits. Additional names beyond five can be added for $45 each. National recognition is given to members in category #1 throughout the year.

2. **Individual Membership ($65)** — for faculty, administrators, and other professionals who are involved in or interested in community and public service, internships, and experiential education.

3. **Student Membership ($38)** — for individuals *primarily* engaged as students and currently enrolled in educational institutions. Students join NSIEE to stay abreast of developments in the field, often because of a potential career interest related to experiential education and service-learning.

4. **Sustaining Membership ($500)** — for corporations, institutions, individuals, and philanthropic organizations with a strong commitment to the value of learning through experience. Sustaining members receive the full benefits of membership plus special recognition if desired.

NSIEE Membership Enrollment Form

Please cut along dotted line and return your completed form to NSIEE at the address shown. Duplicate this form if needed.

Membership category: (for one year following enrollment)

❑ Sustaining Membership $ 500   *Please check one:*
❑ Institutional/Organizational $ 225   ❑ New Membership
   Membership (covers 5 people)   ❑ Renewal
❑ Individual Membership $ 65
❑ Student Membership $ 38
   Total Due $____

I believe the work of NSIEE is valuable and warrants a special contribution. I am enclosing an additional amount of:

❑ $20   ❑ $50   ❑ $100   ❑ $500   ❑ $1000   ❑ Other ($____)

Contributions are tax-deductible to the extent allowed by law. NSIEE is a nonprofit organization under Sec. 501(c)(3) of the IRS code. Thank you for your support.

Why are you joining NSIEE? _____

_____

Name_____Title _____

Program/Department _____

Institution/Organization _____

Address _____

City _____State _____Zip _____

Phone (____)_____FAX_____

Electronic mail # _____

Dues must be prepaid. Complete the credit card section or enclose check payable to NSIEE. Foreign membership must be paid through U.S. bank. If outside North America, also add $15 for postage costs.

Credit Cards: _____

Visa _____ Mastercard _____

Card Number _____

Expiration Date _____

Signature _____

Mail to:

National Society for Internships and Experiential Education
3509 Haworth Drive, Suite 207
Raleigh, NC 27609
Phone (919) 787-3263
Federal ID# 52-1010211

Publications of the
National Society for Internships and
Experiential Education

The National Directory of Internships

edited by Amy S. Butterworth and Sally A. Migliore. Complete descriptions of over 28,000 internship opportunities across the country for students from high school through graduate school and beyond. Also lists opportunities for young people and adults not enrolled in school. Openings in government, nonprofit organizations, and corporate settings. Divided by type of host organization. Complete indexes by field of interest, location, and name of host organization. 350 pp., $18 NSIEE members, $22 non-members.

Quantity ____

The Experienced Hand:
A Student Manual for Making the Most of an Internship

by Timothy K. Stanton and Kamil Ali. Ten steps show how to acquire a satisfactory internship for learners of all ages. Contains chapters on making the internship the most satisfying experience possible. Also useful as a text in courses with internship components. 96 pp., $8.95 NSIEE members, $12.95 non-members.

Quantity ____

Combining Service and Learning:
A Resource Book for Community and Public Service

edited by Jane C. Kendall. Published by NSIEE with the Babcock and Kettering Foundations and 90 other national and regional organizations. For faculty, administrators, policymakers, and students in colleges and universities and K-12 schools; leaders in government, community, or corporate settings; lawmakers; foundations; and others interested in community and public service, youth service, voluntarism, leadership, civic awareness, or cross-cultural learning.

Volume I - Principles of good practice; rationales; theories, research; public policy and institutional issues plus strategies for gaining support; education for civic and social responsibility, for cross-cultural awareness, and for intellectual, moral, ethical, career, and leadership development. 693 pp., $29 NSIEE members, $32 for members of Cooperating Organizations, $45 non-members.

Quantity ____

Volume II - Practical issues and ideas for programs and courses — integration into the curriculum, recruitment, orientation, supervision, evaluation, school/community relations, legal issues, moni-

To order publications, photocopy this form or cut along the dotted line and return.

toring and assessing both service and learning outcomes. 528 pp., $29 NSIEE members, $32 for members of Cooperating Organizations, $45 non-members. Quantity ____

Volume III - An extensive annotated bibliography of the literature from the past three decades. Edited by Janet Luce with Jennifer Anderson, Jane Permaul, Rob Shumer, Timothy Stanton, Sally Migliore. 81 pp., $10 NSIEE members, $13 for members of Cooperating Organizations, $15 non-members. Quantity ____

Strengthening Experiential Education within Your Institution

by Jane C. Kendall, John S. Duley, Thomas C. Little, Jane S. Permaul, and Sharon Rubin. A sourcebook for college and university faculty and administrators. Includes chapters on integrating community service or other types of experiential learning into the institution's mission, curriculum, faculty roles, evaluation system, administrative and financial structures. 154 pp., $17 NSIEE members, $25 non-members.
Quantity ____

Facts and Faith: A Status Report on Youth Service

by Anne C. Lewis with commentary by Jane C. Kendall. From "Youth and America's Future: The William T. Grant Foundation Commission on Work, Family and Citizenship." 42 pp., $5.
Quantity ____

Knowing and Doing: Learning from Experience

edited by Pat Hutchings and Allen Wutzdorff, Alverno College. Shows how several innovative programs help students integrate what they know with what they can do. From Jossey-Bass, Inc., Publishers. 81 pp., $12.95, available only for NSIEE members.
Quantity ____

Preparing Humanists for Work: A National Study of Undergraduate Internships in the Humanities

by Carren O. Kaston with James M. Heffernan, the Washington Center, sponsored by the National Endowment for the Humanities. Results and analysis of a major national study of internship programs offered by humanities departments across the country. 99 pp., $8 NSIEE members, $13 non-members.
Quantity ____

Guide to Environmental Internships: How Environmental Organizations Can Utilize Internships Effectively

by Jane C. Kendall. A concise handbook useful for any organization that hosts interns. 48 pp., $5 for NSIEE members, $8 for non-members.
Quantity ____

NSIEE Occasional Papers and PANEL Resource Papers

Concise papers on major issues to consider in designing, administering, or evaluating programs for experiential learning and community service. Includes papers on theory, practice, and research. $6 each for NSIEE members, $10 each for non-members.

NSIEE Occasional Papers   Quantity

#1   "Toward a Comprehensive Model of Clustering Skills" by J. W. Munce   _____

#2   "The Immediate Usefulness of the Liberal Arts: Variations on a Theme" _____
     by J. M. Bevan

#4   "Field Experience and Stage Theories of Development" by A. Erdynast   _____

#5   "Students at Work: Identifying Learning in Internship Settings" by D. T.
     Moore   _____

#6   "Life Developmental Tasks and Related Learning Needs and Out-
     comes" by J. Arin-Krupp

#8   "Community Service, Civic Arts, Voluntary Action, and Service-Learn-
     ing" edited by R. Sigmon   _____

#9   "Academic Excellence and Community Service: The Integrating Role of
     Undergraduate Internships" by J. Wagner   _____

#10 "Experiential Teaching" by S.G. Rubin   _____

#11 "Strengthening Experiential Education: Three Stories and the Lessons
     They Teach" by S.G. Rubin   _____

#12 "Experiential Education as a Liberating Art" by G. Hesser   _____

PANEL Resource Papers

#1   "History and Rationale for Experiential Learning" by T.C. Little   _____

#2   "Field Experience: How to Start a Program" by R.A. Davis.   _____

#3   "Legal Issues in Experiential Education" by M.G. Goldstein   _____

#4   "Prefield Preparation: What, Why, How?" by T. Stanton & M. Whitham _____

#5   "Monitoring & Supporting Experiential Learning" by J. Permaul   _____

#6   "Learning Outcomes: Measuring & Evaluating Experiential Learning"
     by J. Duley   _____

#7   "Performance Appraisal Practices: A Guide to Better Supervisor Evalu-
     ation Processes" by S.G. Rubin   _____

#8   "Applications of Developmental Theory to the Design and Conduct of
     Quality Field Experience Programs" by M. Whitham & A. Erdynast   _____

#9   "Internships in History" by S. Hoy, R. Sexton, P. Stearns, & J. Tarr _____

#10 "Research Bibliography in Experiential Education" by J. Anderson   _____

#11 "Environmental Internships" by R. Rajagopal   _____

#12 "Experiential Learning and Cultural Models" by E.L. Cerroni-Long &
     S.G. Rubin   _____

#13 "Self-Directed Adult Learners and Learning" by V. R. Griffin   _____

NSIEE Publications Order Form

Please photocopy the order pages or cut along the dotted lines and return this page with the previous three pages.

Total cost of publications	= \$ _____
Plus handling fee (required)	+ \$ _____

Includes 4th class postage and processing costs. For orders:

Up to \$25, add \$2.00
Up to \$50, add \$3.50
Over \$50, add \$5.00

Plus 1st class postage (optional). Because 4th class delivery takes 4-6 weeks, we suggest you add 1st class postage. Add \$2 for the first publication ordered, and \$.50 for each additional publication.　　+ \$ _____

Plus 5% sales tax (NC orders only)	= \$ _____
Total Payment Due	= \$ _____

Name_____Title _____

Program/Department _____

Institution/Organization _____

Address _____

City _____State _____ Zip _____

Phone (_____) _____ Fax _____

Electronic mail # _____

Are you a member of NSIEE? ❑ *yes* ❑ *no*
I would like information about NSIEE membership. ❑

FULL PAYMENT OR CREDIT CARD CHARGES MUST ACCOMPANY ORDER. Make checks payable to NSIEE. Credit card users complete credit card section. All prices subject to change without notice.
Foreign orders: Orders from outside the U.S. must be paid through a U.S. bank. For orders from outside North America, also add \$10 for additional postage costs.

Credit Cards: _____

Visa _____ Mastercard _____

Card Number _____

Expiration Date _____

Signature _____

Mail to: _____

National Society for Internships and Experiential Education
3509 Haworth Drive, Suite 207
Raleigh, NC 27609
Phone (919) 787-3263
Federal ID# 52-1010211

Table of Contents for
Volumes I and III

Table of Contents for Volume I

Table of Contents for Volume III
Service-Learning: An Annotated Bibliography

Index
for
Volume II

Index for Volume II